A Muslim in
Victorian America

A Muslim in Victorian America

The Life of Alexander Russell Webb

UMAR F. ABD-ALLAH

UNIVERSITY PRESS

2006

OXFORD
UNIVERSITY PRESS

Oxford University Press, Inc., publishes works that further
Oxford University's objective of excellence
in research, scholarship, and education.

Oxford   New York
Auckland   Cape Town   Dar es Salaam   Hong Kong   Karachi
Kuala Lumpur   Madrid   Melbourne   Mexico City   Nairobi
New Delhi   Shanghai   Taipei   Toronto

With offices in
Argentina   Austria   Brazil   Chile   Czech Republic   France   Greece
Guatemala   Hungary   Italy   Japan   Poland   Portugal   Singapore
South Korea   Switzerland   Thailand   Turkey   Ukraine   Vietnam

Library of Congress Cataloging-in-Publication Data
Abd-Allah, Umar F.
A Muslim in Victorian America : the life of Alexander Russell Webb /
Umar F. Abd-Allah.
    p. cm.
Includes bibliographical references and index.
ISBN 978-0-19-518728-1
1. Webb, Alexander Russell, 1846–1916.   2. Islam—United States—History—
19th century.   I. Title.
BP80.W43A64 2006
297.092—dc22   2005035280

9 8 7 6 5 4

Printed in the United States of America
on acid-free paper

To my mother, Grace Marian Marmon-Landgraf,
a daughter of the American Revolution

Preface

"Many hands make light work." So many persons worked so open-handedly on this project that I cannot possibly show them the appreciation they deserve. I would like first to extend my thanks to Theo Calderara, Stacey Hamilton, Norma McLemore, Julia TerMaat, and other members and collaborators of the professional staff at Oxford University Press. I am grateful to the Nawawi Foundation of Chicago, where I work as chair and scholar-in-residence, for its passionate backing of this project and steadfast support. I remain obliged to Mr. Timothy Winter of Cambridge for his invaluable assistance, especially in bringing previously unknown material to light, and am always indebted to Drs. Sherman Jackson of the University of Michigan, Ingrid Mattson of Hartford Seminary, and Marcia Hermansen of Loyola University for their encouragement and advice.

I have benefited from the invaluable assistance of dedicated editorial and research assistants. Let me begin by thanking Asra Yousufuddin, Omer Mozaffar, Ibrahim Abusharif, and Asma Tasnim Uddin, all of whom freely expended enormous amounts of time and energy in highly professional editorial assistance. Similar prodigious contributions were made by many others, among them: Adnan Arain, Affan Arain, Dilara Sayeed, Hanane Korchi, Humaira Basith, Lubna Dabbagh, Mazen Asbahi, Mohammed Hasan Ali, Naazish Yarkhan, Nadiah Mohajir, Qaid Hassan, Sabahat Adil, and Tabassum Siraj. For invaluable computer training and assistance, I express my thanks to Tariq Mohajir, Eiman Abdalmoneim, Tanvir Mallick, and Kareem Shelton.

Fareeha Khan, Feryal Salem, Asma Tasnim Uddin, Mohammed Hasan Ali, Omer Mozaffar, Sami Catovic, and Asra Yousufuddin deserve additional thanks for their fruitful labors in searching out, securing, and helping me utilize rare primary and secondary materials. I am obliged to Samina Malik of the Lahori Ahmadiyya Community of Plain City, Ohio, for her assistance in providing primary source materials relevant to Webb's correspondence with Mirza Ghulam Ahmad. I thank Dr. Muhammad Isa Waley, curator of the Persian and Turkish Collections at the British Library, for valuable information on Webb's British colleague Abdulla William Henry Quilliam. I extend my special gratitude to Muhammad Abdullah al-Ahari of Chicago for providing me from his private collection on Islam in America with a copy of Webb's 1892 diary and his two pro-Ottoman booklets. I also thank Edmund Arroyo for accompanying me on a laborious trip to Missouri in 2002, where we toiled in search for relevant historical records on Webb's years there.

I extend my cordial appreciation to Mary Howell, Columbia County historian, who cheerfully gave my research assistant Muhammad Hasan Ali and me many hours of her time, clarified historical details pertinent to Webb's New York background, provided valuable photographs, and was tremendously helpful in directing me to additional archival material. I thank Sally Alderdice and the accommodating staff of the Claverack Free Library and Reading Room. Similar recognition goes out to Joshua Hall, research intern at the Stockbridge, Massachusetts, library's Historical Collection, who spent weeks locating records on the long-obsolete Glendale Home School, where Webb studied as a boy. Sharon Canter of St. Joseph's Historical Collection gladly put at my disposal the valuable historical resources of the St. Joseph Public Library. I found the same supportive spirit from Joe Christopher and Sue Schuermann at the Journalism Library of the University of Missouri, who prepared, of their own accord, all relevant materials available in the School of Journalism so that our time could be utilized to the fullest. At the St. Louis Public Library, Noel Holaback, Joseph Winkler, Keith Zimmer, and other members of the staff of the History and Genealogy Section were immensely cooperative, often bringing to my attention invaluable materials of which I had not been aware, including rare nineteenth-century aerial maps of St. Louis from the time of Webb's residence in the city. My thanks to Randy Blomquist and the other cordial personnel at the St. Louis Historical Society and to Dusty Reese and Tom Gruenenfelder at the Archives Department of St. Louis City Hall. Finally, I would like to express my gratitude to Elaine M. Doak, head librarian of the Special Collections at Truman State University, for helping me locate rare facts relating to Webb's years in Unionville, Missouri, which helped uncover his previously unknown marriage to Laura Conger.

Finally, I express my gratitude to several Turkish colleagues and friends, among them Dr. Ibrahim Özdemir of Ankara University and his associates, who secured for me several documents on Webb from the Ottoman Archives during a visit to Istanbul in 2000. I express my thanks to Dr. Sevket Pamuk, professor of economics at Boğaziçi University, for his unhesitating scholarly assistance in answering questions relative to nineteenth-century Ottoman currencies. Dr. Said Kaya of the Istanbul Center for Islamic Studies provided me with a valuable contemporary study of Webb in Turkish based on Ottoman Archival documents, and my special appreciation to Nukhet Arkasu of the University of Chicago for translating all relevant Ottoman and Modern Turkish materials.

Behind acquisition of the illustrations in this work lay the labors of Humaira Basith and Sabahat Adil. In addition to thanking them both, special words of gratitude are due again to Mary Howell, Columbia County historian, for putting her entire stock of historical photographs at our disposal and freely allowing us to make use of the two illustrations that we finally chose of downtown Hudson and Claverack College as Webb knew them. Chicago's Newberry Library produced the bulk of the photographic work in the book, many of which fell within public domain but were reproduced by the Newberry Library and others of which were provided with the special permission by the Newberry Library from its uniquely rich collection, namely, the 1893 photograph of Webb with turban and a series of illustrations from the Chicago World's Fair: the Ottoman Commissioner, the Ottoman Pavilion, and the Bazaar of Nations and "Streets of Cairo." Newberry reproduced the photographs of Eugene Field pictured with Francis Wilson, Hajee William R. Williamson, and the 1901 photograph of Webb with the fez and Ottoman medallions. I extend particular thanks to the Eugene Field House of St. Louis for generously granting permission to reproduce the Eugene Field photograph just mentioned. Special thanks to the New York Public Library for its provision of the 1892 photograph of Webb in Indian dress along with special permission to use it. Thanks are due Aasil Kazi Ahmad for his skillful portraits—all of which fell within public domain—of William Henry Quilliam, Lord Headley, and Lady Cobbold, from the less-than-ideal originals we found available. Again, I would like to thank Humaira Basith for her reproduction of the coversheet of the 1893 *Moslem World*, which was acquired from the St. Louis Public Library. Finally, abundant thanks for the book's three maps—nineteenth-century New York and environs, Webb in Missouri, and Webb's 1892 tour of the Orient— and the Victorian American Timeline. All were original creations copyrighted to the Nawawi Foundation and resulted from the diligent collaboration of Muhammad Hasan Ali and Hanane Korchi on the maps and Dilara Sayeed and Nadiah Mohajir on the timeline.

Contents

A Muslim in
Victorian America

I

The Yankee Mohammedan

It was late summer 1893. The Chicago World's Fair had reached its final weeks. One of the most imposing of all such fairs, it transformed Chicago into an oasis of "wonders and miracles," as if the city had been reborn like a phoenix from the ashes of the Great Fire of 1871. At center stage stood one of the great events of the nineteenth century: the First World's Parliament of Religions, a major watershed in American cultural history.

The parliament set out to foster religious pluralism to a degree largely unprecedented in the American experience. It captivated enthusiastic audiences with lectures on the world's major religious traditions. For the most part, these presentations were delivered by articulate adherents of Eastern faiths, who came from abroad and were born into the traditions they presented. The presentation on Islam was the exception. Islam's official representative at the parliament was Mohammed Alexander Russell Webb, a prominent native-born American convert to the faith and leader of one of the earliest Islamic movements on American soil.

On September 20, a wet and chilly Wednesday morning, crowds that had gathered outside the parliament's main auditorium, Columbus Hall, rushed in as soon as the doors swung open to hear Mohammed Webb, dubbed in the press as "the Yankee Mohammedan," deliver his first lecture. It was widely known that Webb had served as American consul in the Philippines. His conversion to Islam there in 1888 and his subsequent sponsorship of the American Mission and numerous public lectures in the Orient had won him national and international notoriety.

Webb unapologetically espoused his newly adopted faith in terms that made clear he saw no contradiction between it and his deeply rooted American identity. Many of his Victorian American contemporaries had heard of him in the press and wanted to hear the story of his religious odyssey. Although Webb's speech that morning, as on the following day, was occasionally disrupted by the corpulent and bothersome Boston missionary Reverend Joseph Cook and his followers—whose outbursts proved to be an annoyance for many other representatives of nontraditional religions and purveyors of unconventional opinions at the parliament—Webb's audience was, for the most part, "intelligent, sympathetic, quick to appreciate, and applaud."[1] He identified with them naturally and emphasized his belief in their fairness: "I have faith in the American intellect, in the American intelligence, and in the American love of fair play, and will defy any intelligent man to understand Islam and not love it." Webb repeatedly emphasized that Islam and "the Arabian Prophet" had for generations been misrepresented to Americans, making it difficult for them to comprehend his new faith or why he had chosen it. Still he proclaimed his faith in the American character: "I feel that Americans, as a rule, are disposed to go to the bottom of facts and to ascertain really what Mohammed was and what he did, and when they have done so, I feel we shall have a universal system which will elevate our social system to the position where it belongs."[2]

Alexander Russell Webb (1846–1916) believed himself to have gone "to the bottom of the facts" regarding Islam. Having adopted it as a private faith and personal fulfillment of his identity as an American, he stands as one of the outstanding figures in the early history of Islam in the United States, and his legacy constitutes a valuable point of reference for all Americans today, and especially for those in the growing Muslim community of the United States. Webb was born and raised in Hudson, New York. His character and religious disposition bore the stamp of religious individualism and nonconformity typical of the Mid-Atlantic cultural ethos of nineteenth-century New York.

After the Civil War, Webb made his way west to Chicago, established a jewelry business, but lost everything in the Great Fire of 1871. Although his home was not in the fire's path, Webb's first wife, Laura Conger, disappeared in the chaos of that terrible night. No subsequent record of her has been found, and the story of Webb's first marriage remains one of the unsolved mysteries of his biography.

Webb's next major move came in 1874, when, with the financial support of Laura Conger's father, he moved to Missouri and got started in the newspaper business. Through the next fourteen years, he made a name for himself in Missouri journalism at a time when the state was taking a leading role in defining the standards of modern American journalism.

Webb regarded himself as a liberal and lifelong ardent supporter of the Democratic Party. In 1887, President Cleveland, the first Democrat to be elected president since the end of Reconstruction, appointed Webb as American consul to the Philippines; he served in Manila until 1892. Webb did not seek the position for purely political reasons. By the time of his appointment, Webb's career in St. Louis had spanned more than a decade, and, during these years, he became deeply involved in the city's Theosophical Society, through which he developed an avid interest in spiritualism and world religions. Like many of his generation, Webb looked upon the Orient as the romantic embodiment of the deepest and most lasting religious truths. With profound conviction, Webb believed that his appointment to the Philippines would give him direct access to the spiritual wisdom of the East. No doubt, this choice was naïve, for the Philippines at the time were under Spanish colonial control. The Catholic Church was dominant and did not look with favor on the presence of non-Catholic missions or representatives of non-Christian faiths.

The Philippines did, nevertheless, afford Webb access to information about Islam that he had not had in the United States. Shortly after his arrival in Manila, he decided to embrace Islam, having already contemplated that possibility in St. Louis without taking the final step. In Manila, Webb discovered the writings of prominent Muslim modernists of India from the Aligarh Movement, especially Sayyed Ameer Ali. In 1891, Webb began to correspond with the *Allahabad Review* in India about Islam, setting in motion a series of steps that would lead to his resignation as U.S. consul and his attempt to set up the American Mission.[3]

Through the press and personal correspondence, Webb was able to link with a number of prominent Indian Muslim merchants who promised to sponsor his mission with five years of financial support. At their behest in 1892, Webb resigned his diplomatic post and made a tour of Rangoon and various cities in India, promoting and seeking support for his mission.

Webb returned to New York in February 1893 and set about establishing his mission in Manhattan, immediately attracting front-page headlines in the *New York Times* and other American newspapers. Webb's movement lasted from 1893 until early 1896. He worked diligently, speaking extensively at private parlor gatherings—his preferred means of discourse—and delivering public lectures in a number of different states. His Moslem World Press published Islamic journals of good quality and offered for sale a wide selection of other publications on Islam.

Webb's reception in America was generally positive. Subscriptions and letters of support came from all parts of the country. Webb's chief obstacle, however, was inadequate financial patronage. Webb was probably overconfident in his assessment that his mission could be financially self-sufficient in five years, and his Indian supporters were unable to maintain their commitments for more than a few months. It became clear to Webb toward the end of 1893 that he could not depend upon his Indian patrons. He turned to the Ottoman embassy in Washington to keep the mission alive. He visited the Ottoman ambassador, Mavroyani Bey, in Washington, forged a lasting friendship with him, and earnestly implored him for Ottoman support to keep the mission alive. Mavroyani Bey's correspondence with Istanbul reflects the esteem he felt for Webb and the urgency of the aid he requested. Turkish aid did finally come, but it was too little and too late. Financial squabbles divided Webb's poorly paid staff, some of whom accused Webb of misusing funds.

The *New York Times* seized on the allegations, although ultimately it exonerated Webb after one of its reporters discovered him and his family in the Catskills living destitute in Ulster Park, New York, and attempting to keep the mission alive through correspondence and publication of a highly abridged form of its journal. After enduring poverty and suffering loss of personal status and family prestige, Webb suspended his mission in 1896.

He moved to Rutherford, New Jersey, where he resumed earlier careers in journalism and commerce, frequently commuting to New York on business. Webb lived the last twenty years of his life in Rutherford. He took active part in civic life and quickly attained standing in the New Jersey Democratic Party. The party nominated him to run for U.S. Congress in 1898, but he deferred in favor of another candidate, William Hughes. Appointed as Honorary Ottoman Consul General to New York in 1901, Webb traveled to Istanbul on special state invitation. Sultan Abdul-Hamid II gave him the honorific title of "Bey" [Sir] and decorated him with two Ottoman orders of merit. Webb is the only American to ever receive such an honor.

Webb was generally well-liked, and his genial personality won him friends wherever he went. In 1902, shortly after his return from Turkey, Webb presented a public lecture in Rutherford titled "Constantinople and Turkish Home Life." The local press assured readers that despite Webb's many honors and awards, he remained the same "pleasing personality" familiar to the people of Rutherford.[4]

Webb never returned to his earlier Islamic missionary work, but he remained a Muslim until the end of his life and made no effort to hide his identity as "an American Mohammedan."[5] During his last years, Webb suffered from diabetes; he succumbed to the disease at the age of seventy in his Rutherford home after an exhausting commute from New York on October 1, 1916.[6]

Catching the Public's Eye

Webb was handsome and had a pleasant voice. Physical appearance has various meanings in different times and cultures, but looks were indeed one of several Victorian preoccupations. "Phrenology," the study of facial features for signs of mental ability and character, was a widely accepted popular "science."

Modern American culture tends to emphasize pure physical attraction, but Victorian America was interested in appearance as a fundamental indicator of the inner self. For Victorians, sketches, photographs, and verbal descriptions of Webb were not incidental details; they were telling pieces of scientific evidence disclosing hidden insight into his intelligence and integrity.[7] Victorians did not only want to hear what Webb had to say but also wanted to see what he looked like and how he dressed.

Webb was not hampered by any lack of self-esteem and advertised "fine half-tone portraits" of himself for 15 cents, postage included.[8] Fortunately, his looks left a positive phrenological impression. He was photogenic, and, by the standards of the time, his photographs came out remarkably free of the rigidity and "crushing dignity" characteristic of many Victorian portraits, which left later generations with the impression that they never smiled. In fact, Victorians were not encouraged to smile while being photographed. It is hard to hold a smile for long, and exposures took several minutes. Photographers generally advised against smiling and often clamped their customers' heads in iron braces to ensure firm posture.[9]

FIGURE I.I. Mohammed Alexander Russell Webb (1893)

One Victorian phrenologist writing under the pen name Stiletto provided a full "scientific" statement of Webb's physiognomy for *Frank Leslie's Illustrated*, one of America's earliest and most popular illustrated journals. Stiletto's observations were based on the 1893 portrait of Webb dressed in white turban and Western suit, gazing romantically toward the horizon. The portrait was displayed alongside Stiletto's analysis:[10]

> A face indicating a calm and deliberate mind, a nature never super-
> ficial in its emotions or intentions. When stirred it is deeply and
> overwhelmingly moved, and an intention once conceived is steadily
> and patiently carried out. His eyebrows indicate thought and some
> degree of shrewd calculation. Ideality is largely developed where the
> head broadens on either side of the brow, and there is suggested a
> species of mental inertia or dreaminess, while the listening ears drink
> in high-sounding words and rolling phrases. Beneath his eyes is a gift
> of language. Not of sparkling, brilliant, or rippling words, but a slow,
> steady, and deliberate utterance, forcible because the speaker is ap-
> parently swayed by convictions and emotions so intense that their
> depth checks rapidity and seeks outlet in impressive rather than
> dashing eloquence. There is a distinct absence of definite expression
> in his countenance, and yet the mind is capable and ready, the in-
> tellect deliberate and stable. Such absence of expression can only be
> explained by motives deep-seated and subtle intentions, and is prob-
> ably the keynote of the entire nature. He will only permit to be visible
> that which he wishes to be seen, and wears his countenance as a
> mask to his personality rather than as an indication of the individ-
> uality of the inner man.[11]

Most people concurred that Webb was attractive and dignified. William Williamson, a young Englishman whom Webb helped escape torture at the hands of Spanish colonial prison guards in Manila (and who later embraced Islam independently of Webb's influence), remembered him as "a pleasant-looking man."[12] The *New York Herald* described Webb as "florid faced, with big, sparkling eyes and a luxuriant beard."[13] The *New York Times* portrayed him as a man of poise and presence, although it insinuated that there might be some question about his racial pedigree:

> A person of dignified though gracious bearing. His skin is tanned, and
> there is about him, especially in his movements, an Oriental air. He
> has large brown eyes and a dark brown beard of moderate length. He
> speaks easily and with directness and earnestness. He is of aver-
> age height, and just a trifle stout. There is a suggestion of supple-
> ness rather than briskness in his gait. His face is almost dark enough

for him to be mistaken for a light Hindu, and he talks with a slight foreign accent. With a fez he would easily pass for a Mohammedan.[14]

Emory Tunison, an early Muslim American biographer of Webb, represented him as a "dark, sturdy [man, of] medium height," while, for Clay Lancaster, he was a "handsome [man] with finely chiseled features."[15]

It is said that Victorian American men and women "dressed to the teeth." But more attention was probably given to the face and head than anything else, and both genders displayed "striking imagination in designing their own heads."[16] Webb was no different and often designed his head imaginatively with various types of Muslim head coverings. He wore glasses, at least while reading, but preferred to be photographed without them.[17]

Webb kept a beard all of his life. Keeping a beard is obligatory in Islamic law, but, for nineteenth-century American men, beards and mustaches were standard. It only became customary to be clean-shaven in the next century.[18] On seeing an as yet unidentified photograph of Webb, Nadirah Florence Ives Osman, another early Muslim American biographer of Webb, remarked: "I have been touched by the sight of his last photograph, taken shortly before he passed away, a likeness that displays his shining, resigned face, crowned with snowy hair, as he stands in the midst of his family, his beard still uncut in the shaven America of 1916."[19] Here, Osman is clearly inferring from Webb's bearded appearance as an old man that he had remained loyal to his faith, a matter that his family confirmed for her.

Tunison and several others had the impression that Webb appeared before the Parliament of Religions "dressed in turban and robe."[20] The Chicago Tribune drew a caricature of Webb in a turban, robe, and Oriental sandals.[21] In fact, Webb appeared at his parliament speeches in a red fez and a Western suit.[22] He did, occasionally, don full "Oriental garb," but it was not his habit. A reporter from Calcutta's Mohammedan Observer paid Webb a private visit for an interview at his guesthouse in the city and found him "dressed in Mohammadan [sic] costume."[23] The photograph of Webb in the frontispiece of his book The Three Lectures portrayed him in full Indian Muslim dress, and many of his contemporaries and later researchers—some of them, no doubt, basing their opinion on the photograph in The Three Lectures—were under the impression that he preferred traditional Muslim dress. The San Francisco Argonaut described Webb as one who, "to signify his change of belief, has decked himself in Oriental fashion."[24]

Richard Turner draws the conclusion that Webb "always wore Indian clothing, including a white turban." In Turner's view, Webb preferred Indian clothing because he regarded Western attire as a sign of decadence and believed that wearing it "could ultimately lead to the moral corruption of Muslims."[25] Webb in fact held no such view and almost always wore Western garb. He did, however, indicate some distaste for Oriental Muslims' aping of Western dress and discarding their traditional customs. In India, he repeatedly expressed his dislike of Westernization and its effect on colonized Muslims, one hallmark of which was Western dress. He viewed Muslims who blindly imitated the West, adopted its dress, and abandoned their own as servile and unworthy of their rich heritage. He believed them to be the furthest removed from a genuine Islamic ethos: "The only Mohammedans in all the East who drink intoxicating beverages are those who have been educated in England and wear European clothes. Their contact with Christian nations has demoralized them, and they have drifted away from their religion."[26]

But in America and abroad, Webb rarely appeared publicly in full Oriental dress, which sometimes disappointed his audiences. After one of his first parlor appearances in New York to speak "of the beauties of the Mohammedan religion," the *New York Herald* remarked with surprise and apparent regret that Webb had presented himself that night in stylish Western "evening clothes" and not the "Arab dress" they had expected.[27] In India, when a "fanatical Mussulman" insisted that it was Webb's "duty to adopt the Mussulman dress at once lest [he] should be mistaken for a Kafir [disbeliever]," Webb's reaction was: "Poor, benighted creatures! They have no more idea of the true spirit of Islam than the cows or horses."[28] When a popular Sufi in India remarked during an initial visit that he would prefer to see Webb wearing "Arab costume" in their next meeting, Webb jotted down in his diary: "I hardly think he will."[29]

In the Middle of It All

Webb's life was steeped in Americana. Despite his later affinity to the Turks in particular and the Muslim world in general after his conversion to Islam, he continued indisputably to identify himself as an American. From his first years onward, Webb moved in proximity to many of the settings, symbols, and historic personages that shaped American identity and were crucial parts of the nation's history. When I began work on his biography, I was impressed from the outset with his penchant for always ending up "in the middle of it all." To give an account of Webb's life is not only to discover an unexplored chapter in the history of Islam in America but to walk with him down some of the momentous corridors in our national history.

Webb regarded himself to be an average American. He was not overly educated and never an outstanding financial success. He was an astute spectator but rarely, if ever, a principal actor in the events that transpired around him. Yet Webb's biography repeatedly finds him either in the midst or proximity of the significant events of the time. On hearing these details of Webb's life, one of my friends commented in good humor that Webb was a sort of Muslim Forrest Gump. The parallel does a disservice to Webb's intelligence but is not without a ring of truth.

Martin Van Buren was the favorite son of Webb's native Columbia County, and, although Van Buren's estate was a few miles away in Kinderhook, he spent much time in Hudson. His son John, New York's attorney general, was also a familiar face in Hudson. John Van Buren was a leading national figure in the Democratic Party and could have succeeded his father to national prominence had it not been for his early death.[30] Former President Van Buren was an active member of the First Presbyterian Church, to which the Webb family belonged. As a young man, Webb must have seen the Van Burens frequently.

A prominent Webb family then living in neighboring Claverack preserved the Bible upon which General Washington was said to have taken his presidential oath of office. It was an heirloom of the family's forebear, General Samuel Webb, one of Washington's aides in the revolutionary war. During his youth, Webb often walked by the Old Courthouse on Hudson's outskirts, where Alexander Hamilton and Aaron Burr practiced law.[31] The Revolutionary War hero Marquis de Lafayette visited Hudson in 1824 during his tour of the United States and was given a festive banquet in the city, which unfurled a banner over his seat of honor:

> We bow not the head,
> We bend not the knee,
> But our hearts, Lafayette,
> We surrender to thee.[32]

Hudson's native soil was imbued with images imbedded in the national consciousness and early American literature. Washington Irving's celebrated stories "The Legend of Sleepy Hollow" and "Rip Van Winkle" had familiar settings for Webb. Van Winkle belonged to the lore of Catskill, just across the Hudson River, and the same village was coincidentally associated with Samuel Wilson, whose story, according to local tradition, inspired the national emblem of "Uncle Sam."[33] James Fennimore Cooper's *The Last of the Mohicans* was set even closer to home. The Hudson River Valley was Mohican territory, and the tribe's last stand had taken place just outside Hudson in a seventeenth-century battle with the Iroquois.[34] The *Clermont*, Robert Fulton's early steam-powered craft, was funded by Robert Livingston of Columbia County and took its name from his Clermont Estate, not far from Hudson. During its maiden voyage up the Hudson, the *Clermont* made a historic stop at Livingston's estate to take on firewood.[35] Once a busy whaling port, Hudson took pride in its old Nantucket roots. Melville's epic *Moby Dick* appeared during Webb's boyhood, and its theme and Nantucket setting evoked tangible associations in Hudson's collective memory.

Most of Webb's adult life before his conversion to Islam was spent in Missouri journalism, where, at the pinnacle of his career, he worked at the

Missouri Republican, where Mark Twain had begun his career much earlier. Webb apparently knew Twain and personally invited him and several other dignitaries to one of his first highly publicized parlor talks on Islam in February 1893. By that time, Webb had become a popular, though amusing subject in the *New York Times* and other American newspapers. Mark Twain knew of Webb's mission, and his well-known reference to "Missouri Moslems" in *Tom Sawyer Abroad,* which appeared in 1894, a year after the parliament, may well have been written with Webb in mind and probably evoked images of Webb for many American readers of the book in the 1890s. In Twain's narrative, Huck Finn asks Tom Sawyer about "Moslems" after their encounter with a troupe of whirling dervishes in Egypt. Huck recounts: "And when I asked him what a Moslem was, he said it was a person that wasn't a Presbyterian. So there is plenty of them in Missouri, though I didn't know it before."[36]

Webb grew up at a time when New York State and neighboring Massachusetts had established themselves as pioneers in American culture, actively shaping national consciousness and laying the foundations of a distinctive national identity. During the generation before Webb's birth, American national culture began to come into its own, taking a course independent of the European models that had dominated the colonial period.[37]

The Hudson River School (1825–1875) was the earliest distinctive post-revolutionary school of American art and architecture. Webb's native Hudson-on-the-Hudson was one of the movement's principal centers and an artists' haven during Webb's childhood and early manhood. Frederic Edwin Church, a leading figure of the school, was closely identified with the city, often resided there, and remodeled the First Presbyterian Church to which the Webb family belonged. Like the literary movement of the time, the Hudson River School drew its inspiration from the New World's natural beauty, especially that of the Hudson Valley and the adjoining mountains of western New England. Proudly nationalistic, it immortalized on canvas many stunning views of the Catskills panorama as seen from Church's Persian-styled Olana Manor, three miles outside Hudson. For Webb, such stunning views were familiar sights.[38]

When Alexis de Tocqueville visited America in the 1830s, he failed to notice its budding literary movement and wrote, "The literary genius of Great Britain still casts its rays deep in the forests of the New World." But within a decade and shortly before Webb's birth, Tocqueville revised his assessment by taking note of Washington Irving, James Fennimore Cooper, and William Ellery Channing, the American "apostle of Unitarianism."[39] Webb was an avid reader from childhood and knew well the national literary figures of the time, but, in addition to their general appeal as works of art, the emerging American literature of the time spoke powerfully to Webb's consciousness because its setting was often the surroundings of his native region.

Webb's Life	Political Developments	Cultural Developments
○ 1846: Webb's birth.		○ 1847: Hudson's whaling economy cannot be revived. ○ 1847: Frederick Douglas publishes *North Star*. ○ 1851: Death of James Fennimore Cooper.
○ 1864: Webb enrolls in Claverack College. ○ 1869: Webb goes to Chicago.	○ 1850: Enactment of Fugitive Slave Law. ○ 1854: Bleeding Kansas. ○ 1857: *Dred Scott* decision. ○ 1859 Abolitionist John Brown raids Harpers Ferry.	○ 1852: Harriet Beecher Stowe publishes *Uncle Tom's Cabin*.
○ 1870: Webb marries Laura Conger. ○ 1871: Webb's business burned out in Chicago Fire. ○ 1871: Laura Conger disappears from records. ○ 1872: Webb Loses religion.	○ 1861–1865: The Civil War.	○ 1859: Darwin publishes *The Origins of Species*. ○ 1860–1861: Pony Express (St. Joseph, Missouri). ○ 1862: Death of Henry David Thoreau. ○ 1864: Death of Nathaniel Hawthorne.
○ 1874: Webb comes to Missouri; editor of *Unionville Republican*. ○ 1876: Webb at *St. Joseph Gazette*. ○ 1877: Webb enters St. Louis Journalism. Marries Ella Hotchkiss.	○ 1865–1877: Reconstruction. ○ 1876: Little Bighorn, Custer's last stand. ○ 1877: End of Reconstruction. Beginning of the "Jim Crow" Era.	○ 1869: Trans-Continental Railway completed.
		○ 1881: Death of Ralph Waldo Emerson. ○ 1885: Chicago builds first skyscraper. ○ 1886: Completion of Statue of Liberty.
○ 1881–1883: Webb leaves journalism for the circus and the stage. ○ 1881: Webb begins study of Oriental religions. Becomes a Buddhist. ○ ca. 1883: Webb joins the Theosophical Society. ○ 1888–1887: Webb returns to journalism at the *Missouri Republican*. ○ 1888–1892: Webb appointed U.S. consul to the Philippines. ○ 1888: Webb converts to Islam. ○ 1890–1892: Webb corresponds with Indian Muslims. ○ 1892: Abdulla Arab, Indian Muslim merchant, visits Webb in Manila, to lay the foundations of the American Mission. ○ 1892: Webb's Oriental tour. ○ 1893: Webb inaugurates the American Mission in Manhattan.	○ 1890: Massacre of Wounded Knee.	○ 1891: Death of Herman Melville. ○ 1890s: The telephone has become an indispensable part of American Life. ○ 1892: Death of Walt Whitman. ○ 1893: Chicago World's Fair and Parliament of Religions.
○ 1893: Webb represents Islam at the Parliament of Religions. ○ 1896: The end of Webb's American Mission.	○ 1896: *Plessy v Ferguson Decision* establishes racial segregation as national policy.	○ 1903: Orville and Wilbur Wright—flight at Kitty Hawk. ○ 1910: Death of Mark Twain. ○ 1912: Sinking of *Titanic*. ○ 1915: Alexander Graham Bell inaugurates first transcontinental telephone service.
○ 1901: Webb appointed Honorary Turkish Consul General to New York. Visits Turkey. ○ 1916: Webb's death.	○ 1914–1918: World War I. United States does not enter until 1917.	○ 1916: Henry Ford's "Model T" has become a national mania.

FIGURE I.2. Rough Victorian American Timeline

Early Victorian Period 1820–1850

Middle Victorian Period 1850–1870

Late Victorian Period 1870–1901

Cooper and Irving were New Yorkers and broke the ground for a distinctive American literature, inscribing the themes and imagery of their native state on the American imagination. Irving's humorous *History of New York* appeared in 1809. Its narrator, the fictional Diedrich Knickerbocker—as much a pedant as Ichabod Crane—presented his own eccentric history of New York since the world's creation. In *Sketches*, which came out in 1820 and contained "The Legend of Sleepy Hollow" and "Rip Van Winkle," Irving experimented with the short story, helping to craft it into one of American literature's most successful genres. Cooper grew up in the Alleghenies in a frontier town northwest of Hudson and fostered a romantic picture of the wilderness and its people in *The Last of the Mohicans* (1826) and *Deerslayer* (1841).

Interestingly, both Irving and Cooper took note of Muslims. Cooper hailed a 1645 victory over the Barbary pirates by a crew of Massachusetts seamen as "the first American naval battle." It prefigured the nation's triumph over the North African regency of Tripoli in 1815, which in many eyes established the young republic's status as a nation among nations. In *Salmagundi*, Irving created the character of "Mustapha Rub-a-Dub Keli Khan," a fictional Barbary pirate on parole in New York, who, in his sundry reflections on public manners and morality, determines that America is more a "logacracy" or "government of words" than a government of the people. While serving as diplomatic attaché to Madrid from 1826 to 1829, Irving fell in love with the lore of medieval Muslim Spain and wrote *The Conquest of Granada* (1829) and *The Alhambra* (1832), both of which left their mark on Webb. Later, as ambassador to Spain, Irving published an influential but hastily written and poorly researched work titled *Mahomet and His Successors*, which Webb knew and frequently commented on.[40]

Nathaniel Hawthorne, Ralph Waldo Emerson, and Henry David Thoreau—all New Englanders from Massachusetts—built on the broad literary foundations of Irving and Cooper. In *The Scarlet Letter* (1850), Hawthorne confronted the unforgiving legalism of Puritan religiosity. Emerson, an eminent Unitarian turned Transcendentalist, greatly influenced the literary expression and religious thought of his contemporaries, including Webb. Emerson advocated that each person seek an intensely individual path to religious truth, an ideal that Webb himself would emulate. Thoreau, Emerson's friend and disciple, undertook his own spiritual journey and recorded it in *Walden* (1854).

Herman Melville and Walt Whitman, New Yorkers roughly of Webb's generation, were particularly successful in molding the American literary imagination and articulating the nation's sense of self. In truly Mid-Atlantic spirit, both rejected institutionalized religion as the overseer of America's conscience. They celebrated the majesty of America's unspoiled nature and the native virtue and wisdom of its common people.[41] Whitman was deeply influenced by Elias Hicks, an early abolitionist and Quaker leader whose radical theology had even divided the local Quaker congregation of Hudson, New York. Webb liked to quote from Whitman's *Leaves of Grass*, which typified the individualistic and nonconformist spirit of nineteenth-century New York. Whitman "[cocked] his hat as [he] pleased indoors or out" and found God's signs in everything, even a handful of grass: "I guess it is the handkerchief of the Lord / ... Or I guess it is a uniform hieroglyphic."[42]

Where Webb Belongs in History

Although *A Muslim in Victorian America* is the first in-depth study of Webb's life, his importance has been recognized for some time, especially in academic circles. More than twenty years ago, Akbar Muhammad emphasized the need for exhaustive research on Webb "to illuminate the early social and intellectual history of Islam in the United States."[43] In the wake of the terrorist attacks of September 11, 2001, an examination of Webb's legacy for American Islam has taken on additional significance in light of Webb's relatively broad-minded spirit, his frank opposition to fanaticism, and his lasting civic commitment. But where exactly does Webb belong in the history of Islam in America?

In 1945, Dr. Emory Tunison, an American convert to Islam and secretary of the New York Islamic Center, resoundingly proclaimed Webb to have been "the first American Muslim."[44] Although unique in Muslim American history, Webb was not the first Muslim on American soil, nor was he even the first Anglo-American to adopt Islam or dream of bringing it into the consciousnesses of other Americans. Tunison lived half a century before the presence of West African Muslims among America's slave population came to general attention in the late twentieth century. Although they represented a small percentage of the enslaved Africans brought to America, West African Muslims made up a "distinctive minority" because they were often literate and came from relatively cosmopolitan backgrounds, as exemplified in the lives of Job son of Solomon, Yarrow Mamout, and "Prince" Ibrahim.[45] Seeking to rectify this oversight with regard to Webb, Fareeha Khan, who did her master's thesis on him at the University of Chicago, describes him as an early white convert to Islam in the United States and noteworthy example of an American who embraced Islam with no links, direct or indirect, to the older legacy of the religion among the enslaved Africans of the antebellum era.[46]

The earliest records of indigenous European-American conversion to Islam have been found in Canada. Although little is known about them, John Love, a native of Ontario, and John and Martha Simon, a couple who immigrated to Ontario from the United States, registered themselves as "Mahometans" in the Canadian census around 1871.[47] A few years later but still several years before Webb's conversion, an American missionary identified only as the Reverend Norman embraced Islam in Turkey and returned home with the intent of establishing an Islamic mission. In 1896, the eminent British Orientalist Thomas Arnold referred to Webb's conversion in the first edition of his classic work *The Preaching of Islam*, but he carefully noted that a Methodist clergyman named Norman had been sent to Turkey from the United States as a Christian missionary but ultimately embraced Islam instead. In 1875, the Reverend Norman returned to the United States to propagate his newfound Islamic faith.[48]

Arnold took his information from a French Orientalist, Joseph Garcin de Tassy, who had mentioned Norman in an annual review of Indian literature for the year 1875. Citing the British Indian press, Garcin de Tassy noted the shocking discovery of several British conversions to Islam in India. Also expressing alarm at the precedent, the *Bengalore Examiner* declared: "Few people will be able to believe that Europeans in Hindustan have abandoned the Christian religion in order to turn themselves into Mussulmans and have thus dishonored their countries; but the matter is only too true." Garcin de Tassy then cited the *Indian Mail*'s report of the Reverend Norman scandal: "What is even more astonishing is the perversion of a Methodist missionary named Norman, who had gone to Constantinople to preach the Gospel but who embraced Islamism and is now preaching it in America."[49] In 1984, Akbar Muhammad first drew scholarly attention to Norman's story. But other scholars were slow to take note, and it is not uncommon even today to find references in their works to Webb as the first American convert to Islam and indigenous propagator of his adopted faith.[50]

I wavered a long time myself before assigning Webb a label. It seemed wise at the outset to liberate him, insofar as possible, from the contentious adjective "first" and to look instead for something less impassioned, such as "early American spokesperson of Islam." All the same, Webb does deserve the prestige of standing first and foremost in several areas of the modern history of Islam in America. The vision and scope of Webb's work were distinctive. In 1895, when he and his family were living in penury in the Catskill Mountains and his mission was on the brink of total financial failure, an Indian Muslim reader of Webb's *Moslem World* wrote to assure him: "I am sure that you will, in spite of all the opposition and difficulties in your way, push on and not at all care for people who go against justice and honesty. There is no doubt that God will help you, and that in the history of the Islamic propaganda in America your name will stand first and foremost."[51] A month later, Webb's good friend and supporter Hajee Abdulla Browne, a British convert who was editing the *Egyptian Herald* in Cairo, offered similarly encouraging sentiments:

Dear Brother Webb:
　Peace be with you.
　Very many thanks for the always welcome *Moslem World*, a valuable aid to the good work you have so nobly undertaken.

No one knows better than I the many difficulties that surround such efforts as yours, and I trust that the day is coming when all Islam will recognize the services you are rendering to the cause we all have at heart. If our Moslem brethren generally could grasp the true value of your labors, they could not but enter heart and soul into the task of aiding you, and I trust and hope that the time is not far off when they will do so; till then you must only labor on, but ever with the certainty that the best and surest reward awaits you in the here-after.

With salutations to all the brethren in America,

Hajee A. Browne[52]

In other ways, too, Webb stood first and foremost in the history of Islam in America. From the beginning, he sought to give his work an international perspective by creating a link between America and the Muslim world. Seira Shalton, who wrote her master's thesis on Webb at Arizona State University, emphasizes the international dynamic of his vision: "From the podium and in the press, Webb assumed the responsibility of becoming Islam's spokes-person in America and a liaison to the rest of the Islamic world."[53] This perspective is reflected throughout Webb's speeches and writings and cul-minated in his appointment as Honorary Turkish Consul General to United States in 1901. Richard Seager, an authority on the First World's Parliament of Religions, notes that this Ottoman honor reflected the status Webb had attained in the eyes of the contemporary Muslim world.[54]

As a pioneering herald of Islam in the United States, Webb may rightfully be called America's first Muslim editor and the founder of the North Amer-ican Islamic press. His newspapers and journals were widely read not only in the United States but also in Europe, Asia, and Africa. Their period of cir-culation (1893 until early 1896) was relatively short, yet few attempts at Muslim journalism in America lasted longer until the latter part of the twentieth century, when the American Islamic press came into its own.[55] Webb's editorial work was of credible quality and even today compares ad-mirably with North American Muslim journalism.

Webb's participation in the First World's Parliament of Religions of 1893 constituted a singular claim to fame. As indicated earlier, he was the only Muslim—and an indigenous one at that—to represent Islam at that great watershed in American cultural history. But his public appearances on Islam's behalf extended far beyond the parliament, and he evinced a readiness to travel widely throughout the country to lecture on his faith. Like many Victorians, Webb had a preference for informal parlor talks at private homes but also lectured in diverse public arenas and gave regular weekly presentations in the opulent lecture room of his Moslem World Building at 458 West Twentieth Street in Manhattan.

With reading circles in New York, Washington, D.C., and California, Webb's Islamic society demonstrated a distinctive structure and an interesting strategy that antedated by a full generation America's early-twentieth-century Islamic missions.[56] In light of Webb's organizational work, Jane Smith and others have designated him as the founder of New York's "first documented Islamic institution."[57] Smith adds that he established the "first Muslim house of worship" in America.[58] Webb's Manhattan mosque on the third floor of the Moslem World Building in Chelsea was, in fact, inaugurated a full seven years before the Syrian and Lebanese Muslim immigrants of Ross, North Dakota, began to hold communal prayer services in their homes in 1900. The mosque in Ross, sometimes called "the first American mosque," was not built until 1920, two years before the construction of the so-called "mother mosque" of Cedar Rapids, Iowa, which remains functional today.[59]

Webb's speeches, pamphlets, and books frequently drew attention to his spiritual journey to Islam, and, in light of this work, he has been characterized as one of the precursors of Islamic conversion narrative in the West.[60] But, perhaps as much as for anything else, Mohammed Alexander Russell Webb deserves to be counted first and foremost among American Muslims as a public representative of the faith who attempted to take interpretative control over his faith and speak of it with personal authority; he attempted to forge a viable Islamic self-definition and authentic indigenous identity within the norms of an increasingly pluralistic world.

Jane Smith concludes that, although Webb was "extremely serious in his dedication to Islam and his desire to bring its message to his native country and city," his efforts left no "lasting effect on the religious culture of America."[61] Similarly, J. Gordon Melton observes that although Webb, like the proponents of America's first Buddhist and Hindu missions, used the Parliament of Religions as a platform for announcing his mission, his undertaking, unlike theirs, never succeeded in establishing a lasting movement with an unbroken spiritual pedigree traceable to the parliament. Webb's legacy, in Melton's view, was largely forgotten after his death.[62]

Much of what Smith and Melton say can be conceded for the short term. Although the story of Webb's conversion and Islamic mission in America were hot items in the early 1890s press, Webb faded quickly from public memory, and his legacy long remained hidden below academic radar. Five years before Webb's death, Samuel Zwemer established a Protestant missionary journal bearing the same title as Webb's journal, the *Moslem World*, but it was dedicated to diametrically opposing goals. Between 1920 and 1960, both it and the *International Review of Missions* presented several studies on Islam in America without a single reference to Mohammed Alexander Russell Webb.[63] Strikingly, no mention of Webb, not even an obituary, appeared in the early issues of the London-based *Islamic Review*, which began in 1913, or in its American counterpart, *The Moslem Sunrise*, which was inaugurated in 1921.

All the same, Webb was not utterly forgotten after his death, and his life served as an inspiration for at least a few Muslim Americans. In 1943, the Webb Memorial Committee held a tribute in his honor at Manhattan's Steinway Hall.[64] There had probably been at least one earlier Webb memorial, although the 1943 meeting appears to have been the last.[65] Two Muslim American converts spoke in Webb's commemoration at Steinway Hall: Dr. Emory Tunison and Nadirah Florence Ives Osman. Osman had come to know of Webb in 1931 while in Turkey after someone in India mailed her a copy of Mirza Ghulam Ahmad's *Teachings of Islam*. The preface had been written in 1910 by Muhammad Ali, a prominent Lahori Ahmadiyya[66] leader and scholar. Ali paid tribute to Webb, whom he identified as a New Jersey resident, and thanked him for valuable editorial assistance in the final draft of Ali's English translation of the Qur'an. Osman exuberantly declared:

> No one can imagine how joyful I was to see this reference to an American convert to Islam from New Jersey, for I had been born in that state myself, and many of my relatives were still living there. It comforted me, far away in a distant land, as though he were approving the position I had taken, as a convert to Islam. It is always remarkable, even to myself, why I did not write immediately, or even later, directly to Muhammad Ali to enquire about him. However, 1910 was a long way removed from 1931. A whole war lay between. I had the feeling that he must be dead. It was only later, when I met Dr. Tunison, that I found in his enthusiasm again the echo of Muhammad Webb's name. Since then I have found, with Dr. Tunison, the simple stone that marks his grave, and seen the vine of ivy that swards his resting place.[67]

In the end, though, Webb's merit does not hinge on his having been first in various aspects of American Islamic history, nor has it been diminished by the fading of his memory for most of the twentieth century. Webb's very human and very American biography is edifying for its own sake. Until his death, he remained a prototype of pluralism and civic involvement. More generally, his life constitutes a true-to-life reflection of Victorian American history.

His adoption of Islam in late-nineteenth-century America was utterly out of the ordinary, but the manner in which he pursued it was not. Webb embraced Islam in the spirit of classical American individual initiative in religion.[68] Moreover, Webb regarded his conversion as a perfectly natural alternative for himself and any other American who chose it. He never became deeply learned in Islam yet was creative in his application of what he knew. With an instinctive

American naturalness, he assumed authority in the interpretation of his adopted religion, rejected "fanaticism" and bigotry, and never felt himself duty-bound to follow any "irrational or backward" formulations associated with the faith wherever he might encounter them. Webb founded his life and his vision for Islam in America on the same broad spiritual ethos through which he himself initially made his journey to the faith.

2

Hudson Valley Roots

The Big Picture: Victorian America

The lives of human beings reflect the times in which they live, and one can see clearly the influence of the Victorian period on Webb. Not only was he characteristically Victorian in outlook and behavior, but many aspects of his biography make full sense only within the Victorian context.

Like other historical eras, the Victorian age is a construct of historians. They differ in their dating of it, although the lengthy reign of Queen Victoria (1837–1901) always constitutes a convenient reference. Webb was born in the era's early phase, attained manhood during its middle period, and lived out most of the remainder of his life during the late stage.

The Victorian age was a "crucial turning point" in modern history, a major transition from the largely agrarian, premodern past to massive industrialization and urbanization. It was an era of imperialist global expansion, a self-consciously new age marked by distinctly novel ways of looking at the world. Although Victorian America remained an epoch of Protestant hegemony and its core values emanated from the dominant culture's belief in work and progress, Webb's generation was one often engaged in radical reinterpretations of society, nature, the self, and society.[1]

It was during the Victorian period that America came of age, gradually emerging as a world power and a major player in international affairs.[2] Webb witnessed these changes firsthand, although his four years as U.S. consul in the Philippines reminded him repeatedly that, in the eyes of established powers, the United States was still far from ranking as a peer.

During Webb's childhood, the nation completed its continental expansion from Atlantic to Pacific. A year before his birth, President James Polk annexed Texas and triggered the Mexican War (1846–1848), which ended in a humiliating defeat for Mexico and cession of most of its northwestern territories to the United States. Such monumental changes had local significance for Webb. Hudson's General William J. Worth, a hero of the War of 1812, won national acclaim in the Mexican War and served as Mexico City's military governor.[3] By coincidence, a prominent nineteenth-century memorial to General Worth stood in Manhattan directly in front of the location of Webb's first mission office at 1122 Broadway. By 1912, four years before Webb's death, the forty-eight contiguous states had become a single union, making the United States one of the largest and potentially most powerful nations on earth.[4]

The unprecedented metamorphosis from a rural to an urban nation of burgeoning industrial cities was one of the principal revolutions of the period.[5] The Hudson Valley of Webb's childhood was little different from the agrarian landscape familiar to George Washington. All of that changed with the Civil War, which marked the beginning of industrial America and the emergence of new technologies and ways of thinking. The nation moved rapidly toward urbanization, and, by the time Webb reached old age, the number of American towns and cities had increased sevenfold.[6] In high buildings, elevators supplemented staircases and ushered in a panorama of unprecedented towering structures. City skylines extended upward toward the clouds, and, in 1885, Chicago inaugurated the era of the skyscraper.[7]

Life on the Hudson River

To tell Webb's story without speaking of the Hudson River would be like writing about Mark Twain without mentioning the Mississippi. Webb grew up only a few minutes' walk from the great river's banks, and his identity was deeply rooted in the river and its history. Like other Hudson youths, he could have recounted at length an array of river stories and legends, including those of the Nantucket whalers who first settled his town. Like most of the city's children, however, he saw the river not as a historical symbol but as a focal point of fun. Throughout the year, it offered a variety of sports and games. Year-round fishing opportunities included ice fishing when the river froze over. The river was excellent for swimming and boating, and, in the dead of winter, it provided ice skating and ice boating. The river's main channel was usually open to navigation, and boats were required to cross the river itself. In harsh winters, however, the river occasionally froze over, providing a special occasion for Hudson families, who seized the opportunity to cross the river on foot, sleds, in sleighs, or on iceboats. There were no bridges, and daily ferries transported people, announcing their comings and goings with deafening whistle blasts that filled the streets of Hudson.[8]

Webb's native Hudson-on-the-Hudson owed its existence to the river. During his childhood, the Hudson ranked indisputably among America's most vital waterways. It was not only the backdrop of Webb's sense of himself but was central to America's emerging national consciousness. It was the central symbol of the Hudson River School, for which the city of Hudson was a principal center, and was a key image in early American literature.

Located about a hundred miles north of New York's Upper Bay, Hudson-on-the-Hudson was established in 1785. Its history did not go back to the colonial period, but the city had been chartered just two years after independence and prided itself on being among the first municipalities incorporated in the newly established United States.[9] What colonial roots the city might boast of were rooted in New England and not New York, since its founding fathers were mostly pacifist Quaker seamen from Nantucket.

After the Revolutionary War, England's continued hostility toward its former colony exposed the American merchant marine to regular predations. As in the story of Melville's *Billy Budd*, British men-of-war would seize American ships, impose heavy taxes upon their owners, and press their crews into service. Because of its location far out in the Atlantic, Nantucket was dangerously exposed to English attacks.

For Nantucket Quakers, armed resistance was out of the question, but their economic losses were also unacceptable. In 1783, their leaders banded together to find a commercially viable haven. They decided upon Hudson, which at the time was a small Dutch waterfront known as Claverack Landing. Many of the new families came to Hudson by sea. Some dismantled their old houses in New England, numbered the timbers and frames, loaded them on their ships, and brought them upriver to be reassembled in Hudson.[10]

Webb was born in Hudson at a time when history had already begun to pass it by, but, as was the case with many up-and-coming cities, there had been little indication of Hudson's looming fall from greatness during the early period. Soon after its foundation, it had moved into the forefront as a prominent American seaport, and from 1790 until 1815 it was designated an official port of entry to the United States. Famous ships from around the world docked in its port, which could accommodate more than twenty-five seaworthy ships at a time and boasted a number of first-rate shipyards. Hudson became a magnet for regional commerce and international trade and was praised throughout the nation for its precociousness. The *New York Journal* spoke of its rapid growth as "something unheard-of and marvelous."[11]

Hudson's commerce was primarily based on regional products. New York City was its major market, although the port also traded actively with the Old South and the Caribbean and maintained commercial links with Europe.

Whaling had never prospered in Hudson as it had in Nantucket, and even before Webb's birth it was more a matter of nostalgia than profitability. Still, Hudson outfitted many great whaling ships that plied the southern seas, often returning with tales richer than their catch. But Hudson's attachment to whaling was strong, and in 1829 it made a concerted attempt to revive the industry, which led to the formation of the Hudson Whaling Company. A year before Webb's birth, the corporation failed suddenly, bringing huge financial loss and an abrupt end to Hudson's whaling dreams.

By 1847, economic decline had set in and the city's maritime greatness faded into little more than a memory. One Hudsoner despaired: "The days of [Hudson's] prosperity have long since passed away. Its wealth has diminished, its business sources have dried up, and almost every vestige of its former glory has disappeared."[12]

As Hudson turned away from the sea, its aspirations turned inland, especially toward the vast wilderness beyond the Alleghenies. The new-fashioned railroads interceded to fulfill its westward-looking dreams, rendering obsolete what remained of the city's maritime past. By the 1850s, the old waterfront was virtually closed for business.

During the first decade of Webb's life, Hudson undertook major railway construction. In 1851, Webb probably took part with Hudson's other children in the grand festivities welcoming the Albany–New York line. Speeches and celebrations lasted through the day, culminating in a grand public banquet for more than fourteen hundred. A local reporter declared: "We reached Hudson amid the booming of cannon and the cheering of thousands. There was more enthusiasm manifested here than at any previous stopping-place. Banners and flags waved in every direction, and the utmost enthusiasm prevailed." Soon, Hudson emerged as a central cog in the New York rail system. By the time Webb was a young man, he could board a train in Hudson for Buffalo and from there proceed to Chicago.[13]

New York and the Mid-Atlantic Cultural Genius

One of the most important developments in America's English-speaking colonies—a phenomenon with parallels throughout the British colonies—was the subtle development of cultural undercurrents. This cultural drift ultimately led to the creation of a viable, indigenous sense of New World identity sufficient to wean America from its transatlantic roots and enable it to negotiate New World challenges on its own. Such cultural developments not only made it possible for British American colonies to survive in the wilderness but laid the foundation for revolution and a coherent nation-state.[14]

I opened this chapter by saying Webb was a Victorian. He was, more precisely, a Victorian from America's Mid-Atlantic cultural zone. To understand

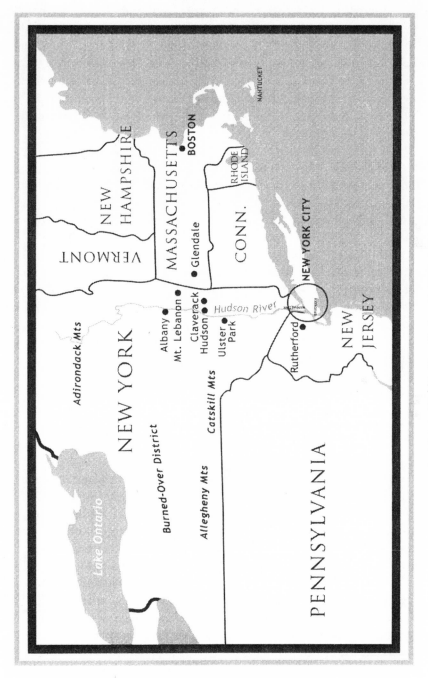

FIGURE 2.1. Webb's New York and Surrounding Area

him, it is important to have an appreciation of those qualities of the Mid-Atlantic that make it distinct from anywhere else.

In the thirteen British American colonies along the Atlantic seaboard, three zones of pan-British (early American) culture emerged: New England, the Mid-Atlantic, and the Old South. Each region matured into one of the core areas of American cultural genesis. Webb's New York, in company with New Jersey, Pennsylvania, and Delaware, constituted the Mid-Atlantic.[15] Each main cultural area corresponded to a primary center of seventeenth-century Protestant settlement: Massachusetts (Puritan), New York (Dutch Reformed), and Virginia (Episcopalian).[16]

By the time independence came, certain outlooks had become characteristic of each zone. In New England, Puritanism engendered introspection, a commitment to external moral conventions, and serious civic commitment. The Mid-Atlantic was markedly different. It had a deeply innovative religious character, one that was as heterodox if not as heretical as New England was orthodox. The Mid-Atlantic was also known for its Yankee pragmatism and robust individualism embodied by Walt Whitman. Given its overwhelmingly agrarian nature and dependence upon slave labor, the Old South was inherently conservative, patriarchal, and elitist. Its cultural ethos was also, not surprisingly, linked to the imperative of preserving white exclusivity and racial supremacy.[17]

Webb's township and the Hudson Valley in general constituted a distinctive subcultural zone of the Mid-Atlantic. Hudson had ethnic and cultural roots in Nantucket, which were further strengthened by proximity to the Massachusetts and Vermont borders of New England. This special relation to New England made Hudson and much of the Hudson Valley an overlapping cultural zone, where Mid-Atlantic and New England culture came together.[18]

In addition to Hudson's Nantucket roots, it was also the case, more generally, that most British Americans who settled the Hudson Valley during the late eighteenth century had originated from New England. American cultural historians often mention the theory of "first effective settlement" to explain local regional consistencies. According to the theory, the initial groups to settle a region—the Puritans of New England or Dutch of New York, for example—generally set primary cultural norms that affect the assimilation of newcomers, whatever their background. In Webb's region, the first effective settlers were Dutch Protestants, and they left a stamp of pragmatism, relative broadmindedness, and a "religious civility" surpassing other colonies.[19] Hudson's first effective settlement, however, had been at the hands of the Nantucket Quakers, and they made it a point to imprint the city with their own distinctively New England flavor, which, although blended with the region's overall Mid-Atlantic temperament, can still be sensed in the city today.[20]

Mid-Atlantic Religious Innovation
and Webb's Formative Period

Hudson's religious institutions represented the most common Mid-Atlantic denominations: Presbyterians, Methodists, Dutch Reformed, Lutherans, and Baptists. As founders of the city, Quakers were especially strong. The Hudson's Proprietors—the leading members of its founding families—were mostly members of the Society of Friends (Quakers), and the Quaker Meeting House was, naturally, the city's oldest church. True to Quaker tradition, the Proprietors welcomed all denominations to the city and donated sites for their houses of worship and religious schools.[21] The Freemasons, a quasi-religious society, were an important part of Hudson, as they were elsewhere in the United States, and established a lodge there in 1786. Roman Catholics arrived in 1847, a year after Webb's birth, and founded a thriving congregation. In 1855, the city's African-American minority established the Zion Methodist Episcopal Church and continued to expand their numbers during Webb's early manhood. A small group of Jews, apparently newcomers to Hudson, incorporated as an official congregation in 1868, shortly before Webb left for Chicago, and built a synagogue two blocks from his home.[22]

The First Presbyterian Church was Hudson's second-oldest congregation and is one of its largest and most prominent churches even today. As mentioned earlier, former President Martin Van Buren was an active member, often officiating in various minor capacities.[23] Although reared as a Presbyterian, Webb made during his early manhood what appears to be his first independent religious choice: he joined Hudson's Episcopalian Church. He claimed, however, that the change had been motivated not by theological considerations but by consideration of the attractiveness of the congregation's young ladies.[24]

Religion has always been deeply rooted in the American experience. Tocqueville, who visited America during the Second Great Awakening, observed that religious commitment exercised more influence over the United States than any nation on earth: "It is religion that gave birth to the Anglo-American societies: one must never forget this; in the United States religion is therefore intermingled with all national habits and all the sentiments to which a native country gives birth; that gives it a particular strength."[25] Webb's formative period took place during the last years of the Second Great Awakening, a time when "religious exuberance was at an unusual pitch" and the "democratization" of Old World Christianity was brought to its completion.[26] The religious expression of the time was as highly diverse as it was individualistic, presenting "alternative views of religion, the rights of women, patterns of eugenics, and the like."[27]

The Second Awakening was an age of "uncompromising dreamers." Religious millenarians and utopians multiplied throughout the United States, seeking a new moral order and "taking their models from some perfect past and their direction from some perfect future." They spread out over the nation to establish religious communes where the pious, often after "long treks to the new promised colonies or kingdoms," could make a new beginning. Townships grew up around their religious experiments and still bear names like Zion, Aurora, Bethel, and Zoar, which reveal their religious origins in the spiritual enthusiasm of the period. Such communities were so widespread during Webb's formative period that it would have been difficult to find an American who had neither participated in nor lived within range of them.[28]

Webb grew up in ready proximity to some of the most important religious experiments of nineteenth-century America: Shakers, Mormons, Adventists, and Perfectionists. There is no question that the religious ambience of the times helped form the attitudes and expectations that guided Webb through life.

Columbia County and eastern New York were rich in religious enthusiasm, but over the Catskills in central and western New York lay the "burned-over district," so-called by later historians because of the frequency with which it was "struck by evangelical lightning." The district witnessed the "first major *intra*-American blending and fusion of regional cultures" and, remarkably, it matched the old core area of the Iroquois Confederacy, which fostered marriage alliances and other contacts with white settlers.[29] It was also a springboard for westward migration and a major source of Midwestern culture. Few other parts of America generated such diversity of consequential religious movements and intense followers, and the fervor of religious renewal did not persist anywhere as long as it did there.[30]

New York's religious movements manifested characteristics typical of the evangelical individualism of the Second Awakening, combining a powerful sense of personal biblical authority with original interpretation. This independent evangelical spirit empowered ordinary Christians to take direct part in the world of preaching, revival, and missionary work. The Second Great Awakening created democratic religious communities that nurtured a strong "we-feeling" within their ranks and often succeeded in spreading their missions abroad by producing "tremendous expansionary energy" in their followers, but which, to the displeasure of many mainstream Protestants, also fueled communitarian and exclusivist sentiment.[31]

Presbyterians, representing the predominant Mid-Atlantic denomination, were major participants in the First and Second Great Awakenings and were among the earliest churches to master the "competitive revivalism" of American religion and adopt "a New World orientation." They were predictably nationalistic and made little attempt to maintain ties with their denominational brethren across the Atlantic. Ambrose Searle, a British colonial governor of New York, "smelled Presbyterians at the bottom of the colonial conspiracy," and, after the outbreak of war, the English sometimes referred to the revolution as "the Presbyterian Rebellion."[32]

The Hudson Quakers were theologically active before and during Webb's life and had important affinities with the Columbia County Shakers, a Quaker offshoot who were at the heart of the American Shaker movement. Women played a prominent role in the Quaker community, as they did among the Shakers. The minister Hannah Barnard rose to prominence among the Hudson Quakers within a decade of the city's founding. Barnard, known for her inquisitive mind and eloquence, was a comely woman with "eyes black, keen, and penetrating" who espoused "ideas and principles in advance of her day," according to a nineteenth-century local historian. She visited the Quakers of England around the turn of the eighteenth century, but her outspoken nature and unconventional teachings won her their disapproval. She returned home in 1801 to find that the Quakers of Hudson, in response to the complaints and directives of their English brethren, had disavowed her leadership and views.[33]

Almost thirty years later, the teachings of Quaker Elias Hicks, Walt Whitman's mentor, gained ground in Hudson and caused divisions among the Quakers, who separated into the "Orthodox Friends (Quakers)" and "Hicksite Friends." Around 1828, the Hicksites prevailed and won about three-fourths of the local fellowship. The "Orthodox Friends" implored their brethren in London for help and, with their assistance, purchased new property for an independent meeting hall.[34]

The Shakers—officially, the Millennial Church of the United Society of Believers in Christ's Second Appearing—lasted more than two hundred years and were among the most influential religious movements of nineteenth-century America, occupying a central place in the religious history of the United States. They were known for their ecstatic religious practices, which included dancing and sometimes even whirling like dervishes. They were called "Shaking Quakers" because of their religious ecstasies, and from that name came the popular form, "Shakers." "Mother Ann" Lee, originally a radical English Quaker, established the movement's first colony at Watervliet, New York, in 1774. After her death, the movement's national center moved to Mount Lebanon in the northeastern corner of Columbia County, about thirty miles from Hudson; it remained the center throughout the movement's history. The Shakers reached their zenith around the time of Webb's birth and continued to flourish until the Civil War, but their prevalence began to diminish during the 1870s in the wake of the Civil War and the rise of American industrialism. By the early twentieth century, the Shakers were a thing of the past and had become virtually extinct.[35]

Gender equality and Ann Lee's person were central to Shaker theology. "Mother Ann" was "the chosen female," "the spiritual Mother in Israel," the second incarnation of "the Christ Spirit," and "the female Messiah." Her advent constituted one of the major dispensations of universal religious history. Through her, "the Christ Spirit [had been] exhibited a second time," the pristine state of Eden before the fall had been restored, and men and women had again become equals.[36]

The deity in Shaker belief was "dual in being," the "primary fountain of male and female." Shaker social organization reflected a corresponding dual order of government, based on gender equality. But for Shakers, the divine grace that renewed perfect equality between men and women required total sexual abstinence. There was no place in their communes for either marriage or procreation. They kept their communities alive by attracting converts and adopting children.[37]

Like their Quaker brethren, Shakers were pacifists. In Shaker belief, war and other social evils were the consequences of "physical and mental lust from abnormal passions." For hostility to cease and peace to reign, a true state of gender equality on Shaker principles had to be attained. There was no private property in the communes. All possessions were held in common, as in the first Christian communities. Shakers taught hard work, and every member perfected a selection of crafts and skills. Intense daily labor generated wealth and open-handed generosity.[38] In addition to physical labor, Shakers devoted themselves to cultivating their minds and educating others. They developed excellent schools and libraries, replete with the latest newspapers and magazines as well as religious and secular literature. Attainment of true simplicity was the fundamental goal of Shaker spirituality and was reflected in everything about them, especially their matchless carpentry and architecture. The famous Shaker composition " 'Tis the Gift to Be Simple" has become a popular contemporary song:[39]

> 'Tis the gift to be simple, 'tis the gift to be free,
> 'Tis the gift to come down where we ought to be,
> And when we find ourselves in the place just right,
> 'Twill be in the valley of love and delight.[40]

The Church of Jesus Christ of Latter-Day Saints (Mormons) has been called "the most peculiarly American religious movement to originate prior to the Civil War."[41] The church's founder, Joseph Smith, grew up in the burned-over district and was repelled by the "sectarian anarchy" he found around him in New York. In 1829, he published *The Book of Mormon*, alleging to have translated it from golden angelic tablets discovered near his home. Alexander Campbell, a minister of the Disciples of Christ, observed that Smith's revelation, notwithstanding its claim to antiquity, succeeded remarkably in debating "every error and almost every truth discussed in New York for the last ten years." In 1830, local hostility forced the Mormons to leave New York for the Midwest. But hostility followed them wherever they went, and Joseph Smith and his brother Hyrum were killed by a mob in Illinois in 1844.[42]

Brigham Young succeeded Joseph Smith as the church's president and began the process of resettling the Mormons in the Utah Territory. The great trek to Salt Lake City, an American hegira of sorts, began two years after Webb's birth.[43]

The Church of Jesus Christ of Latter-Day Saints was surrounded by controversy from the beginning, less for its theology than for its appeal to "theocratic authority," which generated strong communal solidarity and threatened to create a powerful Mormon bloc. Mormons looked upon the United States with a "double vision." They endorsed the Constitution as "divinely inspired" but believed the Mormon kingdom of God on earth would supersede it. When Joseph Smith won the Illinois presidential nomination in 1844, his victory brought to the surface deep fears of Mormon dominance. The social order Brigham Young established in Utah was widely viewed as a theocracy. President James Buchanan saw it as a direct threat to U.S. sovereignty and, in 1857, declared the "Utah" or "Mormon War" to reestablish federal authority.[44]

When, in 1852, it became public knowledge that Mormons practiced plural marriage, it helped make fear of polygamy the great negative fixation of the Victorian American mind-set, a fixation that Webb, as a Victorian Muslim, would continually encounter. The practice of polygamy further alienated non-Mormons but was controversial among the Mormons themselves and divided the movement. The Supreme Court declared polygamy unconstitutional in repudiation of Mormon practice, and Utah was admitted to statehood in 1890 only after the Church of Latter-Day Saints officially rejected the practice.[45]

Polygamy was one of several points of contact between Mormonism and Islam, and few Americans failed to see the resemblance. Comparisons between Islam and Mormonism—generally at the expense of both—continued to be drawn well into the twentieth century. In 1917, Bruce Kiney published a highly prejudicial work titled *Mormonism: The Islam of America*. In his review of the book, Samuel Zwemer, the prominent Protestant missionary, contended that Joseph Smith had claimed in 1838 that he "would be a second Mohammed to his generation." Zwemer carried the comparison further:

> Mormonism has also had its Hegira, makes much of its sacred
> book, which also is often unintelligible because of its stilted and dif-
> fuse style. Yet like the Koran, the book of the Mormons is the key-
> stone of their religion; it also has glaring discrepancies which are
> accounted for by a doctrine of abrogation. Its ethical code as regards
> the seventh and ninth commandments of the Decalogue remind one
> of Al Bokhari. On the other hand the contrasts are no less dis-
> tinct: the Moslem idea of God is not only higher than that of
> Mormonism . . . but Moslems would shrink from the blasphe-
> mies here recorded.[46]

Given the religious enthusiasm of the Second Great Awakening, mille-
narian fervor, the expectation of Christ's return, was almost universal during
the decade of Webb's birth. Revivalists saw the moral deterioration of the
social order as a certain sign of Christ's pending advent. The Adventists were
one of these movements and not only anticipated the rapture enthusiastically
but set a date. William Miller established the movement in northeastern New
York but drew most of his followers from the burned-over district. In 1831, he
began to proclaim that Christ's advent would take place in twelve years. Seven
years later, he published *Evidence from Scripture and History of the Second
Coming of Christ, about the Year 1843*. Within a year, the national best-seller
had attracted a flock of "Millerites," despite the fact that mainstream ministers condemned Miller's teaching. During 1842 and 1843, as the advent
approached and intensity increased, Miller held a flurry of fervent camp
meetings. His sermons electrified entire communities:[47]

> Behold, the heavens grow black with clouds; the sun has veiled
> himself; the moon, pale and forsaken, hangs in middle air; the hail
> descends; the seven thunders utter loud their voices; the lightnings
> send their vivid gleams and sulphurous flames abroad; and the great
> city of the nations falls to rise no more forever and forever! At this
> dread moment, look! The clouds have burst asunder; the heavens
> appear; the great white throne is in sight! Amazement fills the
> Universe with awe! He comes!—He comes!—Behold the Saviour [sic]
> comes!—Lift up your heads, ye saints—He comes! He comes! He
> comes![48]

Miller's predictions missed Christ's advent twice. A March 1843 date was
deferred to March 1844. Then, after the spring equinox of 1844, "a gray pall of
gloom settled over the Millerites." An undaunted few reset calculations for
October 22, 1844, the Jewish Day of Atonement that year. The fervid preaching
resumed, and the faithful congregated in churches and houses or on hilltops,
awaiting Christ's Second Coming. The final failure led to "the Great Disappointment," all the more for those who had sold their farms and livestock.
Most found their way back to the Protestant mainstream. Some abandoned
religion altogether. The remaining Millerites convened a general assembly in
Albany in 1845. The staunchly faithful asserted that the Second Coming had,
as predicted, taken place in 1844 but in heaven and not on earth. Others
formed the Seventh-Day Adventists, officially incorporated in 1863, declaring
the Second Coming at hand but carefully avoiding dates.[49]

The Sanctified Perfectionists of John Humphrey Noyes had their roots on
Webb's side of the Hudson but were transplanted to the burned-over district.[50]
Noyes's theology was predicated on a widely criticized doctrine of the Second
Coming, namely, that Christ's return had taken place during the Apostolic Age,
seventy years after Christ's birth. Without knowing it, Christians had been

living in the millennium for nearly two thousand years. Noyes taught that perfect communion with Christ—notably that of Noyes and his followers—removed the effect of all sin. As early as 1834, Noyes proclaimed that "he was no longer a sinner" and had been given the power to distinguish between the "perfect" and those who remained sinners.[51]

Noyes declared himself a new "Prophet of Christ" and instituted a commune in Vermont that aspired to establish "the Kingdom of God on earth" and live "only under Jesus Christ." The commune strived to realize a single "church-state," unifying the religious and the secular. They renounced the United States because it "tyrannized Indians and Negroes" and envisioned a universal government of the world, although, as pacifists, the Perfectionists disavowed war as a means to rectify social injustice or establish a new order.[52]

Members of the Noyes community were industrious and held all possessions in common but espoused views on marriage and sexuality that clashed with traditional Christian values. Noyes instituted a system of "complex marriages" on the basis "that it is not a sin for any sanctified man and woman to have intercourse." Sanctification abrogated the need for marriage, and, for those in that state, there was "no more reason why sexual intercourse should be restrained by law than why eating and drinking should be—and there [was] as little occasion for shame in the one case as in the other." The community offered its members relatively easy access to gratification: "The marriage supper of the Lamb [Christ] is a feast at which every dish is free to every guest." What the Noyes Perfectionists referred to as "a regularized form of bonding in which all the communitarians were married to each other in Christ" was denounced outside the community as "free love." In 1847, Noyes fled to New York to avoid prosecution for adultery and resettled his commune in the burned-over district, where they continued as the Oneida Association well into the 1870s, although they were forced to repudiate their doctrine of complex marriage in 1879.[53]

Race and Ethnicity in Pre–Civil War Hudson

The America that Webb knew comprised three main racial groups: British Americans (whites), African Americans (blacks), and Native Americans (Indians). Status, rights, or the lack of them were strictly hierarchical.[54] Tocqueville observed that Indians and blacks were "alike in their misfortunes," although they were substantially different in group psychology and in other ways. He foresaw the genocide of the former but a different destiny for the latter. White America could not dispense with African American labor but would hardly be able to assimilate them either. Their presence at the heart of American society would ultimately confront the United States with the greatest challenge to its civic values and democratic principles.[55]

Most whites were of "Anglo-Saxon" Protestant background with a significant mixture of Continental Protestants, largely western European. The
"great deluge" of non-Protestant whites, Catholic and Jewish, became a reality
only toward the end of Webb's life. Between 1901 and 1910, almost nine
million immigrants were admitted to the United States, the great majority of
whom were Catholics and Jews.

In Webb's time, Harlem was an elite white suburb in Upper Manhattan.
Only shortly before his death did Harlem's demographics begin to change.
New York City rapidly gained a population that was almost half foreign-born,
and a dramatic influx of Caribbean and rural southern blacks transformed
Harlem into the world's greatest black city and triggered the Harlem Re-
naissance within a decade after Webb's passing.[56]

Hudson and Columbia County presented a cross-section of the primary
groups that made up nineteenth-century America. The city's founders and
core population were, of course, British Americans from New England.
Claverack, a township lying a few miles east of Hudson, was originally a Dutch
settlement, and it was in Claverack that Webb completed his formal education.
In Webb's time, Claverack was still dominated by the Dutch Reformed Church,
although its population was an even mix of Dutch and British American
Protestants. Nearby Kinderhook, Martin Van Buren's birthplace, had been
a principal nucleus of Dutch and Swedish settlement in the seventeenth century.[57] Palatine Germans made up the fundamental ethnic stratum of Germantown, about 25 miles southwest of Hudson, having been brought to
America by Queen Anne during the colonial period. The Rockefellers made up
one of Germantown's more notable Palatine families.[58]

Hudson's economy benefited from considerable investments in southern
slavery, based on Hudson manufactured goods that were shipped by sea to
southern ports. Clark's Clothing Factory, a block from the Webb family
printing shop, was a primary producer of slave clothing, which it shipped to
New Orleans. With the outbreak of Civil War, the factory promptly went
bankrupt.[59] In 1810, black slaves made up 1 percent of Hudson's population.[60]
A decade after the Civil War, about 3 percent of Columbia County's population was black. That ratio was more than twice as large as the African-
American minority of New York City.[61] Hudson's blacks were free during
Webb's life and were segregated in a waterfront area near the red-light district.
Most of them descended from the area's colonial slave population, often
bearing the family names of Dutch landowners such as Van Allen and Van
Ness.[62]

By the majority standards of the time, Hudson's African-American minority was deemed relatively "well treated." In the local social hierarchy, they
were put more or less on the same footing as the city's Native Americans.[63]
Columbia County was not inclined to enfranchise local blacks and, on the eve
of the Civil War, voted three to one to reject equal suffrage for its "colored

persons."[64] But Hudson's African Americans had access to education before and after the war. Black children could attend the racially mixed Lancaster Society School for the poor.[65] In 1828, a school especially for black children, called the African School, was opened under the direction of the Lancaster trustees. Despite its name, the African School was also racially mixed. At the outset, it met with strong opposition, primarily out of fear that it would take funds from the older Lancaster School.[66]

In the wilds south of Hudson between the townships of Taghkanic and Gallatin lived a "border people" known as the "Pondshiners" or "Bush-whackers," whose skin color varied from light to dark. Their origins were said to go back to colonial Palatine, Dutch, and New England tenant farmers who found Columbia County's quasi-feudal rental policies unbearable and broke away to live in more inaccessible areas, where they "set up for themselves." They probably mixed with Native Americans (presumably Mohicans).[67]

The Bushwhackers were hardy, "[asking] odds of no man and [desiring] only to be let alone." On long winter nights, they would earn their living through storytelling and were known widely for their tales of witches and witchcraft. They dug simple dwellings in the hillsides and lived much like Native Americans. Because of their livelihood, they were also known as Eastern Indian "Basket-makers." They would collect young white ash branches just before the appearance of the new moon and pound them in preparation for weaving baskets. Local historians speculated that their name, "Bush-whackers," was taken from their beating branches to make baskets, although the word was already widespread in early nineteenth-century parlance for backwoodsmen or people who "beat the bush" in order to ambush enemies.[68]

National discord over slavery and perpetual "Indian" trouble interspersed by frontier wars pervaded Webb's early years. Consolidation of the West meant unabated conflict with Native Americans, the original owners of the land. Most of Webb's life transpired during the great "Indian Wars" and tribal "last stands," a period stretching roughly from 1840 till 1890. After the Civil War, the fight for Indian territory became the "big newspaper story." In 1876, Sitting Bull and Crazy Horse routed George Armstrong Custer at the Little Bighorn. The city of St. Joseph, Missouri, was the Army's principal point of contact with Custer and Montana Territory. Shortly after Custer's last stand, Webb began work in St. Joseph as a reporter. In 1890, news came of the massacre at Wounded Knee, which destroyed the remnants of Sitting Bull's Sioux Nation and brought an end to the Indian wars.[69]

Slavery had been an explosive issue since independence. America's rapid western expansion during Webb's boyhood lit the fuse again. Newly acquired Texas and the vast lands of the Southwest created an insatiable demand for slave labor. The addition of new lands inevitably raised a question: Would slavery be extended into the new territories? In their support for extending slavery, southern congressmen attacked the Declaration of Independence as an "instrument which taught the false doctrine that all men are created equal." They asserted vehemently that the Constitution granted Congress no authority to legislate against slavery. Abolitionists like William Lloyd Garrison vindicated the Declaration of Independence and the right of all humans to resist the state on grounds of conscience. Garrison held public burnings of the Constitution, and his newspaper, the *Liberator*, carried the slogan under its title: "The United States Constitution is a covenant with death and an agreement with hell." In 1854, when Webb was a boy, the Kansas-Nebraska Act repealed the Missouri Compromise of 1820, an action that effectively opened Kansas for settlement but left the issue of slavery in the settlers' hands. Overnight, the antislavery Jayhawkers and their enemies, the pro-Southern Bushwhackers, turned "Bleeding Kansas" into an ominous portent of civil war.[70]

During Webb's childhood, Frederick Douglass, the celebrated black orator and human rights advocate, was based in Rochester, New York. His autobiography, *Narrative of the Life of Frederick Douglass*, came out the year Webb was born, and Douglass began publishing his Abolitionist newspaper, the *North Star*, in Rochester the following year. The nefarious Fugitive Slave Law (1850) ruthlessly empowered slave hunters to track down runaway blacks in the North, which often resulted in the enslavement of free African Americans presumed to be escaped slaves. The law put Douglass's own life in danger, forcing him to leave Rochester and go abroad. The Fugitive Slave Law prompted Harriet Beecher Stowe to begin writing *Uncle Tom's Cabin* in 1851, believing that Northerners would tolerate the law only as long as its evil was not made a "living dramatic reality."[71] When Webb was eleven, the Supreme Court upheld a Missouri court's decision against Dred Scott, a Missouri slave who claimed freedom by right of traveling with his master to a free state. The ruling gave a patent victory to the South by conferring an air of legitimacy on slavery throughout the United States.[72] Years later, as a journalist in St. Joseph and St. Louis, Webb developed a long friendship with poet and fellow journalist Eugene Field, son of Scott's defense lawyer. Shortly after turning thirteen, Webb would surely have heard of John Brown's raid on Harper's Ferry, where the radical Abolitionist and his band of twenty-one men attempted to invade the South and liberate the slaves. Brown's martyrdom on the gallows radicalized Northern opinion. In the North and South alike, John Brown was seen as "a human omen." Herman Melville called him "the meteor of war."[73]

Although most Northerners opposed slavery, few of them were open to the inclusion of blacks in white society on an equal footing. For almost all whites, North and South, any mixing of the races was unthinkable, socially or otherwise.[74] The North began to abolish slavery in its own regions after independence but never put an end to discrimination. Tocqueville noted: "Racial prejudice appears to me stronger in the states that have abolished slavery than in those where slavery still exists, and nowhere is it shown to be as intolerant as in states where servitude has always been unknown."[75]

During the colonial period, slavery was practiced in all the thirteen colonies. In New York, it was abolished in stages. Similar policies obtained elsewhere in the North and allowed Yankee slaveholders to sell their slaves in southern markets, while avoiding economic loss or the creation of a substantial resident population of free blacks. "In the North," Tocqueville observed, "slavery and the slaves are driven out at the same time."[76] New York prohibited the sale of slaves within its borders in 1788. In 1799, it declared slave children born in the state to be free but provided only for the gradual abolition of the institution. Generally in New York, manumission of adult slaves was allowed only if they could produce proof of financial support to the "overseers of the poor" in their local townships. Slavery as such was not permanently put to an end in New York until 1827, hardly three decades before the Civil War.[77]

Opposition to slavery and support of the Union were strong in Hudson. Sympathy for radical Abolitionism was not. It is safe to say that Hudson's general outlook and that of Webb himself followed the political line of the county's "favorite son," Democratic President Martin Van Buren. Van Buren had little sympathy for Abolitionism, which, as a rule, held that the abolition of slavery should take precedence over the preservation of the Union. Van Buren adamantly supported the undivided integrity of the Union, although he opposed the further extension of slavery beyond the Old South. He voted against annexing Texas in opposition to the Southern wing of the Democratic Party, which wanted Texas admitted to the Union as a slave state. Van Buren formed a new political party called the Free-Soil Party, which held a convention in 1848 under the slogan that "Congress has no more power to make a slave than to make a king." From 1853 till 1855, Van Buren toured Europe, speaking urgently of the need to preserve the Union in the case of civil war. He died in Columbia County in 1862, after hostilities had begun.[78]

In Columbia County, the war was called "the Great War of the Rebellion." One of Webb's obituaries maintained that he had served in the war, but it is virtually certain that Webb was not a Civil War veteran.[79] The war went much worse than expected. President Abraham Lincoln observed later that each side had anticipated swift victory, and no one expected the war to be as long or bloody as it was.[80] Technologically, it was one of the first modern wars. But weaponry was far more advanced than modes of combat. Modern arms combined with outdated strategies and protocols led to immeasurable slaughter and vast destruction.

Long before the outbreak of war, civil discord over slavery tore most Protestant churches apart. Southern clergymen insisted on the "plain teaching of Scripture," which, in their view, upheld the institution of slavery. To preach against slavery was to flout biblical teaching. "In a world cursed by sin," they argued, slavery was a necessary evil for attaining human progress. They often added that a Christian slaveholder should treat slaves as immortal spirits rather than brutes but that to seek slavery's abolition would be to deprive blacks of the "benefits of Christian civilization and culture." Northern clergymen fiercely rejected such arguments and argued that slavery was un-Christian and that Southern ministers who used the Bible to justify it were scriptural literalists with no understanding of the true spirit of biblical teaching. In the late 1830s, Presbyterians divided into "New School" (antislavery) and "Old School" (proslavery) factions along North-South lines. Methodists soon separated regionally over slavery. In 1845, the national Baptist Church split into Northern and Southern Baptists, and the formal division remains a reality until the present.[81]

With the coming of war, most churches threw their weight behind their respective regional governments and made all their spiritual resources available for the conflict.[82] Modern historians often interpret the Civil War as essentially an economic struggle between the industrial North and agrarian South. For those who fought the war, however, it had powerful religious overtones. Both Northern opposition to slavery and Southern backing for it were seen as Christian causes by each opposing party in its own way. Most Protestant churches divided bitterly over the issue and their biblical interpretations regarding it in an unyielding theological battle. For Southern Protestants, opposition to slavery was un-Christian, and their religious fervor over the matter was no less ardent than their Northern counterparts and fellow churchmen, who saw slavery as an irreligious violation of biblical truth. For both sides, the Civil War was a religious war, and each believed that God was on their side.[83] "Few wars in modern history," Clifton Olmstead asserts, "have received such overwhelming approval from religious institutions as the Civil War."[84] Northern and Southern ministers alike held camp revivals on the battlefield, rallied their troops to war, and assured them of victory by virtue of God's sanction for their cause.[85]

President Abraham Lincoln found such selective use of religion repugnant and invited the nation to put itself on the Lord's side without each warring party claiming God to be on its side. After the Union defeat at Bull Run in 1862, the war's low point from a Northern perspective, Lincoln declared: "The will of God prevails. In great contests each party claims to act in accordance with the will of God. Both *may* be and one *must* be wrong. God cannot be *for*, and *against* the same thing at the same time."[86] Three years later, he repeated in his Second Inaugural Address (1865), sometimes called "Lincoln's Sermon on the Mount," that both sides read the same Bible and prayed to the same God, invoking his aid against the other. Yet "the prayers of both could not be answered," and, indeed, the prayers of neither side had been answered in full.[87]

The conflicting theologies of the Protestant churches on the Civil War and their inability to mitigate the conflict left long-lasting unintended consequences after the war. An air of cynicism and religious skepticism pervaded the country during the second half of the nineteenth century to an unprecedented degree. In the words of Louis Menand, "agnosticism was then riding its high horse, and was frowning superbly upon all metaphysics." Many of the core religious commitments that had constituted the foundations of both Northern and Southern culture had been called into question, and post–Civil War America lost its cultural moorings and was in search of something new.[88] The religious ambivalence of the post–Civil War period and the new alternatives that the Late Victorian Period created in religion and thought are an essential part of the Webb story. He undertook his spiritual odyssey during the 1870s and 1880s at a time when many of his contemporaries were embarking upon similar searches of their own. Webb completely rejected traditional faith in the early 1870s but became newly interested in religion in the 1880s with exposure to novel forms of spirituality and, eventually, to Oriental traditions, which ultimately brought him to Islam.

Webb's Family

Family ties were greatly valued in Victorian America, and personal fulfillment was generally sought in domestic life. Children were an essential part of the home, but guests and boarders were welcomed. The Victorian family unit was more cohesive than was the typical family unit in the preceding period. In part, their strength was a response to emerging industrialization and its destabilization of society. Previously, there had been less mobility; people knew each other intimately, and they intermingled daily in work and play. Industrialization ushered in an age of transience and impersonality in towns and cities. The Victorian family became a sanctuary for emotional support and interpersonal affection.[89]

It is customary to stereotype Victorians as sexually inhibited. In reality, marital affection and intimate family bonds were central to their culture. Husbands and wives made frequent expressions of their love for each other; they cultivated lasting unions for the sake of joy and to remove the isolation of modern life. An unmarried life, even after the death of a spouse, was unconventional. Children were regarded as the essential fruit of marriage and were relied upon for happiness and to offset personal hardship. The father-daughter relation was especially strong; it constituted "the essence of Victorian patriarchal culture." The mother-son relationship was correspondingly deep and reflected mutual reliance.[90]

Nadirah Osman asserts that Alexander Russell Webb enjoyed "a rich family life" as a child and adult.[91] His mother was Caroline Elizabeth Lefferts. He was named after his father, Alexander Nelson Webb. Both parents were New York State natives, although neither came from Hudson.[92] Caroline Lefferts was born in New York State in 1818. The actual town and county are not given, although she had some connection to Saratoga County and the township of Galway, where she was married and returned to live toward the end of her life. Alexander Nelson Webb was born in Onondaga Hollow, New York, in 1816. Webb's grandparents had migrated to New York from Connecticut, following the normal pattern of late-eighteenth-century British American immigration to New York from New England.[93]

Webb's family lived at 338 Diamond Street (today Columbia Street), not far from the family printing shop and the Presbyterian church to which they belonged.[94] During the era, it was common for Victorian families to house relatives and take on boarders.[95] "Live-in maids" were an essential mark of middle-class affluence.[96] Census records of the Webbs show signs of prosperity. In the 1850 census, the Webb family had three boarders: an older woman and two males. One of the boarders seems to have been Franklin H. Webb, who seems to have been part of Webb's extended family, although the relationship is not clear. Later, Franklin Webb became an independent printer in Hudson and author of a noted Claverack history. There were also two black female servants.[97] The 1860 census valued Alexander Nelson Webb's estate at $5,000, a substantial sum at the time. There were no longer any boarders by then, but the census lists two female servants, one Irish and another black.[98]

Alexander Nelson Webb and Caroline Webb had eleven children, the fourth of whom was Alexander Russell:[99]

- Edward Cook Webb, born January 25, 1841
- Caroline Elizabeth Webb, born January 28, 1843
- Ellen Louisa Webb, born September 1, 1845
- Alexander Russell Webb, November 20, 1846
- Henry Lefferts Webb, born May 21, 1849
- Herbert Nelson Webb, born July 20, 1852
- Carrie Lefferts Webb, born November 30, 1854
- Nina Louise Webb, born December 18, 1856
- Anna May Webb, born March 9, 1859
- Willie Bunker Webb, born October 11, 1861

His mother bore almost twice the average number of children at the time, but child mortality rates were generally high, which was also true for the Webb family.[100] Almost half of Webb's siblings died as children.[101]

The Webbs of Hudson were known as printers. Alexander Nelson Webb ran a printing shop and was both proprietor and editor of the *Hudson Daily Star*, which was one of Hudson's oldest newspapers, dating to the city's incorporation in 1785.[102] During the early period of American journalism, most newspapers were weeklies. The *Hudson Daily Star* had begun as a weekly but was one of the earliest newspapers in America to print a daily edition. Webb's father was credited with introducing the new daily edition in 1847, although

FIGURE 2.2. Downtown Hudson as Webb Knew It, Showing the General
Warren Street Location of the Webb Family Printing Shop

he continued to produce a weekly edition simultaneously.[103] Later in life,
Alexander Russell Webb showed great skill as a daily journalist, which he
probably owed to his father's tutelage.

Throughout Webb's life, newspapers were the principal form of com-
municative media. Reading newspapers was a vital part of Victorian culture
and virtually an obligatory "civic activity."[104] During Webb's childhood, numerous periodicals were published in Hudson, which took pride in having
produced a "phenomenal number of journalistic ventures through the
years."[105] The *Rural Repository*, a local journal, set a high standard for national
and international news and was also devoted to polite literature. A "Fort-
nightly Club" met in Hudson to discuss newsworthy events and cultural
developments.[106] James W. Webb of Claverack, son of General Samuel Webb,
became a major figure in New York journalism and founded the *New York
World*, which decades later would attain national fame for its editor Joseph
Pulitzer.[107]

Tocqueville observed that even for the American pioneer, plunging "into
the wilderness of the New World," his supply of newspapers was only secondary in importance to his Bible and hatchet.[108] He also observed: "One
encounters in America at once more associations and more newspapers than
any other country in the world."[109] Politics and the press were closely linked.
During most of the nineteenth century, newspapers were "generally violently

partisan in character and teemed with the grossest personal abuse of political opponents."[110] The *Hudson Daily Star* was no exception. It was proudly "Republican [i.e., Jeffersonian Democratic] in politics," and its editorials were "outspoken and fearless on all matters of public interest."[111] This centrality of journalism to early American life and its close association with politics constituted crucial elements in Webb's own makeup. Growing up in the family of a prominent and innovative editor and adopting the profession as his own personal career reflects another dimension of Webb's intimate association with the prevailing American culture of the time. It also explains his abiding interest and involvement in politics throughout most of his life.

Claverack College

Little detailed information is available on Webb's education, which began in Hudson's public schools and was completed in private schools. It is not clear when he began his private schooling, though he eventually left the public schools of Hudson and enrolled in the Home School of Glendale, Massachusetts, in the Berkshire Mountains several miles east of Columbia County.[112] At the time, Glendale was an important center for public and private education and took boarding students from surrounding regions. Today, however, the Glendale Home School has been long forgotten. There is only a scant record of the school's existence and probably none of Webb's enrollment. Such information gaps are commonplace, since school records were rarely kept during this period.[113]

Webb returned to Columbia County after studying in Massachusetts and finished his education at the Claverack College and Hudson River Institute. Again, sources give no clear indication of when or how long Webb studied at Claverack or what degree, if any, he obtained. According to Nadirah Osman, he studied there until the end of the Civil War. I found his name in the school register only for the term that started January 1, 1864. He studied English grammar, dictation, arithmetic, and history. Like all male students, he was also required to train as a cadet, was issued a government regulation uniform, and trained with a Springfield rifle. The Claverack girls took gymnastics and calisthenics instead.[114]

The college began as a seminary during the Revolutionary War. In 1830, after a period of decline, it was converted into the Claverack Academy, which rose to new academic heights and "exerted a controlling influence in education for more than twenty years." In 1854, the academy was expanded and renamed the Claverack College and Hudson River Institute. It soon became renowned for academic excellence.[115] By today's criteria, Claverack College would be comparable to a junior college, but such a comparison would be misleading in the context of the times. Institutions of higher education were still relatively few in America. By antebellum standards, Claverack offered a high degree of education. Moreover, it was closely affiliated with Yale, and its male graduates could go there if they desired to complete their bachelor's degree after an additional year of study. Although identical opportunities were not available to women, Claverack College began shortly after the Civil War to offer the degree of "mistress of arts" to women graduates.[116]

For most Americans of that time, education rarely went beyond the basics—reading, writing, and arithmetic—and offered little or nothing toward the acquisition of broader skills that would enable them to succeed at their careers. Primary instruction was within the reach of most whites, but higher education was beyond the means of virtually everyone but the wealthy. Most Americans began their adult careers at the age of fifteen. (Mark Twain, who was about a decade older than Webb, received even less formal education and started his career in printing at the age of thirteen.)[117] Tocqueville observed: "[American] education most often ends in the period when ours begins." No nation on earth, he concluded, had fewer men who were completely ignorant than America, while none had such a lack of the truly well educated.[118] It was only after the Civil War that America underwent the radical changes that would create the national education system we are familiar with today. The modern American university system emerged in the second half of the century, bringing with it an unprecedented "culture of professionals and professionalism," which restructured the middle class along lines of credentials and careers.[119]

Claverack College was based on the English "form system," with six form levels, instead of the grade structure customary to American schools. Scholastic progress rather than age determined the level at which students were enrolled.[120] Students were encouraged to express themselves and engage in active discussion. Early on, Webb developed a love for writing and is said to have composed essays and short stories before he was sixteen.[121] His exposure to Claverack College undoubtedly fostered those interests. Each Friday evening, the institute's six forms debated "the live questions of the day" in order to train "students for duties that would devolve upon them in life as responsible American citizens." Every Friday afternoon, students presented weekly literary essays on subjects assigned at the beginning of each week. Student monitors were appointed to "note the slightest errors and correct them, including pronunciation and delivery." Lively group discussions followed the presentations, and all students joined in critiquing their subject matter, style, and educational value.[122]

Claverack College exercised a conspicuous influence on Hudson and Columbia County that extended beyond its internal academic services, and such influences would have been a part of Webb's life from early childhood long before his enrollment in the college. Claverack provided a number of local public services; for example, the college enlisted its student body to teach reading and writing to the children and adults of the county, especially the poor, who could not afford an education. It also exposed residents to many of the greatest minds and speakers of the day, organizing frequent public lectures and hosting such speakers as Horace Greeley, William Lloyd Garrison, and Bishop John Henry Newman.[123]

Claverack College was a boarding school. So although it had a number of day students, like Webb, who commuted from surrounding areas, the college also attracted students from various parts of the United States, including the Deep South, and foreign students from as far away as Mexico, Cuba, and the Caribbean.[124] Claverack boasted of producing "many splendid and purposeful men and women."[125] Former President Martin Van Buren was among its alumni, as were many other members of the "prominent families of Columbia County."[126] In the decades following Webb's study at Claverack, it took pride in having among its graduates the famous illustrator Arthur Burdett Frost, the novelist Stephen Crane, and the prominent feminist Margaret Sanger.[127]

Female boarders were often accompanied by brothers who were simultaneously enrolled at the school. Males and females resided in separate wings off the central building. Each floor of the men's dormitory was under the moral, academic, and spiritual supervision of a "professor." "Lady principals of culture and experience" oversaw female students and "their moral and physical training, and [instructed] them with reference to health, order, neatness, politeness and the elements of pure and noble womanhood," according to the school's official records.[128]

Students were expected to deport themselves as "ladies and gentlemen." One of the chief purposes of coeducation at Claverack College, however, was to encourage marriages among the students by enabling them to meet their future spouses under controlled circumstances. In fact, many of the institute's students did marry one another, and parents were attracted to the school by the likelihood that a student would find there a worthy partner. Males and females were allowed to congregate several times each day. They gathered each morning for chapel and were required to attend Sunday services together, although males and females sat on different sides of the chapel. Classes were mixed, as were the three daily meals served in a large dining hall. Boys and girls were also allowed to meet in a college parlor under the supervision of chaperones.[129]

Webb's education at Claverack was undoubtedly one of the most important factors in his formation. The school emphasized intellectual freedom and the exploration of new ideas. It had a diverse student body and an excellent staff of highly trained men and women.

In Webb's time, the college was especially known for the dynamic personality of its principal, the Reverend Alonzo Flack of North Carolina, who began his tenure in 1854 and continued until his unexpected death in 1876. Randall Saunders, a local historian, reports that Flack's sudden loss was "a blow from which the school never fully recovered."[130] Claverack's students

FIGURE 2.3. Claverack College

loved Flack and held him in esteem. He created strong bonds with them, which he maintained for years after graduation. In addition to his administrative duties, Flack taught classes on philosophy as "promulgated through the ages." He encouraged the free discussion of ideas, and his classes were "delightfully controversial."[131] The academic freedom that Flack promoted at Claverack College must have constituted a fundamental element in Webb's intellectual formation.

Moreover, Webb's exposure through the college to some of the leading personalities of the time must have imparted a sense of distinction and self-esteem beyond mere interest in their ideas. The college encouraged his love of reading and honed his ability to interact effectively in society. Its commitment to coeducation and the active engagement of women in education and critical discourse affected his attitude toward women at a time when social space was sharply segregated by gender and women, as a rule, were viewed as biologically as well a socially subordinate to men.

Claverack College was closed in 1902. Although historical markers in Claverack draw attention to the school's importance in its time, a visitor to the area can only determine with some difficulty where the school used to stand. Claverack began to decline toward the end of the nineteenth century, and all attempts to revive it were unsuccessful. Finally, all of its buildings were torn down, and the materials were sold as scrap in Hudson.[132]

3

Webb's Journey to Islam

Webb was born during the Second Great Awakening, which lasted until the Civil War and constituted a high point of American religious intensity. The mood following the war was very different, and there was general spiritual demoralization and cultural decline in the North and South alike. Instead of spiritual awakening, the postwar period was a time of secular numbness. Most of the nation—again, both North and South—underwent a period of questioning and doubt, and traditional religious commitment ebbed to a nadir. The contours of American religion began to change rapidly. Yet, although the waves of cynicism brought irreligion, they also produced an unprecedented openness to new ideas and traditions.[1]

The Civil War destroyed more than the material culture of the Old South. It destroyed the paradigms that underlay the antebellum worldviews of North and South alike and shook the very foundations of America's moral and intellectual culture. The war discredited the beliefs that had failed to prevent it and the very religious establishments that had beaten the drums of war, polarized the conflict, and made the rush to war unstoppable. Church attendance declined, and traditional religious institutions faltered.[2]

In the North, many Christians gravitated away from the church and searched for inner spirituality along unconventional paths. Even in the South, strains of secularism ran through postwar society.[3] In 1872, when Webb shifted his focus from traditional religion to materialism, his actions mirrored the malaise of his generation. A few years later, after his interlude of "spiritual vagabondage" as a materialist, Webb became interested in religion again and began investigating spiritualism, Theosophy, and non-Western faiths. Once again, his newfound interest in the religious search after a period of spiritual doubt and rejection was akin to the experiences of many of his Victorian contemporaries.

Growing up Presbyterian

Although Webb was not the first American convert to Islam, none of those who came before him—so far as we know—wrote a conversion narrative.[4] In his biography of Malcolm X, Louis DeCaro defends Malcolm's conversion narrative against the "antisupernatural presuppositions of psychoanalysis" and insists that Malcolm's account "be respected as testimony to an authentic religious experience."[5] Similarly, Webb's conversion narrative contains complexities common to conversion narratives and other elements that lend themselves to psychoanalysis. Like Malcolm's account of his conversion, however, Webb's story deserves to be approached impartially, balancing as far as possible a respect for his intimate spiritual experience with the legitimate concerns of historical, social, and psychological analysis.

For both Webb and Malcolm X, the personal dimension of their religious experiences is inseparably linked to a conspicuous social component, namely, the missionary desire of both to make their conversion narratives convincing to others. Both men, in different ways, were public personas with religious and social commitments on which their conversions had profound bearing. It is clear, therefore, that Webb's conversion narrative was never strictly autobiographical but also written and employed to invite others to join him in his faith. Consequently, Webb had a vested interest in presenting his conversion in a compelling manner. This consideration does not exclude the possibility that he also had real and compelling spiritual experiences that led to his conversion, although it acknowledges that the internal complexity of Webb's account is augmented by the fact that he wrote it from the perspective of a Muslim missionary.

Webb began his conversion narrative with his boyhood, presenting himself as an amiable, nonconformist child who was endowed with remarkable common sense. After his conversion to Islam, Webb often insisted that the Christian doctrine of the Trinity was irrational. In his conversion narrative, however, he portrays himself as having perceived the dogma's irrationality and that of certain other church teachings while still a boy, contending that he never found traditional Christian doctrine fully plausible. Back-projections are characteristic of conversion narratives, and contradictions in Webb's biography make it appear that something of that element informs Webb's recollection of his religious experience as a child. It is clear, however, that, as an adult, Webb saw himself as eminently rational and questioning by nature. Even after conversion to Islam, Webb's diary repeatedly portrays him as neither credulous nor given to gullibility, continually looking critically at the spiritual claims of Muslim holy men and others.

Webb's portrayal of his boyhood, however endearing a boy he might have been, served the objective of his conversion narrative. Boyhood in the middle Victorian period was greatly influenced by images of Tom Sawyer and Huck Finn: two naturally good boys who went against the grain but outshined others in the end by virtue of their redeeming qualities.[6] Webb, who as an adult often used a Twainian type of humor and imitated Twain in habits of smoking and dress, portrayed himself throughout his conversion narrative in the image of boyhood celebrated in Twain's accounts of Tom Sawyer and Huck Finn. The image would not only have appealed to his audience and helped them identify with Webb but also served to prod them, as adults, to exercise the same individualism and ideological freedom that Webb described himself as having had as a boy.

Webb averred that he was not a "fervently religious" child or "even a good boy" such as one whom mothers pointed out as a "shining example" to their sons.[7] Accepting Webb's account at face value, Osman interpreted the statements as indicating that he was "a very human little boy."[8] The religious ambivalence that Webb assigns his boyhood, however, takes on the aspect of a "master role," introducing the motif of holding religious claims to close scrutiny. The picture of Webb as a dissenter from boyhood not only puts him at a distance from the devotional aspects of his Presbyterian upbringing but emphasizes Webb's precociousness, on the one hand, and relegates standard Protestant theology as unworthy of serious consideration on the other.[9]

In an 1892 interview with the *Mohammedan Observer* of Calcutta, Webb insisted that he never once in his life truly believed in the Christian religion.[10] Webb emphasized his religious disaffection in antebellum America by referring to himself as "an American, born in a country which [was] nominally Christian, and reared 'under the drippings' of an orthodox Presbyterian pulpit."[11] At this point, Webb's account of his boyhood is difficult to accept. The claim that he was never serious about religion as a boy conflicts with the assertion that he lost religion as a young adult. Moreover, the description of the United States as "nominally Christian" may have been valid for large parts of its population in the post–Civil War period, especially around the time that Webb wrote his conversion narrative. It was certainly not, however, a justifiable depiction of the nation during the Second Great Awakening and the religious intensity that Webb witnessed on the eve of the Civil War.

Victorian children were expected to attend church services regularly, and doing so was taken as an important measure of their piety.[12] As a boy, Webb conformed to this pattern, although he insisted in his conversion narrative that he found the routine spiritually suffocating. He said also that he sought continually to find means of escape from church to retreat to the natural settings around Hudson, to which he found himself powerfully drawn. The Hudson city limits were then and remain today in proximity to nature. Even now, the First Presbyterian Church of Hudson, which Webb attended, is only a few minutes' walk from beautiful woods and glens filled with wildlife:[13]

> I attended the Presbyterian Sunday School of my native town, when I couldn't avoid it, and listened with weariness and impatience to the long, abstruse discourses of the minister, while I longed to get out into the glad sunshine and hear the more satisfying sermons preached by God Himself through the murmuring brooks, the gorgeous flowers and the joyous birds.[14]

Webb contended that he took issue with church dogma from an early age and "listened incredulously" to the doctrine he heard from the pulpit.[15] Finding nothing to attract him to church teachings, he drifted away from them at an early age:

> As a boy I found nothing in the system taught me in church and Sunday-school calculated to win me to it, nor did I find it any more attractive in later years, when I came to investigate it carefully and thoroughly. I found its moral ethics most commendable, but no different from those of every other system, while its superstitions, its grave errors, and its inefficiency as a means of securing salvation, or of elevating and purifying the human character, caused me to wonder why any thoughtful, honest and intelligent person could accept it seriously.[16]

Continuing in the same vein, he averred that, almost from the time he was born, his natural skepticism regarding standard Protestant doctrine had become his basic disposition:

> I listened incredulously to the story of the immaculate conception; and the dramatic tale of the vicarious atonement failed to arouse in me a thrill of tearful emotion, because I doubted the truth of both dogmas. Of course the narrow-minded Church Christian will say at once, that the scriptural bogey-man, Satan, had me in his clutches as soon as I was born.[17]

Such incredulity would certainly be rare in a boy of the antebellum period, especially if not prompted by a circle of adults already of that disposition. Webb was, in fact, influenced by a circle of universalists after the war. In addition, Webb's reference to "the immaculate conception" is an indication that there is an element of back projection in his narrative. Webb would have never heard the doctrine of Immaculate Conception preached from a Presbyterian pulpit or any other mainstream Protestant pulpit in America at the time. The Immaculate Conception is a distinctly Roman Catholic doctrine associated with the birth of Mary—not Jesus—and which Pope Pius IX enunciated "as a doctrine revealed by God" in 1854, when Webb was eight years old.[18] If anything, Webb would have heard the dogma assailed from the "orthodox Presbyterian" pulpit of his boyhood and certainly not espoused. In all likelihood, Webb, in writing his conversion narrative, confused the Immaculate Conception with the doctrine of Incarnation or Virgin Birth and probably the former and not the latter, since the Virgin Birth is a standard Islamic belief as well. In any case, it is clear that Webb has added to the narrative some elements that do not accurately describe events as they actually transpired.

When speaking of his early manhood, Webb portrays an image of himself consistent with the early picture of his boyhood, describing himself as a young man blessed with an inquiring mind and common sense. This is, however, an apparent contradiction in Webb's conversion narrative. He states explicitly that he fell away from his doctrinal convictions as a young man, yet these were the same doctrines to which he had listened only "incredulously" as a boy. Perhaps, Webb meant to imply not that his incredulity was new, but that he had now begun to ask questions that he had not previously voiced: "I was emotional in later years, but not mawkishly sentimental, and always demanded a reason for everything."[19] Again, he linked his rejection of "irrational" church doctrine to his innate rationality and good sense:

> Fortunately I was of an enquiring turn of mind—I wanted a reasonable foundation for everything—and I found that neither laymen nor clergy could give me any rational explanation of their faith; that when I asked them about God and the trinity, and life and death, they told me either that such things were mysteries, or were beyond the comprehension of ordinary mortals.[20]

With early manhood, according to the conversion narrative, Webb dismissed Christianity altogether and turned away from it:

> I abandoned the system improperly called Christianity, soon after I attained my majority, because its teachers could not give me a convincing reason for the faith that was in them. When I was asked to believe that one was really three, and that a just and merciful Creator committed an act of unnatural cruelty simply to gratify a mere whim, I demanded corroborative testimony and was told that none had ever been filed. This very grave omission compelled me to throw the case out of court.[21]

The idyllic scene of Webb taking in the "glad sunshine and hear[ing] the more satisfying sermons preached by God Himself through the murmuring brooks, the gorgeous flowers and the joyous birds" is now replaced by Webb's allurement to "the nice-looking girls," whose presence at church justified his own:

> When I was young I went to Sunday school. In those days I was a
> pretty wild kind of a boy, and I used to go to church simply for the
> sake of seeing nice-looking girls and escorting them home. It was a
> most delightful task. When I was a little older, I changed from the
> Presbyterian church, to the Episcopal one, as there were equally nice
> young ladies to look at in the latter church.[22]

Taken aback, a correspondent of the *Mohammedan Observer* who interviewed
Webb in 1892 followed up by asking Webb if, indeed, he went to church in
those days only "to look at young ladies," and Webb responded: "Yes. I gave
religion no thought."[23]

Webb dated his taking mastery over his life to 1866, when he was twenty,
perhaps around the time of his graduation from Claverack College.[24] In his
interview with the *Mohammedan Observer* in 1892, Webb indicated that his
intellectual discontent with religion began at this time, when a family of
Universalists "began to preach religion to me, and I began to think of religion.
The more I thought of it, the more absurd it seemed to me."[25]

Spiritual Vagabond

Emory Tunison contended that Webb rejected Christianity in 1872 and became
"a spiritual vagabond" for a time.[26] Hassan Ali, Webb's companion in India,
may have been Tunison's source, since he too stated that Webb "gave up
Christianity" in 1872 and "for some years" had no religion at all.[27] Webb
described his intellectual disillusion with Christianity, however, as taking place
much earlier, in 1866, although his subsequent spiritual history was apparently one of increasing skepticism to the point of irreligion: "I drifted into
materialism; and, for several years, had no religion at all except the golden rule,
which I followed as closely as the average Christian follows it."[28]

Webb's conversion narrative gives no indication of sharp breaks between
youthful religiosity and later loss of faith, since he portrayed himself as having
had problems with Christian theology from the beginning. In Webb's case,
therefore, there was no distinct "spiritual moratorium"—a waiting period of
suspended religious activity—between rejection of the old religion and acceptance of the new. According to Webb's portrayal of his formative period, his
entire youth and young adulthood was one of suspended religious activity. The
irreligion of 1872 was not a radical departure from Webb's past in anything
other than a qualitative sense. His indifference toward religion became a
genuine antipathy toward it—in that sense marking a new episode in his life, a
type of spiritual moratorium—which lasted until he accepted Buddhism more
than eight years later. In his interview with the *Mohammedan Observer*, Webb
stated: "For nine years I had no religion. I followed the old materialistic idea."[29]

Webb replaced "the old materialistic idea" with Buddhism, and his attraction to that faith seems to have come around the time of his adoption of Theosophy. In January 1892, while Webb was still employed as U.S. Consul in Manila, he wrote an evidently anonymous autobiographical account of himself about a spiritual experience that he may have had some time prior to his adoption of Theosophy. The story is about a St. Louis reporter who is in the process of moving to the city from St. Joseph. The spiritual happening he describes took place "about five years before" the reporter "had even heard of Theosophy." The anonymous reporter's early life is remarkably similar to Webb's. The reporter's early years "were tinctured with the old orthodox Presbyterian training," a training he later rejected:

> By the time [he] reached manhood [he] had learned to look upon the
> prevailing forms of religion as irksome, erroneous and absurd: devoid
> of everything calculated to commend them to a thoughtful, intelli-
> gent, matter-of-fact person's salvation—granting that salvation was
> possible—whose principal virtue was their effectiveness in securing
> for their followers social standing and respectability.[30]

The essence of the anonymous reporter's materialism was that he "believed that when death came to us it was a complete annihilation of our consciousness and individuality, a putting out of the light of life as effectively as the flame of that gas jet is extinguished."[31] The reporter's materialism was also a period of hedonistic pleasure: "I was devoted to the world and its pleasures and managed to get no small degree of physical comfort out of it."[32]

At least in retrospect, Webb did not take lightly the disbelief that underlay his materialistic hedonism and spoke of the dangerous "drift out into the dark and forbidding waters of atheism."[33] After a few years of materialism, Webb moved away from it, just as he had inclined away from Christianity earlier, because it could not give answers to fundamental questions about the meaning of life and matters of the soul:

> It could tell me the name of every bone, muscle, nerve and organ
> of the human body, as well as its position and purpose of func-
> tion; but it could *not* tell me the real difference between a live man
> and a dead one . . . it could not tell me how and why the tree grew and
> the flower bloomed. . . . Whence [man] came and whither he went
> were riddles which [scientists] confessed themselves utterly unable to
> solve. . . . "Those matters belong to the Church," said a scientist
> to me. "But the Church knows absolutely nothing of them," I re-
> plied. "Nor do I—nor does science," was the helpless, hopeless way
> in which he dismissed the question from the conversation.[34]

In his Calcutta interview, Webb indicated that his path to spirituality had begun around 1872 as soon as his attraction began to "the old materialistic idea." In that year, Webb read the work *Zanoni* by the Victorian novelist Baron Edward Bulwer-Lytton, and, according to the article, it "excited his curiosity" in Islam.[35] There is little doubt that Webb referred to *Zanoni* in the interview, since it is not the kind of reference that a reporter would jot down inadvertently. The book may, indeed, have aroused Webb's interest in Islam by virtue of its vague Middle Eastern associations and references to Oriental mystic truths. It is more likely, however, that *Zanoni* aroused in Webb a general interest in spirituality and opened the door to his later Theosophical interests. Dating Webb's spiritual odyssey as beginning in 1872 when he read *Zanoni* is clearly problematic. It is the kind of minor detail his Calcutta editor might easily have mistaken. Taken literally, however, it contradicts Webb's other reference to this period as the time his materialism began, while Webb dated his spiritual journey in earnest as beginning almost a decade later. In looking back on *Zanoni*, however, Webb may have seen it as planting the seeds that would later come to fruition when he turned to Theosophy.

Although not concerned with Islam per se, the plot of *Zanoni* centers on two "mystic" figures of apparently Near Eastern background—Zanoni and Mejnour—both of whom are heirs to the esoteric and magical wisdom of the East. The book stresses the imperative of belief in the Supreme Being, life after death, and a moral system derived from God. The book is distinctly antimaterialistic, stressing the inherent conflict between the spirit and material reality. It presents a symbolic tale of the soul's ascent to God through divine love and mystical experience. It explores a number of eclectic and esoteric issues that would later make up the essence of Webb's religious outlook, including the idea that conversion to true faith requires personal sacrifice.[36] In all likelihood, *Zanoni* prepared the ground for Webb's study of Oriental religion and his subsequent adoption of Theosophy, after which he came to Islam.

The irreligion that came with Webb's materialism and rejection of religion paradoxically propelled his spiritual quest forward by liberating him from subservience to creeds and enabling him to undertake what he believed to be a dispassionate and objective search for the truth:

> My mind was in a peculiarly receptive, yet exacting and analytical, condition, absolutely free from the prejudices of all creeds, and ready to absorb the truth, no matter where it might be found. Firmly materialistic, I looked at first to the advanced school of materialistic science and found that it was just as completely immersed in the darkness of ignorance as I was.[37]

Returning again to the anonymous St. Louis reporter, it is noteworthy that he suffered from neuralgia, acute paroxysmal pain along the nerves, and would take an "elixir of opium" to relieve the suffering. If the reporter is

Webb, he took opium for neuralgic pain; there is, however, no indication of that in Webb's diary.

The reporter was severely afflicted by the disorder en route from St. Joseph to St. Louis but did not have access to his medication until after arriving. After taking the opium and falling asleep, he perceived his spirit in "clear and vivid" consciousness separate from his body and standing at the foot of the bed, his body seeming "only half awake." After coming back to consciousness, the reporter concluded that he had been "the victim of a mental and optical illusion." About five years later, now a Theosophist, he attributed the phenomenon to the "temporary separation of the astral body from the physical," which he interpreted as proof of the "independence of our consciousness of its bodily vehicle, and its ability to function outside of and beyond it."

The account of the opium-induced experience seems to have had a profound effect on Webb, cast doubt on his purely materialistic conception of reality, and constituted an important step toward his investigation of new spiritual alternatives.[38] If *Zanoni* had awakened Webb intellectually to the immaterial world of the unseen, the anonymous reporter's out-of-body experience opened the door to him for Theosophy and a variety of spiritual studies and investigations that would preoccupy much of the remainder of his life and also serve as the vehicle for bringing him to Islam.

Searching for Alternatives

Webb saw himself as part of "liberal progressive America," often counterpoising "American liberalism" against "the spirit of Puritanism and fanaticism."[39] His liberalism was reflected in the direction he took in his search for spiritual alternatives after his loss of faith and renewal of interest in religion. The search did not begin with Theosophy but ultimately led there. The spiritual alternatives Webb explored—Theosophy, Buddhism, and spiritualism—were popular in his time, especially among the "idealistic and liberally minded" like himself.[40] Webb referred to "the almost universal disposition, among liberal-minded Americans, to know more of the Oriental religions than their ancestors knew," which he believed helped people to break with "soul-destroying religious superstitions" and had led to "the development of an independent, fearless spirit of thought and investigation, which is gradually becoming the aggressive and relentless enemy of the mental slavery of creeds."[41]

Such eclecticism and spiritual liberalism were not uncommon in Webb's time.[42] His personal openness in matters of religion and doctrine, however, probably also owed a particular debt to his education at Claverack College and especially the influence of Alonzo Flack, who, while cultivating in his students a respect for "the philosophies promulgated through the ages," also encouraged them to look upon new concepts and beliefs with candid minds.[43]

Nineteenth-century secularization and science diminished the theological intelligibility of Victorian religion and placed shrouds of uncertainty and doubt over the convictions of earlier generations, but few Victorians remained spiritually indifferent. Many were stirred to venture beyond traditional religious practice in search of the secrets of the occult, often attempting to commune with the invisible world of spirits and the dead through spiritual experimentation, séances, and other means.[44] Public séances with spirits and "clairvoyant communication with the dead" were nowhere in the United States more popular than in the burned-over district of New York.[45] Webb began his search with spiritualism, by attending séances in St. Louis under a local medium named Cordingly.[46] Webb's attraction to spiritualism and the occult continued for years and is reflected in his advertisements of books on the subject in his journals.[47]

There is evidence of similar interest in spiritualism as well as Theosophy among Victorian converts to Islam in Britain. In his study of Abdulla Quilliam's Muslim community in Liverpool, John Pool encountered a British woman who had been an ardent Theosophist before converting to Islam.[48] Early issues of the *Islamic Review* reflect an abiding interest in esotericism, spiritualism, and Theosophy and the conviction that such perspectives were commendable and not merely compatible with the Islamic mission in the West.[49] In 1915, the *Islamic Review* proudly heralded Annie Besant, then international president of the Theosophical Society, and a lecture she had given titled "Islam in the Light of Theosophy."[50] Victorian American converts to Buddhism and adepts of Vedanta Hinduism reflected similar interests in spiritualism and the occult and often passed through them and through Theosophy on their path to Buddhism and other Oriental traditions. Webb gravitated toward the Buddhist converts, with whom he had strong affinities in particular, and joined their ranks.[51]

Compared with earlier periods, the Victorian era presented Americans with a much broader array of spiritual alternatives. In addition to spiritualism and the occult, Buddhism was well represented. Between 1879 and 1912, a dynamic discourse developed between Buddhism and the populations of America, Great Britain, and Continental Europe. Many either embraced Buddhism or developed strong sympathy for it.[52] The formative period of American Hinduism was a little later and came into its own between 1893 and the 1930s, although the movement survived the 1930s with considerable difficulty and minimal social acceptance.[53]

The availability of a rich and growing body of translations was key to the discourse that the Buddhist and Hindu traditions carried on with the Victorian world. The translations presented interpretations of their tenets in a manner generally compatible with Victorian sentiments, making the two faiths attractive and viable religious options for the spiritually disillusioned. In 1844, Henry David Thoreau became one of the earliest translators of Buddhist texts from French into English.[54] In 1888, one of the earliest American converts to Buddhism, Herman Vetterling, established the *Buddhist Ray*, the mouthpiece of the American Buddhist movement.[55] Webb knew and respected the journal and quoted from it in the *Moslem World*.[56]

American religious liberals—Unitarians, Transcendentalists, Free Religionists, and others—generally showed sympathy with Buddhism, although they were often disquieted by certain elements of the faith that seemed to run contrary to the Victorian ethos. In particular, the belief that Buddhism failed to affirm a personal God, buttress Victorian social optimism, or show a commitment to individualism and progress were major obstacles to the faith's progress.[57] But both Buddhism and Hinduism benefited from the general spiritual malaise of Victorian America and strengthened their appeal through unequivocal endorsement of inclusive universalism in opposition to exclusivism and intolerance.[58] To a great extent, it was for this reason that Hindus taking part in the Parliament of Religions were perceived as charismatic figures by their American audience. The Indian religious reformer Swami Vivekananda was the most popular, and in his lectures he eloquently espoused the underlying unity of all religions. Vivekananda founded the Ramakrishna Mission in 1897 and pioneered the way for an indigenous Hinduism in America. His mission presented itself as essentially humanitarian and—similar to the Aligarh Muslim movement, which inspired Webb—preached a revived and modernist Hinduism, which greatly appealed to Americans.[59]

Webb apparently came to Theosophy at a time when the Theosophical Society was developing a significant following in St. Louis.[60] Around 1881, he turned his attention to "Oriental religions and spiritual philosophies," adopting Buddhism as his preference.[61] He "became interested in the study of the Oriental religions, beginning with Buddhism as students of the Eastern systems usually do."[62] Webb never lost his sympathy for Buddhism, although he ultimately found the religion to be inadequate for his purposes. Later, as a Muslim missionary to America, he looked upon the small and growing Buddhist Mission of America as a natural friend and ally. Paul Carus was among the most important figures in the popularization of Buddhism in Victorian America, and Webb said of him in *The Moslem World and Voice of Islam*: "We cordially commend to students of the Oriental religions 'The Gospel of Buddha,' taken from some of the oldest records by Dr. Paul Carus, editor of *The Monist*. It presents, in a more lucid and satisfactory form than any work we know of, the true spirit of the doctrines of Buddhism."[63]

In St. Louis, Webb had access to about 13,000 books on spiritual matters at a library whose name and location he never identified. The collection provided him with books on religion that he would not otherwise have been able to find. It was the printed word—no doubt, such as he found in this library—that brought him to Buddhism, and it was the printed word that would bring him to Islam some years later. Webb described himself as spending from four to seven hours a day poring over his books, "intensely in earnest in [his] efforts to solve the mysteries of life and death, and to know what relation the religious systems of the world bore to these mysteries."[64] His absorption was so strong, it threatened his health: "So intensely absorbed did I become in my studies and experiments, that I devoted four and five hours a day to them, often taking for that purpose time that I really needed for sleep."[65] Col. Henry Steel Olcott, cofounder of the Theosophical Society with whom Webb met in India in 1892, testified to Webb's devotion to Buddhism, describing him as "a strenuous advocate" of the faith up to a few months before his acceptance of Islam.[66]

The initial period of spiritual search for Webb was from 1881 till 1884, which overlapped with the interval when he left journalism and turned to jewelry salesmanship and circus work publicity. He also tried his hand as a playwright and drama director. Nadirah Osman writes that Webb became so engrossed in spiritual studies at this time that he "decided to terminate his journalistic activities, which did not give him enough free time to do all that he desired." This comment is obviously a reference to the break in Webb's career, although Osman conceived of Webb as having the good fortune to secure his appointment as consul to Manila around that time, whereas Webb's interlude outside journalism actually ended when he resumed his journalistic career; the diplomatic appointment came four years later.

Webb may have come to Theosophy and Buddhism sometime around 1881 or 1882, that is, about five years after moving to St. Louis.[67] Other reports indicate, though, that his attraction to the Theosophical Society came some time after his introduction to Buddhism.[68] Webb's portrayal of his spiritual search, as described in his second letter to Mirza Ahmad, dated February 24, 1887, asserted, however, that he had been "seeking" for three years prior to writing and that he had "found much."[69] Just as Webb's loss of faith followed stages of increasing intensity, the same was probably true of his spiritual quest.

Buddhism and Theosophy were integrally linked during the late nineteenth century, and it is not surprising that Webb's interest in Buddhism would ultimately tie into Theosophy. The Theosophical Society was established in New York in 1878, although not officially chartered until 1886. Its founders were Helena Petrovna Blavatsky, a Russian writer and spiritualist, and Col. Henry Steel Olcott, an American lawyer and spiritualist.[70] The goal of the society was to popularize the teachings of esoteric Buddhism and Hinduism. Its link with Buddhism was especially strong, to the extent that thousands of the society's members who considered themselves Buddhist converts regarded esoteric Buddhism and Theosophy to be indistinguishable. Madame Blavatsky attempted to resolve the misunderstanding and asserted that Theosophy and Buddhism, in her view, were compatible but distinct. She insisted, however, that the "secret" religious teachings and lofty ethical principles of the Buddha were, indeed, identical with Theosophy.[71]

The Theosophical Society encouraged the study of comparative religion, again with emphasis on Buddhism and the Eastern faiths, and it endorsed the principle of the "esoteric" unity of all faiths, espousing as well the universal brotherhood of humankind regardless of class, gender, and race.[72] Theosophical Buddhists were especially adept at adding esoteric Hinduism to their sources of Oriental inspiration. Olcott's introduction to Buddhism, *A Buddhist Catechism*, was an example of such eclecticism. The Ramakrishna Hindu mission also asserted that its goals were fundamentally compatible with those of the Theosophical Society.[73] Webb joined into the chorus on behalf of Islam. From the time of his conversion and throughout the remainder of his life, he insisted that Islam and Theosophy were in basic agreement.[74] He reiterated his attachment to Theosophy shortly after arriving in New York in 1893: "I am myself a member of the American Theosophical Society and a firm believer in the knowledge and honesty of the late Mme. Blavatsky. Theosophy and esoteric Mohammedanism are almost identical."[75] William Quan Judge, head of the American Theosophical Society, testified to Webb's fidelity in holding to basic Theosophical teaching even after his conversion to Islam.[76] Theosophy became and remained a major element in Webb's spiritual quest and his fully developed religious life.[77]

According to the *Missouri Republican*, Webb became an adherent of Theosophy at a time when it enjoyed wide popularity among his friends. They soon tired of it, but Webb remained engaged in its pursuit: "Webb, however, was the one student out of the whole bunch, which included some of the best-known people in the city, who stuck." Webb soon began to alter his lifestyle, and it soon came to staff's attention that he had changed his habits:

> Quietly and without the least ostentation, Webb separated himself from all his former intimacies. There was nothing in the least pretentious about the way he did it. In ordinary work he was the same earnest and indefatigable worker; but it came to be a matter of comment that he was "purifying himself." This showed itself first in the trivial incident of his midnight lunches. He quit running down to the saloon for a glass of beer; brought his lunch from home, and always it was very light, and always of a delicate character—almost entirely fruits. It became known in a little while that Alex. Webb had taken up Theosophy.[78]

"Hadji Erinn"—a Turkish Muslim pen name among several used by William Quan Judge, chief director of the American Theosophical Society during the 1880s and 1890s—wrote in defense of Islam in 1893 and declared that "Bro. Webb [was] still a member of the Society, with interest in its progress." Judge also said that Webb had discovered Muslims in India who belonged to the Theosophical Society, many of whom possessed "much knowledge of formerly so-called esoteric doctrines, which are common to all religions."[79] L. Grebsonal, one of the important primary journalistic sources for Webb, affirmed in his profile Webb's lasting commitment to Theosophy:

> Mr. Webb is an old member of the Theosophic Society, and in his lecture recently given before the Aryan branch of the society in this city he endeavored to show that Mohammed not only understood and followed the teachings of the ancient Eastern philosophers, but that he clearly taught these doctrines to his followers—or those of them who were sufficiently developed spiritually to understand them. In fact, the lecture treated largely on theosophical ideas, and showed there was a close connection between them and the true Islamic system.[80]

Theosophy had enabled the deepest and most lasting changes in Webb's life. It offered him spiritual insight, criteria for judging spiritual experiences and other religions, and, most important of all, access through reading and lectures to the various religious traditions of the world. Theosophy helped bring Webb to Islam, while providing him criteria by which he could navigate and interpret the faith once he had accepted it. It was probably his experience of Theosophy that convinced him that Islam—like other non-Western religions—could constitute a valid religious alternative for other Americans like himself.

One of Webb's first steps toward Islam, however, occurred in St. Louis and, insofar as we know, without direct connection to the Theosophical Society. Two years before his move to the Philippines, where he accepted Islam, Webb initiated a remarkable correspondence about Islam with the Indian Muslim scholar Mirza Ghulam Ahmad. Mirza Ahmad would soon become the object of great controversy, but that was not yet the case when Webb wrote him. At the time, Mirza Ahmad was recognized as one of the foremost Muslim scholars of India and was actively involved in making Islam known to the West, especially through personal correspondence with prominent Westerners. Webb came to know of Mirza Ghulam Ahmad's interest in corresponding with persons interested in Islam and wrote a letter to him. The Webb–Mirza Ahmad letters are an essential part of Webb's biography and are of great note because they were a prelude to Webb's later correspondence with Indian Muslims and presaged many of his later concerns about Islam, even the possibility of creating an Islamic mission in America.

The Mirza Ghulam Ahmad Correspondence

Correspondence played a vital role at every stage of Webb's spiritual search. He wrote to "noted people of [the Theosophical Society] in this country and in foreign lands," which led to his discovery and acceptance of Theosophy. It was apparently through writing to his Theosophical colleagues that Webb became convinced of the efficacy of pursuing a consular appointment in the Philippines as a means of gaining access to the wisdom of the Orient.[81] His correspondence from Manila with Indian Muslims and Anglo-Indian journals underlay the articulation of his Islamic faith and the formation of his American mission. Webb's first clear step toward Islam, however, was expressed in his correspondence between 1886 and 1887 with Mirza Ahmad.

Today, Mirza Ahmad stands out as one of the most controversial Muslim religious leaders of the modern period. The controversy was only in its initial stages when Webb wrote to him, and he probably knew nothing of it. Webb's 1886–1887 correspondence with Mirza Ahmad came at a time when the debate about him was just beginning, and Mirza Ahmad was still widely regarded among Indian Muslims as a legitimate and highly learned scholar. During the 1870s, Mirza Ahmad had attained wide fame in the subcontinent as one of Islam's foremost champions against the inroads of colonial missionaries and similar groups critical of Islam or committed to the conversion of Muslims. In 1882, he proclaimed himself to be Islam's "Centennial Renewer" (*Mujaddid*). It was the first of Mirza Ahmad's many claims, but, although contentious, it was not heretical in itself.[82] It was not until 1891, just months before Webb's Oriental tour, that Mirza Ahmad came to be held in disrepute by large segments of the Indian Muslim population by virtue of proclaiming himself to be not only the Messiah Jesus returned to the world but also the reincarnation of Krishna and embodiment of the spirit of the Prophet Muhammad.[83] Consequently, the clamor surrounding Mirza Ahmad in 1892 during the Indian tour was sufficient to keep Webb from visiting him. Even the uproar over Mirza Ahmad that year paled before the riotous tumult that would surround him in 1898 and throughout the remainder of his life.[84]

There are different accounts of how Webb's correspondence with Mirza Ahmad began. According to one account, Webb decided to write to him regarding Islam in 1886 after reading a letter that the latter had written to one of Webb's American acquaintances. Another report states that Webb initiated the correspondence after reading an advertisement of one of Mirza Ahmad's principal works with an offer of several thousand dollars for anyone who could rebut the author's arguments in favor of the divine nature of the Qur'an and the authenticity of the Prophet Muhammad's claim to prophethood.[85] As indicated above, Mirza Ahmad was an enthusiastic letter writer and was noted for his copious correspondence with prominent Americans and Europeans. Among these were a number of Christian missionary leaders, including John Dowie, a famous Evangelical faith healer and strident anti-Islamic propagandist.[86]

Webb's correspondence with Mirza Ahmad consisted of four letters, two from Webb and two replies from Mirza Ahmad. The only known record of the correspondence today is in a work by Mirza Ahmad titled *Shahna-e Haqq* [The

Burden of Truth]. The only text given is for Webb's second letter. There is an Urdu summary of the content of Webb's first letter and Mirza Ahmad's response, and there is an Urdu version of Mirza Ahmad's second reply. Webb's second letter to Mirza Ahmad is dated February 24, 1887. It indicated that he received a response from Mirza Ahmad on December 17, 1886, along with several brochures about Islam.[87] *Shahna-e Haqq* contains only a synopsis in Urdu of Webb's initial letter. The book presents the full English text of Webb's second letter with Urdu translation and gives Mirza Ahmad's Urdu response to the second letter with an English translation.[88]

Although evidence for the Webb-Mirza Ahmad correspondence comes exclusively from Ahmadiyya sources, there is no reason to doubt its authenticity. One indication of its validity is the correct citation of Webb's St. Louis address in early Ahmadiyya sources at a time when access to such knowledge would have been difficult to obtain. *Shahna-e Haqq* records Webb's return address as 3021 Easton Avenue, St. Louis, Missouri (today 3021 Dr. Martin Luther King Drive).[89] Hassan Ali made reference to the letters in his preface to Webb's lectures. Webb knew the text well and gave no evidence of having found it inaccurate or otherwise objectionable. Ali had Ahmadiyya sympathies and is said to have become a follower of Mirza Ahmad within the years following Webb's visit to India. He had apparently not yet taken that step when he wrote in the preface: "Four years ago I had the pleasure of seeing one of [Webb's] letters addressed to Mirza Golam Ahmad of Kadian in Punjab, when I had gone there on my missionary tour. In this letter he had expressed his faith in Islam."[90] Although Webb's correspondence indicated that he was inclined toward Islam, it did not, in fact, give any indication that he had accepted the religion. The date of Ali's visit, though, is apposite, since it would have occurred sometime in 1888, the year following the end of the exchange and the year that Mirza Ahmad published *Shahna-e Haqq*, in which it was contained.

The Ahmadiyya attach considerable importance to the Webb–Mirza Ahmad correspondence, especially as an indication of the role Mirza Ahmad played in calling Westerners to Islam. The Ahmadiyya maintain that Mirza Ahmad was instrumental in Webb's conversion. They do not, however, claim that Webb became one of his followers.[91] Jane Smith, who seems to give credence to the Webb–Mirza Ahmad letters, acknowledges the Ahmadiyya claim that Webb's correspondence with Mirza Ahmad was "key to his conversion to Islam."[92] Robert Dannin notes that Webb made no public mention of Mirza Ahmad and asserts further that no distinctively Ahmadiyya eschatology appears in Webb's published work.[93] It is true that Webb made no known public pronouncements about Mirza Ahmad and that his published works show no evidence of Ahmadiyya theology. The *New York Herald* did, however, attribute an intriguing statement to Webb shortly after his return from India that probably indicates Ahmadiyya influence. Speaking of Christ's last years on earth after the Resurrection—a distinctive element of Ahmadiyya belief—Webb made vague reference to matters concerning that period of Jesus' life that were beyond the pale of official church doctrine, although he refused to elaborate.[94]

Whatever degree of influence the Ahmadiyya might have exercised on Webb, neither the Lahori nor Qadiani factions of the movement numbered him as a follower nor wrote of him or his mission during his later years or after his death. The early decades of the *Islamic Review*, which was Lahori, and *Moslem Sunrise*, which was Qadiani, evinced no knowledge of Webb, and neither journal printed an obituary of him upon his passing.[95] The *Moslem Sunrise* was based in the United States and clearly did not regard Webb as its first American convert. Instead, it announced in 1921 that a certain Mirza Ahmad Anderson, who had begun to correspond with the Ahmadiyya as early as 1901, was the first Ahmadiyya convert to Islam in America.[96] Furthermore, the Qadiani faction of the Ahmadiyya had a conspicuous presence in the Chicago World Fellowship of Faiths of 1933, billed as "A Second Parliament of Religions." It was an appropriate occasion for mentioning Webb, Islam's representative at the First Parliament of Religions, especially if he had been a follower of Mirza Ahmad, but the Qadiani delegation made no mention of him and appears to have been ignorant of his legacy.[97]

Webb's initial letter, for which there is only an Urdu synopsis in *Shahna-e Haqq*, mentioned that he had seen a letter of Mirza Ahmad in an American newspaper, in which Mirza Ahmad had invited readers to a demonstration of the truth (*haqq*), inspiring Webb to write him. Webb indicated that he had made extensive study of Buddhism and Hinduism and had attempted to make a study of the teachings of Zoroaster and Confucius. He had, however, only been able to learn a little about Muhammad. The synopsis described Webb as still wavering (*muzabzab*) about the true path and unable to discern it. It portrayed him as the "leader of a Christian church group (*mēñ 'īsā'ī garōh kē ēk girjā kā imām hūñ*)," although he had only been able to teach them basic moral values and character building. Webb concluded that "he [was] sincerely in search of the truth."[98] Mirza Ahmad's reply to Webb's first letter is not given, although Webb's second letter indicated that he received it on December 17, 1886, with the various pamphlets about Islam.[99]

Webb's second letter expressed his earnestness to submit to the truth, once he found it: "God, who can read all hearts, knows that I am seeking for the truth, that I am ready and eager to embrace it wherever I can find it."[100] Webb also emphasized his willingness to do God's work:

> God has blessed me abundantly, and I want to do His work earnestly
> and faithfully. How to do it is what has moved me, how to do it
> so that the most good may be accomplished. I pray to Him that the
> way may be pointed out clearly to me so that I may not go astray.[101]

He also requested more literature on Islam:

> I shall be happy to receive from you at any time matter which you
> may have for general circulation, and, if you should see fit to use my
> services to further the aims of truth in the country, they will be freely
> at your disposal, provided, of course, that I am capable of receiv-
> ing your ideas and that they convince me of their truth.[102]

Webb also alluded to his financial limitations. After mentioning that he would
like to come to India to meet Mirza Ahmad and study Islam, he noted that he
lacked the wherewithal:

> But I am so situated that it seems almost an impossibility. I am
> married and have three children. For nearly two years, I have been
> living a life of celibacy and shall continue to do so as long as I live.
> My income is not sufficient to justify me in giving up my busi-
> ness as it requires all that I can make to support my family; there-
> fore, even if I had sufficient means to enable me to make the journey
> to India, I would not be able to furnish support for my family during
> my absence.[103]

Webb concluded:

> However, I am impressed to believe that God will provide a way if
> I try to deserve His love. Blessed be His holy name and I hope
> that I may hear from you and that we again may some day meet in
> spirit, even if we cannot meet in the body. May the peace of God
> be with you and with those who listen to your words. I pray that all
> your hopes and plans may be realized. With reverence and esteem,
> I am, yours respectfully, Alex. R. Webb.[104]

In his reply to the second letter, Mirza Ahmad avoided Webb's questions
but stated that the letter had been an inspiration for him, especially regarding
Mirza Ahmad's lifelong hope that "the light of truth" not be confined to the
East but be furthered in Europe and America as well. He promised to keep in
touch with Webb and satisfy "his thirst after the investigation of truth,"
concluding that he was finishing a study of the Qur'an, which he hoped to
have translated into English. He would then send a copy to Webb for his
edification and with the hope that it would answer his questions and "bring
full and final conviction."[105]

Although Webb expressed his interest in Islam in both letters, in neither
of them did he indicate that he had become a Muslim. Interestingly, Webb's
second letter explicitly expressed his commitment to undertake an Islamic
mission in America, if he were to be convinced of the religion's truth: "It
occurred to me that I might through your aid assist in spreading the truth
here."[106] He noted that Americans were open to Buddhism and other Oriental

religions and that the "public mind" of America would be equally well-suited to accept Islam:

> If, as you say, the Mohammedan is the only true religion, why could I not act as its apostle or promulgator in America? My opportunities for doing so seem to me very good, if I had some one to lead me aright at first. I have been led to believe that not only Mohammed but also Jesus, Gautama Buddha, Zoroaster and many others taught the truth, that we should, however, worship God and not men. If I could only know what Mohammed really taught that was superior to the teachings of others, I could then be in a position to defend and pro-mulgate the Mohammedan religion above all others. But the little I do know of his teaching is not sufficient for me to do effective work with.[107]

As a Theosophist believing in the underlying unity of all religions, Webb expressed his misgivings about Islamic exclusivism:

> I am already well satisfied that Mohammed taught the truth, that he pointed out the way to salvation and that those who follow his teach-ings will attain to a condition of eternal bliss. But did not Jesus Christ also teach the way? Now suppose I should follow the way pointed out by Jesus, would not my salvation be as perfectly assured as if I fol-lowed Islam? I ask with a desire to know that truth and not to dispute or argue. I am seeking the truth, not to defend my theory. I think I understand you to be a follower of the esoteric teachings of Mo-hammed, and not what is known to the masses of the people as Mohammedanism; that you recognize the truths that underlie all religions and not their exoteric features which have been added by men. I too regret very much that I cannot understand your language, nor you mine; for I feel quite assured that you could tell me many things which I much desire to know.[108]

Again, however, Webb emphasized his willingness to follow Mirza Ahmad: "If you can lead me into its blessed light you will find me not only a willing pupil but an anxious one."[109]

Taking the Big Step

As should be clear by now, Webb's conversion was actually a series of con-versions. First, he adopted materialism, which he rejected for Buddhism in a search for new spirituality. Then, he adopted Theosophy and made changes in his eating habits and lifestyle. Finally, he embraced Islam. Although he gave up the first two choices, he remained loyal to Theosophy and Islam for the rest of his life.

The Webb-Mirza Ahmad correspondence makes clear that, by the time it ended in 1887, Webb had not embraced Islam, and there is no reason to believe that Webb had entered the faith prior to his appointment as consul to the Philippines toward the end of that year. In his interview with the *Mohammedan Observer* in the fall of 1892, he stated that he had been a Muslim for five years, which would mean that he had embraced the faith toward the beginning of 1888, around the time that he assumed his post in the Philippines.[110] The *New York Times* confirmed similarly that it was in Manila that Webb had become "actively interested in Mohammedanism."[111] Emory Tunison specified that the conversion took place in Manila, shortly after Webb's arrival there, when he "declared in 1888 that Islam was the only acceptable faith for himself."[112]

Webb embraced Islam in the Philippines without ever having seen a Muslim. According to Hassan Ali, Hajee Abdulla Arab, a prosperous Calcutta merchant who would prove central to Webb's Islamic spiritual life and his undertaking of an Islamic mission to America, was the first Muslim Webb saw, to which Ali added cajolingly, "I am glad that he saw the best Mussulman in India."[113] Webb's wife and family also converted. When Arab came to Manila, "he was also very much pleased to see Mr. Webb and his little family. The good-natured wife of Mr. Webb and her three children [were] also Moslems."[114]

Although correspondence played a role in Webb's conversion, books were the chief vehicle by which he came to the faith; as one profile of Webb puts it, he came "all by himself, from books, without ever having seen a Muhammadan."[115] Even in his letters to Mirza Ahmad, Webb requested books. Grebsonal attributed Webb's conversion to books, stating that about a year after his arrival in Manila, "he came into possession of books and documents, the works of Mohammedan authors, which aroused in him the most intense interest in the Islamic system, and he at once gave himself up entirely to its study, so far as his official duties would permit."[116] Tunison maintained that Webb discovered in Manila "works by several honest Muslim authors" and became immediately engaged in their study.[117]

It is customary to distinguish between "rational" and "emotional" religious conversions. The former are thought out, often during a "spiritual moratorium" of several years, while the latter takes place suddenly and often unexpectedly as the result of an overpowering emotional experience. Western conversions to Islam tend to fall within the rational category, while there is a propensity for emotional conversion among those who embrace Christianity or are reborn in the Christian faith.[118]

Having developed over a number of years and after considerable reflection, Webb's conversion followed the rational paradigm. It also came after a lengthy spiritual moratorium, although it is difficult to define the moratorium's beginning because of Webb's ambivalence about ever having been spiritually committed to Christianity. Webb interpreted the Islamic faith as an affirmation of an essentially Victorian moral code, which allowed him a rational belief in God's unity, while looking upon the world in a manner which he regarded as in keeping with modern science. As such, Webb's adoption of the Islamic faith validated much of his former Christianity while shearing it of all "irrational" aspects of dogma.

Stressing that his conversion to Islam had been the result of a long rational process and not emotional fervor, Webb emphasized that he had come to the faith through "protracted study," which finally brought him to the conclusion that Islam met "the spiritual needs of humanity." He concluded his presentation on the same note:

> I have spoken so much of myself in order to show you that adoption of Islam was not the result of misguided sentiment, blind credulity, or sudden emotional impulse, but that it was born of earnest, honest, persistent, unprejudiced study and investigation, and an intense desire to know the truth.[119]

Webb emphasized his exercise of discrimination in discerning what he found praiseworthy and worthy of imitation in Islam and what he found to be unacceptable. It was Islam's "pure and perfect" esoteric dimension, its "higher philosophy," which had won his commitment by convincing him that it was far superior to the materialistic philosophy of the day: "And I tell you frankly, that it was through this exalted philosophy that I was brought to Islam."[120] At the same, he had found and rejected much dross in the Islamic tradition which he did not believe convincing or worthy of being followed:

> And let me assure you that in seeking for the truths I have found, I have had to overturn a vast deal of rubbish in the shape of false history, false opinions, and false reasoning, before I caught the faint gleam of that priceless jewel which has been preserved to man through all the ages, although the bigots and Pharisees of orthodoxy have striven most earnestly to destroy it.[121]

In his study of Western conversion to Islam, Larry Poston identifies five principal attractions that the faith generally presents to the neophyte: simplicity, rationality, divine unicity, practical morality, and a direct relation to God.[122] All of them are to be found in Webb's description of his conversion, making him fit neatly within Poston's paradigm. The idea of Islam as "simple and pure" was one of Webb's frequent themes, which he attributed to both Islamic theology and ritual practice and often invoked in rhetorical flourishes against Christian dogma and practice. Webb regarded Islam as eminently commonsensical and advanced its "rationality" as its primary appeal in an age of advanced science and critical thought. Islam was, in his view, the antithesis of various types of superstition, and he insisted that his adopted faith required no one to believe what their intellect could not accept as demonstrably true. Webb regarded Islam as the "natural religion" and linked its "primordiality" to its faithfulness to ancient prophetic tradition. Webb believed that all religions had exoteric and esoteric aspects that originally complemented each other. This archetypical exoteric-esoteric dichotomy was, in Webb's view, well-preserved in the Islamic religion but had lost its original gospel clarity in the tradition of the Christian church.[123]

Islam's theology of divine unicity, the faith's third major attraction to Western converts, is often linked in their minds with what they perceive to be its "humanistic corollary," the unity or "universal brotherhood" of humankind. Both aspects are explicit in Webb, who stressed the clarity of Islam's unitarian theology while invoking "universal fraternity" as its theological corollary. In *Islam in America*, he mistakenly deemed the "universal brotherhood of man" to be Islam's fourth pillar. Islam's practical morality and its "this-worldly focus" on humanity and social problems constituted one of the basic objectives of Webb's Islamic mission. This exoteric dimension of the faith was, in his belief, suitable to all classes of human beings. Webb emphasized Islam's lack of priests and other intermediating agents between the Muslim worshipper and God and brought this aspect of the faith to bear against the doctrine of "vicarious atonement," which he believed vitiated social morality and destroyed individual accountability.

The primary reasons that Webb gave for his conversion were the inadequacy he found in traditional Christian religion and its inability to confront the skepticism produced by modern science. By contrast, he found Islamic theology internally consistent and capable of answering the questions of modern science. When placed within the context of Webb's personal life, other questions come to mind as possible motives for his series of spiritual conversions leading ultimately to Islam. Among these motives would be the general skepticism in traditional religion that grew up in the United States in the wake of the Civil War. On a personal level, several of Webb's biographers set 1872 as the date that he made a radical rejection of Christianity, as opposed to the apparent indifference of his earlier years. That year came in the wake of three major events in Webb's life: the Chicago fire, the loss of his business in the fire, and the unexplained termination of his first marriage to Laura Conger. It is notable that Webb mentioned none of these matters as underlying reasons for his rising doubts or his subsequent spiritual odyssey to resolve them. His diary and published writings make no mention of the Civil War at all. Webb was, however, the product of his time, and the unconscious ethos of an era cannot be ignored as a powerful, although unspoken, force underlying Webb's behavior. He undoubtedly reflected the unabated spiritual crisis of his century, one that had become so strong by the time of the

Parliament of Religions in 1893 that even the most isolated and uninformed of Americans had at least an inkling of it and knew that "something [was] going on out there."[124] Although nothing specific is known about how Webb lost his first wife, the fact that Webb never talked about it indicates that its memory must have been uncomfortable and comprised an important element of his subconscious.

Webb made frequent mention of the new science, although his conversion narrative made no particular mention of Charles Darwin or evolutionary theory. Darwin's *On the Origin of Species* first appeared in 1859, when Webb was entering his teens, and *The Descent of Man* appeared in 1871, the year of the Chicago fire. It was, coincidentally, shortly afterward that Webb exchanged his Christian beliefs for "materialism."

By the time Webb was a young man, science, not theology, had become the dominant discourse of American intellectual life. It had displaced Christianity as the "vital ideal" of Victorian Americans, creating an acute sense of disequilibrium from which many never recovered. The new scientific spirit extended beyond material science to other fields of critical inquiry with direct bearing on religion, including archaeology, biblical criticism, and comparative religions. Here too the new inquiries raised profound questions about traditional religious authority.[125] Skepticism and agnosticism became rife in all walks of life, and O. B. Frothingham, an American Transcendentalist, wrote in 1872: "Ours is an age of restatements and reconstructions, of conversions and 'new departments' in many directions. There is an uneasy feeling in regard to the foundation of belief. The old foundations have been sorely shaken."[126]

The Victorian spiritual crisis peaked during the 1870s with "agnosticism," to use Menand's image, "riding its high horse, and...frowning superbly upon all metaphysics." Unknown to Webb, it was in his year of greatest spiritual crisis, 1872, that William James, Charles Peirce, Oliver Wendell Holmes Jr., and other members of Boston's intellectual elite "half-ironically, half-defiantly" formed their "Metaphysical Club," inaugurating a process of philosophical examination that, by the close of the century, would lead to the formation of the Pragmatist School and finally give Victorian America a new sense of direction.[127]

Although a time of spiritual questioning and doubt, the Victorian era was also a time of great optimism. Many doubted church teachings, but, like Webb, they rarely doubted their personal ability to discern the truth once they found it. One of the most fundamental Victorian traits, as historian Anne Rose notes, was self-assured temperament that enabled them to turn away from "inherited religious definitions of meanings" of life in their personal search for "answers to questions of life's purposes that they devised themselves."[128] This general Victorian outlook in response to the spiritual crisis of the time also explains to a great extent why so many of Webb's countrymen and women were willing to give him a hearing, even if with mixed emotions, and why his enemies—especially Protestant missionaries—feared that Webb's American mission constituted a danger to Christianity in America.

Since standard religious formulas had failed and long-standing answers were rarely tenable, Victorians often sought in their self-confident searches distinctly personal solutions to their spiritual crises. Each seeker invented "a formula of his own for the universe."[129] There were countless alternatives from which to choose, many of which would have been unimaginable in an earlier age. Webb's Islamic option was exotic, but, in essence, it was no different from many other serious alternatives of the time: spiritualism, Theosophy, Buddhism, Hinduism, Transcendentalism, and Free Religion. Indeed, the broad appeal of the Parliament of Religions was a reflection of such wide-ranging religious curiosity and the Victorian penchant for the eclectic.[130] Not all Victorians turned to new forms of religion as a response to their spiritual crisis. Many of them, while maintaining a nominal commitment to church theology, turned zealously to the pursuit of secular success, which they now took up with the same sense of personal reward that religion had once provided.[131]

Comparing Analogues

Webb's conversion had several parallels among Victorian converts to Islam and Buddhism, where Webb himself had begun his spiritual odyssey. From the time when Webb inaugurated his American mission until roughly the end of the first decade of the twentieth century, as many as three thousand Americans considered themselves converts to Buddhism. Those who were active sympathizers with the faith numbered in the tens of thousands.[132] Perhaps because of his earlier association with American Buddhism, Webb understood fully the importance of those who sympathized with his mission. Buddhist sympathizers, while not actually embracing Buddhism, expressed profound attraction to it, endorsed its mission, and, in some cases, even gave monetary support. They often attended lectures on Buddhism and came to its defense in writing and speech.[133] The sympathizer phenomenon is especially important for both Webb and the Buddhists, because the sympathizer represented an invaluable bridge between the newly emerging community and the dominant majority at large.

Buddhist sympathizers tended to be concentrated in the Northeast and along the Pacific Coast. The wealthy industrialist Andrew Carnegie was among the most influential of them, although other prominent American businessmen and civic leaders were equally generous in support. One of the most important sympathizers on the West Coast was a certain Alexander Russell, who was a wealthy San Francisco sales manager of Bowers Rubber Works.[134]

The spiritual crisis of the age played as conspicuous a role in the American Buddhist missions as it did anywhere else. Like Webb, American converts to Buddhism acknowledged having been brought to their new faith through spiritual crisis. They were inclined to seek spiritual solutions, not just at the individual level, but within the nexus of newly formed religious communities, which embodied and reinforced their novel values and ultimate concerns.[135] Similar generalizations seem to hold for American converts to Hinduism during the same period.[136]

Women played a notable role in Webb's mission and tended to predominate among American Buddhists as well, where their proportion was especially high among converts to esoteric Buddhism, although somewhat less among spiritualists, Theosophists, and the early Baha'is. Victorian women often found that such alternative types of spirituality were better suited to their needs, and in fact that they often endorsed ideas of gender equality.[137] American women were well represented in the Ramakrishna Movement.[138] In terms of class affiliation, the American Hindu mission generally appealed to those in the white middle and upper classes, especially "spiritual seekers" of Protestant background, many of whom were foreign-born and not, like Webb, members of long-established American Protestant families.[139] There was also a notable countercultural element among American Buddhist converts, which does not appear to have been pronounced among Webb and his colleagues in the American Mission, despite their critique of organized Christianity, the West, and the travails of modernity. Webb's somewhat older contemporary, Dyer Daniel Lum, who is often regarded as the first American convert to Buddhism, threw his energy into the American Buddhist mission. Lum, however, was also known for his commitment to the radical politics of anarchism.[140]

No similarly exhaustive study has been done of Muslim converts in Victorian America or Britain, but Webb had several Western Muslim analogues in and shortly after his time. The little-known Reverend Norman is certainly among the most intriguing, since he was not only before Webb but was also an American, while most of the Muslim converts of the period were British or Continental. As mentioned earlier, Norman is said to have embraced Islam in Turkey in 1875 while working there as a Methodist missionary. He then returned to America to establish a Muslim mission.[141] Webb gave no indication of knowing Norman's story, although he related a rumor of a U.S. minister to Turkey who had embraced Islam. Webb had a diplomatic minister of state in mind, someone like himself, although the rumor, assuming it had some basis in truth, may have confused the Methodist minister with an anonymous minister of state.[142]

Webb's ties to British Muslim converts were an important facet of his mission. Quilliam and Browne were the most significant of them, and Webb alluded to the assistance and encouragement of many others. William Richard Williamson (Haji Abdullah Williamson), whom Webb helped escape torture and imprisonment in the Philippines, later embraced Islam under Quilliam's influence and contributed to Webb's journal under the name of Abdallah bin Fadle the American (despite his English background). Williamson's active life inspired one of the most remarkable conversion narratives of the period.[143] Another British convert who assisted Webb was A. W. Obeid-Ullah Cunliffe. He submitted a poem, titled "A Moslem Prayer," which Webb published. Cunliffe also wrote a book called *The Disintegration of Christianity*, which Webb advertised for sale.[144] Webb acclaimed the South African Hajee Omar J. F. Chamberlain for his commitment to the faith and thanked him for his "generous aid in our efforts to establish Islam in America."[145]

The early decades of the twentieth century witnessed numerous conversions to Islam in Britain and America, and, although they belonged to a different age in some respects and will be mentioned only in passing, such converts still lived in a world affected by the Victorian ethos and not radically different from the worlds of Webb and Quilliam. The first decades of *The Islamic Review* and *The Moslem Sunrise* are filled with photographs and stories of Western converts to Islam on both sides of the Atlantic. Lord Headley figured most prominently among the British converts of the time, and no doubt his conversion and active participation in the Woking Mosque outside London and the *Islamic Review*, which it published, were underlying factors in many of those conversions.[146]

Abdulla William Henry Quilliam (1856–1932) was probably the most important analogue for Webb and is an essential part of Webb's story. The connection between the two will be discussed in greater detail later. Quilliam's work and thought clearly influenced Webb, but their relationship does not appear to have been especially warm. Indeed, there are indications of an element of rivalry between the two. Quilliam was a lawyer ("solicitor") by profession and is said to have been the first recorded "native-born Briton who converted to Islam and openly declared himself a Muslim in England."[147] Quilliam, ten years younger than Webb, embraced Islam four years before Webb after a visit to North Africa.[148] He was struck there with "the apparent sincerity of the followers of Islam, and with the absence in Moslem cities of the vices so prevalent in large centers of population in Great Britain." After his return, Quilliam devoted himself to the study of the Qur'an and, as John Pool, a late-nineteenth-century writer on Islam put it, of "every other work he could procure upon the subject, *pro* or *con*, with the result that he was at last convinced that of all the religions of the world Islamism was the best." He then "had the courage of his convictions, and openly confessed himself a convert to Mohammedanism, while he formally renounced Christianity."[149]

Quilliam established his "Church of Islam" in his native Liverpool, launching an Islamic Mission, which lasted many years and was remarkably successful by the standards of the time.[150] Quilliam adopted "vigorous and active methods of propaganda," delivering public lectures, organizing groups of "open-air preachers," circulating pamphlets, and publishing books and

FIGURE 3.1. William Henry Quilliam (1893)

journals. The precedent Quilliam set was the chief inspiration and model for Webb's mission. Quilliam initiated a British Islamic press and brought out a weekly, the *Crescent*, and a monthly, the *Islamic World*. Yahya-en-Nasr Parkinson, himself a British convert and follower of Quilliam, wrote that the *Crescent* appeared regularly from 1893 until 1908. It recorded the "doings of the Association, work accomplished, financial statements, meetings held for prayer and instruction, public lectures, etc." Parkinson gave no similar details about the *Islamic World*.[151]

According to Thomas Arnold, Quilliam claimed to have thirty converts to Islam within five years of his mission's inception. That number is said to have grown to more than one hundred over the following five years.[152] When Pool visited Quilliam's community in 1891, he found more than fifty members.[153] Quilliam, like Webb, captured the attention of the Muslim world for a time, especially the Muslims of British India. He was decorated in Istanbul by Sultan Abdul Hamid II and commissioned in 1894 "to be the bearer of a decoration from the Sultan to a Muslim merchant who had erected a mosque in Lagos."[154] By the turn of the century, the Liverpool Muslim Institute numbered about one hundred and fifty people—mostly English men, women, and children from all walks of life. There was a boarding school for boys and a day school for girls called the Medina Home for Children. There was a library, reading room, museum, and science laboratory.[155] According to Parkinson, the majority of Quilliam's followers were "working men, not millionaires."[156]

Quilliam and his following sometimes confronted strong opposition from the surrounding community. The association disbanded in 1908.[157] Quilliam left Liverpool and immigrated to Ottoman Turkey. The buildings were vacated, and the group dispersed. A number of former members moved to the Woking Mosque, took part in its activities, and contributed to the *Islamic Review*. Quilliam returned to England years later and died in London in 1932. He was buried in the Brookwood Cemetery in Surrey, where Muhammad Marmaduke Pickthall, another British convert to Islam, is also buried.[158]

Little is known of Hajee Abdulla Browne, but he was also a prominent English convert of the time and active in various Muslim societies in London. Browne was close to Webb and is more conspicuous in Webb's journals than Quilliam. Browne stood firmly behind Webb and offered him moral and monetary support.[159] Webb commented in connection with Browne that "the number of English Mussulmans [was] rapidly increasing, and [Browne's society] the London Anjumani-Islam [was] doing most excellent work there."[160] The society was not primarily English but consisted mainly of "Indian gentlemen."[161] Its goals, however, were "to promote the study, and propagate the knowledge of Islam (or Mohammedanism, as it is sometimes improperly termed) as a religious, social and political system."[162] The society sought the establishment of a reading room and library.[163] Webb referred to him as "our earnest brother Moslem" and "one of the most earnest and devout of English Moslems" and "a most capable, well-informed and careful writer."[164] Webb printed an article by Browne, "The Evidences of Islam: The Religion of the Mussulman Clearly of Divine Origin."[165] He later offered an offprint of Browne's *Evidences of Islam* for sale, published by Webb's Moslem World Company, contending that it enjoyed "a very extensive circulation in the United States."[166] In 1893, Webb listed Browne as the *Moslem World*'s chief agent in London.[167]

Browne insisted that the Islamic faith was "based upon the free exercise of the judgment and reasoning powers, and claims acceptance from men— not upon the authority of tradition, but upon that of the visible and incontestable evidence it offers for their consideration." His "evidence" closely paralleled Webb's own reasoning on the matter, although it is more academic and less polemical in tone. Browne generally invoked the same sort of arguments that Christian missionaries used as proofs of their faith, but he used them in Islam's favor. He cited, for example, their contention that the historical preservation of the Bible was a proof of the Christian religion. Like many Victorians, Browne doubted their assertion but insisted that the argument applied well to the Qur'an, which he insisted upon as proof of Islam's validity. Christian missionaries drew attention to the extensive spread of their faith through the world. Browne noted that, if proliferation of a faith were a proof of religious truth, it would surely stand as Islam's claim to fame. He argued that while missionaries spent millions of pounds "to win a score or two of converts," Muslims spent nothing but received "a thousand" in return. He argued that the Christian missions in India and the East had, in fact, only served to awaken people "to a sense of the folly of the old religions and lead them to the acceptance—not of Christianity but of Islam." Like Webb, he noted the church's legacy of militancy and intolerance, which culminated in the Inquisition. He also argued that Islam provided a powerful call to the reformation of sound morality, whereas Christianity had shown itself powerless "to stem the tide of open sin and vice."[168]

Like Quilliam and Webb, Browne focused on the medium of public lectures:

Competent lecturers on the Religious, Moral and Social aspects of Islam, the manners and customs of Moslem peoples, and kindred topics, will be supplied to public institutes &c [sic, i.e. etc.], on terms which can be learned on application, and lecturers will invariably treat their subjects in an historical or descriptive manner, for, as the acceptance of Islam, to be valid, must be entirely spontaneous.[169]

Browne also solicited for his presentations all Britons serving in the British Empire's Muslim colonies:

It is earnestly hoped that journalists, clergymen and missionaries of all denominations, religious enquirers, and members of Her Majesty's service liable to serve in India and other countries where a large proportion of the population are Moslems will avail themselves of the advantages offered by the society.[170]

Browne later moved to Egypt, where he was the "guest of Mahmoud Salem Bey, Judge of the Mixed Tribunal." Webb stated that Browne intended to produce in Egypt "some translations of Islamic literature that promise to attract widespread attention in the English-speaking world."[171] A few months later, Webb said that Browne had just completed the "last of three works on the history and doctrines of Islam, which he will soon publish."[172] By the end of the summer of 1895, Browne established and edited a weekly journal in Cairo called the *Egyptian Herald*, which Webb regarded as "one of the most commendable of English Islamic publications." The journal advocated the administrative autonomy of Egypt and other interests of Islam throughout the world. Webb wrote:

Hajee Browne has for many years been an earnest and consistent advocate of three political principles of vital importance to the international interests of Europe and Asia, viz. [i.e., namely]: The preservation of the Ottoman empire; the integrity of all Moslem peoples and the promotion of friendly relations between the followers of Islam and the British empire. In his advocacy of these principles we feel assured he will have the countenance and support of all American Moslems.[173]

Webb noted that Browne had always championed "His Imperial Majesty, the Sultan of Turkey," Sultan Abdul Hamid II, whom he regarded as "a greater statesman than Gladstone and Bismarck."[174]

Sir Rowland George Allison, or Lord Headley, belonged to Webb and Quilliam's generation. He formally entered the Islamic faith in 1913, three years before Webb's death.[175] The *Islamic Review* reported that Headley declared in 1923, while in Cairo en route to the pilgrimage, that he was no new convert to Islam but, in fact, had been "a Moslem at heart for fifty years, but at [that] time it would have been unkind—in fact, cruel—to declare his belief." *The Islamic Review* continued to explain that Headley waited until 1913 to declare his conversion, because by that time "all the old people whom he had had to consider had gone, and he did not care a penny for what the young people thought, so he felt that it was time for him to come out and declare himself in his true colours."[176] Taking the *Islamic Review* literally, Headley's conversion of heart would have taken place sometime around 1873, which would place it prior to the conversion of Reverend Norman and long before Quilliam and Webb. In most respects, Headley and Webb's outlooks were very similar. Like Webb, Headley placed great emphasis on the principle of fraternity. He wrote a poem titled "The Brothers in Islam" on January 5, 1914, with the concluding stanzas:

> Great Allah, Lord, our God our King,
> Who knowest what for us is best,
> We praise Thy Name and loudly sing
> The fusion of the East and West.

The same issue carries a second poem by Headley titled "Muslim Equality."[177] As the titles and content of his poems indicate, Headley, despite his aristocratic background, was powerfully attracted by the Islamic ideals of fraternity and equality.[178]

Like Webb's conversions two decades earlier, Headley's conversion shocked Christian missionaries. Zwemer's *Moslem World* sounded the alarms in missionary circles and claimed that the "Irish peer's" conversion "called attention to the existence of an organized endeavour to carry on a Moslem Mission in England." Writing on behalf of Zwemer's *Moslem World*, H. U. Weitbrecht attempted to explain away both Quilliam's and Headley's conversions in terms of their not having been suitably Christian. Both, in his view, had been Deists before embracing Islam. Weitbrecht asserted, "It is

FIGURE 3.2. Lord Headley with Khwaja Kamaluddin, Director of the
Woking Mosque (1913)

sufficiently obvious that a nominal Christian Deist who is ready to swallow the
historical contradictions of Islam, has but a very short step to take in order to
become a Moslem; and having already emptied the Christian faith of its
specific content, he may regard himself, as Lord Headley professes, to be still
a Christian after he has embraced Islam."[179]

Like Quilliam and Webb, Headley was convinced that Islam had a future
in the West. Like them also, he devoted his energy and resources to fostering
an Islamic mission and wrote optimistically of the possibility of Islam's
spreading in England:

I feel sure that if the people of England fully grasped what Islam really is, common sense, and the natural desire we all have to use our
reasoning faculties as well as our emotions, it would do much to
remove the misunderstandings which exist. It is, I think, much to
the discredit of certain persons that they have willfully spread abroad
incorrect accounts of Muhammad's work and teaching, and have
generally misrepresented Islam to Western nations. To show that
Islam stands on a firm foundation and is a religion appealing

strongly to the intellect as well as to the natural sentiments engrafted in human nature, should now be our closest duty.[180]

Like Webb, Headley stressed his belief in the compatibility of Islam with the
original teaching of Christ and the early church. The *Islamic Review* insisted that
"although [Headley] had accepted Mohammedanism, he was still a Christian in
so far as believing in Christ and following the teachings of Christ." Affirming
that Headley's attitude toward Christ was typical of Muslims in general, the
Islamic Review proudly notes: "Needless to add that Lord Headley is not the only
Muslim who is also a Christian. Muslims all the world over believe in the
Prophethood of Jesus as much as that of Muhammad, and so every Muslim is at
the same time a Christian."[181] Headley stated: "I repeat with confidence that
'Islam is Christianity shorn of useless and pernicious dogmas.' "[182] The *Inver-
ness Courier* reported in the spring of 1925 that the Muslims of Albania had
requested that Headley—as a Muslim convert and British nobleman—assume
the Albanian throne, which Headley graciously declined.[183]

One of the most extraordinary Western converts to Islam of the early
twentieth century was Lady Evelyn Cobbold, who took the name Zeinab and
was closely associated with Headley until his death, although she came to
Islam independently of his influence. The eldest daughter of the seventh Earl

FIGURE 3.3. Lady Evelyn Zeinab Cobbold (ca. 1930)

of Dunmore, Cobbold, whose family had the custom of spending the winters in Algeria, learned Arabic and a few rudiments of Islam as a child. Once, as an adult, in a personal audience with the pope arranged by a group of Cobbold's Italian cohorts, he asked her to which denomination she belonged. Cobbold had not formally embraced Islam at the time but responded as if involuntarily: "I am a Moslem." Cobbold's spontaneous answer shocked her, although probably not as much as it shocked the pope and Cobbold's friends: "What possessed me I don't pretend to know, as I had not given a thought to Islam for many years. A match was lit, and then and there I determined to read up and study." She added: "The more I read and the more I studied, the more convinced I became that Islam was the most practical religion, and the one most calculated to solve the world's many perplexing problems, and bring humanity peace and happiness."[184] Later in life, whenever asked when she had adopted Islam, Lady Cobbold would say: "I can only reply that I do not know the precise moment when the truth of Islam dawned on me. It seems I have always been a Moslem."[185]

Another noteworthy British convert to Islam of the period was Muhammad Marmaduke Pickthall, who was also closely associated with Lord Headley; Pickthall was followed into Islam by his wife and brother Rudolf, who took active part in supporting the Woking Mosque.[186] In France, René Guénon (Shaykh 'Abd-al-Wahid Yahya) and, in the Austro-Hungarian Empire, Leopold Weiss (Muhammad Asad) entered Islam during the century's early decades. Each exercised a notable but very different influence on their contemporaries and subsequent generations. Their Islamic acumen and intellectual insight greatly enhanced the level of discourse among converts, and each, in his own way, became a leading interpreter of Islam to the West.[187]

4

Go West, Young Man

Chicago: Ordeal by Fire

As Webb grew up, he could not help feeling the pull of America's expanding frontier beyond the Alleghenies. Even before the Civil War, many young men and sometimes whole families were pulling up their roots in Hudson and moving westward, especially to Michigan.[1] The Civil War slowed down the nation's western thrust, but after the war Webb's generation turned west with new vigor.

Many in the postwar North and South alike looked toward the frontier to start new lives and shake off the disillusionment of civil war. The world beyond the horizon became a land not only of economic opportunity but also of a profoundly needed spiritual regeneration.[2] The words of Horace Greeley resonated in their ears: "Go West, young man, and grow up with the nation." Webb himself, in all likelihood, had heard Greeley in person at the Claverack College addresses.[3]

Webb's first move was to Chicago, then a booming prairie city on the shores of Lake Michigan, and to a job as a jeweler, using skills he learned at an early age.[4] It is noteworthy that Webb avoided the family profession of journalism there. Though he ended up working most of his life as a journalist, it was more out of sheer financial necessity than from love of the work. In Victorian culture, fathers often insisted that their sons follow them in their line of work, but young men frequently responded by seeking entirely different vocations. Such an inclination may well explain Webb's lifelong flirtation with the jewelry business, a line of work that rarely brought him success but always seemed worth another try.[5]

Before the Civil War, Chicago was the major transportation hub and wholesale center of the nation's interior. Once the war ended, Chicago quickly surpassed St. Louis, its regional rival, and became not only the financial fulcrum of the Midwest but an American global city second only to New York.[6]

The "Can-Do City" was pulsating with promise when Webb arrived in 1869. Like others of his generation, Webb probably welcomed his move to Chicago with great expectations of making a new beginning for himself and earning substantial wealth. The fact that he was hoping to find riches is reflected in the rash investments that he undertook with his father-in-law. Had it not been for the intervention of the Great Fire of 1871, which destroyed their inventory, their huge outlays of borrowed capital and merchandise would surely have ruined them both.

Webb joined the Giles Brothers jewelry house at 142 Lake Street and appears to have continued in jewelry for the remainder of his stay in the city.[7] One of Webb's expectations must have been to get married and start a family, and it was not long before he found Laura Cordelia Conger. Laura's father, Lucian West Conger, hailed from New York and was well-to-do. Like Webb, Conger had a hand in the jewelry business, and the two became partners and established a joint venture as "watchmakers and jewelers."[8] They began with an investment of $3,000 and opened their shop in the Loop at 135 Clark (Chicago streets did not have North-South designations at the time).[9] The investment capital probably came entirely from Conger, since census records listed him as wealthy but show Webb as possessing no property of note.[10]

Webb and Conger lost everything in the fire,[11] but the fire saved them financially. In the partners' early euphoria, they had "allowed drummers and glib-tongued salesmen to stock them up with goods of every sort and kind until they had a stock of more that $25,000 in value in their store." The amount was unbelievable for the time, and a Webb obituary recorded years later that the partners had breathed "a sigh of relief" because the fire had destroyed their luckless inventory and erased all financial liability.[12]

When Webb married Laura Conger in Chicago on May 4, 1870, she was seventeen.[13] What became of her on the night of the fire, October 8, 1871, is unclear. No divorce or obituary records have come to light, and there is no evidence that she abandoned Webb.[14] The home that she and her paternal family shared with Webb on 5 Forest Avenue (today 31st Street and Indiana) on Chicago's South Side was almost twenty blocks south of the fire's main path. Had Laura been at home that night, she would have been safe, and census records indicate that her mother, father, and siblings survived the fire, making her disappearance from subsequent records all the more unusual.[15] There is no telling where she had been or what she might have been doing during the universal panic that engulfed the city along with the flames, and we can only guess at her demise.

The Great Fire actually was not a single fire, but a chaotic accretion of dozens of separate conflagrations that were set off more or less simultaneously as thousands of firebrands were being wafted by the strong winds from one part of the city to another. The fire's course tended to follow the winds, but panic and chaos reigned everywhere. By 2:30 A.M., Chicago's business district was caught up in the blaze. By daybreak, it was clear that the fire was unstoppable, and there was little to do but wait until it burned itself out.[16]

Whatever became of Laura Conger and Webb's marriage, its termination and the events surrounding the fire were decisive: it was only a matter of months before he "lost [his] religion," underwent fundamental psychological changes, became "a spiritual vagabond," and entered a period of cynical hedonism that would continue several years.

There are few substantial records regarding Webb's life during the initial years—1872–1874—following the Chicago fire. The special *Fire Edition* of the Chicago directory, which appeared shortly afterward and listed surviving persons and businesses that remained in the devastated city, makes no mention of Conger, Webb, or their business, indicating that they left the city immediately afterward.[17] Webb appears to have returned to New York. Although the chronology is not clear, he worked for a time at selling jewelry at the House of Tiffany in New York City and as a journalist in Hudson at his father's newspaper. During the fire's aftermath, he came back to Chicago once or twice. Sometime in 1872 and possibly 1873, he owned and managed a billiards hall on Michigan Avenue.[18] He is then said to have become a Chicago agent of a "large jewelry concern," presumably Tiffany of New York.[19] Webb's stint as a Tiffany salesman must not have lasted more than a few months. Sometime in 1873, he returned to Hudson, where he wrote for his father's *Hudson Daily Star*. This was apparently the last job Webb held before his move to Missouri in January 1874; it was ostensibly his success at the Hudson paper that made him an attractive candidate as an editor in Unionville.

Unionville, Missouri: Starting All Over

Since Victorian family attachments were strong, family members were often torn between the impulse to make their mark in the world and the emotional need to remain behind with family. Pulling up roots and heading out to unfamiliar places often led to emotional and spiritual crises, which were sometimes exacerbated by the disillusionment following the Civil War.[20] Webb was apparently the "mobile member" of his family; he first demonstrated his ability to venture out into the world by his move to Chicago.

For Webb, the emotional strains of leaving his New York family behind were resolved in Unionville, where he renewed his companionship with his former father-in-law and former business partner, Lucian Conger. On January 8, 1874, Webb officially joined the *Unionville Republican* and began a long career in Missouri journalism.[21] An announcement in the *Unionville Republican* welcomed him as "an experienced Newspaper man" from the *Hudson Daily Star*. It made no reference to his father's ownership of the Hudson paper, Webb's Chicago past, or his former partnership with Conger in the Chicago jewelry business. Conger was by then a leading Unionville citizen and instrumental in bringing Webb to town.[22]

Victorian families often followed their mobile members, attempting to preserve the integrity of the family unit in the face of rapid social change.[23] Within a short time, Webb's entire immediate family joined him in Missouri. His oldest brother, Edward, would ultimately move from Unionville to California.[24] In 1876, Herbert Nelson Webb, a younger brother, became coeditor of the *Unionville Republican*. Their father, Alexander Nelson Webb, died in March 1877, shortly after the move, at age sixty-one.[25]

Webb joined the *Unionville Republican* as coeditor and coproprietor in partnership with the paper's founder, W. T. O'Bryant.[26] Like most American newspapers at the time, the *Unionville Republican* was a weekly. O'Bryant had established it thirteen years earlier, shortly after the outbreak of the Civil War, as a Republican organ, replacing the *Unionville Weekly Argus*. Webb's partnership with O'Bryant lasted the remainder of the year. In contrast to the *Unionville Republican*, the *Argus* had been pro-Southern and strongly Jeffersonian Democratic, seething against "blasphemous" politicians who prayed "for an anti-slavery Bible and to an anti-slavery God."[27]

Unionville, the seat of Putnam County, is in north-central Missouri, not far from the Iowa border. The Civil War had paralyzed its economy and terrorized its citizens. But the Burlington and Southwestern Railroad had come to the town in 1873, and its presence had promoted a speedy economic revival. By 1874, when Webb arrived, Unionville was undergoing dynamic growth that seemed likely to surpass its antebellum prosperity.[28] Webb's opening editorial proclaimed confidence in the town's "brilliant future," trusting that Unionville would "yet take a place among the notable cities of this country."[29]

Generally speaking, Republican sentiment was strong in Unionville and Putnam County. Most people were antislavery and pro-Union. The town's name and monuments still bear witness to its pro-Union allegiance. Graves of Civil War veterans are proudly dedicated to the Missouri Grand Army of the Republic. One large memorial proclaims: "To the Volunteer Soldier of America This Monument is Respectfully Dedicated: One Country and One Flag." But Missouri's cultural and political fault lines persisted in Putnam County as elsewhere in the state.[30]

FIGURE 4.1. Webb in Missouri (1874–1887)

By moving to Missouri, Webb entered the different world that lay south of the Mason-Dixon Line. He came to the state during the final years of Reconstruction (1865–1877), during which Radical Republicans, albeit in conjunction with rampant graft and corruption, had attempted to empower the South's newly freed blacks. In 1871, Congress outlawed the Ku Klux Klan, and four years later, it passed a noteworthy Civil Rights Act. Neither law was popular in Missouri, which had been settled primarily by Southerners and entered the Union as a slave state.

Like Webb's native Hudson Valley, Missouri stood at the confluence of different cultural swells. In the Hudson Valley, the cultural mix of New England and the Mid-Atlantic met harmoniously. It was different in Missouri, where the powerful undercurrent of the formerly slaveholding South tended to overwhelm the state's largely Mid-Atlantic Unionist components.[31] With the outbreak of the Civil War, Missouri first opted for neutrality but was immediately placed under federal occupation, strengthening pro-Confederate sentiment even among some former Unionists. Missouri became one of four border states, and, as in Kentucky, two governments were established in the state—one Unionist, the other Confederate. The divisions ignited violent civil strife.

Almost a decade after the war, old wounds remained open, often manifesting themselves in the state's contentious political divisions. Missouri had been reunited administratively, but hearts were still divided, and their animosities generated the burning issues that engrossed the regional press.

Like all Americans, Webb had followed the Civil War closely. By coming south of the Mason-Dixon Line and especially to a border state, he had, for the first time in his life, entered into a former war zone where combatants were not outsiders but often from the region itself. As a Unionville editor, he wrote for victors and vanquished alike. Reconstruction was almost a decade old and would last another three years. For six years, Reconstruction policy had denied Missouri's ex-Confederate majority the right to vote, turning them into a "helpless majority" by empowering the state's Liberal and Radical Republican minority. Three years before Webb's arrival in Missouri, however, the ex-Confederates secured the right to vote. Their enfranchisement put the Reconstruction on the defensive by bringing the Democratic Party back to life. Soon Missouri Democrats had taken control of the state legislature and turned both Liberal and Radical Republicans into a "hopeless minority."[32]

During the remainder of his years in Missouri, Webb would witness the death of Reconstruction and the institution of "Jim Crow" racial segregation and racism that would continue long after his death.[33] Webb—like his future colleague Joseph Pulitzer of St. Louis—supported the newly reconstituted Democratic Party, and there is little evidence that he took offense at the new developments that were taking place south of the Mason-Dixon Line. Whatever Webb's position on the matter, the fact is that the Jim Crow era of the late nineteenth and first half of the twentieth century was made possible only by the full complicity of the North. On both sides of the Mason-Dixon Line, whites willingly complied with segregation, hoping, in many cases, that their complicity would bring about the "reconciliation" of all American whites by "removing race from the table."[34] In 1883, while Webb was living in St. Louis, the Supreme Court refused to prosecute a Tennessee lynch mob and declared earlier Reconstruction legislation outlawing the Ku Klux Klan to be unconstitutional. The same year, in its "egregiously misnamed" civil rights cases, the Court systematically struck down every noteworthy achievement of the Civil Rights Act of 1875, decrying the act for having made blacks "the special favorites of the law."[35]

During his Missouri career, Webb worked for Republican and Democratic newspapers but insisted that the latter was always his preference. The *Missouri*

Republican, where he later worked in St. Louis, claimed that Webb's dedication to the Democratic Party was a lifelong allegiance and forever close to his heart.[36] It should be noted that Webb brought his Democratic proclivities with him from New York, and his affiliation to the party was not something that he developed in Missouri. His political inclinations were almost certainly akin to those of Martin Van Buren, Columbia County's favorite son. Webb's father had run a Democratic newspaper, and, with one exception, his native Columbia County voted consistently Democratic in presidential elections from 1856 till 1876.[37]

During Webb's first year at the *Unionville Republican*, the paper "worked in a measure against the Republican Party, and in favor of the Democracy"— that is, in support of the Democratic Party.[38] In his "Salutatory" as the new associate editor, Webb thanked Unionville citizens for their hearty reception of him and expressed his goal of setting the best course in journalism, one that would keep them not only informed but also remain subservient to "the interests of morality." "I shall probably commit errors," he added, "but they will be of judgment and not of the heart."[39]

By coming to the *Unionville Republican*, Webb filled an opening created by the recent death of G. S. Nicholas, its former coeditor and coproprietor.[40] Nadirah Osman contends that Webb's business ventures had finally prospered after his initial disappointment in Chicago, earning him the money with which to purchase the Unionville paper.[41] Emory Tunison states similarly that Webb "purchased and managed" the Unionville paper.[42] In fact, Webb was never a chief editor or sole proprietor at the *Unionville Republican* or any other Missouri newspaper. An obituary reports with less glamour but, perhaps, greater accuracy that "after the Chicago fire Webb gravitated toward the printing business."[43]

Webb's part-ownership of the *Unionville Republican* is ascribable directly to his father-in-law and former business partner, Lucian W. Conger, who was on the verge of helping to found the Putnam County Bank; Conger put up the money for Webb's interest in the paper.[44] Conger bought out Nicholas's share in the paper and placed it "in the hands of his son-in-law, A. R. Webb," according to a local history.[45] Throughout Webb's tenure at the *Unionville Republican*, the Conger family remained in the picture. Lucian Conger's son, Clarence La Fayette Conger, succeeded O'Bryant at the end of 1874.[46] Then, after only a few months, Clarence sold his interests to O. J. Brown, another nephew of Lucian Conger on his sister's side.[47]

In March 1876, after Webb had been at the paper for more than two years, his younger brother Herbert, who was six years younger than Webb, took over Brown's interest and became its new business manager. In announcing Herbert's appointment to the public, the *Unionville Republican* wrote that it hoped that his addition would help make the paper "one of the best, if not the best county paper in North Missouri" and make it "adhere strictly to the principles of Republicanism."[48]

For a short time, the *Unionville Republican* was run under the aegis of "the Webb Bros." When Alexander R. Webb first joined the paper, its motto was: "We Work for Ourselves, Town, County, State and Nation."[49] With Herbert's arrival, the motto changed: "Devoted to News, Literature, and the Interests of the Republican Party."[50] Soon the paper declared: "In the future, as in the past, we shall adhere strictly to the principles of Republicanism."[51] In July 1876, on the eve of the presidential election, the Webb brothers cosigned an editorial titled "Campaign Republican" endorsing Rutherford B. Hayes's candidacy and calling for the creation of a Republican campaign paper.[52]

Trouble had begun to brew around Alexander Russell Webb because of his Democratic leanings. The friction peaked rapidly and brought his Unionville career to an end before the election. The internal affairs of the *Unionville Republican* are not clear, but Webb had clearly been losing influence to his brother and Clarence Conger. A local history speaks of Clarence Conger as "ousting" Webb from the paper that summer. Webb, no longer content to remain at the paper, sold his interests to a Republican editor, J. F. Frankey. The paper's new editorial staff later announced triumphantly that Frankey "made the paper thoroughly Republican" and used it successfully to remove a number of local Democrats from office.[53]

Fraternal squabbles between the Webb brothers must have been heated. It was not just a matter of party affiliation; former regional loyalties were involved. The Democratic candidate, New York governor Samuel J. Tilden, was from Columbia County.[54] Ultimately, Tilden lost the election of 1876. Republicans had their ballots from Florida, Louisiana, South Carolina, and Oregon counted twice. Tilden still got the most votes but lost in the electoral college. Tilden became the first presidential candidate in American history to win the popular vote but lose the election.

After the abrupt culmination in Unionville, Webb set out for St. Joseph, Missouri. Almost a year later, the *Unionville Republican* declared triumphantly that Herbert Nelson Webb had "always been identified with the Republican Party." It observed further that all efforts to organize the Republicans of Putnam County had failed earlier, "owing to division at the county seat [Unionville]." Apparently hinting at Alexander Russell Webb, it assured readers that the "cause of trouble having disappeared, perhaps mainly through the efforts of this office, there is nothing to hinder a perfect organization of the party in this county."[55]

Herbert Webb's antagonism must have anguished his brother. Herbert took sole charge of the paper in May 1877 "and at once took an aggressive stand relative to the management of certain county affairs—a position which subsequently involved him in slight personal difficulty."[56] Herbert died of an unspecified cause on March 11, 1886, at the age of thirty-four.[57] Records are silent, and it is not known how Alexander Webb responded to his younger brother's untimely death. Perhaps, he was as taciturn about it as he was regarding his first wife. Nevertheless, Herbert's death must have affected him deeply and came at a time when Webb's religious search was becoming its most intense. Herbert's wife took charge of the *Unionville Republican* and ran it about four months in conjunction with a Mr. G. H. Gardner. When she sold the newspaper that July, it had become, in the words of a local history, "one of the best papers in northern Missouri."[58]

St. Joseph Interlude

Perched above the Missouri River and overlooking the Kansas plains, St. Joseph was one of the great river towns of the Old West. In Webb's time, its mention evoked rich associations: wagon trains, the Pony Express, and Jesse James. Modern railways rendered wagon trains and the Pony Express obsolete, but this Missouri town remained in the general spotlight as a national railway hub and steamboat center.

On average, seventy passenger trains arrived daily, while as many as eighty steamboats plied their way along the Missouri River, which linked St. Joseph to St. Louis in the east and the Montana Territory to the northwest.[59] Webb's interlude in St. Joseph lasted only a few months and was probably more like a vacation than an established residence. It is not clear why Webb remained in St. Joseph or why he worked so briefly as a reporter for the *St. Joseph Gazette.* More than likely, his St. Joseph interval was just a short transition from the hostile and unexpectedly rapid developments that forced him to leave Unionville for the better circumstances that he soon found in St. Louis. The same Democratic sympathies that led to Webb's expulsion from Unionville likely made him welcome in St. Joseph, where they would have counted as an asset and at least allowed him to bide his time there until more auspicious employment opportunities arose.

Although Webb's stay in St. Joseph was short, his days there must have been among the most memorable of his early manhood. For much of the nineteenth century, St. Joseph was the nation's most famous western outpost. To leave the city and cross the Missouri River into Kansas meant to leave the United States for Indian Territory. The gold rush of 1849 turned St. Joseph into "the gateway of the West" and filled its streets with forty-niners heading across the Great Plains and Rocky Mountains to seek their fortunes in California. The city became renowned for the "St. Jo Road," which led across the prairie to the California and Oregon Trails. For the pioneers, St. Joseph was the foremost "jumping-off town" along the Missouri River. Each spring, covered wagons converged upon it by the thousands, stretching back along the city's neatly cobbled streets for miles and waiting, often for days on end, to be ferried across the river to the vast frontier on the other side.[60]

As was the case elsewhere in Missouri, the city's economy had been ruined by the Civil War but showed immediate signs of bouncing back after the war's end. St. Joseph soon became a major banking center, dominating the regional wholesale trade and reestablishing its economic importance nationally.

Webb witnessed the city at a time of dramatic growth. When he arrived in the late summer of 1876, St. Joseph's population numbered around thirty thousand and was growing rapidly. For the remainder of the decade, the press would often speak of St. Joseph as a "modern wonder." Within a few years, its population tripled, trade and industry flourished, and St. Joseph rivaled its regional competitors: Chicago, Kansas City, and Omaha.[61]

St. Joseph's connection to the South was as deep as its links with the frontier were strong. Unlike Unionville, St. Joseph was a former Confederate city, and public sentiment remained overwhelmingly pro-Southern. The majority of St. Joseph's newspaper readers counted themselves among the vanquished of the war, not the victors. War memories were very much alive, Reconstruction was in effect, and federal troops still occupied much of the South.[62]

When Webb arrived in St. Joseph, few households were willing to fly the American flag, which they regarded as a symbol of defeat and Reconstruction. The Fourth of July had not been celebrated for fifteen years, nor would it be celebrated locally until a year after Webb left.

Upon the outbreak of war in 1861, St. Joseph's citizens tore down the federal flag flying from the post office and brandished Confederate banners and decorations from their homes and along streets and avenues. When, in 1865, news of President Lincoln's assassination reached St. Joseph, it was received with great thanksgiving. Local citizens recalled proudly how, just a year earlier, John Wilkes Booth presented a dramatic reading in the city. St. Joseph resumed celebration of the Fourth of July in 1877. Reconstruction had come to an end, and the St. Joseph Gazette declared: "The Patriotic people all over the Union are making greater preparation for the celebration of the Fourth of July, 1877, than at any time since the war. The reason is obvious: Tyranny is dethroned and the government of [1776] is partially restored. By all means, let us celebrate."[63]

The James Gang was at its peak when Webb arrived in St. Joseph. The defiance of Jesse James, an ex-Confederate, had direct ties to the Civil War. Throughout Missouri, attitudes toward the James brothers mirrored regional loyalties. James hailed from outside St. Joseph, and there was extensive sympathy for him in the city. Many saw him not as an outlaw but as a symbol of Southern pride and simmering discontent. Most Americans, whatever their sympathies, followed the James story with great interest. It was one of the most newsworthy items in the press. As a reporter for the *St. Joseph Gazette,* Webb surely knew the story as well as anyone and probably even reported on it.[64]

The *St. Joseph Gazette* was the oldest newspaper in the city.[65] It had been staunchly proslavery during the antebellum period, and local Republican interests established the *Morning Herald* during the early phase of the war to counteract its influence. After the war, the *St. Joseph Gazette* remained uncompromisingly Democratic, pro-Southern, and anti-Reconstructionist, in opposition to its local rival.[66] As a "democratic journal," it declared itself an "advocate of good government," an opponent of "Radical [Republican] corruptions, and in favor of the overthrow of military power and corrupt rule," all anti-Reconstructionist catchwords.[67]

Like many American newspapers at the time, the *St. Joseph Gazette* began as a weekly but added a daily edition in 1875. Publishing separate weekly and daily editions required an expanded staff, and Webb helped meet that need.[68] Though he had been an editor in Unionville, he began at the bottom in St. Joseph as a typesetter, but was soon promoted to reporter and finally became an editor of the daily edition.[69]

For the rest of his career in Missouri journalism, Webb would be primarily associated with "daily journalism" as opposed to the "weekly journalism" that he had practiced in Unionville. The *New York Times* speaks of him as having "drifted into daily journalism" in St. Joseph.[70] Some reports overstate his description as the paper's editor.[71] Others refer to him more accurately as a "city editor," which was tantamount to saying "daily editor." Daily editions, for the most part, were locally distributed, while the weekly editions of the *St. Joseph Gazette* were written for wider distribution and enjoyed great popularity as far away as Nebraska.[72]

Nadirah Osman states that Webb developed a friendship at the *St. Joseph Gazette* with Eugene Field, one of the most noteworthy American journalists of the nineteenth century and a popular Victorian poet.[73] Although Osman gives no details about the relationship, it is clear that Field, who was four years Webb's junior, worked at the paper from 1875 until 1876—roughly the same period as Webb's employment there—before both journalists moved on to St. Louis, where presumably their friendship continued. St. Joseph left a lasting impression on Field, who commemorated his courtship there in the well-liked Victorian poem "Lovers' Lane St. Jo."[74] Field's memories of the city were marred, however, by the tragedy of his first child's death, which inspired "Little Boy Blue," one of the most widely read poems of the era (and not to be confused with the nursery rhyme by the same name).[75]

Another poem, "The St. Joseph Gazette," spoke approvingly of the period when he worked on its daily edition, "the local." Field recalls fondly that he was "upon familiar terms" with all he met there (doubtless including

FIGURE 4.2. Eugene Field (right) and Close Friend Actor Francis Wilson
(early 1890s)

Webb), and that "there never was a smarter lot of editors" than his associates
there:

> "THE ST. JO GAZETTE"
> When I helped 'em run the local on the "St. Jo Gazette,"
> I was upon familiar terms with every one I met—
> A votary of Mammon, I hustled round and sweat,
> And helped 'em run the local on the "St. Jo Gazette"—
> And frequently an invitation to a meal I'd get
> When I helped 'em run the local on the "St. Jo Gazette."
> There never was a smarter lot of editors, I'll bet,
> Than we who whooped up locals on the "St. Jo Gazette"—
> My thoughts turn ever fondly to that time in Old St. Jo
>   The years that sped so fleetly
>   Have blotted out completely
> All else than that which still remains to solace me so sweetly;
> The friendships of that time,—ah me! They are as precious yet
> As when I was a local on the "St. Jo Gazette."[76]

Field moved on to the *Times-Journal* in St. Louis in 1876 and worked there
for four years before moving to Chicago.[77] Webb came to the city shortly after
Field and, during his first year, probably working simultaneously at the *St.
Louis Post-Dispatch* and *Times-Journal*. Although little certain can be said about
Webb's relation to Field or what influence they may have had on each other,
Webb's association with him is another example of his proclivity for ending

up "in the middle of it all." Field was not only one of the great American journalists and poets of the late Victorian period but was also the son of the distinguished Vermont lawyer Roswell Martin Field, who defended Dred Scott in the Missouri court system and doggedly pursued his case to the Supreme Court. When the court ruled against Scott in 1857, the loss was regarded as an ominous harbinger of the Civil War.[78] Not only did Webb benefit from association with one of the most talented writers of the period but, through his knowledge of him, also had access to Field's knowledge of his father's experience in the pivotal Dred Scott case.

St. Louis: Making It Big

Of the almost fourteen years Webb lived in Missouri, more than a decade was spent in St. Louis. It was there that Webb came into his own, claiming a reputable place in Missouri journalism. When President Cleveland chose him to represent the United States as consul in the Philippines, his appointment was widely heralded as a triumph for Missouri journalists as a whole. It was also in St. Louis that Webb began in earnest the spiritual journey that would lead him to Theosophy and ultimately bring him to Islam.

Webb's Missouri years—1874 till 1887—roughly coincided with one of the greatest periods in Missouri journalism, the dynamic fifteen years from 1875 till 1890. Towering figures like Joseph Pulitzer made the Missouri press a national leader and helped lay the foundations of modern American journalism. Prior to that, American journalism had been unabashedly factional and made little pretense of fairness. Pulitzer led the way in forging standards predicated not just on careful exploratory reporting but also on a principled editorial policy based on impartiality and the search for justice.[79] In St. Louis, Webb came under the influence of two of the greatest editors of the time, Pulitzer and "Little Mack" McCullagh.

St. Louis was one of America's largest and fastest growing cities when Webb arrived. It ranked behind New York and Philadelphia but proudly vied with Chicago, its Midwest rival. By the early 1870s, it had begun a healthy recovery from the Civil War and was beginning to reassert itself as a center of industry, trade, and commerce. As Julian Rammelkamp notes, the burgeoning city "sprawled nineteen miles along the [Mississippi] river front," and its population, although exaggerated by inaccurate statistics, was several times greater than St. Joseph's. Boasting its inflated population statistics, St. Louis laid claim to being "*the* metropolis of the Upper Mississippi Valley," the "final Great City of the world," and "the great city of futurity."[80] The Chicago press, on the other hand, routinely scoffed at St. Louis's pretensions, emphasizing widespread stereotypes of the city's conservatism and its reputation for being "a sleepy place, slow-going, and overcautious."[81]

It was in St. Louis that Webb first beheld the outward signs of early-twentieth-century technology. Shortly after his arrival there, he could walk the streets at night illuminated as never before by the marvel of electric lighting.[82] Cable cars arrived a decade later, and one of the new routes ran past his house down Easton Avenue.[83] The era when ferries were the principal means of crossing rivers had also come to an end, and Webb could journey easily over St. Louis's newly constructed iron bridge, which spanned the Mississippi, directly connecting for the first time St. Louis with East St. Louis. Webb had known railroads since his childhood, but they had now become such a vital part of the American economy that they virtually put an end to the era of the Mississippi steamboats, just as, years earlier, competition from the New York railway system had brought an end to the economic vitality of Hudson city's port. Mark Twain commemorated the bygone era of the great riverboats in *Life on the Mississippi* (1883).[84] On a return visit to St. Louis in the 1880s, Twain complained that he could find only six steamboats on its waterfront and that they were "fast asleep," while he called to mind a time only a few years earlier when "a solid mile of wide-awake ones" were to be found along the city's wharfs.[85]

Like New Orleans, St. Louis prided itself on its French colonial past. Its long-standing families were known for conservative ways, which had given them the reputation of being unreceptive to change. Although electric lighting had finally come, it had been long resisted out of fear that overhead wires would kill the city's trees and "so much electricity in the air would cause sickness."[86]

German culture was also a conspicuous part of St. Louis. When Webb came to the city, German-speakers constituted its largest homogenous community, making up more than a third of the total population. The number of German-speakers in St. Louis was triple the population of St. Joseph as a whole. The St. Louis Germans came primarily from the Rhineland, and many had come there during the antebellum period.[87]

Political liberalism was strong among St. Louis's German-speakers, since many of them had some connection to Germany's failed democratic revolution of 1848. Not surprisingly, the city supported a thriving and enlightened German press. Joseph Pulitzer personified the classic American success story. He had come to St. Louis after the Civil War as a penniless German-speaking Jew from Hungary, unable to form a proper English sentence. Having started his career as an unskilled laborer in the local German press, he worked up through the ranks and, in 1874, purchased the city's leading German-language newspaper, *Die Staats-Zeitung*. From that time on, Pulitzer was a prominent player in Missouri journalism and soon achieved national fame.[88]

Like St. Joseph, St. Louis was a bastion of Confederate sympathies. Municipal monuments still testify to the fact. One in Forest Park is dedicated "To the Memory of the Soldiers and Sailors of the Southern Confederacy, who fought to uphold the right declared by the pen of Jefferson and achieved by the sword of Washington."[89] During the Reconstruction period, St. Louis's general populace, including Pulitzer and prominent German liberals like the former revolutionary leader Carl Schurz, played a major role in overthrowing the Radical Republicans, helped bring about the reenfranchisement of ex-Confederates, and laid the foundations of the modern Democratic Party.[90]

Most of Webb's time in St. Louis was spent as a journalist. From late 1876 or early 1877 until sometime in 1880, he worked for three local newspapers. He then turned his back on daily journalism for about three years from 1880 till 1883, hoping to be done with the profession forever. During this intriguing interlude, Webb worked with limited success as a jewelry salesman, circus publicity manager, drama director, and playwright. Ultimately finding no escape from journalism, he resumed work briefly as a drama critic but was ultimately constrained to return to daily journalism. In St. Louis, Webb wrote for four local newspapers. He began at the *St. Louis Post-Dispatch* and the *Times-Journal*, apparently working simultaneously for both papers until 1878, when he began to work exclusively for the *Times-Journal*. In 1879, he moved on to the *Globe Democrat,* from which he resigned in 1880. At this point, Webb began his interlude of seeking a fulfilling livelihood outside journalism, and, interestingly, the period also overlaps with his attempt to rediscover a meaningful spiritual life. Toward the end of 1882, he returned to thematic journalism as the editor and dramatic critic at the newly established *St. Louis Dramatic Critic,* but this episode was also short-lived. In 1883, Webb was financially constrained to return to daily journalism at the *Missouri Republican,* where he remained for the rest of his years in St. Louis.

Webb first appears in the St. Louis city directory in 1878 but probably had begun living in the city before the end of 1876.[91] It is certain that he was in the city by the summer of 1877, since he married Ella Hotchkiss there on June 27, 1877. Webb had received a share of his father's inheritance a few months before, in March 1877,[92] and his new family probably lived comfortably. The 1880 census shows that they had two live-in servants, one an Englishwoman and the other a black woman from Illinois.[93]

For both the Webbs, the marriage was a second marriage. There was no secret of Ella's first marriage, which produced a child, Elizabeth. As we have seen, Webb's second marriage is the only one mentioned in available biographical accounts, and he never seems to have spoken of his first marriage. Ella's maiden name remains unknown; Hotchkiss was the surname of her deceased husband.[94] Webb spent the rest of his life with Ella and looked upon his adopted daughter as his own.[95] Webb was thirty at the time of their marriage, and Ella was roughly the same age, possibly two years younger.[96] By Victorian standards, there was nothing unusual about the second marriage of either spouse, since Victorians were not averse to the remarriage of widows or widowers.[97]

Ella was a schoolteacher from Cincinnati. She was a schoolteacher in St. Louis when Webb met her, and she continued to work at her profession during the greater part of Webb's St. Louis days, although she does not seem to have resumed teaching after the birth of Webb's second child by her.[98]

Elizabeth ("Bessie") was seven when her mother remarried.[99] Ella subsequently bore a son and two daughters. The two born in St. Louis were Russell Lorenzo Webb (May 1879) and Mary C. Webb (May 1885).[100] Nala D. Webb was born in Manila (February 1888), shortly after Webb assumed his diplomatic post there. Her unusual name was Arabic (Nāla in Arabic means "gift") and reflects the Eastern influences that were working on Webb at the time.[101]

The bonds between Alexander Russell Webb, his wife, his adopted daughter, and his three natural children seem to have been strong and comparable to the relationships of his childhood family. Webb's diary, written during his solitary 1892 travels in Burma and India, speaks repeatedly of his loneliness and emotional need for his wife and family. His first entry reveals his delight at having "received 5 letters from my darling wife yesterday. She's a good woman. God bless her." He continues: "It is singular that I have been more or less ill since the 8th of June last, the day on which my wife and precious babies left Manila for the States. I think that my wife's presence is necessary to me. I am certainly very lonely without her."[102]

"Daily journalism" was Webb's main job and may have been the key to his rapid promotion in St. Joseph before coming to St. Louis. When he came to the St. Louis Post-Dispatch and the Times-Journal, he was employed as a "day journalist" at both papers.[103] It is a challenge to identify what Webb or most journalists of the time actually wrote, since their newspaper contributions generally were anonymous. In many cases, papers did not disclose even their editors' names. The Unionville Republican was an exception to this rule, perhaps, because it was a small town newspaper and its staff would have been common knowledge and accessible in any case. The big-city newspapers of St. Joseph and St. Louis conformed to the rule of general secrecy. City directories contain information about proprietors and editors, although they make little or no mention of lower ranking editors, reporters, and general staff.[104]

Journalistic anonymity reflected the old style of American journalism, when editors, in particular, had to be rugged individualists to survive. Each had to wield a vitriolic pen but never lose the ability to "swing a punishing fist, and, on occasion, [show] considerable skill in handling a gun."[105] Newspapers inspired devotion in their supporters but inflamed the hostility of their enemies. As a consequence, newspaper culture protected editors and writers by withholding their names.[106] Eugene Field conveyed the general state of affairs in "The Fighting Editor," an idyll dedicated to Solomon Burch of the St. Louis Journal of Commerce:

Solomon he sat in his office—
His nose running blood, his
    Eyes swelled and black
His clothing all torn, his body all bruised,
    With great purple welts all over his back.[107]

It has been said that Webb's involvement in journalism was tantamount to a simultaneous career in politics.[108] In Victorian America, journalism and politics were virtually inseparable, and all the Missouri newspapers Webb worked for upheld distinct political ideologies. The extent of his personal involvement in Missouri politics, however, is difficult to determine and was conspicuous only in the *Unionville Republican*. The fact that President Cleveland appointed Webb as consul to the Philippines indicates that Webb possessed a certain amount of political capital, although his personal reasons for seeking the post were not purely political but also motivated by his spiritual quest to discover religious enlightenment in the Orient.

Webb worked briefly at the *St. Louis Post-Dispatch*, which was called the *Evening Dispatch* at the time.[109] The 1878 city directory lists him as working simultaneously as a city editor for both the *St. Louis Post-Dispatch* and the *Times-Journal*. The directory for the following year lists him as a reporter for the *Times-Journal* exclusively.[110]

Pulitzer purchased the *St. Louis Post-Dispatch* in 1878 and turned it into an immediate success. By the time Pulitzer left St. Louis in 1883 for the *New York World*, he had become St. Louis's undisputed and most dynamic voice of reform. It is not clear how well, if at all, Pulitzer and Webb knew each other, but the *New York World* extended a warm welcome in 1893 to Webb's newly founded Islamic mission in Manhattan.

Although Webb began working at the *St. Louis-Post Dispatch* as soon as he came to St. Louis, he did not work there under the editorship of Joseph Pulitzer or only for a short time if he did. Pulitzer took over the paper in 1878 and remained its editor until 1883. Thus, Pulitzer took over the *Post-Dispatch* the same year that Webb transferred full-time to the *Times-Journal*. Still, Webb, like other St. Louis journalists, could not have escaped the profound influence that Pulitzer's editorial prominence exercised on the entire city and ultimately the nation.

The *St. Louis Post-Dispatch* literally became the laboratory for Pulitzer's journalistic experiments, which would eventually "revolutionize the American newspaper," and his influence quickly spread nationwide. Webb surely was among the countless Americans who read Pulitzer's convictions in earnest, including his declaration on June 5, 1882, that newspapers must become truly independent, standing above political parties and special interests and proving themselves to be "agreeable to none except those who lead an honest life."[111] A free press, in Pulitzer's view, had to uphold "the injured, the oppressed, the downtrodden, the law-abiding, but it must be true and just above all." He set forth in the *St. Louis Post-Dispatch* his conception of the ideal editor, "shrouded in judicial impartiality," with "no associations, or political ties that will warp his judgment of public men or measures, no social entanglements to crowd out the news because it may be offensive to Mrs. Snobb or Miss Toady or to her favorite biped poodle."[112]

At the time that Pulitzer took over the *St. Louis Post-Dispatch* and began to model it according to his editorial philosophy, the *Times-Journal* was also undergoing a process of vigorous expansion and sweeping renovation. Its rapid growth required new ideas and an expanded staff, which may explain why Webb found it lucrative to work there.[113] Eugene Field's presence on the staff may also have encouraged Webb to join the paper, and the two continued to work together until Field moved in 1879 to Chicago, where he made his name as one of the most innovative writers in American journalism. That same year, Webb left the *Times-Journal* and moved on to the *St. Louis Globe Democrat*.[114]

Webb began at the *Globe-Democrat* as a reporter and continued working at the paper for several years. It was during this period that the newspaper realized its greatest success.[115] Its management was under the direction of Joseph Burbridge McCullagh (1842–1896), "Little Mack," one of the foremost editors of the era. Field dedicated a poem to McCullagh titled "Little Mack," contending that he equaled the best journalists in the East.[116] McCullagh was known for his audacious methods, which were credited with making his paper the wealthiest and fastest growing newspaper in St. Louis at the time Webb joined it.[117]

It is no easy task to keep track of the various papers for which Webb worked or identify their political leanings. Newspaper names changed constantly through amalgamations, and, in any case, were often misleading in indicating political loyalties. For example, the *St. Louis Globe-Democrat* was "Republican in politics and true to the party," while the *Missouri Republican* was staunchly Democratic.[118] Thus, Webb's years at the *St. Louis Globe-Democrat* were spent at a Republican establishment as much devoted to the party's cause as the *Unionville Republican* had ever been. Little Mack, Webb's editor, was not only dedicated to the Republican Party but expected his workforce to be "a veritable army of reporters armed with a catechism of politics."[119] It is not clear how Webb felt about working for such an ideologically Republican organ, but his years at the paper concluded with a temporary resignation from journalism altogether. Nevertheless, given Little Mack's ideological demands, Webb's employment at the paper reflected a less than uncompromising Democratic allegiance, although probably consistent with the earlier role he played at the *Unionville Republican*.

As mentioned earlier, monetary need, not an idealistic commitment to journalism, often determined the course of Webb's newspaper career, and that may have been the case at the *Globe-Democrat*. Sometime in 1880, after a year or two at the newspaper, Webb made a break from journalism, but he was compelled to return out of financial necessity in 1883. During the interlude, he tried his hand again at the jewelry business and made an attempt at the circus and the stage. At the end of this interlude, Webb returned to writing as a drama critic, but financial failure forced him to return to daily journalism at the *Missouri Republican*.

Webb began his break from journalism by working as a jeweler and diamond salesman for Merod, Jaccard, and Company and for E. Jaccard and Company, both of which ranked among St. Louis's largest jewelry establishments. Webb stayed with them only briefly, and his return to the jewelry business did not meet with great success.[120]

The following year, Webb appeared in the St. Louis directory as a "traveler," one who earns his livelihood by travel.[121] The purpose of Webb's travel is not clear and may have been connected with the jewelry business. But it more likely reflected Webb's newfound calling in the circus. As Webb was standing behind the diamond counter one day, he struck up a conversation with some "show people" browsing in his shop, and they convinced Webb to leave jewelry and sign on with the circus. One of Webb's colleagues later at the *Missouri Republican* asserted that "the virus of show business [had] always [been] in his veins." Overnight, Webb became a "theatrical and circus advance man," taking charge of the circus's advance publicity. Later, he worked as a "theatrical manager and player," and, according to his colleague, was "a noted success" in the theater and circus, possessing "the nerve to 'go broke' twice in the theatrical business as his own manager."[122]

Webb handled advance publicity for the famous actors, Robson and Crane, "for a number of seasons." He became popular on the circuits himself: "For Alex could tell a dandy story, was a wonderful mixer and could 'hold his own' and a little more in any company, be it ever so fast or ever so fashionable," the colleague said. Webb then left Robson-Crane and "went on the road ahead of one of the big circuses."[123]

Confident of his ability, Webb set up his own traveling theater in partnership with another "old-time newspaper man," Robert Morris Yost. Together, they wrote and produced a play called *Brentwood*, especially scripted for Pearl Eytinge, daughter of the famous actress Rose Eytinge. Webb and Yost are said to have "newspaperized" their play in the "most extravagant language." To advertise *Brentwood*, Webb proudly hit on a sound byte: "a poem, a sermon, a song."[124]

The production ended in failure, costing Webb's investors dearly. Webb's own financial losses forced him to return part-time to journalism as a copy editor for the *Missouri Republican*, but he remained active as a theatrical advance man. During this period, he also became the first editor of a newly created theatrical journal, the *St. Louis Dramatic Critic*, inaugurated on

December 21, 1882.[125] The 1883 St. Louis directory listed Webb as a "dramatic critic," and it was a role he presumably performed with some skill, since *The Missouri Republican* wrote in 1887 that Webb's "literary research and accomplishments [had] long been recognized in the literary circles of St. Louis."[126]

Sometime after the *Brentwood* debacle, Webb and Yost made a second ill-fated bid for fame on the stage, this time by directing a comedy starring a donkey. They called the play *Calamity Jane* after the famous frontierswoman, Martha "Calamity Jane" Cannary. The production failed utterly and caused Webb to go bankrupt again, forcing him and Yost back to their newspaper desks, which both men "fondly hoped they had abandoned forever," in the words of a newspaper colleague.[127]

Webb worked full time as a reporter at the *Missouri Republican* until 1885, when he was promoted to assistant city editor, a position he kept until his consular appointment in September 1887.[128]

Founded in 1808, the *Missouri Republican* was one of America's oldest newspapers and, when Webb joined it, had just added a widely circulated daily edition. It also helped pioneer the Sunday edition as a new genre in American journalism. The *Missouri Republican* had been Democratic from the beginning, and its front-page banner proudly proclaimed: "A staunch Democratic Journal." In Webb's time, its chief rival was the *St. Louis Globe-Democrat*. The *Missouri Republican's* name was, in fact, older than the Republican Party and reflected the paper's espousal of the Jeffersonian republican principles underlying the Democratic Party. It prided itself on its connection with Mark Twain, who began his career there in 1853 at the age of eighteen and was in his ascendance as a national figure when Webb came to work at the paper.[129]

The *Missouri Republican* opposed the election of Abraham Lincoln in 1860 but also rejected the Confederate policy of secession that followed it. After the war, it worked diligently for the reenfranchisement of the ex-Confederates. With their reenfranchisement in 1871 and rejuvenation of the Democratic Party, the *Missouri Republican* became exceptionally powerful and earned the reputation of being an "organ of wealth and money." It exercised extensive control over the Democratic politics of St. Louis and was regarded to be the voice of the city's conservative oligarchy and the preferred paper of its "best citizens." At the same time, however, it cultivated the reputation of being progressive.[130]

A colleague at the *Missouri Republican* recalled that Webb never undertook anything "meretriciously brilliant" as a journalist but still was a valuable man for any newspaper to have, because he was "safe" and preeminently "clean." Webb avoided sensationalism, used plain English, wrote good copy, and knew what to say and how to say it.[131] Most knew him only as a journalist. He did not lead a "double life" but played many different parts in his life. Many knew him intimately but only "in one or another of his 'roles' or spheres of activity," the colleague said.[132] "When [Webb] switched from one calling to another he completely divorced himself from the old and became entirely absorbed in the new, to the total exclusion of all previous alliances and associations," he said. "In life [Webb] played many parts and played most of them more than passing well."[133]

After fourteen years in Missouri journalism, a profession that Webb had mixed emotions about, he was now on the verge of the most radical change of his life. He was about to begin a new interlude that would go on for eight years, and he would embark upon a spiritual odyssey that would last the rest of his life. And that would be made possible by his journalistic support of the Democratic party and personal connections in Washington, which opened up for him the door to the world of diplomacy.

In late 1887, a Democratic administration came into office under President Grover Cleveland and asked Webb to fill the position for U.S. consul to the Philippines. Webb's colleagues in Missouri celebrated his appointment as a Democratic victory and tribute to the state's journalists. Yet, although Webb's appointment may have appeared to his colleagues as a political victory for the Democratic party, Webb's deeper motives reflected his abiding Theosophical interests, which he had cultivated in St. Louis for more than half a decade until they became one of his chief preoccupations. Like many Theosophists and religious thinkers of the time, Webb saw the Orient as the residuary of primordial religious truth, and he saw his appointment in the Philippines an opportunity to gain access to the spiritual truth he was seeking.

His four years of service in Manila constituted the exasperating beginning of a short-lived and less than promising diplomatic career. Further, the solidly Catholic Philippines did not extend to him the opportunities to study Oriental religion as he had hoped. Yet it was in Manila that Webb discovered the teachings of Islam by coming across literature on the faith that was attractive and, to his mind, more authentic than anything he had previously read in the United States. Within a relatively short time after his arrival in the Philippines, Webb, his wife, and children embraced Islam without having met a single Muslim. Within a few years he began in Manila to lay the foundations for his Islamic mission to America, which would dominate the coming years and constitute the most memorable episode of his life.

5

Diplomatic Post in the Orient

After his career in Missouri journalism, Webb found that he had
been projected into the political limelight as never before by his appointment as U.S. consul to the Philippines. Though his journalistic
attachment to Democratic politics and his personal connections in
St. Louis and Washington led to the selection, Webb was personally
motivated to seek a position in the Orient, convinced that life in
the East would give him direct access to the spiritual treasures of
the East.

On September 29, 1887, Webb was appointed U.S. consul
to Manila—then under Spanish colonial control—by President
Grover Cleveland (1885–1889), the first Democratic president
since Reconstruction. Webb retained the position under the
succeeding Republican administration of President Benjamin Harrison (1889–1893).[1]

It took Webb and his family about a month to pack up and
finish business in St. Louis. They set out for San Francisco by
train, where, on November 9, 1887, they boarded the steamship
Gaelic for the Philippines. They arrived in Manila about five
weeks later.

Webb immediately met with the first of his many frustrations
at the hands of the Spanish colonial bureaucracy, which kept him
from assuming his official duties until January 1, 1888.[2] Spanish
authorities refused to recognize his diplomatic passport or extend
customary protocol to him and his family. "When I arrived at this
port in Dec. last my trunks as well as those of my family were sub-
jected to examination at the Custom House, and, at Hong Kong,

the Spanish Consul exacted a fee of $3.00 for a passport notwithstanding the fact that I exhibited a special passport from the Department of State," he says.[3] At the time, Americans were often treated badly in the Philippines, and Webb's diplomatic credentials did not make him an exception. From the moment of his arrival, Webb developed a dislike of the Spanish colonial officials and frequently voiced grievances against them to Washington.[4]

Webb spent, in all, about four and a half years in the Philippines. His career in the U.S. Foreign Service began and ended there. Richard Seager mistakenly describes him as "a former American diplomat in Smyrna," and others mention Turkey as one of his diplomatic assignments.[5] Obituaries occasionally refer to Webb as "former U.S. Consul to Manila and Con-stantinople" or "Consul in Turkey and Manila during the Administration of President Cleveland."[6] Toward the end of his services in Manila, Webb ur-gently requested Washington to transfer him to a more attractive post, Turkey among them, but he was never given such an appointment. More than likely, confusion over Webb's assignment to Turkey arose from his 1901 designation as Honorary Turkish Consul General to New York—an Ottoman post, not an American one—in addition to his journey to that country as an official guest the same year.

Robert Dannin engages in elaborate speculation about Webb, whom he suggests was a shadowy figure caught up in elaborate schemes of domestic and international intrigue, a "journalist turned a diplomat who perhaps en-gaged in espionage." He links Webb with an American diplomat in Istanbul, John Porter Brown, with whom he believes Webb associated in Turkey as part of a cabalistic "circle of Arabists," forming a "tight clan within the U.S. dip-lomatic corps."[7]

In fact, John Porter Brown died sixteen years before Webb's entry into diplomatic service or conversion to Islam. Webb was never assigned to Turkey as an American diplomat and did not even visit Turkey until after the turn of the century. He lacked higher education and was certainly no Arabist. Whenever alluding to Arabic in his diary, writings, or speeches, Webb in-variably made glaring mistakes of the most rudimentary nature. Never having learned even the basics of Arabic or, for that matter, any of the other tradi-tional languages of the Muslim peoples, Webb failed consistently to distin-guish Persian from Arabic. Indian Muslims, with whom Webb was closely associated, freely combined Arabic and Persian terminologies in their Islamic discourse. Their linguistic usage was totally lost on Webb, who invariably mistook all the Islamic formulaics that he picked up from them as Arabic. Webb did have some knowledge of Spanish, which he presumably picked up in the Philippines. It was the only foreign language that he knew.

Both Grebsonal and the *New York Herald* contended, based on interviews with Webb, that he joined the diplomatic service in the East to study "Oriental religions and spiritual philosophies." Grebsonal added that Webb did in fact devote himself as much to religious study in Manila as duties permitted.[8] The *New York Herald* asserted that Webb had always been "a student on religious lines and [had] read about Buddhism and Islamism and the other isms of the Orient." Consequently, he had sought "a Consulate to the [F]ar East and got appointed to the Philippine Islands."[9] The Ottoman Archives, basing its claim on the *New York Herald* article, stated that Webb had sought his consular appointment to study Islam in his free time, which he did faithfully until finally dedicating himself entirely to its study.[10]

Webb's diplomatic correspondence documents his desire to journey to the East to study Oriental religions, and, since he found the Philippines inadequate for such study, he explicitly mentioned his longing as a chief argument for seeking a transfer to a new post. Toward the end of his tenure in Manila, an impoverished and disenchanted Webb, his family in declining health, requested a transfer to "Singapore, Colombo, Calcutta, Bangkok, Nagasaki or Osaka and Hiogo . . . or a post in Spain or Italy or to Tangier, Gibraltar, Beirut, Constantinople, Jerusalem or Smyrna." He then disclosed that his "original purpose in coming to the East [was] to pursue, during [his] leisure time the study of the Oriental religions." He complained that the Catholic Church reigned supreme in the Philippines and allowed no other religion adequate representation. "For this purpose, therefore, I could not be more unfavorably situated. There are Buddhists, and Mohammedans, and one Parsee here . . . but they are not of the classes with which I desire to come in contact, and are unable to teach me what I desire to know of their religion."[11]

Webb, Politics, and Presidential Appointment

Grover Cleveland carried Missouri in the presidential election of 1884, and the *Missouri Republican*, where Webb worked, gave his candidacy full editorial backing.[12] When President Cleveland appointed Webb as consul to the Philippines, the staunchly Democratic paper sang Webb's praises, proudly declaring that he had always been a Democrat, taken great interest in the party's success, and that his appointment could not fail to bring satisfaction to all Missouri.[13] Featuring a sketch of a young, thin, trim-bearded Webb, the paper announced: "A telegram was received from Washington last night announcing the appointment of Mr. Alex R. Webb, Assistant city editor of the *Republican*, to the consulship at Manila, the chief city of the Philippine Islands." It said that St. Louis newspapermen hailed the appointment with enthusiasm, since they had "known and respected Mr. Webb during his long residence here," and that "all those citizens who had information of [Webb's] recognition at Washington" also approved highly of his appointment.[14]

Most reports specify that President Cleveland appointed Webb to his consulship without indicating who initiated the request.[15] The *New York Herald*, however, stated that Webb himself had solicited the position.[16] His obituary in the *Missouri Republican* said that Webb "went after the position," possibly spurred on by his Theosophical interest in the Orient. It added, however, that Webb enjoyed a personal connection with Daniel S. Lamont, later to become Cleveland's Secretary of War, and that Lamont had written to Cleveland on Webb's behalf.[17] Although Webb sought his appointment with hopes of pursuing his study of Oriental religions in the East, his desire to journey abroad was a common Victorian aspiration; many American men of that era seized upon work opportunities that would take them far away to foreign lands. Research and diplomatic service were common avenues toward that end.[18]

Despite Webb's underlying motive of making his consular appointment the great milestone in his spiritual odyssey, his religious interests were personal and secondary to his secular duties in Manila, which he took very seriously. Webb's life before and after the Manila appointment demonstrates that he held politics and civic service in high esteem.

Webb's positive outlook on politics and diplomatic service was, like so much of his character, true to Victorian form. Although Victorians decried political corruption and understood it to be a common evil of government, they looked favorably upon political involvement as an essential dimension of a healthy social ethic.[19] For them, politics was the most respected medium of public discourse and constituted a civic happening of greatest consequence. Victorians insisted that their actions—including public participation in politics—take on moral value beyond the prosaic concerns of exercising power. They were not far removed from the Republic's formative period, and their minds were filled with heroic and compelling images of the Founding Fathers. Many Victorian Americans looked upon the Civil War as a massive failure of political discourse. Unlike the Founding Fathers, America's Civil War–era politicians had failed to find a peaceful solution to their national discords. At the same time, the war tended to reinforce the American political instinct to restore the democratic process, and it underscored the need for political professionalism.[20]

Life in Manila

Although there were times of excitement in Manila, Webb's work was usually tedious, and his tour of duty was hardly romantic. His dispatches are a repertoire of grumbles: inadequate pay, exposure to disease, and indignities at the hands of colonial authorities. To all of this, Washington usually turned a deaf ear. Manila in the late 1880s and early 1890s was still a diplomatic backwater for the United States. The State Department showed limited interest in the Philippines and revealed even less knowledge of where exactly the islands were located and what they were like.

Unlike the American consuls immediately before and after him, Webb came to Manila with his entire family of six, making his family a quarter of the registered American expatriates in the Philippines.[21] Daily expenses were exorbitant, and Webb's salary, $2,000 a year, was hardly adequate for even a single man. Having his dependents with him plus the constant fear of disease made his residence in Manila trying. He wrote to Washington after two years of service:

So much has been said by my predecessors concerning the insuffi-ciency of the salary at this port, one of the most expensive in the East, that it may seem unnecessary for me to refer to the subject. It is only by the exercise of the most rigid economy that I can meet the current expense of the support of my family without attempting to maintain a social position such as is held here by the paid Con-suls of other nations whose salaries are from three to four times larger than that of the American Consul.[22]

A year later, he registered a similar complaint:

My salary is most discouragingly inadequate to the support of my family and the [maintenance] of such a social position as it seems to me an American Consul should maintain. The Consuls of the other nations, without exception, keep horses and carriage, entertain with dinner and receptions and use wines, liquors and other expensive luxuries. We have never indulged in these things and have no incli-nation to do so. Our manner of life has been plain and unostentatious in the extreme, and it has seemed to me that further economy was not possible. But I find that it will be necessary to retrench even further in order to avoid going beyond my income this year. An unmarried man might be able to live here comfortably, upon the income even now.[23]

Julius G. Voigt preceded Webb as American consul in Manila but had left his wife and children in Brooklyn. Voigt's allegations foreshadowed those of Webb. One dispatch complained that Voigt had performed "over four years of unremitted service."[24] Charles H. Cowan replaced Webb in 1892. Like Voigt, he came without family but immediately found himself in financial straits and informed Washington despondently: "I live at the English club, but occupy a bed in the alcove at the end of corridor, out of sight, as per diagram. I am alone: i.e. no family here, have no residence." Cowan enlisted the Henry Peabody Company as a proxy in support of his request for a better salary. The Peabody report emphasized that an annual salary of $2,000 was insufficient in Manila:

From our experience as to living expenses in that locality we think it would be practically impossible for you to support yourself and family on this amount, and we regret that our government cannot be more liberal in the payment of their representatives abroad; at all events, it seems to us that they should allow them sufficient compensation to enable them to make at least a bare living out of the office.[25]

Webb's monetary troubles alone would have sufficed to make life in Manila harsher than imagined, but he faced other challenges as well. There was the constant concern of communicable and often fatal diseases at a time when still very little was known about how to prevent or treat them. Consul Voigt had been scheduled to set out for the United States on December 31, 1887, but missed his ship due to "pestilent health" and died before the next boat arrived. Webb wrote to his superiors that Voigt's five years of service in the tropical climate had "reduced his strength." Webb added that Voigt had hoped a "long voyage and bracing sea air would restore him to health" but suffered an attack of diarrhea that turned into dysentery, which, Webb noted, was "almost invariably fatal here." Webb remained by Voigt's side as he wasted away and died.[26]

Another American national, Joseph C. Tyler, who assisted Webb as a consular agent in the Caroline Islands, arrived in Manila in the spring of 1890, took ill, and suddenly died. Webb reported to Washington that Tyler contracted a bad cough, began hemorrhaging from the lungs, and soon wasted away to "a mere skeleton."[27]

Webb's official correspondence emphasized great fear for his family's health. He wrote in the summer of 1891 that his wife and one of the children had been suffering for months from "the debilitating effects of the climate to an extent which causes me considerable anxiety, and I am satisfied that they need a change, even if it is only to some other port in the East in order to restore them to health."[28] Webb finally sent his family to California in early June 1892, where they stayed with his elder brother, Edward, and he complained to the State Department of his own deteriorating health.[29] Webb continued to work at his consular duties until late summer of that year, when the State Department finally confirmed his replacement.

Consular Business

Under the Cleveland administration, Webb's diplomatic dispatches were generally addressed to Assistant Secretary of State George L. Rives, who was replaced by William F. Wharton under President Harrison. Though Rives showed little interest in the Philippines, Wharton was more engaged, especially with matters pertaining to agriculture, commerce, and industry. However, his queries revealed abysmal ignorance of the Philippines, even the fact that they were a collection of islands.

Webb required consular help, but the pay he could offer was uninviting, and none of the three qualified Americans in Manila could be induced to assist him as vice consul, because they "consider the salary of Consul so small that it would not pay them to accept an appointment."[30] Webb turned instead to his family members for various office jobs. His wife and her daughter Bessie served alternatively as Webb's clerks for most of his Manila years.[31] Occasionally, the State Department refused to reimburse him for their clerical help, and Webb ended up doing the work himself. He insisted that consular regulations allowed him $400 a year for clerical help, but Washington refused to allot even a quarter of that sum.[32]

Bessie was the first to work at the consulate and began on January 1, 1888, the day Webb officially assumed his duties.[33] Webb wrote a year later:

> The position of clerk has been heretofore held by my daughter, who is 19 years of age and has discharged her duties most satisfactorily. I would ask, therefore, that, if it is within the power of the Department, a special allowance of $200 be given her for her services as clerk for September and December quarters of 1889.[34]

The State Department bickered over her salary, forcing Webb to do the clerical work himself for a few months, but she returned to her work by year's end and was given a salary of $500 for the next year, which was renewed in late 1891 for the next fiscal year.[35]

Webb employed his son Russell, who was nine years old when the Webbs arrived in Manila, for messenger services.[36] It was customary for young boys to work in the Victorian period, and, in America, boys younger than Russell typically "hawked newspapers and journals."[37] Consul Cowan, Webb's replacement, retained a messenger boy for a year but at his own expense for $120.[38] Webb wrote in 1889 to Assistant Secretary of State Wharton, who had given him an allowance for messenger service:

> I have entered into an agreement with Russell Lorenzo Webb to supply said service for the remaining three quarters of the current year. He has been acting in a similar capacity at this Consulate for the past eighteen months without a fixed compensation and as the allowance is made for the fiscal year, it seems proper that he should draw for the quarter just ended, the regular accounts and returns for which were mailed before your instructions were received. I have therefore negotiated my draft No. 18 on the Department of State for $150 in favor of the Hong Kong and Shanghai Banking Corporation.[39]

The messenger service resumed at an allowance of $120 per year. Russell continued to perform the services, which were renewed at the same rate in late 1891 for the new fiscal year.[40]

Upon arrival in Manila, Webb was dissatisfied with the consulate's location and changed it without delay. He continued to find new and more "centrally located" sites during his years in Manila and relocated the consulate several times, informing Washington that each area was better than the one before.

Consulate papers were in a state of total neglect. American diplomatic records in the Philippines went back to 1801, and they were all in "exceedingly unsatisfactory condition," unlisted, unindexed, and "wrapped in bundles and packed in three wooden boxes." Because of the humidity, most were mildewed and some decayed. Webb complained that his search for documents "among such masses as filled these boxes was anything but agreeable."[41] He requested and received funds for their proper restoration, and, applying his editorial skills, organized their contents and had them bound in ninety volumes.[42]

Webb's first major order of business was to look into the possibility of establishing an American consular agency on the Pacific island of Ponape (Pohnpei) in the Spanish-controlled Caroline Islands (today the Federated States of Micronesia). American Protestant missionaries had established a foothold there and were pressuring the State Department to defend their interests. After requesting time to study the matter, Webb related to the Department of State in June 1888 that there was no need for such an undertaking. Never a lover of the missionaries, he reported that he had consulted "reliable persons" and found that their views were "diametrically opposed" to the contentions of the chief local missionary, Rev. E. T. Doane:

> The missionaries at Ponape undoubtedly want a Consular Agency
> there as they feel that it would be an additional protection to their
> rights and privileges, and in this they are heartily supported by their
> American friends who have heard only Mr. Doane's side of the case.
> I regret, therefore, that I cannot make a recommendation more in
> accord with their wishes.[43]

Although an official consular agent was sent to the island, no consul was established there. In July 1890, rebellion broke out in the Carolines. As Webb duly reported to the State Department, the mutiny began with the massacre of two colonial officers and thirty-seven soldiers. The Spanish held the American missionaries responsible and began arresting a number of Westerners on the islands.[44] Trouble in the Carolines continued throughout Webb's service in Manila and forced him to become directly involved in seeking the release of American prisoners whom the Spanish brought to their central prison in Manila.

The Manila consulate was invariably concerned with American shipping interests in the region. Yankee whalers and steamers had to know whether the port of Manila was "clean" or "dirty," that is, contagion-free or infected.

Consequently, one of Webb's continual tasks was to keep Washington posted on local sanitary conditions, especially outbreaks of cholera and smallpox. There were also national interests relating to agriculture, trade, and commerce, and the State Department kept Webb running innumerable errands at its behest and that of other government agencies, including the Department of Agriculture, which requested reports on animal diseases, and the California State Board of Horticulture. He was once charged, for example, with collecting every variety of Philippine coconuts and sending them, properly crated, to the State Department. Washington asked him to send a report on Philippine hemp along with an assortment of its seed. Webb advised that the plant was grown from suckers—not seed—and probably would not do well in the United States anyway. In response to an official inquiry about Philippine silk worms and regional silk production, Webb reported that the Philippines produced no silk at all, despite the fact that Americans and Europeans associated it with "Piña silk," which was produced by weaving imported Chinese silk into native pineapple fiber. Washington assigned him in 1891 to collect a number of Philippine exhibits in preparation for the Chicago World's Fair of 1893. At the time, he had no idea that he would attending the fair as Islam's chief spokesman or that he would be able to view some of these exhibits that he had collected.[45]

Washington was interested particularly in trade possibilities and asked about rubber, refrigerators, lead, zinc, and other materials. Asked to describe the railroads, Webb informed Washington that no railways existed in the Philippines, although the British were beginning to develop a rudimentary rail network in Manila. Roads in the islands were so bad, he continued, that people traveled primarily by bull cart. When asked about the canals, Webb reported that the Philippines were a group of islands—apparently new information for some within the State Department—and had no canals or any need of them.

Webb's work sometimes required long excursions on small boats into the sometimes treacherous waters of Manila Bay, inspections of mutinies and shipwrecks, and the investigation of outbreaks of contagious diseases on American ships. Filing reports on American ships and sailors in Philippine waters was one of his unceasing labors. Americans entering Manila Bay anchored their ships far from shore. Visiting the ships was part of Webb's job, and he took it in stride, even developing personal connections with some of the captains. His chief concern with respect to this aspect of duty was to secure a dependable steam launch. The harbor, he explained, was about twenty-seven miles in diameter and often rough, making it "exceedingly unpleasant and dangerous to keep going out on small boats:"

All our ships are anchored in Manila Bay from two-and-a-half to three miles from the mouth of the Pasig River. It is necessary to traverse a distance of nearly a mile down the river before reaching the bay. The only means of communicating with the ships is by a number of steam launches, most of which are owned by Compradores [purchasers, i.e., special agents] and the native boats or "bankers" which are simply canoes hewn of logs, and are unsafe in rough weather.[46]

He generally rented launches from the local "Compradores" for $4:

I infer that this was the method adopted by my predecessor in visiting ships. But as there are three Compradores here, actively engaged in trying to cut each other's throats in a business way, I do not think it wise to place myself under obligations to either of them in order to save $4.00 occasionally.[47]

Webb continually dealt with shanghaied American sailors, "barefoot and utterly destitute," who turned up in Manila after jumping ship or having been abandoned on some distant Pacific island by their captains as hopeless sailors. He provided them with room and board and arranged for them to be sent to Hong Kong and shipped back to the United States from there. He wrote in 1889:

During the past sixteen months, seventeen destitute seamen have arrived at this Consulate from the Caroline and Marianas Islands where they were left by or deserted from American whaling vessels on which they shipped at San Francisco. With two exceptions all were utterly unexperienced [sic] as sailors and according to their statements had been "shanghaied" on board the vessels or induced to ship by misrepresentation, several of them being put ashore penniless and in some cases sick, when it was found that they were unable to do duty as able seamen. I enclose herewith for your information a tabulated list of these cases with the idea that a remedy may be possible for what appears at present to be not only gross injustice to the men but an expense to the government which might have been saved.[48]

Webb appears to have been so openhanded in his treatment of the sailors that Washington suspected him of abetting their desertion. He countered that American sailors almost never deserted their ships in Manila itself, but, when they did so elsewhere, they came to him with allegations of "ill-treatment and poor or insufficient food." He added, "I feel justified, therefore, in expressing the opinion that the present administration of the relief law, in its application to deserters, does not increase the number of desertions." He urged Washington to adopt a generous policy toward such men.[49]

Another of Webb's common duties was to secure freedom for American prisoners in colonial custody. The work was not only demanding of Webb's time and patience but also underappreciated by those whom he was able to free. One of the most difficult cases was that of Albert Geesa, whom Spanish authorities believed to have been involved in the disturbances on the Caroline Islands; he had been denied a fair trial. When, after weeks of labor, Webb finally secured Geesa's release, the latter appeared at the consulate and gave Webb a good cursing before stowing away on an outgoing steamer. Webb complained to the State Department that Geesa behaved "in such an insolent and insulting manner that I was compelled to order him to leave the premises."[50]

Perhaps the most extraordinary prisoner case was that of an adventurous English teenager from Bristol, William Richard Williamson, who, like Geesa, had been brought to Manila in chains under suspicion of fomenting rebellion in the Carolines. Williamson's account is worth telling for many reasons. In addition to its dramatic value, there is the unique coincidence that Williamson embraced Islam a few years after his escape, although Webb does not seem to have played a role in his conversion. The Williamson story also provides singular insight into Webb's character. Webb did not hesitate to come to Williamson's aid and see to his safe escape from Manila, although Williamson was not an American national, and it was beyond Webb's call of duty—probably even diplomatic protocol—to help him as he did. Because the Williamson case fell outside Webb's official duties, he made no mention of the incident in his official correspondence with the State Department. Instead, the story comes exclusively from Williamson's biography.

Webb made frequent visits to the Manila prison on behalf of the Americans imprisoned there, and is probable that Williamson came to know of him there. When Williamson finally made his daring prison break, he wisely chose to make a mad dash to Webb at the American consulate and not to the British authorities, who seem to have taken little interest in his case anyway. Williamson was only eighteen when imprisoned in Manila but had already done more than most people do in a lifetime. Too unruly for boarding school, his parents had sent him to sea on a tea-clipper at thirteen as punishment with the hope that discipline and hard work would teach him to behave and understand the benefits of a good education. Instead, Williamson resolved never to return to England and spent the rest of his youth roaming the world in search of adventure.

His travels took him to California, where he worked for an aunt, and quickly developed a liking for the Southwest, soon becoming an experienced cowhand who was able to cut cattle and handle a gun. In light of this background, combined with Williamson's aversion to England, Webb probably looked upon him as a true-blue American.[51]

Williamson took part in a Nevada gold rush and also proved himself a first-rate amateur boxer. During a San Francisco boxing championship one night, after Williamson took the first of three bouts, he unwittingly accepted an opium-laced beer and woke up the next day to find himself shanghaied on the *Sitka Brave*. After a long and involved series of events, he ended up in the

FIGURE 5.1. William Richard Williamson (late 1890s)

Caroline Islands on the eve of the Pohnpei rebellion, trading in sea cucumbers, an Oriental delicacy.

Spanish authorities found him offshore on his outrigger, harvesting sea cucumbers, and detained him under the pretext that he was selling arms to the local tribesmen.[52] Webb took a different view of how the Caroline tribesmen had come by their rifles. Shortly after the outbreak and long before the Williamson incident in Manila, his lengthy dispatch to the State Department explained in detail how the "natives" had taken their several dozen Remington rifles off the bodies of the colonial troops they massacred.[53]

Williamson was imprisoned in Manila awaiting trial, and described those days as the worst of his life. Like other prisoners, he lived in constant fear of torture and death and was placed for several hours in a metal tank filled with water, where he could save himself only by desperately pumping the water out before the tank filled. He finally managed to escape by bribing a guard and fled to the American consulate under hot pursuit from his Spanish guards. Webb granted him refuge without hesitation:[54]

A pleasant-looking man, dressed in white, rose from a seat in the doorway of the Consulate and removed a Manila cheroot from his lips. Young Williamson darted in beside him. There was no time for explanation. Three or four of the Spanish guards were rushing toward the building. He gasped out two words: "Help me!" The American Consul did not pause to answer. He thrust him inside, slammed the large wooden door and bolted it.[55]

Williamson described Webb as "a man of outstanding character and integrity." His impression was more than casual sentiment. After refusing adamantly to turn Williamson over to the Spanish, Webb proved to be a generous host, and he helped Williamson to escape from the Philippines.[56]

Webb provided Williamson with a safe room on the upper floor of the consulate and gave him an escape plan over the housetops of the surrounding buildings, should the Spanish return unexpectedly.[57] Webb set out directly to the British consulate, expecting that the British would grant Williamson protection, but he returned "fuming with anger." The British consul wanted nothing to do with "people who got themselves mixed up in rebellions and internal disputes." He refused to help Williamson in any way and insisted that, pending judgment in the local court, Williamson should be sent back to prison. Webb related to Williamson: "I told him, son, you were innocent—and I hold to that belief. He said 'the fellow must return to prison and stand his trial.' That got my goat. 'What kind of justice do you reckon he'll get from these goddam Spaniards?' I asked him. It cut no ice. Your Consul only repeated what he'd said before, and we both got kind of hot under the collar before I came away."[58]

Webb assured Williamson that he would get him out of Manila safely:

Russell Webb [sic] dropped into his chair. "Sit down, my boy," he ordered. "Between you and me, I hate these yellow-bellied dagoes. Yours is not the first case from that damn prison that's got under my skin. Take it from me: I'll not let them play around with you. If your own Consul won't act, I'll see this through for you myself."[59]

Webb sought help elsewhere, and when he returned to the American consulate he had with him a British shipmaster, Captain Gurney of the SS Elwold, who agreed to slip Williamson out. The captain was "a jovial type with a boisterous sense of humour" and as "clear-cut in his opinion of the Spaniards like the Consul himself, and forthright about his intentions if trouble occurred." After Webb determined that it was safe to move, Captain Gurney and Williamson made their escape, disguising Williamson as a drunken sailor.

Williamson embraced Islam in Aden a few years later. His conversion was ascribable, in part, to the writings of the British Muslim leader Abdulla Quilliam rather than to Webb's direct influence. In fact, Williamson was not aware of

Webb's beliefs until after his own conversion to Islam. Williamson performed the pilgrimage to Mecca in 1895 and wrote a letter to Webb about life in Arabia, which Webb published in the *Moslem World*.[60] "Years later," W. E. Stanton-Hope narrated, "when [Williamson] was established firmly in Arabia and had embraced the Islamic Faith, he learnt with surprise the coincidental fact that his American benefactor had also joined a Moslem community."[61]

Webb never found the direct access to Oriental traditions in Manila that he had romantically hoped to discover there. Nevertheless, his consular work, as exasperating as it was at times, generally left him free time to read and write when off duty, and Webb spent much of his time reading about his newly adopted faith in addition, no doubt, to the Theosophical researches that never failed to captivate his mind. He also engaged in correspondence about Islam and its future in America with Indian Muslims and in the Indian Muslim press. Like Webb's involvement in the Williamson case, his religious undertakings in Manila were a private matter, but during his last years in the Philippines, Webb not only grew confident of his commitment to Islam but also resolved to bring it to the knowledge of other Americans. His correspondence and ultimately the private visit in Manila of his most enthusiastic Indian Muslim supporter led to the establishment of his American Mission in New York, beginning with a preliminary tour of Muslim communities in Burma and India.

The Indian Connection

Webb's conversion to Islam took place early during his consular service in Manila, where his Islamic mission to America was also conceived. A "Parsee gentleman" from Bombay, possibly the one referred to above in Webb's July 26, 1891, dispatch to the State Department, came to know of Webb and his newly adopted faith. Carrying a letter from Webb, the Parsee put him in contact with a prominent Muslim merchant in Bombay, Budruddin Kur. Shortly afterward, a lively correspondence ensued.

Although Webb contended that the exchange "was commenced for mutual instruction," it quickly went beyond points of faith to touch upon Webb's personal interest in promoting Islam in America. Webb himself suggested to Kur that "someone should go to preach Islam in the free country of America."[62] While Webb was corresponding with Kur, he published several articles and open letters in the *Allahabad Review*, expressing his conviction that an Islamic mission would succeed in America, his belief that "educated, broad-minded liberal Moslems" in India had an obligation to support it, and his willingness to be a part of such an undertaking.[63]

Kur published his correspondence with Webb in the Indian press as well, creating a greater stir among Indian Muslims about the highly placed

American convert and the possibility of sending "a Mohammedan Mission to the American Continent."[64] Kur brought Webb to the attention of several friends, among whom was Hajee Abdulla Arab, a prosperous Memon merchant from Calcutta with extensive business interests in India and abroad who was known for his devotion to Islamic causes. Although based in the Arabian cities of Medina and Jeddah, Arab happened to be visiting India at the time and zealously "took up the matter" of Webb's interest in mission work, entering into correspondence with him sometime around March 1891.[65] Webb invited Arab to Manila, where the two conferred together. The American Mission evolved directly out of their meeting.[66]

According to Kur, Webb "expressed his desire to resign his post of Consul-General at Manilla [sic] and devote his whole life to the propagation of Islam in the United States of America."[67] Once the matter came to Arab's attention, he had a letter drafted to Webb in English (Arab was not proficient in the language himself) expressing his support for the idea of an Islamic mission to America.[68] Webb reciprocated with enthusiasm, inviting Arab to visit him in Manila. Arab agreed and invited Hassan Ali, a noted Muslim missionary from Bihar and one of the first Indian Muslims to "discourse effectively in the English language on Islam," to accompany him as a translator. Since Ali was unable to travel, Arab set out for Manila with a translator, and they arrived in mid-March 1892. The translator was Serajuddin Ahmad, a convert of unspecified European background, who lived in India and spoke English "perfectly."[69] Arab spent a week as a guest in Webb's house, which Webb referred to as "the happiest week I have ever passed in this benighted country."[70]

Given Webb's previous proposal of the mission idea, Arab's visit to Manila was not for the purpose of convincing Webb to undertake the mission but to work out its details. An official contract was drawn up and signed at the American consulate in Manila in the presence of "an upright, honorable witness from Bombay."[71] Arab asked Webb to give him an estimate of yearly mission expenses over the next five years, and Webb complied with his request.[72] Webb was convinced that the mission would stand on its own feet after five years and would not require indefinite support: "[A] sufficient sum [had] been guaranteed in Bombay to keep the weekly, the publishing house, and the other branches in full operation for five years, and by that time I think Islam will be on a sufficiently firm footing here to take care of itself."[73]

As part of their five-year contract with Webb, Indian backers promised to provide $13,000 during the initial year to establish the mission in New York and support Webb's family. They were to send an additional $10,000 annually over the subsequent four years to keep the mission running on the supposition that Webb could support it independently after that time.[74] Arab promised to donate one third of his personal wealth to the project and "was confident that others would come forward and contribute freely to the cause."[75] Months later in India, a funding committee was created for the mission, "composed of some of the wealthiest and most influential Mohammedan merchants of Bombay" with Kur as its secretary. The committee pledged itself to "furnish all the money necessary for the [mission's] purpose." Arab was designated as a member but given no executive authority.[76]

Having concluded the Manila agreement, Webb was told to await word from Arab that preliminary preparations were in place before resigning his post and embarking on the Oriental tour to Burma and India for raising funds. Arab promised to join Webb in Rangoon, and from there they would proceed together to India. Arab also directed Webb to visit Quilliam's English Muslim convert community in Liverpool on his return trip to America to establish "friendly contact" with the Muslims there.[77]

Arab returned to India from his Manila visit, where he succeeded in gathering a few thousand dollars in Hyderabad. According to Hassan Ali, Arab was swept away by enthusiasm after the initial success in Hyderabad and felt assured that future fundraising would be equally promising. He immediately wired Webb—apparently in opposition to Ali's counsel—telling him to resign his post and begin preparations for the tour. Ali deemed Arab's decision as precipitous, suggesting to him that more extensive funding should be collected before giving Webb the signal to leave his post.[78] Webb received the telegram on June 20, 1892, "informing [him] that the arrangements for starting the American mission were completed." Webb immediately wrote his resignation and began to prepare for his Oriental tour.[79]

During his tour, Webb was welcomed to Bombay with a banner proclaiming: "The fact that you have voluntarily sustained a serious loss, by resigning your honourable and lucrative post of Consul General at Manila, conclusively proves the deep interest you take for establishing a mission on the American continent."[80] Three years later, however, when Webb's Islamic movement was on the verge of total collapse, he would impugn Arab for the loss of his diplomatic post, which Webb maintained he might otherwise have held indefinitely. He stated that Arab had approached him in Manila, "acting on behalf of himself and a number of other wealthy Mussulmans," and persuaded him to give up his position.[81] Although Arab may be impugned for excessive enthusiasm and hastiness, it was Webb himself who orchestrated the creation of the mission and sought an alternative to his post. His work in Manila had been a long-standing source of dissatisfaction, as his complaints about pay and conditions make clear. Webb's correspondence with Kur left no doubt that the mission proposal had originated with Webb:

> I am impatient to meet you and talk freely with you concerning the matter, for I feel sure that you will agree with me not only that the object is of the grandest importance, but that there has been something more than ordinary human agencies at work in bringing the

project to its present condition. God is great, and will surely guide his servants in the right way.[82]

Given Webb's history of failed undertakings, one might be inclined to interpret his advocacy of the American Mission as another of his less-than-brilliant ventures in search of gainful employment. It would be simplistic, however, to say that finding employment or seeking self-enrichment was his sole motive or principal incentive. To begin with, Webb agreed to an annual salary of $2,400 for mission work, not considerably higher than the inadequate $2,000 a year that he received as consul in Manila.[83] Moreover, Webb continued to work for the mission while living in poverty after his Indian backers failed to deliver the support they promised. Such commitment gives clear demonstration of a dedication deeper than mere pecuniary enrichment.

Webb's character had an unmistakable missionary side. Colonel Henry Steel Olcott of the Theosophical Society, who met Webb when he visited Madras for a few days in 1892, recognized that quality in Webb. Olcott asserted that Webb had been "a strenuous advocate of Buddhism" until his acceptance of Islam. Even after accepting Islam, Webb remained, in Olcott's view, "an ardent Theosophist," committed to its propagation and convinced that Islam and Theosophy were "distinctly in accord."[84] The same missionary disposition appeared earlier in Webb's 1887 correspondence with Mirza Ahmad, where Webb spoke of his readiness to be part of a mission for "spreading the truth" in America.

Webb expressed his missionary readiness even before he had become fully convinced of the truth of Islam: "If I could only know what Mohammed really taught that was superior to the teachings of others, I could then be in a position to defend and promulgate the Mohammedan religion above all others."[85] Webb's correspondence with Kur had much the same spirit and asserted that his commitment to spread Islam in America had preceded his correspondence with Kur, although Webb had resigned himself to the fact that he would probably have to rely on personal resources: "It seemed that I was destined to work out quietly, and in my own way the bringing of my countrymen to a knowledge of Islam, and it hardly seemed probable then that any other way was open."[86]

Webb's Resignation

Webb's official communications with Washington were fairly transparent. He did not hesitate to inform the State Department of the spiritual interests that underlay his desire to accept a consular post in the East, although his Washington communications also reflect some indecision. Webb never hid his dissatisfaction with his pay and living conditions. He filed no official report of his conversion to Islam or desire to launch an Islamic mission in America but probably saw nothing duplicitous about keeping both matters to himself as essentially private and not official concerns.

Although Webb took definite steps to start his American Islamic mission, he had not completely given up hope of continued government service. His diplomatic correspondence reflects that he almost certainly had a double mind about the prospect of continuing in his diplomatic career. At the same time that he was laying the groundwork for the mission, he was requesting the State Department to transfer him to a more amenable post, preferably in a Muslim country. His preference for a post in a Muslim land testifies to his attachment to his newly adopted faith and his certain desire to gain greater knowledge of it. No doubt, Webb also entertained misgivings about the feasibility of his mission plans, as indicated by his diary entry when he finally set out on the Asian tour to secure financial backing: "I returned to the hotel wishing that I was going straight to San Francisco instead of to Singapore [the first leg of the journey]. Well, God's will be done."[87]

Webb had begun seeking a transfer from Manila in July of 1891: "In view of the conditions prevalent at this port and the impaired health of my wife and one of my children I would respectfully ask to be transferred to another post where the climate is less enervating and where the cost of living is less than it is here."[88] The State Department promised it would give the request due consideration.[89] Having received, on the one hand, Arab's telegram on June 20, 1892, indicating that the groundwork for the mission had been set in place and failing to receive, on the other, a satisfactory response from Washington, Webb handed in his resignation.[90] He wrote to Assistant Secretary of State Wharton, on July 7, 1892, requesting immediate authority, confirmed by telegraph, to appoint an acting consul in his place. Referring to a June dispatch, he informed Washington:

> I regret to say that it is imperative that I should leave Manila at the earliest moment possible. My family has already gone and I am waiting with no little anxiety, to turn the office over to someone else. Therefore, I would most respectfully ask that, if it is found impossible to get anyone to come here and be here not later than the 1st of October, I be given authority by telegraph to appoint William A. Daland Esq to act as Consul until my successor arrives.
>
> Mr. Daland is an American, a native of Brooklyn, N.Y. and is engaged in business as a broker but will have ample time to attend to the duties of the office with the assistance of a clerk. He is the only American here who is qualified to take the position and is so situated that he can do so without moving the office into a commercial house. He is not engaged in trade and would make a most

creditable representative of our government. If his nomination meets with your approval please telegraph the word "Nominate".

I am, Sir,

> Your Obedient Servant,
> Alex. R. Webb
> U.S. Consul[91]

Webb resigned from service and handed the consulate over to William Daland on September 5, 1892, just days before his voyage to Singapore, Burma, and India. He wrote in his diary the day before: "This is my last day as Consul. To-morrow I will be a plain American citizen."[92] After turning over the keys, he wrote his last dispatch to Washington:

> I have the honor to report that under the authority given by your telegram of the 20th ult [i.e., of last month] I have this day turned over to William A. Daland Esq all the archives and Government property in this Consulate and he has entered upon the discharge of his duties as acting Consul. I also transmit herewith the inventory and certificate as required by Article 9 of the Consular Regulations.
>
> I am, Sir,
>
> > Your Obedient Servant,
> > Alex. R. Webb
> > U.S. Consul[93]

Webb auctioned off a few belongings for $84.75, concluded his consular duties by arresting two pirates, and, on September 5, said his goodbyes. That evening, to his unspoken chagrin, a group of friends called upon him at his hotel with a heavy package of books to be delivered to Singapore. Before dropping off to sleep, Webb jotted down in his diary that the barometer had fallen sharply, winds had picked up to gale force, rain was pouring down in torrents, and a typhoon threatened.[94] Standing on the threshold of his Islamic mission to America, Webb was now ready to embark on his passage to India.

6

Passage to India

Just before handing in his resignation, Webb wrote in his diary: "This is my last day as Consul. To-morrow I will be a plain American citizen."[1] On the contrary, he would never be a "plain American citizen" again. As a former American consul, his conversion to Islam and Oriental tour put him more directly in the public eye than ever before and brought him considerable notoriety in the American and international press. As he set out from Manila for the tour, he began a journey that would last almost half a year and would constitute one of the most unforgettable experiences of his life.

The first step on Webb's Oriental tour to gain support for his American Mission took him to Burma by way of Singapore. He then continued on to India, his chief destination, where he spent almost half the journey. The excursion kept him in the public eye and introduced him well to the practice of public lecturing, a craft that would be of great service to him in America. Naturally, he caught the attention of the Indian press, but he was hardly overlooked by American reporters, whose stories created considerable notoriety for him in the United States.[2]

Webb, less than elated with the trip's prospects, set out on the journey alone; his family was still in San Francisco with his brother Edward.[3] His diary gives a detailed account of his tour— no other source approaches it in value—and also provides an intimate and invaluable portrayal of Webb himself. It was the first diary Webb kept: "I have never tried to keep a journal before and am too lazy I guess to make a success of it. There's nothing in the

world to write about."[4] As a professional journalist, however, Webb soon discovered much to record after musing over his opening entries:

> All this reads very much like a school girl's diary but I feel so little
> like writing and there is so very little to write about that I can hardly
> make it much better. After all events it is not intended for anyone's
> eyes but mine and as a sort of note-book for future writing.[5]

Unfortunately, only two volumes of the diary have been discovered. There
was at least another volume, its existence clearly indicated by the fact that the
second breaks off in midsentence two weeks prior to the journey's end.
The lost volume would portray one of the most critical junctures of the tour,
Webb's journey from Agra to Lahore, where the question arose of possibly
visiting Mirza Ghulam Ahmad in Qadian.

According to Ahmadiyya sources, Hassan Ali, who later became a follower of Mirza Ghulam Ahmad, related some time afterward that Webb expressed an interest in visiting Mirza Ahmad during their stay in Hyderabad,
remarking that Mirza Ahmad had done him "a great favor" by bringing him
to Islam. Webb consulted with Hassan Ali and Abdulla Arab about the possibility of such a visit, although the three decided against it because of Mirza
Ahmad's growing ill repute: "To go to meet such a reviled man . . . would
result in damage to the work of the propagation of Islam." Ali continued that
Webb decided, instead, to write a letter to Mirza Ahmad, to which he received
an eight-page reply in Urdu, which Hassan Ali translated for him. When in
Lahore, Webb carefully avoided visiting Mirza Ahmad in Qadian, although the
township lay at a short distance from Lahore.[6] The two extant volumes of
Webb's diary make no mention of such a discussion in Hyderabad or anything else relevant to Mirza Ahmad.

After Lahore, Webb returned to Bombay, where he was ceremoniously
seen off to America. His journey home took him by way of the Suez Canal and
the Straits of Gibraltar to England, where his sponsors had hoped he would
visit Quilliam's community in Liverpool before continuing back to New York.
Quilliam's journals report no such visit.[7] Again, however, the lost volume of
Webb's diary certainly recorded the details of his stops along the last leg of his
journey back to America, including his layover in England.[8]

Journey's Course

Webb's five years in the Philippines had hardly been without fears and hardships but also constituted one of the main episodes of his life. Despite lengthy
official complaints to the contrary, Webb also admitted personally to happy
days and memorable occasions in the Philippines. More important, it was in
Manila that Webb underwent the major transformation of his life. The years of

private study and spiritual quest, which had begun in St. Louis, culminated in Manila with his conversion to Islam and conception of an Islamic mission to America. Though relieved to leave Manila on September 6, 1892, Webb could not help feeling nostalgic as his ship set out for Singapore and he gazed back, watching Manila Harbor recede forever into the past:

> It was not without a slight feeling of regret and sadness that I saw Manila fading away in the distance forever. I had spent many happy hours there as well as unhappy ones. It had been my home for 5 years and a good home too. Now all was broken up and I was about to begin the world anew.[9]

The voyage began inelegantly on the Spanish steamer *España*: "We had a cargo of copra [dried coconut meat] on board the odor of which added to the usual nastiness of a Spanish steamer made the cabin unbearable."[10] Victorians stressed cleanliness, taking it to be a sign of righteousness, and Webb shared their fastidious spirit, detesting untidiness and bad smells.[11] The stench of copra mixed with the excrement of pigs, dogs, and cats on board made the first leg of his journey unbearable. The filth annoyed him all the more because it appeared not to trouble the crew: "The men walk over it without taking the least notice of it." The seas were rough, the food seemed to get continually worse, and after a few days, Webb wrote facetiously, "The ship gets nastier every day and will be ready to breed a pestilence by the time we reach Singapore."[12] Webb was relieved to arrive in Singapore, finding himself in "a more oriental city" than any he had seen before with "Chinese, Hindus, Malays and almost all Eastern types" waiting at the dock.[13] He spent about a week in the city, exploring it on foot, looking up an old friend named Ong Kim Cheow, and pronouncing Singapore "a most beautiful and comely city" and "a great improvement on Manila."[14]

The *Patria*, the British steamer that took Webb to Rangoon, met his expectations for cleanliness. After setting out from Singapore, the ship passed through the Straits of Malacca, making a brief but enjoyable stop at Penang farther along the way.[15] The *Patria* reached the Burmese coast at the break of dawn on September 28, steaming up the Irrawaddy River to Rangoon. The river's muddy waters made Webb reminisce on the Mississippi.[16] When he reached Rangoon, there was an immense crowd of Muslims waiting to welcome him:

> As we neared the wharf I noticed a large number of Mohammedans awaiting our arrival but did not suppose they were waiting for me. But as soon as the gang-plank was put off quite a number of them came aboard and I was soon surrounded by a crowd of Moslem brethren who seized my hand as fast as I could take theirs and gave me a most cordial welcome. I was not prepared for such a reception

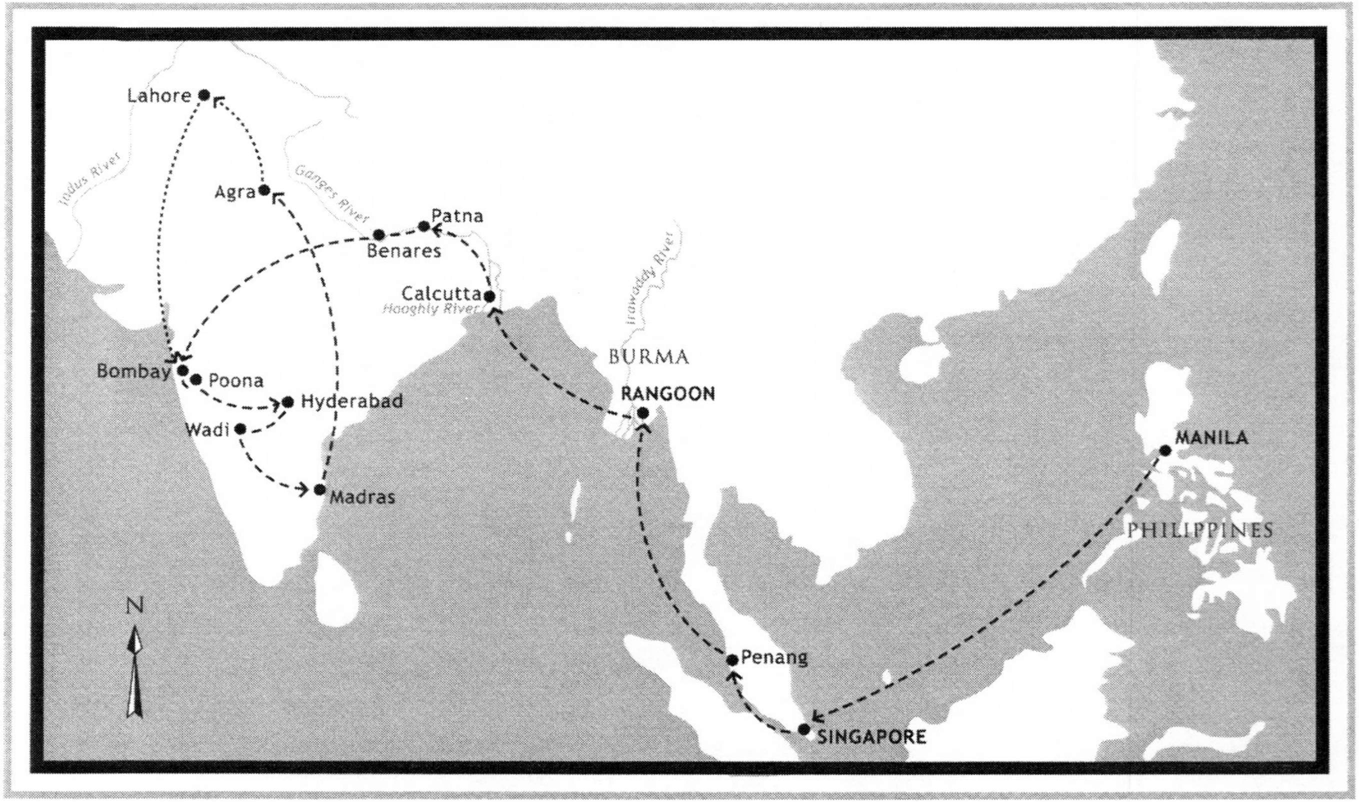

FIGURE 6.1. Webb's Oriental Tour (1892)

and my astonishment increased when I found that there were
fully 500 Mussulmen on the wharf waiting to receive me. As soon as
I had made ready my luggage I was escorted to the wharf where
I passed through a long line of Mussulmen all anxious to take me by
the hand. After them were two lines of school children who sang a
song of welcome in Hindustanee [sic]. The reception showed a true
spirit of brotherhood which was very pleasing to me.[17]

Webb's host spirited him off by carriage to the Rangoon central mosque,
and they were followed by the enthusiastic crowd of Muslims, who stared at him
through the carriage window, occasionally reaching in their hands to shake his.
At the mosque, he spoke to "the vast gathering" and was given an official
welcome on behalf of the Muslims of Rangoon, who congratulated him "upon
having become a follower of Islam."[18] A prominent Muslim of the city put him
up in a guesthouse. Newly furnished for Webb's exclusive use, it was "large and
cool and nestled among great Jack fruit and other large shade trees."[19]

Over the next two weeks, Webb met the leaders of the Rangoon Muslim
community, paid visits to mosques and Islamic schools, and imbibed memories that he assured himself would never be forgotten.[20]

As promised, Hajee Abdulla Arab joined Webb in Rangoon and remained
with him for the remainder of the tour. On the morning of Arab's arrival,
Webb's host eagerly informed him over breakfast that the *Africa*, which was
bringing Arab, had been sighted and would soon anchor at the wharf:

After breakfast we started off and reached the office down town just
as Abdulla alighted from his gharry [horse-drawn cab]. The dear
old man looked as lovable and good as ever and it was a pleasure
to meet him again. He is far and away the best looking Mohammedan I have yet seen.[21]

After spending a week together in Rangoon, Webb and Arab set sail for
Calcutta.[22] As in Rangoon, an immense crowd of Muslims awaited Webb's
arrival; this time, a number of them in a sampan pulled alongside Webb's
boat as it steamed up the Hooghly River to Calcutta. Once more, Webb's host
had prepared an elegant carriage, which conveyed them to "very pleasant
quarters." Webb spent the next ten days there.[23] He found Calcutta "very
handsome [and] well-kept" but complained of the mosquitoes that kept him
from sleeping, turning him into "a total wreck" and forcing him to pass "most
of the morning in sleep on a lounge in the parlor."[24]

After Calcutta, Webb and Arab set out for Bombay by train. On October
23, they set out for Patna, traveling to Webb's delight along the Ganges River
by way of Benares. Webb was struck by the great flocks of spectacular birds along
the Ganges, but he was disappointed to find that Benares had forgotten its
ancient greatness and was now in a neglected state with "the most persistent

beggars in the world."[25] Budruddin Kur sent a telegram to Webb saying that he would meet Webb and Arab by train and join their party at Kalyan, just outside Bombay.[26] When Webb and Arab reached Bombay on October 28, hundreds of Muslims gathered to receive them.

The Bombay welcoming seemed to Webb even more cordial than previous receptions: "Hundreds of Mussulmans pressed forward to shake hands with me while a long line of school boys sang a song of welcome in Urdu. Then two teachers and others hung garlands of flowers about my neck and filled my hands with beautiful boquets [sic]." The crowds were so large that the carriage waiting for Webb and Arab could hardly move but finally made its way to the "handsome residence" that Kur had put at their disposal.[27]

Bombay appeared to Webb more beautiful and "well-regulated" than Calcutta, and he noted that he would prefer to live in Bombay.[28] He spent the next twenty days in Bombay with regular outings to the beach, an occasional sailing or deep-sea fishing excursion, and even a visit to the historic caves of Elephanta Island. Hassan Ali also joined Webb's party in Bombay and served as his translator for most of the remainder of the journey.[29] Despite Kur's generosity, Webb became dreadfully bored in Bombay and faulted Kur for failing to make good use of their time.[30] Cultural shock and fatigue began to take their toll. Webb's patience waned, and, with each passing day, he became more bad-tempered.

Webb left Bombay on November 17, setting out for the highland town of Poona en route to Hyderabad. In Poona, Webb was received by an enthusiastic crowd as before, and his party was taken "in a handsome carriage to the bungalow assigned for our use."[31] He fell in love with the city: "My first view of Poona impressed me very strongly with the beauty of the streets and the tasteful arrangement of the place."[32] He observed the following day: "Poona proper is a quaint old place and is the most Oriental town I have seen yet."[33] On November 20 after an arduous trip, Webb arrived in Hyderabad, a key city on his journey:

> When we arrived to within about 100 yards of the platform quite a number of Mussulmans put in an appearance and some of them entered the car and greeted me cordially. At the platform there was a vast crowd in waiting to receive me and I was escorted to a handsome carriage—evidently a state vehicle—and under an escort of mounted native soldiers was driven to the Nizam's Club. The cavalcade presented quite a showy appearance. A gaily caparisoned elephant was also in attendance and gave the scene a very oriental aspect. I was struck with the general oriental appearance of the town as we passed through the streets. At the club I was presented to a large number of well-dressed, Europeanized Mussulmans, who were

apparently of a higher order of intelligence and refinement than any I had yet seen.[34]

Each city Webb visited seemed more beautiful and Oriental than the ones before. Webb never tired of this city's beauty: "Hyderabad is full of interest to me and I would like to stay here a long time if I could only go about on foot."[35] The old city held a special attraction and seemed to be "the first really oriental city seen" in his travels:

The old walls, turretted [sic] buildings among the trees, narrow streets, little shops, arches over the street, elephants, plodding along with bells on their sides and half a dozen people on their backs, gaily colored dresses and turbans, odd-looking bullock carts and gharries gave the place a novel and attractive appearance.[36]

Among other things, Webb was treated to a ride on a royal elephant, which "fatigued [him] considerably" and alarmed him when his elephant "passed a plebian elephant carrying a load of hay—smelled of our elephant to see if we were all right, much to my nervousness."[37]

In Hyderabad, Webb's disappointment with poor planning, broken promises, and general wastage of time surpassed his frustration in Bombay. His party had hoped that Hyderabad's Muslim ruler, the Nizam, would meet with Webb and support his mission. Webb quickly lost patience with the Nizam and his secretary, who was forever making vague promises for appointments. Webb noted: "These little six-penny monarchs are very difficult to approach except by good-looking actresses."[38] When, on December 6, an exact appointment with the Nizam was finally granted, Webb refused to go, and Arab and Ali missed the scheduled time:

Hajee Abdulla and Hassan Ali returned about 11, completely crest-fallen—had arrived at the palace too late—had agreed to be there at 7:30, but had to stop on the way to pick up the poet—he was late, of course, everybody is out here, and when they got to the palace it was 8:30—Secretary had gone in to the Nizam leaving word that he would see them "some other day." Very unfortunate but a good lesson if those concerned will only take it to themselves. Procrastination and utter unreliability are the curses of the people of this country—after laziness, hypocrisy and a few other curses.[39]

Having had enough of Hyderabad, Webb insisted on moving on to Madras, the next stop on their tour. Still entertaining hopes of meeting the Nizam, Arab and Ali were unwilling to leave the city. After quarrelling with Ali, Webb left Hyderabad in a huff, setting out for Madras by train on his own.

Pleased to get away and be by himself, Webb enjoyed the view of the rolling plains from his compartment. Finally, the train stopped for the night at a remote, isolated station called Wadi, where he would have to await another train for Madras due the following morning:

> We arrived at Wadi about 1 and much to my disappointment I found there was no hotel there—what had been called a hotel was only a refreshment room—there wasn't a bed to rent in the town—town consisted of about 50 mud and stone huts. A fresh young man at the station told me I could sleep in the lavatory, which was a stone cell on the ground floor which had a mirror, a washstand, a washbowl full of dirty water and a stone bath tub which had never been used in it, but no bed. The place had been whitewashed, apparently, some months previously and the spatterings of lime and dirt had never been removed—besides it had a disagreeable odor and I did not receive favorably the suggestion that I could haul one of the public benches inside and sleep there. Had a very good tiffin [luncheon] in the refreshment room and was told by the waiter that if I could get the station master's permission I could sleep in the ladies' waiting room. Presently the telegraph clerk—a Mussulman—discovered me and told two or three other Mussulmans. After he had bored me awhile he said he would go but would see me again after the train had gone. I made up my mind that he wouldn't if I could prevent it—but he did, about 5 o'clock and, with the assistance of a friend began to pump me. I endured it for a while and then shut him up by telling him that I had come to Wadi to get rid of people who bored me at Hyderabad and that it made me very nervous to talk. He took the hint and finally slid off. I then took a walk about the town; or, rather, up and down the R. R. tracks, feeling very blue. I regretted my hasty and stubborn action in leaving Hyderabad and looked forward to a night on a hard wooden bench with anything but pleasant anticipations. When I went to the refreshment room to get dinner at 6:15 I asked the Supt. [i.e., superintendent] if I could haul a bench in there and sleep. He said, no, but that the station master would probably allow me to sleep in a first-class coach if I asked him. I remembered my unpleasant experience with the station master when we changed cars at Wadi about 3 weeks ago on our way to Hyderabad and I didn't like the prospect. However as the Supt. wanted to take me to him I went and found the young man very affable. He quite promptly consented and ordered a yard-man to put a light in a first-class coach and show me to it. Compared to a hard bench it was luxurious. I gave the yard-man and his assistant one rupee each and the latter brought my traps from the refreshment room. By 7 I was as

comfortably fixed as anyone could have asked. Rolled up in my rug with my spring overcoat and gray undercoat for a pillow and turned in at 8.[40]

Arab arrived the next morning, bringing "an impertinent letter" from Ali, who, to Webb's liking, had chosen to stay another day in Hyderabad "to bark" at a public gathering that day, never able to "resist the chance to talk." Arab gave Webb "the gratifying intelligence that he desired to go on to Bombay and attend to some business and wanted to know if [Webb] objected to going on to Madras alone," to which Webb replied: "Not a bit of it." Webb and Arab spent "the greater part of the forenoon in settling" their plans, until their trains arrived.[41]

Webb arrived alone in Madras on December 10, and the Muslims of the city turned out to greet him as usual. Webb was no longer excited, and simply noted that "the usual crowd was at the station to receive me and the usual hand-shaking process was gone through with."[42] Almost immediately after arrival, Webb went to visit the Madras Theosophical Society and the society's cofounder Col. Henry Steel Olcott.[43] Webb became fond of Madras, describing it as "far ahead" of the other Indian cities he had seen, with wide, well-paved streets, "plenty of shade and good sea air."[44] Nevertheless, he complained of mosquitoes, a hard bed, and bad food, for which he faulted his hosting committee, whom he described as "old fossils" who "meant well" but did not know how to go about anything properly.[45] The crows of Rangoon had annoyed Webb immensely, but he found those of Madras just as audacious: "Crows very numerous here and very cunning—when floor cloths were laid out to air they tried to carry them away. These crows would steal a hot stove if they could carry it off."[46]

Webb did not have much time to himself in Madras. Ali arrived the next day: "Hassan Ali put in an appearance about 9, as greasy and complacent as ever. He's a good-natured idiot after all. I hardly think he means any harm—he's simply lazy and no good generally."[47] Webb insisted that his stay in Madras last no longer than three days, making it his shortest stay in the major Indian cities on his tour. On December 12, he set out alone for Agra. Arriving three days later, Webb found the city bracingly cool but gray and dusty. He enjoyed touring the city, taking in the remnants of its Mughal glory, and hired a Hindu guide who spoke English well and "seemed, at first, quite a treasure":

But as soon as he saw me taking notes he was seized with the idea that I intended to write a book, and with an intense longing to have his name appear in that book. When I assured him that his name would appear he became consumed by a desire to have me put down regularly and in his own language everything he told me. He turned out to be quite an ass.[48]

It is at this point that volume two of the diary ends in midsentence, and the record of Webb's journey breaks off. Arab and Ali presumably joined him again in Lahore, before he returned to Bombay and set off for home.[49]

Webb and His Inner Circle

In spite of the large crowds and their enthusiasm for Webb, some Indians were suspicious about the fundraising associated with his tour, and controversy over the integrity of Webb's mission erupted in the Indian press. Webb noted in Bombay that accusations had appeared alleging that he had come to India seeking personal gain: "Saw in 'Times of India' communication signed 'A Mohammedan' advising his brethren to keep their money for the poor of India rather than put it into the American Mission."[50] That morning, Webb chanced upon Arab busily preparing a response, which Kur intercepted surreptitiously:

> Hajee Abdulla, Mohammed and another man spent the greater part of the forenoon in constructing a letter to the Gazette to the effect that my visit to India was not for the purpose of collecting money. But it fell into the hands of Budruddin and did not get into the paper as it was calculated to deprive him of some of the glory of my discovery. He has a perfect mania for notoriety and an utter lack of honor and fairness.[51]

Before the day was over, Kur had tailored a response in his own name and had it printed in both the *Bombay Gazette* and the *Times of India*. The letters, which are reprinted in the Bombay and Lahore editions of Webb's Indian lectures, give the general background of his conversion and interest in an Islamic mission in America and argue that critics should "ascertain facts" first and understand that "the field [of charity] is, indeed, a boundless one."[52]

Although fundraising was the tour's explicit purpose from its inception, Arab, Kur, and Ali went to great length to deny that objective publicly.[53] Webb himself disowned it in an interview with the *Mohammedan Observer* in Calcutta. When asked about his intentions in Bombay, he replied: "Nothing. I am neither a missionary nor a theological Juggler. I have only come down here to make the acquaintance of my Mohammadan [sic] friends, and not to convert people."[54] Nonetheless, Webb met frequently with potential donors, although his diary accounts show that he found such presentations boring and took minimal interest in collecting or managing funds. He welcomed every opportunity to excuse himself from fund-related meetings, leaving the discussion for others. One night in Bombay after a large dinner in Webb's honor, Arab and Ali retired with guests to promote the American Mission, but Webb typically excused himself and made his way to the veranda, where he sat contentedly enjoying the moonlit evening.[55]

During the tour, Webb came to know Arab, Kur, and Ali well. His reverential attitude toward Arab continued unchanged, but he developed a distinct dislike for the other two, finding faults in them and other supporters as well. Since the defects that Webb was convinced he had found pertained to issues of personal integrity and competence, they were shortcomings which, if true, would likely endanger the mission further down the line. Oddly enough, Webb, despite his observations, rarely expressed anxiety in his diary that such failings, as exasperating as he found them to be, might ultimately impede the mission.

Perhaps Webb's shortsightedness regarding his patronage can be explained by his unshaken faith in Arab, who remained for Webb a saintlike figure. After seeing a local "Mohammedan saint" in Madras, Webb saw the reflection of Arab mirrored in the saint and referred to him as a man "of the Hajee Abdulla stamp," who must be "very good."[56] Arab—tall, handsome, and of good character—personified the ideals that Webb felt a true Muslim should epitomize. The fact that Arab stood behind the mission was undoubtedly one of the main reasons why Webb did not initially doubt its success. Even after financial trouble developed at the end of 1893 and Webb's detractors had, according to Webb, "poisoned" Arab's mind against him, Webb continued to think well of Arab's character, although he would not excuse him for the financial breakdown:

> He is the grandest, noblest specimen of manhood I have ever met, and a living illustration of the fact that it is possible for a man to be rich and active in business and yet be as pure in thought as a child, and as devout a worshipper of the one true God as it is possible to imagine.[57]

As for Kur, the positive impressions Webb had formed of him based on their earlier correspondence faded quickly after they met. As he approached Bombay, Webb anticipated their rendezvous eagerly, referring to Kur in letters and his diary as "my dear brother" and "Bro. Budruddin."[58] After a few days in Bombay, the brother prefix was dropped. In his published writing, Webb referred to Kur respectfully, alluding to his social status and accomplishments as "member of the Municipal Council of Bombay, India, and a scholar of rare attainments."[59] But Kur appeared to be everything distasteful to him, and Webb grew to dislike Kur intensely, concluding that he was "a great liar" and "as slippery and unreliable as an eel:" "Of all the gifted, prolific liars I have met in my life he is the high point."[60]

Initially, Webb interpreted Kur's hollow promises as a generically Indian trait, not a distinctive moral defect in Kur himself:

> Budruddin Kur promised to come yesterday morning to take me out but failed to do so and last night promised to come this morning before 10, *sure.* Of course I knew he wouldn't come—they rarely do—so

a little after 9, I went to the Post Office and mailed some letters and papers. Returned at 10:30 and found, as I expected, that Budruddin had not been here. These Indian people are a good deal like the Spaniards—prompt to promise but slow to fulfill.[61]

Kur's perceived ineptitude annoyed Webb immensely.[62] The poor turnout at Webb's Bombay lecture was ascribed to Kur's "usual stupidity": "As the affair was wholly managed by Budruddin it was, of course, botched."[63] As a result of Kur's inordinate laziness, unhappy scheduling, and penchant for bungling plans, Webb came to see his lengthy stay in Bombay as a colossal waste of time. Although Kur was a wealthy merchant, Webb began to see him as a self-serving miser.[64]

Webb's attitude toward Kur was generous, however, compared to his feelings for Hassan Ali, which eventually exposed one of the worst sides of Webb's personality, bringing out deeply imbedded racist sentiments that were otherwise imperceptible. In print, Webb called Ali "the famous Moulvi Hassan Ali Sahib, the Moslem missionary," "our esteemed brother Hassan Ali, the earnest and faithful Mohammedan missionary," and he confidently referred readers to an essay Ali had written on fasting.[65]

In his private thoughts, Webb had a very different opinion. Bitter daily exchanges took place almost from the beginning, and Webb found Ali to be lazy, scheming, and dishonest. Ali portrayed himself as Webb's mentor: "I tried to increase his knowledge, correct his wrong ideas, and instruct him in the necessary principles as far as I could."[66] But the two had not been together in Bombay for only a few days before falling out over the issue of mentorship. Webb read his draft of "The Faith of Islam" to Ali. Ali's criticisms were unacceptable to Webb and led to "an acrimonious argument," which left Webb "feeling very blue and ashamed the rest of the day."[67]

As the days went by, Webb's remorse turned into disgust: "Hassan Ali usually monopolizes the talk. Of all the lazy worthless fellows I have ever met I think he is one of the most incorrigible."[68] In Hyderabad, the arguments became steadily worse, finally driving Webb, in a fit of bad temper, to set out for Madras on his own. One evening, they returned home and fell into a dispute "about figures of animals on cloth—our mayordomo [Ali] had discerned that my Jap gown had a bird on it."[69] Webb's aversion to Ali now spewed forth the racist sentiments that Ali was a "black fraud" and "a 'slick nigger' ":

Arose at 4:25 and after bath went over to Hajee Abdulla's room to pray. Awoke Hassan Ali who promptly turned over and went to sleep again as usual. Finally insisted upon his getting up and catching the 7 o'clock train when he sleepily informed me that we were not going to Madras; that Shah Saheb had sent a note over at 11 o'clock last night saying that we must stay. I was hot in a minute and declared most positively that I would start by the 7 o'clock train no matter what happened. Hurried the boys off for a bullock-cart and to order the carriage hitched up, much to the dismay of Hajee Abdulla and Hassan Ali; the latter managed to get awake and alive when he saw that I was determined to go. It appeared that Shah Saheb wanted us to stay so that we could hear Mehdi Ali's lecture to-morrow and so that I could be properly "seen off" by a large crowd of hand-shakers at the station on Saturday morning. The absurdity and stupidity of the proposal fairly exasperated me. While we were eating break-fast a man came from Shah Saheb's telling us that he wanted us to stop there on our way to the station. I found that Hassan Ali was scheming to prevent my getting the train and had given orders to delay the bullock-cart. I finally got it started however. Hassan Ali saying that his trunks would go by another cart. He is a "slick nigger" and although lazy and shiftless to the last degree has head enough to keep from starving. He was teaching school in Calcutta at 100 rupees a month and gave up his post in order to serve God—great sacrifice! Last night he received about 300 rupees for 2½ weeks work as a missionary, and admitted that he was doing better now than when teaching school. He is a black fraud. When we arrived at Shah Saheb's instead of being ready to receive us we had to wait 20 minutes for him. In the meantime Hassan Ali sneaked outside so as to avoid acting as interpreter. When Shah Saheb finally appeared he sent for Hassan Ali and a lively argument ensued. I reiterated my determination to start for Madras and was then told that my trunk had been sent back to the Club by Shah Saheb. Then I was fully determined to go in spite of everything as I saw that all except Hajee Abdulla had been scheming to keep me. I hastily, and as politely as I could under the circumstances, said good-bye to Shah Saheb and ran out to the carriage. Hajee Abdulla accompanied me to the station and saw me into a 1st class car—or alleged 1st class. The Nizam's State Railway is a caution. While we were waiting for the train to start up came Hassan Ali and Shah Saheb, and the latter renewed his request for me to stay; or rather, entered a strong protest against my going. The train started while he was talking and, much to my relief I was soon away from Hassan Ali and Hyderabad. In the car with me was the little Secretary of the Nizam Club. He was as calm and lady-like as usual. He accompanied me to Vikarabad, a small station, about two hours' ride from Hyderabad.[70]

"Nigger" occurs twice in Webb's diary, first in the quotation above and second in reference to a few working-class Hindus who Webb believed had stolen one of his oranges.[71] As evidenced in E. M. Forster's *Passage to India*, the British commonly applied "nigger" to Indian "natives" during the colonial period. Like other white Americans, Webb had been exposed to the word since childhood. At that time and for decades afterward, most white children were introduced to the word by parents and teachers. It was customary for white adults to shame children from certain types of conduct by scolding them for behaving "worse than niggers," deserving "no more credit than niggers," or being "as ignorant as niggers."[72] The word "seeped into practically every aspect of American culture, from literature to political debates, from cartoons to song."[73] Whites used the word daily with hardly a thought, just as they taught it to their children in nursery rhymes. Only during the Civil Rights movement of the mid-twentieth century did the word come to be seen as unacceptable.[74] Jenkin Lloyd Jones, probably the most liberal and progressive voice at the World's Parliament of Religions, remarked after hearing two eloquent addresses by an African American bishop and an African representative of Christian missions: "It will be harder than ever to spell negro with two 'g's.'"[75]

Although repugnant, it is not surprising to find this prejudice in Webb. In his time, racism was often stronger in the North than the South. He clearly believed in racial differences and ascribed to "Anglo-Saxon" superiority.[76] Islam, in Webb's view, was "the most perfect system of spiritual development the world has ever known," but he did not hesitate to attribute Muslim backwardness to "climate and racial influence."[77]

As a public persona, however, Webb prided himself on being progressive and liberal and would surely have taken offense at being called a racist. He espoused the principles of Theosophy, which called for "the formation of a universal brotherhood without distinction of race, creed, sex, caste or color."[78] He believed that Islam in America would "ultimately work a revolution in our social system," elevating it "to the position where it belongs."[79] One of the "commendable features" of Islam, in his view, was that all Muslims stood "upon a perfect equality before God"; the only differences among them were such as naturally arose "from personal and moral cleanliness." He proudly cited the verses of the Persian poet Sa'di:[80]

> All Adam's race are members of one frame,
> Since all, at first, from the same essence came;
> When by hard fortune one limb is oppressed,
> The other members lose their wanted rest.
> If thou feel'st not for others' misery,
> A son of Adam is no name for thee.
> Yea, "to love God we must his creatures love."[81]

Webb also decried the popular bigotry that persecuted interracial marriage in America:

In Glendive, Montana, recently a mob of 200 people went to the house where John Orr, white, and Emma Wall, colored, who had been married by Justice Kay during the afternoon, were stopping, took them out, rode them on a rail, and treated Orr to a coat of tar and the woman to a coat of alabastine [*sic*, probably alabastrine]. Then they showered them with rotten eggs, and gave them twenty-four hours in which to leave town. Other houses were visited and the inmates were similarly treated. We have heard a great deal about the "brother-hood of man" as the crowning glory of Church-Christianity, in con-nection with a great strutting and bragging about "The Land of the Free and the Home of the Brave." We must conclude, therefore, that Church-Christianity hasn't reached Montana yet, and that the "Bird of Freedom" has been so busy that he hasn't had time to go out there and shriek.[82]

He derided an Episcopalian rector in South Carolina who had "labor[ed] to prove that negroes, Mongolians, and Indians [did] not belong to the Adamic races" and denounced a racist incident in Louisiana, alleging that it would be unthinkable in a Muslim society:[83]

Down in Louisiana last month some of the white people took a poor negro, who was suspected of murder, and roasted his feet over a blazing fire. When this had been going on a short time it was found that he was not the guilty man, but the roasting continued for the purpose of forcing him to tell who committed the deed. His feet were burned to a crisp and then he was released. Such a crime would be impossible in a Mussulman community, but if it were possible, it would be attributed to the influence of Islam.[84]

However strained his relationship to Hassan Ali became during the In-dian tour, Webb would later speak of him generously in his American jour-nals and publications. In 1895, two years after the Indian tour, Ali died unexpectedly at the age of thirty-nine. Webb reported Ali's untimely death with regret, describing him as descending "from a good and ancient stock" and "ever scrupulously studious to utilize his abilities for the good of the sovereign and of his community."[85]

Hobnobbing

Clearly, Webb was hardly the "plain American citizen" he thought he would be after resigning his consulship; given his former consular status, he remained a person of note and was welcomed by many important people during his tour. Wherever an American consulate was to be found, Webb made a point of paying a visit almost immediately after arrival to check his mail.[86] He visited three consulates in all, those in Singapore, Calcutta, and Bombay. The consul in Singapore took a liking to Webb, hosting him to banquets and other engagements, including a ceremonial dinner in honor of the Sultans of Penang and Jahore.[87] That evening, the consul introduced Webb to an English major general, Sir Charles Warren, who commanded the infantry force at Singapore and had served with distinction in Africa and elsewhere in the East.[88]

In Calcutta, Webb "had a pleasant chat" with the American consul general, finding him "rather stiff at first," although the consul "soon melted" and apparently found humor in Webb's facetious allusion to "American polygamy."[89] Webb described the encounter to the *Mohammedan Observer*:

> I was speaking to the American Consul General in Calcutta, and he
> was horrified that I had turned Mohammadan [*sic*]. He asked me
> whether I believed in Mohammad as well as I believed in Jesus Christ;
> and I said that I most positively did so. Well, he then said that Jesus
> had not half a dozen or more wives; and I said that Mohammad had
> not either. People have to be educated to polygamy. It is not obliga-
> tory at all. It is from childhood that one must be taught the advan-
> tages or otherwise of polygamy. In America there are 90 per cent of
> polygamists.[90]

Webb had a "long chat" with the American consul in Bombay, who attended his lecture in the city.[91] Four days afterward, Webb returned for another "general chat with the Consul"[92] and deposited three trunks at the consulate for retrieval on his return before sailing home from Bombay.[93]

Webb met with consuls and vice consuls from the Ottoman Empire and Persia, in some cases under the auspices of Hajee Arab, who seems to have had good connections with the Ottomans in particular.[94] Webb dined with the Persian consul and his staff at Poona and had repeated contacts with the Ottomans in Bombay and Madras.[95] Webb's first encounter with the Ottoman consul and vice consul of Bombay was at a seaside dinner at Webb's guest residence.[96] Three days later, Webb called upon the consul at his office, where they had tea and prayed the afternoon prayer.[97] Webb developed markedly cordial relations with the Ottoman consul in Madras. After Webb's official lecture in the city, the consul took him for a carriage ride in his "elegant turnout [coach with attendants]" along the seashore on "a fine drive and promenade."[98]

The consul subsequently took Webb to "the new asylum [shelter] of Mohammedan Converts," and Webb presided over the opening ceremony and spoke briefly. Afterward, there was "a most excellent breakfast" at the Turkish consul's residence in a large company of guests. Webb, the consul, and three Englishmen ate in "a nice breezy room in the top story of the house." After breakfast, "a Hindu photographer" took a group shot with Webb in the center.[99] As Webb departed later that day, the Ottoman consul rode with him on the train briefly to the next station, where he said his good-byes and left Webb to proceed on to Agra by himself.[100]

Throughout the tour, Webb met with a number of Muslim scholars and dignitaries, including Khoda Baksh and Cheragh Ali.[101] Khoda Baksh and several associates received Webb a few miles outside Patna and took him to the former's famous "Oriental Library of 3000 volumes in Arabic and Sanscrit [sic] and a quite large English collection."[102] Webb had several meetings with Cheragh Ali in Hyderabad.[103] Cheragh Ali took an interest in Webb, and they had several "general" chats. Ali also presented Webb with a personal copy of his work, "Exposition of the Jihad," from which Webb published lengthy excerpts in the *Moslem World*.[104]

In addition to consuls and religious persons of note, Webb met various and sundry Muslim nawabs, that is, the descendants of former imperial landholders, who seemed to turn up at every occasion. Though he found some of them noteworthy, Webb gave most of them little notice except to disparage their lack of taste or criticize the degree to which they had been "Anglicized" and dispossessed of their proud heritage. In his diary, Webb often referred to Westernized nawabs as "monkeys." Although the image brings to mind Darwinian presumptions of the inferiority of non-whites and Webb's own racial prejudices as indicated earlier, it probably did not carry such overtones with regard to the nawabs in Webb's diary. Instead, it expressed his extreme distaste at how the nawabs "aped" the West, imitating its conventions blindly and at the expense of their own (to his mind superior) culture and history:

> Found the Nawab to be a monkey dressed up uncomfortably in European clothes and most disgustingly Anglicized. The poor fellow suffered torments in his uncomfortable dress and the perspiration poured off his chubby face in streams. A more consummate ass it has not been my misfortune to meet in the East. A young man of good family, liberally educated and possessed of ample means, a fawning lickspittle to the English who despise his whole race and use him only for their own pleasure—a deserter from his ancestral religion and social customs and a pitiable object generally. A briefless barrister who takes pride in showing that he has adopted British weaknesses. His cousin the Nawab of Junjera dressed in a bright canary-colored silk coat and white pants and decorated with diamonds was presented to me. He was a tall young man with a countenance that could not be accused of over-intelligence—one of those decendants [sic] of ancient Indian royalty who have little left of the old nobility and who are gradually dying out and being crowded out of their property by the English.... Why in the world can't these people have some manhood and independence, and cultivate a true manhood, instead of following the brutalizing habits and customs of their conquerors?[105]

Webb admired the ancestral traditions of the East, and his aversion to "Anglicized" Indians sprang in part from his sense that they had no sense of the value of their historical legacy. Throughout the tour, Webb was fascinated to see and learn about all the religious traditions that he encountered—Muslim, Chinese, Hindu, and Buddhist, folk and formal—and insisted that his hosts let him observe them. Although Webb's hosts were willing to take him to Muslim holy men, they generally showed little understanding of his interest in non-Muslims. Webb visited the tombs of Muslim saints and was taken frequently to sit in the circles of Sufis. The Muslim holy men often blessed him and occasionally foretold an illustrious future for his mission:

> We had not long to wait when the saint came out and many of his disciples who had gathered at this time greeted him cordially and kissed his hand. He is said to be 115 years old. He is certainly 80, and perhaps he is as old as his fellows believe him to be. He is a fine looking old man with grey beard, clear eye [sic] and clean face and hands, although he is emaciated and his skin lies in folds on his hands. He also seems to be short of teeth. By the time we were well seated around him fully 50 persons had come in, many of whom were very hysterical. Hassan Ali talked with him and he showed that he knew at least the ethical principles of Islam. His followers seemed to worship him and hung eagerly upon his words, some of the [sic; i.e., them] occasionally breaking out into shouts and violent contortions. After an interview of about half an hour we started to go and our friend asked the old man when he could give me a séance. The latter thought it would be better to have it at once and when he made known his decision the more hysterical ones howled with delight. We then adjourned to the larger meeting place in the neat yard where a scene was enacted something like that in a large spiritualistic séance in America. The old man threw his mantle over his head and dropped into a meditative mood after telling me to close my eyes and think of him. I kept my wits and think I discovered the secret of his longevity. After vainly trying to bring me under the influence he drew aside his mantle and indicated that the séance was at an end. While it was in progress several of the followers, screamed and went into convulsions showing all the evidences of the work of elementals. The old man expressed a desire to see me once more and in Arab costume, but I hardly think he will. Some of his followers are hopelessly mediumistic.[106]

Webb was also taken to a "dervish" outside Hyderabad in "a beautiful place [that] afforded us an extended view of the surrounding landscape—valleys and hills, and rocks and in the far distance a hill with what looked like a castle on its extreme summit":

> In a little room or cell at the left of the picturesque little white mosque we found the dervish, an emaciated little man apparently

about 60 years old crouched upon a bench and wrapped in a cloak of coarse yellowish stuff. His marked cleanliness, both of person and clothing as well as of his cell struck me at once; he was very different in this respect from the Hindu yogis. His hands and face and beard were noticeably clean and well kept and his eyes were clear and intelligent. It is said that he was formerly one of the judges of one of the local courts and was the disciple of a dervish who lives where he lives now. He was so abstemious and economical in his habits that he was considered a miser. About 12 years ago his teacher died and he went to the funeral and never returned. He left wife and children, property, everything and gave himself up to contemplation in the cell of his master. He said that I was born for the work before me and that it would result in great success. He prayed with us and for us and gave Hassan Ali some good advice which probably went in at one ear and out at the other. We drove directly home and I put in the rest of the day in reading.[107]

In Bombay, Webb was taken to "a Moslem mystic" who had become "sensitive, clairvoyant and intuitional":

He predicted full success for the American Mission and said that he saw large numbers of Mussulmans in North America—also saw [the Prophet] Mohammed on my right hand and [his Companion] Omar on my left. His place was up four flights of dark stairs in a bad smelling, smoky tenement. Rather repellant surroundings. A very good man, apparently.[108]

In Madras, a "Mohammedan fakir" (mendicant wonder-worker) forced himself upon Webb's hosts, insisting that he had to see Webb:

While we were waiting up came a Mohammedan fakir and in spite of the efforts of the porter he stripped himself to the waist and began to drive an exaggerated ice-pick into the top of his skull. He had two of these picks, the heavy ends of which were adorned with iron chains. The iron points were about 6 inches long and tapered from ¼ of an inch in diameter down to a sharp point. He placed the point apparently at the juncture of the sutures of the occipital and frontal bones of the skull, and with the heavy end of the other "pick" drove it in until it stood up firmly without his touching it. It seemed to go in an inch.[109]

Webb insisted on inspecting the man very carefully afterward and was surprised to find no evidence of injury.

On at least two occasions, Webb received delegations from the Indian Shi'a community. First, in Calcutta, a group of them "presented their respects." Then, in Bombay, Webb received a second visit from a party of Shi'a and was again favorably impressed: "Received a call from 4 Shi'a—neat turbans—very glad to see me and spoke most encouraging and congratulating words."[110] The first visit in Calcutta coincided with an unpleasant meeting with some Sunni "fanatics." Webb called it the "first case of unreasoning fanaticism" that he encountered in India, and he contrasted the irritable Sunnis with the markedly respectful party of Shi'a.[111]

Webb abhorred fanatics of all faiths, regarding them to be "regrettably benighted." Muslim fanaticism, for Webb, was emblematic of the social "degeneration" of the Muslim community. When he received a letter from a Muslim asking him which sect he belonged to, Webb commented: "The fanatics here commenced to manifest themselves—as usual, we have been here too long. Oh, how wretched and degraded they have become. If Our Prophet could see them now in the flesh, how he would excoriate them."[112] In Hyderabad, "two fanatical Mussulmans" accosted Webb in the bazaar, one insisting that he not wear Western clothing, which made him look like a "kafir" [disbeliever], and the other insisting that Webb's improper "genuflexions at prayer" had "offended the whole Mohammedan population of Hyderabad," Webb responded: "Poor, benighted creatures! They have no more idea of the true spirit of Islam than the cows or horses. Ignorance and superstition have done a fearful work all over India."[113]

Webb was eager to meet all "holy men," Muslim or otherwise, and expressed repeatedly his desire to discover "accomplished yogis" and was shown "three healthy looking yogis" in Calcutta:

> We asked to be taken to an advanced yogi who could do wonders, and were taken down the bank of the river about 50 feet further where found [sic] tall, black, naked yogi with beard twisted into ropes and hair matted. Whole body, face, head to foot covered with dust. Squatted on a mat feeding fire. He wouldn't talk. One bystander who spoke English said he could do wonders and had great powers but wouldn't exercise them because that was God's work. He looked to me like a hopeless lunatic. He too smoked ganja [intoxicating hemp], and was not averse to accepting coppers. Urged wonders, but bystanders said that all the yogis who did these were in Benares or in the jungles—never in city—hid themselves.[114]

Webb continued his fruitless search for "advanced yogis" in Benares but was again told they had gone to the jungles. He wrote his reaction succinctly: "Failure."[115]

In the Public Light

With his first public exposure in Rangoon, Webb, apparently without having prior knowledge or giving his permission, was adorned with a Muslim name.

In Hyderabad, the phenomenon repeated itself, again without his prior knowledge, and he was given a different Muslim name. The first naming came on September 30, 1892, just before he was to deliver an address before about two thousand Muslims at Rangoon's principal mosque after the Friday prayers: "But first [before speaking] I was formally given my Mohammedan name 'Alexander Russell Abdulla Webb,'" to be written 'A. R. Abdulla Webb.'"[116] After the entry, no further mention of the name appears in the diary or any other available source, but he never seems to have taken the name.

The second, more successful appellation came on November 28, 1892, at a banquet in Hyderabad where Webb was the guest of honor. He entered the room to find his new name "Mohammed" spelled out on the table in flower petals and ornamental leaves:

> When we came home we found three or four persons waiting who had come to dine with us, one of the prominent brethren, an ex-judge, who subsequently appeared at the table with his head bundled up in shawls, having made a dinner in my honor. The table was very handsomely set, my name "Mohammed Alexander Russell Webb" being traced out on each side in flower leaves and petals.[117]

The New York Times claimed that Webb was given his Islamic name "Mohammed" in Bombay at the close of his Indian tour just prior to setting sail for home: "Several thousand influential Mussulmans" of the city conferred it upon him during a special reception held in his honor.[118] Most likely, Webb's newly adopted name, "Mohammed," which had not been used during his first visit to the city halfway through the tour, was announced publicly with considerable fanfare during his parting visit. It is also related that Hassan Ali gave Webb the name "Mohammed" along with the honorific "shaykh" [lit.: "elder" or "religious leader"]. Ali is reported to have said: "His name, Sheikh Mohammed, was also given by me."[119] Since Ali was part of the Hyderabad entourage and had a proclivity, often to Webb's chagrin, for directing things behind the scenes, it is likely that he had a hand in designating Webb's name.

The tour kept Webb in the public eye at almost all times. In addition to delivering formal public lectures, he gave private and impromptu presentations at mosques, various societies, children's schools, and private homes. The crowds that gathered on such occasions were often much larger than those attending his formal lectures. Webb recorded several noteworthy episodes. Once at a private home in Bombay, after a superb dinner on the shores of the Indian Ocean, the host invited him to speak to a group of Muslim women whom Webb could not see because they were sequestered in the dark. Although Webb had, up to that point, proven himself to be a good speaker, he became self-conscious and awkward when speaking to the silent female audience hidden in the dark:

FIGURE 6.2. Webb in India (1892) with His Signature Below

On either side of the drawing room was a large room with double doors. Screens were placed in front or in the doorways, and in these rooms, which were dark, were assembled a number of Mohammedan ladies who had come to hear me speak. I addressed them upon the social systems of Europe and America as compared with that of Mohammedan countries but as I could not see my audience I was somewhat embarrassed and did not make a good speech. The host and the other Mohammedans, however, seemed to be very well pleased.[120]

On other occasions, Webb demonstrated impressive oratorical gifts. After a speech by Webb at the famous "Mecca Mosque" in Hyderabad, "one Mussulman became so enthusiastic that he announced the willingness of himself and his brethren to lay down their lives for me if I wanted them to."[121]

Webb delivered at least five "official" lectures: in Rangoon, Calcutta, Bombay, Hyderabad, Madras and possibly a sixth in Lahore. He spent long hours—often the greater part of his day—writing and rewriting them and rehearsing his delivery.[122] Not having had prior experience in lecturing, Webb's speeches and lectures during the Oriental tour served as an indispensable trial run for the lectures he would deliver the following year in Chicago at the World's Parliament of Religions. His poise at the parliament was, to a great extent, the fruit of his Indian experience, and Webb drew heavily from his Oriental addresses for the content of his parliament speeches.

Webb spoke on several occasions in Rangoon. His first formal lecture, titled "The Faith of Islam," was delivered there on October 6, 1892. The local English-language press failed to report it, which Webb attributed to a staff shortage and inefficiency: "No local news; Gazette and Times probably run by two boys and a man."[123] Webb called it his "first lecture" and gave himself good marks: "By God's help it was a success so far as I was concerned and I was surprised at myself. As a lecturer, I'll do."[124]

On his first Friday in Calcutta, Webb addressed an animated gathering of about five thousand Muslims at the city's principal mosque, introducing his proposed Islamic mission to America in a speech translated by a "prominent Mohammedan lawyer."[125] The size and enthusiasm of this first "unofficial" presentation in India alerted British authorities, leading to the cancellation of Webb's official address at the Madrassah Hall scheduled to be delivered that evening. The Indian headmaster had "changed his mind" at the last minute and sent word to him, explaining, in Webb's words, that "as I was an American and might have something about politics in my address, it would not do to allow me to speak in the college hall." Webb did not take the headmaster at face value:

> I suspect that the *real* reason was that missionary influence was
> brought to bear on him. The missionary and the Britisher are all-
> powerful here and there seems to be a general disposition among the
> natives to cringe to [sic] them. A smaller hall, and one not altogether
> comfortable, was secured and my lecture was received with much
> enthusiasm. The usual note of thanks was passed and I was assured
> that I had greatly entertained the gathering.[126]

Webb could be stubborn when irritated. He did not take the cancellation at Madrassah Hall lightly. He was still perturbed over the matter a few days later when a group of prominent Calcutta Muslims approached him and persisted in asking him to deliver another speech at the town hall. Webb had decided to give no more lectures in Calcutta and refused to listen. He wrote in his diary: "[The committee] urged and insisted but I held out. Irish brogue."[127]

Webb presented his Bombay lecture, "Islam," at the Framjee Cowasjee Hall. The Indian editions of his lecture described the gathering as "a very large and influential number of persons of all communities" and estimated attendance at around five hundred.[128] Webb believed that no more than four hundred came and laid the blame for the less-than-capacity turnout at Kur's feet:

> The hall should have been full of people and would have been if he had made it an open lecture free to all; but he advertised it as for Mohammedans only and very few more than those who could speak English came. I was freely congratulated upon my lecture and its delivery.[129]

Two weeks later, Webb presented "Philosophical Islam" at Hyderabad in a large open pavilion in the Public Garden.[130] He estimated attendance at two thousand, although the *Three Lectures* and *New York Times* put the number at three thousand.[131] Webb noted that "the audience seemed to be very well pleased" and that the speech was followed by "the usual hand-shaking ordeal."[132] When Webb rose to speak, there were enthusiastic cheers, and he was frequently interrupted by applause.[133]

Webb delivered a speech called "The Better Way" in Madras on December 11 at the Aziz Bagh House.[134] To his exasperation, the speech began an hour late and was the most poorly attended of the Oriental presentations; the crowd, in Webb's estimation, did not exceed two hundred and fifty.[135] The low turnout was probably ascribable in part to the fact that the original date had been moved up to accommodate Webb's abrupt decision to shorten his visit to Madras to three days. Colonel Olcott shared the stage with Webb in Madras and made a brief presentation. Immediately after Webb's lecture, Olcott leaned over and confided in Webb that he was "a devilish good speaker."[136] On his final day in Madras, Webb recorded tongue-in-cheek that he had presided with "customary grace and dignity" over a gathering at the asylum for Mohammedan converts that had recently opened in the city. It was a good turnout, about two thousand, and Webb had to run "the gauntlet of hand-shaking."[137]

American Family Man Abroad

Throughout the Oriental tour, homesickness and culture shock were Webb's constant companions. Family affections stirred the greater part of his longings for home. Webb often thought of his "loved ones," received their letters with joy, and spent hours writing them back.[138] He noted in Rangoon: "I miss my loved ones more and more every day, it seems. I can hardly become reconciled to this separation. God grant that they may be kept alive and well until I return to them. They are my life and soul or part of me."[139] Noting that he had been "more or less ill" since Ella's departure, he confessed to himself: "My wife's presence is necessary to me. I am certainly very lonely without her."[140]

Small children reminded Webb of his own and increased his sadness and anxiety. When three "rather pretty children" boarded the *Patria* with their father and ailing mother, Webb remarked: "One was a dear little baby about 18 months old. I got hold of it of course and longed for my babies. Homesick again."[141] On the same voyage, he began reading *The History of David Greene* by the noted Victorian authoress (Mary) Humphrey Ward. Its opening in colloquial American English made Webb nostalgic, and he wrote in his diary:

> I longed for my precious babies and went to be feeling quite miserable. I wonder if anyone grows happier as he grows older. There is certainly very little real happiness in this life. I look forward to meeting my babies and feel that I will be happy with them. But they will grow to manhood and womanhood and I will grow old and troublesome and perhaps will know that they will wish me dead and out of the way. Oh, well, God's will be done.[142]

On the steamer to Calcutta, Webb wrote: "Crying Indian baby on board—deck—cries the most melancholy—sends cold chill all over me and makes me think of funerals."[143] He would dream of his children and occasionally have nightmares about them:

> I had a strange and impressive dream last night. I dreamed that the Nannie and Nala went away from the home to play and remained so long that we were alarmed. Presently Nannie returned alone and said that they had been playing on the bank of a pond, that Nala had fallen in and had disappeared. The poor little thing was very much frightened and I was almost wild with grief. My repression of grief awakened me and I was glad to find that it was only a dream. God grant that nothing serious has happened to my precious darlings.[144]

Webb's wife and adopted daughter, Elizabeth, wrote to Webb of Elizabeth's recent marriage. For reasons not known, Webb did not approve of the marriage and commented in his diary, "Poor child, I'm afraid she has made a mess of it."[145]

Webb's travels led him to reminisce on America as well. He liked to refer to his native English as "American" and filled his diary with memories of home. An excellent breakfast on an Indian train reminded him of meals in the States:

> At Arkonam [en route to Madras] at 5:30 [A.M.] had a very good cup of tea, ½ doz oranges and the first fresh grapes—except the Malagas— I have seen since I left America. Very good and very cheap. Also had buttered toast and some crackers—a very good breakfast."[146]

A "beautiful cool morning" in Bombay reminded him of "a late September morning in Missouri."[147] The Calcutta Zoo seemed to be "the most complete and best arranged I have seen outside of America," and its "beautifully laid out" grounds reminded him "very much of the St. Louis Zoological

Garden."[148] Steaming across the Bay of Bengal brought back memories of the Hudson: "Another beautiful day with just a slight ripple on the sea— Wonderful weather for the Bay of Bengal—the voyage as quiet and enjoyable as a sail up the Hudson."[149] The muddy Irrawaddy and Hooghly Rivers reminded Webb of "our Mississippi, clay color and mud," while the "stern-wheel steamers with 2 smoke-stacks forward [looked] like Old Mississippi boats."[150]

Native drums in the Orient brought Native American "tom-toms" to Webb's mind, and when a "very buxom and pretty Hindu girl loaded with jewelry and flashily dressed" danced before Webb at the behest of one of the Muslim nawabs, Webb noted in his diary that she wore a "head dress of roses made like [a] Davy Crockett trapper's cap."[151] The elegant mansion of another nawab reminded Webb of "the White House at Washington" with the qual- ification that the nawab's "refined and elegant side of Mohammedan life" and excellent balance between Oriental and Western styles created a combination more elegant than one would likely find in the White House.[152]

Webb's American tastes often dictated what he liked or disliked about India. An Indian home where "everything [was] so fine and delicate . . . and in good taste" made him happy and brought back memories of home.[153] A prosperous Muslim businessman of Poona inspired Webb's admiration as a "shining example of the self-made man."[154] When he met "an Indian Mo- hammedan" in Calcutta who had lived in the United States five years as a merchant, Webb observed: "Said he was well pleased with the country. I can't imagine why he returned [to India]."[155]

Webb was proud of his ability to "lie like an American," which enabled him easily to "out lie" any Indian or Englishman who tried to pull the wool over his eyes.[156] One evening, he, Kur, and a wealthy young Muslim from Zanzibar went out for a ride:

> This young man is a greater liar than Budruddin—a more artis-
> tic, picturesque liar. He told of a shark killed off Zanzibar that had 36
> human skeletons in his stomach. Budruddin blushed and seemed
> to feel that it was hopeless to try to beat that. Then the other pre-
> varicator rounded up by telling of a fish he saw in the Arabian Sea.
> 80 feet long. I told about a shark killed off Coney Island that had the
> skeletons of 47 horses and 35 full sets of harness in his belly. This
> weaned the Zanzibar man and he became interested in passing ob-
> jects. When an Indian or an Englishman tries to out lie an American
> he has a large job.[157]

Despite all the humor he could muster and his abiding interest in Eastern traditions, the fatigue and cultural shock that Webb experienced during his Oriental tour were often unbearable and continually threatened to mar his relationships with those around him.

Culture Shock

After returning to the States, Webb looked back on his Oriental tour with appreciative eyes, assured that he would never forget the "beautiful days" he had spent among the Muslims of the East, where he believed he had encountered a superior civilization unparalleled in art and architecture. He claimed that his days in India had solidified his faith and left him with a favorable impression of the Orient and its people.[158] During the tour itself, however, Webb often suffered from fatigue and cultural shock. Expressions of disappointment and frustration predominated in his diary. Once, he resolved to be more cheerful: "But I'll stop complaining. It is such a beautiful day that I should be thankful to God for the many blessings we have rather than complain of the little discomforts."[159] But his resolution lasted only momentarily, and Webb soon resumed his refrain of grumbles. People, especially Muslims, were his biggest complaint: "I have seen some very queer specimens since I came to India."[160] He often felt as if he were on exhibition and had become "a martyr to the cause" of his Islamic mission, which forced him to "be seen and inspected by every cranky nuisance that comes along."[161]

Webb had predictable problems with climate, diet, and related things. He tired of his hosts' preference for meat and stood one day at a bazaar, eyeing "a fine display of luscious looking fruits and vegetables" and noting glumly that "our brethren do not seem to use them:"

> My mouth watered as I saw the delicious artis[162] and the guava—
> the finest I ever saw—the yams and sweet potatoes and cucumbers and crisp lettuce. My table has been supplied only with *meat.*
> *meat. meat.* Seasoned beyond my taste and heavy with grease. Oh, for
> a good fruit and vegetable dinner for a change."[163]

At times, Webb found the rain and humidity unbearable, although it could not have been much different from the weather he experienced in the Philippines:

> Rain, rain and still more rain. The air is full of moisture and everything about the house is damp and sticky. This must be a fine house
> in dry weather, but, shut in as it is by the trees the sun has very
> little chance to get to it and it is very damp in the rainy season.[164]

On the other hand, once the rainy season had abated, Webb was pleasantly surprised by Poona's cooler weather in the Western Ghat Mountains:

> After prayers, Hajee Abdulla, Hassan Ali and myself went out for a
> walk. The air was cold and bracing—the first really cold weather I

have felt since I left the States 5 years ago. I got out a pair of woolen pants and a Prince Albert coat which I buttoned up tight. Felt like a new man—the bracing air invigorated me and seemed to give me new life. I walked at a very brisk gait and did not perspire at all.[165]

Inefficiency frustrated Webb continually: "Went to Post Office which is the worst I ever saw anywhere. If one of our frontier offices was managed in that way the post-master would be lynched."[166] He found waste of time as intolerable as it was ubiquitous: "We have been here two weeks and are just about where we were when we arrived. I never saw such a slow, lifeless community."[167] He complained how, in an Indian context, the word "soon" might "mean two days or two months. The delay is simply exasperating and I would terminate it at once but for Hajee Abdulla."[168] Webb also bemoaned his inability to get clear answers about what seemed to him the simplest things:

> While sitting at desk note arrives written in Urdu—all glance at it and remark: "Invitation." I give it to the interpreter and after divining it carefully he lays it down with the remark: "Invitation." "Invitation to what?" I ask after waiting in vain for him to speak. "Oh, invitation to some priestly festival." "But where and when?" "At his house, Thursday." "Whose house and what hour." "Why the man's house who made the invitation. He don't say what hour." And that was all I could get out of him.[169]

The only languages Webb knew were English and Spanish. Knowing no Oriental language other than a few words of Urdu, the language gap in India was one of Webb's greatest sources of exasperation and explains in part his dislike of mission-related meetings, in which the Urdu of his hosts tended to predominate. He was always delighted in discovering someone who could speak English well.[170] The Hindu guide in Agra, who spoke "very good English," seemed "quite a treasure." In Hyderabad, Webb encountered an annoyingly eccentric Muslim whom Webb dubbed "the Bible prophecy crank." From the start, their meeting was frustrated by lack of a common language: "He couldn't speak English so we didn't get on together."[171] Upon meeting an impressive "Mohammedan saint," Webb remarked, "As he could not speak English the interview was not very interesting."[172]

Translators were just as frustrating, either because they did not understand Webb or he did not trust them. After discerning the gravity of the language problem, the "Bible prophecy crank" "remedied his language deficiency" by bringing his own translator to future meetings, but Webb found the translator equally exasperating: "Tried several times to get his opinion of [a] verse but the little Dr [i.e., the translator] steered him off onto something else until I became exasperated and tried the other interpreter with no better result. Specimen of interpreting!"[173]

Although Webb's hosts were hospitable in the lodgings and food they provided, Webb was frustrated by their lack of curiosity in the peoples and customs around them and the furtive methods they often employed to keep him from having access to other traditions. Witnessing a Buddhist procession in Rangoon, he asked his hosts to explain its significance to him but learned that his "Mussulman friends seem[ed] to know nothing of the matter and they [did] not seem inclined to allow me to visit the Buddhist temples."[174] He complained that they could not comprehend his desire to learn about the world around him: "These people seem to think that what is ordinary and commonplace to them must be so to everyone else."[175] He also complained of his hosts' pedestrian tastes. In Rangoon, one of them seemed more concerned with visiting cooking oil mills than Buddhist temples.[176] At times, Webb felt his hosts were conspiring against him:

> Why can't the people show me something that I want to see; they will persist in dragging me about to places that I don't care a rap for and carefully avoid the very things I want to see. On this occasion they dragged me off to see an old pontoon bridge that hadn't the slightest interest to me and could only be seen partially in the dark.[177]

Webb's sense of alienation was intensified by Muslims who held him in suspicion. He soon learned that fellow Western converts to Islam generally had difficulty winning the trust of the indigenous Muslim community. In Calcutta, he visited the European convert, "Bro. Serajjuddin Ahmed," who translated for Hajee Arab in Manila. Webb regarded him to be "a good man," but he noted that "the Moslems here do not like him and tell rather hard stories about him. But I find considerable feeling against the European converts who happen to be here."[178]

The British held Webb to be equally suspect and kept him under surveillance. Webb complained that he could not take a meal without someone from British Intelligence being present.[179] At one nawab's home, he noted that there were twenty guests around a single table, "including the inevitable English spy."[180] Wherever Webb spoke, British agents were present and took careful note of what he said. In some cases, Muslim civil servants who dared attend his public lectures were fired from their posts.[181] At his lecture in Hyderabad, Webb observed: "A company of native soldiers had been sent to preserve the peace, a rumor of a contemplated revolt of the Mohammedans having been put in circulation. They were drawn up in line on one side of the tent and a number of native policemen did guard duty."[182] Speeches were sometimes cancelled or postponed because the "Britishers wouldn't like it." Once, Webb learned indirectly that the chief of police was of the opinion that his speeches "had aroused Mohammedans and that they threatened to kill all the English."[183]

Webb found it necessary to abide by the constraints that the British imposed upon him, because refusal to do so would have exposed him to greater "insult and abuse." Nevertheless, in private, he objected to the colonial status quo and expressed his conviction that Indians could liberate themselves from the British if they acted together.[184]

Early to Bed, Early to Rise

Webb followed an orderly daily routine throughout his Oriental tour and presumably kept a similar routine at home. He arose at dawn, washed, prayed, and went out for an early-morning walk. He preferred to nap during the late morning or afternoon and retired as early after dark as conditions permitted, typically washing again before retiring. During the trip, he sometimes found himself less than energetic and began to feel the passing years, awaking one morning toward the tour's end and "feeling rather old."[185] He was not lazy but tired easily, his exhaustion often brought on by the journey's prolonged physical demands, the muggy climate, mosquito-ridden nights, novel and often unpalatable foods, and tiresome company.

Webb loved to read and write and would spend entire days at either. No doubt, the time he spent in reading and writing during his tour helped to relieve the burden of fatigue and culture shock, as had probably been the case during his years at the Manila post as well. On his visit to Patna, he was busy reading Bosworth Smith's *Mohammed and Mohammedanism*.[186] He passed several days with Humphrey Ward's *History of David Greene* and George Eliot's *Felix Holt*, both by female writers known by masculine pen names. In Hyderabad, he consumed an afternoon looking through a bound volume of *Punch*, a popular journal of English humor: "What stupid brutes the English must be to call such an inane vapid publication humorous; and yet I am told they laugh ready to split their sides over the flat and pointless stuff it contains."[187]

Webb had a profound attraction to beauty and took pains to see ancient relics and works of art in addition to visiting museums and libraries at every opportunity, and he often wrote down his observations.[188] A nature enthusiast, he filled his diaries with descriptions of the Eastern flora and fauna in the wild or various zoological and botanical gardens.[189] He was fascinated by the landscapes he saw, taking pleasure in a "grand view up stream" of the Tungabhadra River en route to Agra or delighting in watching deer race alongside his train in the early morning and suddenly bounding off toward heaps of boulders in various directions.[190] His observations reflected the scientific speculations of his generation. En route to Hyderabad he noted:

> Soon after daylight we came to a part of the country which presented
> a very strange aspect. It was covered with rocks of various sizes
> worn into boulders by the action of water or ice and seemed to in-
> dicate the extreme plausibility of the theory that this section was once

covered by ice-bergs which carried these rocks along. In short it
seemed a corroboration of what science believes to have been
the conditions of the glacial period.[191]

The wild and exotic captivated Webb's attention. While Victorians stressed
self-mastery and total control of "animal instincts," they were fascinated by the
images of untamed nature and "savage" man.[192] Webb shared such a fascination, and his diary abounds in stories of cobras, man-eating tigers, and an
assortment of other creatures, although sometimes tongue-in-cheek. Webb
spent considerable time on deck the *Patria* with its captain, a former British
lieutenant, and a passenger, "the Scotchman from Assam," exchanging stories
about wild tigers and poisonous snakes. The captain told of a woodcutter bitten
by a cobra who sought a snake charmer to save him, but the charmer had to see
the snake for himself, was bitten, and both men died.[193] The captain also
claimed to have had a pet alligator, which one of his friends insisted on ex-
amining up close, losing a finger in the process.[194]

One night in Hyderabad, Webb was startled from sleep with visions of a
man-eater coming through his window:

> Was awakened at 2:30 by hearing rattling of the blinds on the
> other side of the house. I thought of the stories I had heard of cheetas
> [*sic*], leopards, panthers and tigers who came into the com-
> pounds of residences and suspected that one of these animals was
> clawing at the blinds and trying to get in. It proved to be a cat which
> had been shut in the house and was trying to get out, but the noise
> robbed [me] of more than an hour's sleep.[195]

Webb was fond of smoking and, like Mark Twain, was partial to cheroots,
a thin type of cigar cut like a cigarette at both ends. He regretted letting an
evening go by without a cheroot to smoke. He bought himself a "native pipe"
in Calcutta and took pleasure experimenting in Oriental smoking culture,
clearly savoring the "hookah," which he also called the "hubble bubble." In
Rangoon, he wrote: "Smoked the hookah for the first time and found it rather
pleasant."[196]

For all his frustrations, Webb often resorted to humor to make things
easier. When he was introduced to a Muslim "public preacher" named
"Munshi Shaik Husein V. Shaik Chand Joonarkar I," Webb remarked in his
diary, "A man with a name like that ought to be able to do some good in the
world."[197] His humor was often good-natured. Once, accompanied by a
talkative little boy who spoke no English but kept excitedly addressing Webb
in Urdu, Webb responded with the few Urdu words he knew (*hā* and *jīhā*
meaning "yes," and *bēshak*, "undoubtedly"): "[We] got on very well although
we didn't understand each other. I said 'Ha. Ha' and 'Gee ha' and 'Be'sheck'
and that encouraged him so that he chattered away at a great rate."[198] When

the occasion was right, Webb could be mischievous. One afternoon, he found himself in the company of an asinine youth who understood little English but insisted that he understood everything Webb said:

> I went out for a walk having to take that idiotic boy who is in the stamp business, as a guide. He is a confirmed ass. Insists that he speaks English and is always ready to answer "Yes" to every-thing he doesn't understand. He thinks that is a very clever way to delude people into the belief that he comprehends everything. Samples—"What is that?" "Yes." "No, I mean what is that, there?" "Oh, that is—?" "Do the Mohammedans all close their stores at dark?" "Yes." Presently we come to a number of Mohammedan stores open. "I thought you said that all the Mohammedan stores closed at dark?" Calmly "Yes." "How far is it to the next street?" "Yes." "I don't like this climate at all." "Yes." Presently seeing that he didn't understand half I said I asked: "Is that woman a man?" "Yes." "Did you ever see a white black bird?" "Bird, yes plenty here." "What kind?" "Yes." That's the sort of a fellow I had to dig infor-mation out of. I succeeded in buying a native cap and pipe, how-ever, and returned home discouraged.[199]

Living with Financial Constraints

In addition to the burdens of fatigue, cultural shock, and the general difficulty of travel, Webb's diary reflects a recurrent concern with personal and family finances. As a rule, he enjoyed generous room and board, but his diary portrays him as paying out of his own pocket for most travel and day-to-day expenses. He makes no mention of receiving monetary gifts but handled his own money, made personal drafts from banks, converted his dollars to rupees, and shopped for basic needs like eyeglasses, pipes, and underclothing.[200] That he bore such financial burdens is evident in his celebration of the "quite unexpected" generosity of his Madras hosts, the *Anjuman-e Islam*, when they provided him with train fare and some spending money:

> At the station found a large number of Mussulmans waiting to say good-bye. The Anjumani-Islam very generously paid my fare, 1st class to Agra, 90 Rs-10 bi and gave me 45 rupees for feed [*sic*] on the way. This very liberal treatment was quite unexpected. In fact I had nothing to complain of at Madras except the mosquitos and the hard bed and feed at Aziz Bagh.[201]

Webb welcomed gifts, albeit after initial protestations. The "self-made" merchant of Poona, whom Webb greatly admired, offered him an overcoat from his store—the weather in Poona was "bracing"—which Webb accepted, since the merchant "would take no pay for the coat but insisted that I accept it as a present. I did so reluctantly."[202] While visiting the marketplace with a Muslim physician, a Muslim shopkeeper offered Webb two "handsome pairs of slippers" and insisted he accept them gratis. Webb consented and kept both pairs for himself despite the physician's desire to have one also. Webb noted: "One enthusiastic Mussulman insisted upon my accepting two handsome pairs of slippers and I reluctantly did so. The Dr wanted me to share the plunder with him but I was too selfish—I wanted both pairs myself."[203]

Finances—personal and family—were recurrent concerns for Webb. He frequently visited banks to take out drafts, which he sent to his wife and family.[204] The diary portrays him as frugal, delighting in a good bargain but fretting about diminishing monetary resources from the very outset of the trip. In Singapore, a Hindu boy offered to sell him "a Serong, Sash, and other Indian goods." They caught Webb's fancy, but he could not afford them: "Didn't buy anything—too poor and have wife and three nice children to look after."[205] In Bombay, Webb concluded an entry with the anxious words: "The $600 seems to be getting low. Where has it all gone?"[206]

Webb consistently expressed unambiguous ideas about the immorality of profiting monetarily from the pursuit of good works or the service of God. He disapproved of people enriching themselves through benevolent work but expressed the highest respect for persons like Arab, who did such work without remuneration:

> Bro. Hajee Abdulla was out all night at work on the mission mat-
> ter. He is a very good man; there are few in this world who would
> work as he is working, without any hope of earthly reward.[207]

Webb did not expect all benevolent or religious work to be done gratis, and he certainly did not intend to undertake the American Mission without support for himself and his family. Nevertheless, he viewed the quest for unwarranted material gain through religious work as demeaning and was disenchanted with Colonel Olcott in Madras because he seemed preoccupied with money instead of being the "disinterested worker for good" that Webb had expected him to be:

> The Col. is rather disappointing. Thought him more sedate, serious
> and dignified and not given to worldliness. When he said his law
> practice in New York used to yield him a thousand dollars a month
> strange thoughts came into my mind. I'm afraid he is not all a dis-
> interested worker for good.[208]

Webb's aversion to Hassan Ali focused on presumption of greed and lack of selflessness in religious work in addition to a number of other perceived moral faults; as indicated earlier, he noted that Ali had sustained no sacrifice worthy of the name by leaving his schoolteaching job in Calcutta for missionary work that was many times more lucrative.[209]

Prospects Sailing Home

Webb contended in *Islam in America* that no one realized "the magnitude" of his undertaking more fully than he did.[210] How fully he grasped the project's practical side is another question. Remarkably, Webb remained upbeat about the mission's future despite his total exasperation with virtually everyone, except Arab, who was supposed to ensure its financial success. Kur had been appointed the secretary of the finance committee, but Arab had not even taken or been given an executive position. Yet only at the rarest moments during his Oriental tour did Webb ever question the mission's likely success. One of those moments occurred on an uneventful night in Hyderabad:

> Arose at 4:15 and after breakfast took carriage with Hajee Abdulla and Hassan Ali and went to see Mehdi Ali. He was not at home so we went to Shah Saheb's and had a general talk, remaining about an hour and accomplishing nothing, as usual. The movement seems to lack a head and makes little or no progress.[211]

Despite his Victorian admiration for pragmatism and efficiency, Webb's personal business life never proved to be financially practical or efficient. His confidence that his mission would be self-sufficient in five years and not have to depend upon his Indian patrons beyond that was overly optimistic, on the one hand, and an unrealistic assessment of his patrons' on the other, whose promised support would not last more than a single year. Webb's veneration for Arabs and belief in his personal fortune and commitment to the project merged with Webb's general lack of practicality in money matters and probably led Webb to look upon his other patrons as little more than a provisional facet of the final outcome.[212]

Webb had, in addition to a certain lack of practicality, an apparently sincere belief that the mission would prosper by virtue of its intrinsic merit, America's receptivity to it, and God's help. These were the hopes Webb had initially expressed to Kur when writing him from Manila:

> To me, [the mission] is in no sense an experiment likely to result in failure, for I know the general tendency of thought in my country and the general characteristic of my countrymen too well to entertain for a moment the idea that anything but success is possible. Besides I have faith in the power and wisdom of Almighty God (Praised be His name for ever), and as Islam is the true religion. I feel confident that He will guide, direct and support a movement for its propagation which promised such great results as this. I have for several years been convinced that there were unseen influences at work bringing about a condition of things calculated to overthrow the

current erroneous religious systems of the world and establish mankind in the one true system. But which that system was to be was to
me uncertain until I arrived at a comprehension of the character and
doctrines of Islam. I have had some strange experiences of which I
hope to have the privilege of talking with you soon, and which have
seemed to me as evidence that God was guiding me for some great
and wise purpose, the ultimate object of which was the spiritual
benefit of mankind. . . . [C]ircumstances have so shaped themselves in
my life that they have drawn me directly toward the movement in
which I am about to engage with all the earnestness, vigour, and intellectual ability that God has given me . . . . I am impatient to meet
you and talk freely with you concerning the matter, for I feel sure that
you will agree with me not only that the object is of the grandest importance, but that there has been something more than ordinary human agencies at work in bringing the project to its present condition.
God is great, and will surely guide his servants in the right way.[213]

Webb expressed such expectations again in Madras: "[Islam] has found a
firm foothold in Europe [i.e., Quilliam's community], and with God's help we
propose to establish it in liberal progressive America, where, I feel confident,
the masses of people are waiting to receive it."[214] When the correspondent of
the *Mohammedan Observer* asked him if he truly believed Americans would
convert, Webb answered:

Yes, most certainly . . . because during the last 19 or 15 years there has
been a great falling off in confidence in the Christian faith. People
have been drifting away from it, and hence there are so many societies formed, such as the Sectarian Society, the Theosophical Society,
and various others; and the people are anxious to investigate, in order to get to the bottom of the system of religion. Now in St. Louis,
where there is a population of half a million inhabitants, where a
special staff of reporters were sent to take the census of the people
who attended church, it was reported that only 7,000 people did so
out of the half million; and the rest attended the various places of
amusement.[215]

Webb believed he was doing God's work, and therefore, God would
see that the mission survived. Webb could "leave the results and [the mission's] practical operation to God."[216] He stated in the same vein: "I have
repeatedly been asked the question: 'How do you propose to introduce Islam
into America?' As if it was a task in which I alone was interested and in which
God had no part. . . . I believe that the power and influence of Almighty
God may be felt there just as strongly as it can in India or any part of the
world."[217]

A great crowd of enthusiastic supporters and well-wishers saw Webb off on December 31, 1892, as he sailed out of Bombay on his return back to America. The lengthy sea journey would take him across the Indian Ocean to the Red Sea, along the Arabian coast, and through the Suez Canal to the Mediterranean. Webb would then travel along the Mediterranean to the Straits of Gibraltar and from there to the Atlantic, northward to London, and from there to New York. We have no record of Webb's stops along the journey, although it would have been customary for his steamer to make several of them.

Webb finally arrived in New York on February 16, 1893. He arrived unannounced—although quickly discovered by the *New York Times*—and found himself in the midst of one of its most brutal winters on record.[218] What expectations did Webb have for his Islamic mission to America? He surely recorded them in the lost volume of his diary. Whatever secret misgivings he may have harbored, his outlook was probably optimistic, as reflected in his speeches and by the intense activity with which he immediately set about launching his movement.

7

Manhattan Beginnings

Getting Started

After Webb arrived in New York in February 1893, his first order of business was to find a quiet place to live until his family could join him a few months later.[1] His spirit did not shrink from the brutal weather. Plunging temperatures, freezing rain, sleet storms, and blizzards in rapid succession clogged Manhattan's streets, and ice floes choked the harbor and Hudson River.[2] Webb spent his first days "very quietly at the Coleman House," apparently a Manhattan boardinghouse. Toward the end of February, he moved in with a friend, Samuel Brown of Jersey City, and immediately launched his mission from Brown's parlor with a well-publicized talk on Islam.[3]

Webb called his mission by various names, which reflected its evolution over about half a decade. The "American Mission," "American Islamic Propaganda," and "American Moslem Brotherhood" were the most prominent, but it is difficult to assign a single designation to the mission as a whole. From beginning to end, he conceived of his work as a movement and frequently alluded to it as "the movement" or, when addressing sympathizers and coworkers, "our movement." In his one of his earliest Manila letters, Webb asserted that he hoped to establish a "broad, liberal, systematic and well-directed movement," ultimately capable of making Islam "the religion of the world."[4]

While still in the Philippines in 1892, Webb wrote to Abdulla Arab, expressing his eagerness to get the "American mission" started, which, he assured Arab, was "our mission" jointly and surely had God's blessing of ultimate success.[5] Later that year in India, Webb announced the proposed "American Mission" to his audiences and, in his Indian diary, referred to it more frequently by that name than by anything other.[6] But the title "American Mission" did not cross the Atlantic. After returning to the United States, Webb ceased to call his movement by that name, although he did not deny it was a mission and frequently quoted others—sympathizers and detractors alike—who continued to call him a missionary and his movement a mission. Perhaps Webb's inclination not to use the American Mission title any more reflected a desire not to attract unfavorable comparisons between his work and Christian missions, which he distinctly disliked and frequently wrote against. More likely, Webb, despite being an Islamic missionary at heart, found the title inappropriate since he had clearly come to see his mission's first task as educating America through disseminating accurate information about Islam, its Prophet, and its culture to remove deeply embedded Western prejudices and reshape American attitudes and understandings.

It is not surprising that "propaganda" was the word Webb liked best and used most when referring to his mission. The "American Islamic Propaganda" is the only title that could justifiably contend as the movement's official designation from its inception until its end. In Webb's time, "propaganda" was a neutral, perhaps even positive, word, retaining its original sense of simply propagating information and ideas. It had not yet taken on its cynical twentieth-century twist of connoting the intentional fabrication and dissemination of misinformation for ideological purposes. Webb's preference for the "American Islamic Propaganda" accurately expressed his conviction that his movement's primary task was educational and informational. It also reflects Webb's reliance on publications and lectures as his principal mode of operation.

Shortly after concluding his Manila pact with Abdulla Arab, Webb wrote enthusiastically to the *Allahabad Review*, announcing their newly conceived "Mohammedan mission to the United States." Webb expressed his resolve to devote his "time and labor exclusively to the development of the propaganda to full perfection," noting that the idea had been in his mind for the last three years.[7] Shortly afterward, Webb praised Arab's efforts to place the "American Islamic Propaganda" on a solid foundation.[8] Webb's diary occasionally designated the mission as the "American Propaganda," and he frequently used the term after establishing his mission in New York.[9] Webb's first mission book bore the full title *Islam in America: A Brief Statement of Mohammedanism and an Outline of the American Islamic Propaganda*, and its closing chapter elaborated on Webb's vision of this "American Islamic Propaganda."[10] Among supporters, he referred to his movement as "our American Islamic Propaganda."[11] He occasionally shortened it to the "American Propaganda," insisting until the end that the "American Islamic Propaganda" had made lasting contributions despite the hardships it endured.[12]

Islamic fraternity was Webb's favorite theme. But during the initial years, his constant references to Islamic brotherhood were synonymous with the religion itself, especially its community of the faithful, and inferred no allusion to Webb's movement. Webb wrote proudly to the *Allahabad Review* that any Jew, Christian, or person of other background could accept Islamic teaching and readily gain full membership in "the Moslem Brotherhood," but, in this context, he clearly meant the Muslim community, not his proposed movement. He stressed in the same article that Muhammad had insisted upon the fraternal principle of Islam, making it the heart of a "doctrine of universal brotherhood without regard to race, colour, social conditions or previous religious belief." For Webb, the practice of true fraternity was Islam's crown jewel and constituted the "grand ideal of the universal brotherhood of humanity."[13] Writing on the importance of music to the human soul, Webb depicted the Prophet Muhammad as the perfect human embodiment of musical harmony—as opposed to religious fanaticism—and asserted that this musical property of the Prophet's being was the secret behind the fraternity he inspired: "The sublime harmony of a perfect love made him the advocate of a perfect brotherhood of man."[14]

Although Webb did not use "brotherhood" to designate his movement during its first and finest years, he designated the "grand ideal" of Islamic brotherhood as Islam's essential organizational principle and made clear in his earliest Islamic writings that only true brotherhood could constitute the "foundation stone of Mohammedan organization."[15] It was in 1895 that Webb began to call his movement the "American Moslem Brotherhood," a remarkably late date and dismal period in the mission's history. Interestingly, Webb's use of the new organizational name coincided with his encouraging announcement of the recent appearance in New York of the "American Moslem Institute," a subsidiary of Abdulla Quilliam's Moslem Institute in Liverpool.[16] Addressing his followers, Webb now equated "our American Islamic Propaganda" with the newly adopted "American Moslem Brotherhood."[17] During the movement's final episode from 1895 till 1896, the term "American Moslem Brotherhood" eclipsed the "American Islamic Propaganda," and Webb frequently invoked the new usage in official contexts to announce meetings and elections as well as invite Americans to join the movement and establish affiliate circles in their areas.[18]

From the beginning of the mission in 1893 till it was discontinued three years later, Webb and his handful of colleagues created an "Islamic presence" of sorts in the United States, which received notice around the world. The closest parallel was Abdulla William Henry Quilliam's society of British Muslims in Liverpool, which served for Webb as a model and source of inspiration. The efforts of Lord Headley, although begun shortly before Webb's death, also provide a useful analogue for Webb and Quilliam; Headley belonged to the same generation and worked in a comparable Victorian environment. All three confronted substantial problems, but each expressed optimistic views about the potential of their adopted faith in the West.[19]

Historically, Webb's mission—similar generalizations apply to Quilliam and Headley's missions—materialized out of two very different influences: Victorian receptivity to new spiritual possibilities and the Muslim world's reaction to Christian missionary movements in their midst. Webb's conversion and missionary vision were inspired by the first influence, broadly reflected in the reversal of religious polarities then taking place in America. No longer finding traditional Christianity adequate, Webb set out to explore the new spiritual universe that the Victorian age had opened before him. He anticipated—no doubt from insight into his own experience—that Islam would fulfill a similar need for many other Americans.

Regarding the second influence, Webb's Islamic mission was an inadvertent by-product of the extensive and powerful Christian missionary movements that flourished throughout the imperial domains of nineteenth-century colonialism. Western colonial presence in Eurasia and Africa empowered the church to carry its message forcefully to "the heathen," but unwittingly generated a converse response among Muslims, who formed their own Islamic movements organized along Christian mission lines.

Webb was no lover of Christian missions. His personal promotion of non-Christian missions in America was driven, to a considerable extent, by a reaction to what he perceived as the presumptuousness of colonial missionaries, and he delighted in the prospect of giving them a taste of their own medicine at home. In the context of the colonial Muslim world, Webb's corrective psychology that drew him to mission work matched their own and created a powerful resonance among them. It is not coincidental that he found unhesitating, albeit short-lived, support among the Muslims of British India. Nowhere else in the Muslim world were indigenous missionary movements patterned on Christian models more enthusiastically supported than in the Indian subcontinent.[20]

During 1893 and 1894, Webb worked out of three Manhattan offices, frequently relocating because of financial problems. He began at 1122 Broadway, where he established the Oriental Library Bureau and Oriental Publishing Company, which published *Islam in America* and presumably the first five issues of the *Moslem World*.[21] Dannin construes Webb's Oriental Publishing Company and bookstore to have been an influential "Orientalist and occultist" bookstore that lasted well into the 1980s.[22] In reality, it was a modest venture that lasted a matter of months. On October 6, 1893, shortly after returning from the World's Parliament of Religions, Webb moved his headquarters to well-appointed accommodations at 458 West Twentieth Street, which remained the center of activities for the next six months and where to this day a handsome brick building—presumably the same one Webb used—still stands in one of Chelsea's more agreeable neighborhoods. He called the new location the Moslem World Building and moved his press there under the name of the Moslem World Publishing Company. The new press put out the last issues of the *Moslem World* and Webb's prayer book, *A Guide to Namaz.*[23] Webb closed his Twentieth Street offices on June 1, 1894, after severe financial shortages made it impossible to subsidize.[24]

Webb established his third and final Manhattan office in 1894 at 30 East Twenty-Third Street, which lodged the Moslem World Publishing Company and became the home of *The Voice of Islam.* Though the Twentieth Street headquarters had taken up an entire building, the Twenty-Third Street office was on the third floor of an apartment complex.[25] The *New York Times* described the Twenty-Third Street center as decorated with photographs of famous Turkish, Persian, and Indian mosques as well as some "blue and gold inscriptions in Oriental hieroglyphics," presumably an unwitting reference to decorative Arabic calligraphies. Webb's private office was now "not much larger than a closet, and [contained] a roller top desk and a crayon portrait of 'the Torch of Islam,'" probably Webb himself.[26] After the mission's complete financial breakdown in the summer of 1894, all operations of the Moslem World Company including book sales were transferred to Webb's residence at Ulster Park in the Catskills, where he attempted to revive the American Islamic Propaganda over the next two years.[27]

Though the event was little publicized, Webb's Twentieth Street headquarters were given an official grand opening attended by a surprisingly large audience.[28] In that age, buildings were regarded as powerful cultural symbols and were expected to be fitting reflections of the character of the institutions they housed. Webb's opulent midtown headquarters—as opposed to the other two locations—probably seemed to him a fitting symbol of his vision for the American Propaganda, although the excessive overhead and unreliable funding helped bankrupt the organization.[29]

The Moslem World Building was a four-story rental property. Webb set aside the first floor for "Indian missionaries" and unspecified "learned Islamic scholars" whom he expected to visit in the near future to aid his work.[30] Webb reported the imminent arrival of Hassan Ali and several other Indian Muslims, who never came. Among them were to be two Islamic scholars and a cook who were to remain permanently at the mission.[31] Webb dedicated the second story to publication and newspaper work. The third floor was Webb's centerpiece, housing a large, lavishly furnished lecture room—"dedicated to the service of God and truth"—an adjoining library, and a mosque (prayer room). The fourth floor housed the kitchen and dining area.[32]

In his development of the mission, Webb kept his side of the Manila bargain, which he described at Hyderabad in 1892:

Our plan of operation includes the establishment of a weekly high-class journal for the explanation of the Islamic doctrines as well

as the dissemination of general information relative to Mohammedans and Mohammedan social laws; a free library and reading-
room, a book and pamphlet publishing house, and a lecture-room
where lectures will be delivered once or twice a week, or as often as
the circumstances seem to warrant.[33]

The general plan corresponded closely to Quilliam's Moslem Institute, which
was based in "a large old-fashioned house" and had "a library, museum, small
lecture hall, where the members meet for the study of the Koran, for instruction in Eastern languages, and for social meetings of various kinds."
Quilliam's institute also had a mosque in an adjoining back yard building,
which could accommodate about a hundred and fifty worshippers.[34]

At the outset, Webb had great hopes for the lecture hall and the public
lectures to be held there. In the end, it proved not only expensive but coun-
terproductive, since lectures were easily disrupted by the mission's opponents.
Every Friday evening, the mission used the lecture room for addresses "on
Islamic doctrines and customs," while on Sunday afternoons, the hall was
used for brief presentations on Islam. All lectures were followed by a question-and-answer sessions.[35] In his scheduling, Webb appears again to have
taken his cues from Quilliam, who held regular sessions "for the faithful" on
Fridays and presentations "for strangers" on Sundays.[36]

The *Moslem World* gave the following description of Webb's venue:

The lecture room at the American Moslem Headquarters, No. 458
West 20th street . . . is probably one of the coziest and most attractive
assembly rooms of its size in New York. It is seated with neat and
comfortable folding chairs of polished oak and walnut and at the
south end is a platform two feet high and about seven feet wide, car-
peted with green tapestry and with a woolen fringe of the same color
running around the outer edge. It has an adjustable reading desk of
black walnut and an oak chair for the speaker. The room is lighted by
a handsome brass chandelier with ground glass globes, four rich
brass brackets and a pearl-shaped drop light of four burners over the
reading desk. At each end of the hall is a green flag with star and
crescent in the center and on the walls appear a number of artis-
tic half-tone engravings representing some of the most beautiful mosques and tombs of India.[37]

The Moslem World Building was open to "all honest, thoughtful men
and women."[38] Its "free library and reading room" were open to the public
daily from 9 A.M. until 10 P.M.:[39]

In it are a long table for newspapers and periodicals and chairs for
those who desire to sit there and read. At the west end are shelves upon
which numbers of Islamic books and pamphlets are placed at the

disposal of visitors who are welcome there at any time. This room is especially designed for those who desire to investigate and study the tenets and customs of the Islamic system, and it is expected that large numbers of Americans will avail themselves of its privileges this winter.[40]

At the opening ceremony, Webb and a number of his colleagues gave presentations.[41] Emin (Erwin) Nabakoff, "the Russian Muslim" and one of Webb's main helpers, presented an address called "The Mussulman's Religious Motives." John H. Lant, a "new student of Islamic doctrines," though later one of Webb's chief antagonists, commented on Nabakoff's presentation, and Leon Landsberg spoke on the importance of morality and "the honesty, and sobriety illustrated in the everyday life of the Mussulman." Webb followed up by addressing the issue of social reforms in America and what his mission hoped to accomplish in that regard:

It is a mistake to suppose that I am here to convert Christians to the faith of Islam. The moral condition of the people of that faith is higher than ours. Social evils common with us have no place with them. I hope to present the merits of a social system which can be imitated only with profit, and to encourage students of religious philosophy to examine carefully the principles of this faith. We shall endeavor to carry on a school of morality, free for all who may attend, to distribute literature without cost for our own productions, and we have no doubt that the work will do good.[42]

The following Sunday, Webb expounded on Islam, assisted by Anton Haddad, one of the pioneers of Baha'i missionary work in America, who gave a talk titled "Why I Believe in Mohammed."[43]

The New York Times reported that Webb intended to build a traditional mosque in New York once he established his "Mohammedan publishing house." Completion of the mosque was to constitute the "third and last step" of his mission. "The rich Mohammedans of Bombay," the paper asserted, had "guaranteed $150,000" for the project, and it quoted Webb as saying: "Eventually we expect to erect mosques in all the leading cities."[44] Melton and Bektashi note that Webb opened "a short-lived mosque."[45] His "short-lived" mosque was nothing more than the prayer area set aside in his headquarters. In Islam, prayer areas constitute legitimate "mosques," but Webb never succeeded in actually constructing the independent mosque structure he had planned. In all, Webb instituted three different prayer area "mosques" in each of his Manhattan headquarters, the largest and most well-appointed of them being the third floor of the Moslem World Building on Twentieth Street. Webb's mission got off to a promising start. New York had been his personal preference, and, for most of the remainder of 1893, it must have seemed that his choice had been well-taken.

Vision and Strategies

The fact that Webb's return to America brought him to New York and not Boston or Chicago reflected his strategic vision and, in this case, his insistence on the priority of his own indigenous understanding of America over that of his Indian support group. In Bombay, the mission committee had preferred Boston as the best place to start the American Mission, perhaps because the city was widely regarded at the time as America's "cultural capital." Chicago was a second option, but Webb insisted on New York City and proudly told the *New York Times* shortly after his arrival that it was in New York "where we will begin our work."[46]

Webb contended that the mission was "the result of mature deliberation."[47] In his belief, the time was ripe for something new in America, and the old, entrenched attitudes of the past were rapidly changing.[48] However much Webb may have disliked Hassan Ali, he surely agreed with his assessment of the unique possibilities before the American Mission and its Liverpool counterpart: "The age we live in is an age of inquiry and toleration. Religious rancour and hatred [are] dying away before the light of education and the progress of knowledge. Such an age is peculiarly favorable to the triumph of truth."[49] Webb felt assured that his American Propaganda could do as well in America as Quilliam's mission was doing in England: "[Islam] has found a firm foothold in Europe, and with God's help we propose to establish it in liberal progressive America where, I feel confident, the masses of people are waiting to receive it."[50]

Webb believed his mission had a future among "progressive and intelligent" Americans, if Islam were presented to them properly.[51] Such "well-balanced" Americans were "capable of understanding and appreciating what [was] good and reasonable" and would give him an impartial hearing.[52] Even toward the end of his mission, Webb's faith in the American people never wavered. He repeated in 1895 what he had been saying since the beginning: "I have full confidence in the intelligence and justice of the American people, and in their willingness to give a fair and impartial hearing to any claim that may be properly presented to them."[53]

Webb did not advocate targeting the American people as a whole, but framed his strategy according to his beliefs about education and class. The *New York Times* noted at the outset of the mission that "there [were] a few Mussulmans in New York, but they [were] mostly peddlers and low-caste Hindus [sic], and Mohammed Webb [would] not associate himself with them."[54] Instead, Webb directed the "Islamic propaganda" to what he called the "educated and intelligent" classes of the English-speaking world.[55] When a reporter visiting him in Ulster Park asked why Webb had never made an attempt to convert the local rustics, Webb replied: "We can only hope for converts among thinking people, to begin with. The people here are not educated to think."[56]

Webb spoke of his undertaking as "purely educational."[57] The task required good communications and combating misinformation with facts, an assignment perfectly suited to Webb's skills as a professional journalist. In his mind, Islam commended itself to human beings simply on the basis of its intrinsic merits as a religion "founded upon that eternal truth which has been handed down from age to age" and "the only system that [would] satisfy the longings of the soul for a higher existence," while remaining "strictly in harmony with reason and science."[58] Yet no religion had been "more willfully and persistently misrepresented" than Islam, nor had any historical personage been more "imperfectly understood" than Muhammad.[59]

Webb understood that the process of reeducating Americans about his faith would not be easy. Webb felt that few "English-speakers," like himself at the outset of his spiritual journey, were able even to "entertain the suggestion that Islam could be true or worthy at least of careful study":

> There is no religious system of which so little is known, not only among the masses of English-speaking people, but among those who are considered the most learned, as the Islamic. This fact is due to several causes, the most prominent of which is the Mussulman's quite natural aversion to the English language and English-speaking nations, his unwillingness to have Mohammedan literature translated into our language, and the strong prejudice which has, for the past eight or nine centuries, existed among Christians against Mohammedans and Mohammedanism.[60]

Westerners were not to be held responsible for their ignorance of Islam: "You cannot justly blame us Americans nor our European cousins for having these ideas, for they are the results of centuries of malignant misrepresentation born of spiteful jealousy, gross ignorance and wicked fanaticism."[61] Not all were blameless, though, and Webb regarded Christian missionaries as the chief source of continued misunderstanding:

> The most absurd and impossible tales about the Mohammedans in circulation among our Christians have emanated from the missionaries who seem to see all the faults of Mussulmans around them and none of their virtues. If a Mohammedan commits a crime or expresses an absurd superstition, they send a report of it home labeled: "An Article of Mohammedan Faith."[62]

Webb did object, however, to bigotry and double standards. He once told his readers about an incident involving a deranged American Christian who had killed his daughter under the delusion that God had commanded him to sacrifice her just as Abraham had been commanded to sacrifice his son:

Of course he was arrested, tried for murder and sent to a lunatic asylum. I never heard that the report was circulated among Mohammedans that Christians believed in killing their children as sacrifices to God. But let some unbalanced Mohammedan commit an insane act and the chances are that the Western Christians will be told that such acts form a part of the Mohammedan faith.[63]

Complacency combined with misinformation meant that many Americans were doubly ignorant of Islam, having no true knowledge of the faith and its history but equally confident that they did:

Ask almost any American Christian if he knows who and what Mohammed was and what the Islamic system is, and he will promptly answer yes. But when you come to question him as to the sources of his information he will tell you that all he has read upon the subject is [George] Sale [*The Koran*] or [Washington] Irving [*Mahomet and His Successors*], or both, and the letters that some of the misguided Christian missionaries have sent home from the East.[64]

Since Webb intended to focus on "the English-speaking people," his mission required that "everything be printed in English."[65] He hoped his mission would help rectify the deficiency of English-language reading materials through a generous program of sponsored translations.[66] The Moslem World Publishing Company, as Webb envisioned it, would foster reliable new English translations of Islam's sacred texts and the "literature of the Moslems nations," especially those originally in Arabic, Persian, Urdu, and Gujarati.[67] Webb gave no specific examples of works or authors, but frequently cited great Persian poets like Rumi and Sa'di in translation. In order to make English a viable medium for his mission, Webb strove to employ a style of clear and simple English that Americans could "easily understand and relate to."[68]

Webb also insisted that English-language Islamic literature be made available in easily affordable publications and books.[69] The *New York Herald* reported that one of Webb's primary objectives was "to circulate translations of the Koran until one [was] in each house in the United States."[70] Although Webb frequently spoke of the demerits of Sales's translation of the Qur'an, the most readily available in his time, he was happy that it had been "published in cheap form," adding that it might give the reader "at least, an imperfect idea" of the Qur'an's essence.[71] Webb reported to the Ottomans that he had sold numerous translations of the Qur'an and that Americans had shown an abiding interest in translations of Islamic literature, although his financial limitations had made it impossible to meet their demands.[72] All the same, Webb hoped that new and better translations of the Qur'an would be inexpensively produced so that they might soon be within reach of the masses.[73] His interest in a new English translation of the Qur'an remained unabated until the end of his life. He reportedly assisted in editing Muhammad Ali's final draft of his translation, the first edition of which appeared in 1917, a year after Webb's death.[74]

Webb welcomed the news that an Indian Islamic society had undertaken an affordable new English translation of the Qur'an that was supposed to be completed by the end of 1893. When it had not appeared by 1895, he grew impatient and complained:

> What has become of the project to give America a truthful English
> translation of the Holy Koran, which was inaugurated at Madras,
> India, in December, 1892? We were informed, at that time, that
> something like 15,000 rupees had been subscribed for the purpose
> and that the work was to be under the general supervision of the
> famous Moulvi Hassan Ali Sahib, the Moslem missionary. Will
> Moulvi Mohammed Nizamuddin, Khan Bahadur, Secretary of the
> Anjumani-Himayet Islam, at Madras, kindly tell us whether the work
> has been commenced or not?[75]

In October 1895, Webb saluted the efforts of an American scholar, Dr. C. H. S. Davis, editor of *Biblia*, who informed Webb of his own projected English translation of the Qur'an, which he believed to be "the most accurate in the language" and able to "commend itself not only to the Mussulman, but to the Arabic scholar," hopefully without a word that would be "distasteful to the Mussulman."[76]

Although Webb and his sponsors were ultimately committed to conversion, Webb did not speak of it as his mission's primary goal, although he did see himself as preparing the ground for future conversions through education. When asked how many converts he had won after three years of mission work, Webb replied: "I have never tried. I did not start out to make converts. I was only to prepare the way at first by starting people to thinking. The preaching missionaries were to follow."[77] He told the *New York Times*: "It is a mistake to suppose that I am here to convert Christians to the faith of Islam."[78] He wrote in *Islam in America*:

> The primary purpose of this book is not to destroy nor weaken any
> creed or system of theology, nor to make proselytes for Islam, but
> to arouse and encourage among English-speaking Christians a spirit
> of calm, persistent and unprejudiced investigation to be applied to
> their own as well as other systems of religion.[79]

Webb repeated the same idea at the Parliament of Religions, to much applause:

> A gentleman asked me if we had organized a mission in New York. I
> told him yes, but not in the ordinary sense, that we simply wanted

people to study Islam and know what it was. The day of blind belief has passed away.

Intelligent humanity wants a reason for every belief, and I say that that spirit is commendable and should be encouraged wherever it goes, and that is one of the prominent features of the spirit of Islam.[80]

Webb firmly believed Islam would constitute a positive moral force in America. In place of immediate conversions, the moral betterment of society should be the mission's first viable goal, he thought, and it was a goal that many Victorians found commendable.[81] With "an intelligent following" in the United States, Islam would "purge our whole social system and bring us, as a nation, to a more perfect understanding of the glory and power of God, and the necessity of moral development."[82]

Webb referred to the moral teachings of Islam as its "universal system." He believed that all religions had esoteric and exoteric dimensions. Sufism constituted Islam's esoteric side, and its moral system constituted its exoteric aspect. Although Webb regarded esoteric Islam to be superior to anything else in the religion, he held unequivocally that his movement could only succeed if predicated on exoteric Islam:

I will seek to introduce practical and not esoteric Mohammedanism, although I am as deeply interested in the one as the other. I am myself a member of the American Theosophical Society and a firm believer in the knowledge and honesty of the late Mme. Blavatsky. Theosophy and esoteric Mohammedanism are almost identical, but practical Mohammedanism is quite another thing. It is a sensible, pure, every-day religion which we believe to be far superior to Christianity.[83]

He wrote similarly in *Islam in America*:

Of course, at this time, we can consider the Islamic system only in its popular or exoteric aspect. As before stated, it has a deeper, more philosophic aspect than is apparent at a first glance. But its chief beauty, viewed superficially, is its perfect adaptability to the spiritual needs of all classes of humanity, from the humblest laborer to the most advanced thinker and man of letters. There is nothing in it that does violence to reason or common sense, or that is in any degree contrary to the natural instincts of justice and mercy. It requires no belief in the supernatural, nor the adoption of any absurd superstitions or impossible theories.[84]

At the Parliament of Religions, Webb informed his audience that his original topic was Islamic theology. They applauded when he then indicated his preference to speak instead about Islam's practical side: "There are some systems which have in them more theology than religion. Fortunately Islam has more religion than theology."[85] He was roundly applauded again when he asserted: "Let us take that system which will accomplish the best results," insisting that Islam was "elevating and refining in its tendencies, and develop[ed] the higher, nobler elements of humanity when it [was] faithfully, wisely and intelligently followed." Furthermore, he suggested that its exoteric "system" was "so thoroughly elastic, so thoroughly applicable to all the needs of humanity that it seems to me it is exactly the system that we need in our country, and that is why I am here, that is why I am in the United States."[86]

The press was one of Webb's primary means of communicating to the American public. It, in turn, showed significant, although generally amused interest in Webb's beliefs and mission. Express hostility was rare, and several newspapers welcomed Webb's work and showed genuine interest in learning about Islam. In the end, however, Webb would come to feel that the press— especially the *New York Times*—played a primary role in destroying his movement, not through hostility but by exaggerated accounts of his financial support from abroad, which created false expectations and ultimately helped sow discord among his followers when the mission faced its first serious monetary crisis toward the end of 1893.

The Press and Public Reaction

Webb tried to avoid the press after his arrival in Manhattan in the winter of 1893, but the *New York Times* quickly discovered him, bringing a quick end to his initial anonymity. At first, Webb was "disinclined to talk," but the paper finally obtained a full interview, and Webb's mission soon appeared on the front pages of the city's leading newspapers.[87] With his prominence—an American consul embracing Islam—Webb had even gained some notoriety in the American press before his return to America. One paper wrote:

> The news that Alexander Russell Webb, of the American Consular
> Service, had been converted to the religion of Mohammed, caused
> the paragraphic lips of the press of the United States to part in
> smiles about a year ago. The more recent news that he has arrived in
> this country as a Moslem missionary has vanished the smile and
> produced a guffaw. Such is our modesty that we laugh in spite of
> ourselves at the notion that anybody from anywhere can teach us
> anything.[88]

At the World's Parliament of Religions, Chairman John Henry Barrows made reference to Webb's fame in the press when introducing him to speak: "Many of you saw and perhaps shared the smile and exclamation of incredulous amusement over the paragraph which went the rounds of the papers some months ago to the effect that the Mohammedans were preparing to send missionaries and establish a Mohammedan mission in New York City."[89]

Webb received mixed press in America. Some welcomed him, others opposed him, and most regarded him to be humorous. Nothing in the press harmed Webb, however, as much as allegations that he had access to unlimited financial backing from abroad. Webb later reflected, "It was reported as soon as I landed in America that I had millions at my command to convert Americans; and at once sharks began to flock to me from all directions."[90] The headlines of the *New York Times* proclaimed: "Muhammad Webb's Mission to Establish the Faith of Islam Here: The American Mohammedan Sent by Wealthy Mussulmans of the East." It emphasized that Webb had "plenty of money" at his command, and it described his backers as "a syndicate of rich Mohammedans of Bombay" working in collusion with "thousands of rich and influential Moslems." "Backed by unlimited wealth and zeal," it was clear that Webb's mission should be "undertaken in earnest": "No Christian missionary ever started forth to go among the heathen attended by such a concourse of his coreligionists and countrymen." Having invested such great wealth in Webb, "the heathen turned the tables" and hoped now to make their investment pay off.[91]

The *New York Herald* sounded the same refrain. Webb had "returned as a missionary of Mohammed, and with unlimited money at his disposal, supplied by wealthy Moslems of Bombay and Allahabad." Without question, Webb was "liberally backed in his enterprise by Mohammedan money." The "rich Mohammedans of Bombay pledged $150,000 to the work" and "enough money [had] been supplied to keep the movement going for five years. By that time, Mohammed Webb said yesterday, the cause [would] be on a sufficiently firm footing to take care of itself." The paper surmised that Webb's explicit goal to "carry the religion of the Prophet to the people of the United States" might not be his true motive: "It may be possible that there is some great commercial scheme back of it all by which trade will be for the first time opened with the Mohammedan nations, but Mohammed Webb declares he only came here as a missionary to spread the word."[92]

Among the newspapers that welcomed "Brother" Webb was the *San Francisco Argonaut*, seeing a number of positive sides to his mission:

> Mohammed Webb is, we trust, a man of learning, intellectual courage, and vigor. If so, he will be a providential agent for infusing some life into the American pulpit. At present it seems, for the most part, to be in the possession of the mentally lame, halt, and blind. The renewed need for defending the faith against the Saracen would

necessarily impart a fervor of faith which is now painfully absent.

It concluded with the greeting:

> Salaam to Mohammed Webb. The benediction of the Prophet of Islam be on him. May he have luck with his mosque in Chicago [sic], or wheresoever else he shall set up, and prod our clergy to feats of study and preaching which hitherto they have been too indolent to attempt. There is no danger that we can know too much about Mohammedanism or anything else.[93]

The *New York Times* acknowledged that Webb's endeavor might prove a helpful lesson for Christian missionaries by letting them "see themselves as others see them":

> [Christian missionaries] regard an effort to convert them to Islam as a highly-impudent and a highly-ridiculous performance. The wholesome reflection which this ought to suggest is that that is precisely the light in which their own missionary efforts are regarded by the Gentiles whom they, in their turn, are endeavoring to convert to Christianity. Mohammedans certainly hold their hereditary faith as firmly as Christians, and so do the adherents of Buddhism and of the other ancient religions that divide the allegiance of the Oriental world. Christian missionaries, whose devotion is in many cases beyond praise, enter upon the task of converting these people without any of the advantages which Mr. Webb possesses in an undertaking that does not appear feasible except to himself and his Mohammedan backers. He is himself a converted American, he knows the language and manner of thinking of his countrymen, and presumably he knows how to avoid offending them. None of these advantages does the American missionary to Asia possess. At present the American missionary to China, where the strongest and most persistent missionary efforts have been made, labors under a peculiar disadvantage, in that the Nation which he represents, and which professes the religion which he is trying to spread, has notoriously been guilty of a breach of faith so atrocious as to be plain not only to an educated Chinaman but to an untutored savage. We have already suggested that the missionaries to China might advantageously be recalled to pursue their labors among the undeported Chinese in America. In any case, the spectacle of Mr. Webb and his Moslem World ought to be instructive as showing the advocates of foreign missions, by an impressive object lesson, the nature and the difficulty of the obstacles they themselves have to overcome.[94]

The *New York Mercury* and Joseph Pulitzer's *New York World* voiced encouraging words about Webb's mission. The former referred to the spiritual decline of the times and observed that Webb's advocacy of Islam ought to be considered as a real alternative: "We must get into something that we can believe in, at least until we test it and find it fallacious." Webb's commentary in the *Moslem World* was: "Why not, without delay, 'get into' Islam? It is not hard. Simply get out of misery and uncertainty 'into' happiness and security. Try it."[95] The *New York World* welcomed Webb for having "performed a great service to our cause." He, in turn, referred to the *New York World* as "a great paper, and a great preacher of Islam."[96]

When Webb launched his mission, his name had already attained a substantial degree of recognition in the American press. In addition, he was fairly well-connected, as the invitation list to his earliest parlor talks indicate. Mark Twain was among those formally invited to attend the second of Webb's presentations in February 1893.[97] There is no conclusive proof that Twain actually came or took note of Webb or his mission, although the assertion has been made that he knew of Webb and heard him speak about Islam.[98] Given Webb's notoriety, it would be improbable that Twain had not attended to the Webb story. Moreover, both men shared overlapping pasts as former journalists who worked at the *Missouri Republican*, albeit at different times. Twain had also returned to visit St. Louis while Webb was a prominent journalist there in the 1880s.[99] Twain would not have failed to note the comic potential of Webb's conversion, and his allusion to "Missouri Moslems" in *Tom Sawyer Abroad*, referred to earlier, may well be evidence of that. A newspaperman himself, Webb was at home speaking with the press and never failed to recognize the central importance of the printed word for spreading his message. His preferred mode of communication, however, was direct personal contact through tours and lectures but especially through the distinctively Victorian medium of the fireside parlor talk.

Outreach: Tours, Talks, and Lectures

Parlor life was central to Victorian notions of gentility and propriety, and Webb not only preferred but apparently excelled at parlor talks. For all classes of Victorians, the parlor was generally the favorite room. It was where families congregated and received guests. As a rule, it had an open-hearth fireplace and was furnished with an array of davenports, chairs, cabinets, and bookcases. Social mixing in the parlor was "gender distinctive," and men and women knew where they were supposed to sit. There were armed throne-like chairs for "gentlemen," and higher armless chairs for "ladies" to accommodate their full skirts and allow them to sit with their hands folded on their laps according to postural expectations. Children also took part in parlor life but sat on special chairs to the side, where they could be "seen but not heard."[100]

Webb launched his "American Propaganda" with two parlor talks, both well advertised in the press, announcing special invitations to a number of high-profile figures and open invitations to the public. Naturally sociable, Webb was at home in the ambience, and, once he had been introduced to the audience, he "attacked his subject in a conversational way, standing with his back to the fireplace."[101] Both gatherings were held "in Webb's honor." The first was arranged at the home of Samuel Brown in Jersey City, where Webb was residing.[102] The second, a few days later, was hosted by Colonel David B. Sickles, another of Webb's "friends in the city," at his Manhattan residence. Sickles was a former American consul to Siam (Thailand) and may have known Webb through the diplomatic service. The Sickles debut was billed as Webb's formal introduction to the American public, and formal invitations were sent to a number of outstanding personages, most of them prominent literary figures of the time. The engagement was published well in advance so that interested persons in the general public could attend.[103]

Colonel Sickles extended an invitation to George F. Seward, a former U.S. envoy to China. Samuel L. Clemens (Mark Twain) was formally invited, as were other prominent literary figures, such as the popular novelist Francis Marion Crawford; the journalist, humorist, and playwright Bronson Crocker Howard; and Edmund Clarence Stedman and Richard Henry Stoddard, both of whom were prominent New York poets, editors, and literary critics. Invitations included "the great agnostic" Colonel Robert G. Ingersoll, a prominent "free-thinker" and popular public lecturer. Also invited were Paul Dana, director of the *New York Sun*; Frank Hatton, a prominent Chicago newspaper editor and former postmaster general of the United States; John Russell Young, a noted Civil War correspondent, former U.S. minister to China, and noted New York journalist; novelist Charles Insley Pardee; and the famous African explorer Paul Du Chaillu.[104]

Webb's obituary in the *Missouri Republican* indicated he also gave many parlor talks in support of his mission at St. Louis after the Parliament of Religions, remaining in the city for "a number of weeks," allowing no more than twenty invited guests at a time, and requiring each to pay an admission fee of $20.[105] In addition to parlor gatherings, he organized weekly public lectures at his Oriental Library Bureau on Broadway and later at the lecture hall of the Moslem World Building.[106] For reasons as yet unclear, the lecture hall experiment did not prove successful. Referring to the hall's failure, Webb observed in 1895:

> We tried the experiment for about a year and found it productive of
> more harm than good. Our work will be pursued, as it has been
> for the past nine months, by lectures and parlor talks upon the

doctrines of Islam, wherever they may be desired and by the circulation of Islamic literature.[107]

Webb readily "lectured for societies" in the Greater New York area when
requested "for such remuneration as [would] cover expenses."[108] He delivered
a speech in Manhattan at Chickering Hall on September 29, 1893, titled "The
Spirit of Oriental Religions" and addressed the Brooklyn YMCA the following
day. He then lectured at the Lee Avenue Academy of Music (also in Brooklyn),
the New York Theosophical Society, and went on to speak in "five other towns
and cities."[109]

His headquarters also handled out-of-town speaking engagements.[110]
Webb spoke extensively in New York State and in various other parts of the
United States. He spoke twice in Ithaca, New York, to a large audience under
the auspices of a Unitarian minister, Reverend J. M. Scott, who wrote favorably
about Webb's lecture in his publication *Kindly Light*. Webb deemed Scott's
remarks "honest, just and manly" and added that "the average Church-
Christian editor should take a valuable lesson from Mr. Scott." According to
the *Moslem World*, Webb's Ithaca speeches were titled "Mohammed the
Prophet" and "The Tenets and Tendencies of Islam," and each was followed
by a question-and-answer session:

> At the close of the meeting large numbers gathered about him
> thanking him for the information he had imparted to them and
> expressing regret at having so long been in ignorance of the true
> character and teaching of Our Prophet. The fabrics of false-
> hood raised by ignorant and prejudiced Church-Christians against
> Islam and its followers were completely demolished and the intelli-
> gent, broad-minded part of the audience seemed to be heartily glad
> of it.[111]

Webb informed the Ottoman embassy that his meetings and speeches in
different parts of the country had been generally well-received, although lack of
funds often forced him to cancel engagements.[112] The Ottoman Archives described one of Webb's lectures in New York, which he delivered to a large
audience one night, as beginning with the Islamic call to prayer "to demonstrate
its psychological effects." Webb demonstrated how Muslims made ablutions,
made ritual prayer, and supplicated God. He then spoke about God's ninety-
nine most beautiful names and the spiritual benefits granted to anyone who
learned them by heart. Since polygamy was an unavoidable topic in Victorian
America, Webb noted that Muslims rarely took more than one wife, although
they were allowed to take as many as four. He explained that Muslims did not eat
with silverware and that it "accounted for their good health."[113]

Nadirah Osman maintained that Webb "filled public engagements...
throughout the country." The *Moslem World* published a promethean schedule

for the period between October 17, 1893, and March 5, 1894, of forty-three engagements up and down the Atlantic coast, in the Midwest, and even in the Deep South, although it is not known how many of the appointments Webb was actually able to keep.[114] Nevertheless, the diversity of invitations that came to Webb from across the country indicates that his mission quickly aroused nationwide interest. A subsequent issue of Webb's journal modified his schedule:

> Owing to the increase and importance of his office work as well as the cancellation of his agreement with the Oriental Literary Bureau he [will] not be able to give more than four or five lectures per month outside of his own lecture room in this city and he has already arranged for those he is to deliver in December and January.[115]

Webb continued to offer his lecture services during 1895 and 1896, when his mission confronted its most adverse times:

> Mr. Webb will be pleased to make engagements now for the season of 1895–6. His lectures this season have attracted widespread interest and have given thousands of Americans a better idea of the Oriental religious systems than it is possible to obtain from current English literature.... Colleges, Universities, Schools, Literary Societies, and other organizations arranging lecture courses for next season should bear in mind that only a comparatively small portion of Mr. Webb's time is available for lectures and those who desire to place him in a course for next season should apply as early as possible. There are still a few open dates in March and April of this year.[116]

Forging Ties That Bind: The Study Circles

Webb's preference for direct personal contact even went beyond tours, lectures, and parlor talks. One of his distinctive organizational principles was the creation of study circles "of five persons each ... for study and improvement, and with the view of bringing the desired moral influences to bear upon evils now prevalent."[117] In India, he alluded to his goals of establishing "in various cities branch societies to propagate the Islamic Faith," but it is not clear where he got the stratagem of circles as a primary mechanism for the branches.[118] The formation of small study groups is a common custom among Muslims on the Indian subcontinent. Quilliam's Moslem Institute also comes to mind, although an early study of the Liverpool society made no mention of such circles.[119] Nevertheless, the most productive organizer of Webb's circles was A. L. Rawson, a convert from Woodcliff, New Jersey, with close ties to Quilliam. Rawson eventually formed his own American Moslem Institute as a branch of

Quilliam's society, although he continued to contribute to the *Moslem World*, which duly announced the foundation of Rawson's organization.[120] Webb may also have patterned his circles on the "Lotus-Circles" of the Theosophical Society, which William Q. Judge instituted in 1886 as a special type of Sunday school for children.[121]

Webb's conception of the circles, whatever the source of the idea, appears to have been well-developed in his mind from the outset of his work in Manhattan. The *New York Times* reported in February 1893:

> As soon as Muhammed [*sic*] Webb gets the magazine and the pub-
> lishing house under way, missionaries will be sent here from India,
> and he and his aides will proceed to the work of active personal
> evangelization, and when converts are made they will be formed into
> societies or bands. They will be joined in the Moslem Brotherhood,
> and will then be full-fledged Mohammedans.[122]

The primary circle was located in Manhattan and called "The Mecca Circle No. 1 of New York City." It was organized around Rawson and five other men, all "chartered members" of Webb's organization. Rawson organized two more circles of eleven men in Manhattan. A "Capitol Circle No. 4" was organized in Washington, D.C., with five members, including, it was said, a professor and two physicians. According to Nadirah Osman, Webb also established an English circle in London.[123]

Ottoman sources report that Webb initially hoped to form circles in all of America's cities by the end of the summer of 1893. He also intended to establish "Oriental religion societies" during the winter of 1893–1894 and, at the time, was still confident that Muslim scholars would arrive to assist in their foundation. There were, according to the Ottoman Archives, six circles in all. Three were in Manhattan, a fourth in Brooklyn, a fifth in Washington, D.C., and a sixth in California, possibly in Pueblo (Santa Clara).[124] Webb mentioned a "Brother Joseph Larsen" from San Francisco, a Scandinavian immigrant who may have belonged to the West Coast circle. Larsen wrote to Webb of his dream of proclaiming Islam, "the religion of the Prophet of Arabia," in Norway, Denmark, and Sweden.[125] Turner asserts that Webb briefly established his mission on the West Coast, but he provides no additional detail.[126] Akbar Muhammad does not mention California but asserts that Webb "established seven branches called 'circles' of the Moslem Brotherhood or the American Islamic Propaganda in various East Coast and Midwestern cities."[127]

Webb sought to build his movement around the nuclei of the circles, the purpose of which would be the advancement of "the comprehensive study of the life, character, purpose, and teachings of the Prophet." The Manhattan Circle would constitute the "parent society" and furnish the branches with "such literature and information as they might stand in need of."[128] The circles would allow converts and sympathizers to experience a "bond of brotherhood with the vast Moslem world and make use of [their] talents to propagate the true faith wherever possible."[129] Webb envisioned the circles as providing the "moral force" which, in time, would bring about the moral reform of "our whole social system."[130]

Ottoman records state that one did not have to be a Muslim to join the circles.[131] Osman confirmed likewise that no member was required to subscribe to any religious doctrine or accept "any creed or tenet not in harmony with his or her reason and common sense." Nonetheless, the first aim of the circles was "the education of the members in Islamic historical and doctrinal literature." Webb sought to make the circles crucibles for presenting "the Islamic system in its purity, freed from the gross and materialistic ideas which had been engrafted upon it by misguided Muslims."[132]

Webb used his journals to promote the circles: "Those who desire to form circles of the American Moslem Brotherhood will be assisted in their efforts if they will send their names and addresses to this office."[133] On another occasion, he stated:

> Our brothers in various parts of the United States, who desire to be enrolled as members-at-large of the American Moslem Brotherhood, are requested to send their names to Brother H. Ali Lewis, Secretary, No. 566 Hudson Street, New York City. There are no fees nor dues to pay and the chief purpose in making this request is to facilitate communication between members and the circulation of Islamic literature.[134]

Since both statements were published in 1895, they indicate that Webb's circles (or at least his interest in them) continued well after his mission had ceased to be financially feasible in Manhattan. He also noted in 1895 that "organizations taking Moslem names, [are] being formed quite numerously in New York, and elsewhere," speaking "volumes in favor of our American Islamic Propaganda, commenced in this country less than two years ago." Webb alluded to an International Moslem Union on Broadway, indicating that he was "disposed to give it a cordial welcome to the American Moslem Brotherhood," if its real purpose was to "promulgate the truths of Islam."[135]

Like other Oriental missions contemporary to Webb, his mission was predicated on promoting cooperation between converts and sympathizers and creating lasting bonds between them both. Webb extended the mantle of fraternity to both groups, freely applying the term "Brother" to converts and sympathizers alike, to the extent that it is difficult to distinguish between them. "Brother Joseph Larsen" of San Francisco was clearly a convert, but one also encounters Brother Caleb S. Weeks of Brewster, New York; Brother Charles Franklin Howard of Windfall, Indiana; Brother Joseph Wade" of Dorchester, Massachusetts; and others who, in all likelihood, were only sympathizers.[136]

Webb justified his mission and sought to inspire its supporters by frequent references to conversion and to persons, often anonymous, who acknowledged the validity of Islamic teachings privately but were too intimidated to do so publicly. He quoted "an American of widespread reputation, who (for reasons best known to himself) decline[d] to have his name made public" but praised "Islamism." Proclaiming that "the truth shall make you free," Webb's anonymous sympathizer expressed at great length the hope that Islam would inaugurate a promising future in America, contribute to "triumphant" humanity's "residuum of knowledge," and "hasten the day of complete renunciation of old beliefs."[137]

8

Getting Out the Word

Getting out the word about Islam was the primary purpose of Webb's American Islamic Propaganda. As we have seen, he welcomed direct discourse with the public in parlor talks, public speeches, question-and-answer sessions, or informal meetings. Like most Victorians, Webb did not consider speeches and talks to be adequate and regarded the printed word to be his propaganda's principal and indispensable vehicle, since he found "literature far more effective than preaching."[1] Webb had himself come to Buddhism, Theosophy, and then Islam through the written word and naturally insisted that "a journal, published regularly, is the most effective instrument that can be given us and the larger and better it is the greater will be its influence for good."[2] In 1892, he envisioned a mission that would give the written word the centrality it required:

> We intend to establish a high class weekly newspaper to be devoted to the real doctrines of Islam. We propose to establish a place for the issue of pamphlets and books, to establish a free library and reading room for the masses, and a free lecture-room where lectures will be delivered once or twice a week.[3]

In emphasizing the printed word, Webb based his mission on tasks that he, as a professional journalist, was well trained at performing. He produced a number of publications—printed lectures, journals, and books—and offered for sale a wide variety of books on Islam and religious topics, some of which were also available in the mission's reading room and study circles.

The printed word, especially in the form of journalism, was the most effective means of communication at the time. Not only was newspaper journalism central to Victorian culture, it constituted the primary means for
spreading religious ideas and ideological movements. For any movement to
succeed, it was indispensable, according to the logic of the time, that it possess
an official newspaper as its chief organ. All religious movements that flourished in Victorian America were adept at publicity, ran their own newspapers,
and knew how to exploit the press to their advantage.[4] William Q. Judge's
Path was the backbone of the American Theosophical Movement. The
American Buddhist Movement issued the *Buddhist Ray*. Even atheistic and
"free thought" organizations produced official newspapers.[5] In keeping with
such exigencies, Quilliam centered his Islamic mission in Liverpool on the
Crescent, a monthly, and the *Islamic World*, a weekly, both of which were produced for more than two decades. Following Quilliam's lead, Webb intended
the *Moslem World* and the *Voice of Islam*—his two initial journals—to be a
monthly and weekly, respectively, to serve the same purpose.

In addition to independent publishing, editorial exchanges were standard
practice at the time, in accordance with which newspaper editors sent their
publications free of charge to their peers at other journals with the understanding that either party could reprint useful materials gratis. Webb distributed his journals far and wide across the country and around the world,
not just to private readers but to other newspaper editors, whose generally
favorable responses he would print in subsequent editions of his journals.[6]
Extensive reliance on exchanges provided Webb and other editors access to
free advertisement and abundant materials for publication.

Webb drew directly upon materials from Quilliam's publications and from
a number of journals like the *World's Advance Thought and Universal Republic*,
which he described as "one of the most interesting of our exchanges" and
repaid by a short advertisement for that journal. Even as Webb appealed for
financial help in 1895, he took care to inform readers that exchanges with his
journal remained free of charge.[7] In addition to editorial swapping, Webb
seems occasionally to have made gifts of his publications to important collections. He donated *The Three Lectures, Islam in America*, and *A Guide to Namaz* to
Harvard, for example, where they remain in the rare books collection.[8]

Sulayman Nyang singles out Webb for praise as the father of the North
American Islamic press, his publication activities having antedated by decades
any comparable endeavors by other American Muslims. In addition to being
first in the field, Webb stands out for the professional quality of his work.
Webb was able to sustain his publications for only a little more than three
years, but the brevity of his success is not surprising when compared to
similar publishing activity among Arabs and Muslims in America during the
twentieth century. It was not until the last decades of the century that their
publishing enterprises began to enjoy significant continuity and a sense of

lasting achievement. Between the close of the nineteenth century and the beginning of the Great Depression of 1929, more than one hundred Arab American newspapers and journals were launched in the United States, but few succeeded, and their mortality rate was high. Only in the 1920s did the Moorish Science Temple and Ahmadiyya begin to produce Islamic publications with sustained regularity. In the 1960s, the Nation of Islam's *Muhammad Speaks*, under the direction of Minister Malcolm X, met with unparalleled nationwide success, but it was not until the 1960s and 1970s that the American Islamic press can be said to have truly come into its own.[9]

The Oriental lectures do not reflect a consistent terminology regarding how Webb spoke about the Christian church or Islam, which appears later in the *Moslem World* and its successor, the *Moslem World and Voice of Islam*, a third journal that incorporated the initial two in a shorter monthly format.[10] Common themes run through Webb's lectures and writings, and are often repeated within the same text. The critique of "Church-Christianity" is among the strongest and most recurrent and was used consistently to illustrate Islam's superiority by contrast. Among Webb's most common themes was his conviction that Islam was in harmony with reason and science and compatible with progress and civilization. He often revisited his anti-Christian polemic in that context by emphasizing the obstructive role of the medieval church in contrast to the supportive role found in the civilization of Muslim Spain. In the same context, he frequently contended that "the Islamic system" constituted the best alternative for America's future.[11] Webb was especially enamored of "the Arabian Prophet," Muhammad, and made frequent references to his character and biography, emphasizing his exemplary stature and the primordial truth of his message. Webb had a penchant for discussing the nature of religion, especially the universal esoteric-exoteric dichotomy in world faiths, and he frequently spoke of the "religious instinct" in human beings, while asserting the inability of modern materialism and science to fulfill spiritual needs.

Webb's competence as an editor is clear in his selection of articles for his journals. In fact, he was more proficient as an editor than as a writer. Though his own writing is generally attractive, there are many factual errors—especially regarding the specifics of Islamic belief and practice—and much repetition. His style tends, nonetheless, to be engaging, especially when using humor and anecdotes, for which he had an obvious inclination. In one instance, he speaks of an Englishman he met in India who insisted that every Muslim he had seen in the Orient was "duck-legged and [had] knees in his trousers from sitting on his legs and feet so much in prayer." To adopt Islam as a faith was simply inconceivable for the English man because the daily prayer ritual would break the crease in his trousers. Webb responded: "In my opinion, it is very much more to one's advantage to go into Paradise duck-legged and with knees in his trousers than not to get in at all." Webb concluded the anecdote by telling his audience: "And since that time whenever I see a Mussulman who is duck-legged and has knees in his trousers I, at once, have a feeling of respect for him for I know that he is attending to his religious duties."[12]

Common themes run through Webb's lectures and writings, and in the *Moslem World* and its successor, the *Moslem World and Voice of Islam*, he adopted a fairly consistent terminology. For example, he uses "Church-Christianity" to distinguish the target of his criticisms from the original teachings of Jesus, which he professes to follow. Webb's earlier writings in *The Three Lectures*, published from lectures that were delivered in India in 1892, focus on the same themes but without an uniform terminology.[13] This difference reflects the fact that Webb in 1892 was still in the process of learning his new faith and the best words to communicate it to English-speakers.

Published Lectures

The Three Lectures, delivered during Webb's Indian tour, reflected the beginning stage of the American Mission. Although published in India, the work was readily available to Webb in America and constituted one of the key publications advertised in his journals in support of his movement. The book does not give a complete record of Webb's official speeches in India but is restricted to those delivered in Bombay, Hyderabad, and Madras. Because of its wide dissemination, *The Three Lectures* remains one of the easiest of Webb's books to find.[14] The collection was published by Hassan Ali, who also wrote a preface repeating much of the information on Webb's conversion that Webb presented in his Calcutta lecture and that reappears in his *Islam in America*.[15] The Calcutta lecture was published separately, and the Bombay lecture was reprinted at least twice.[16]

Webb wrote out his lectures in longhand and allowed publishers to copy them. The editor of Calcutta's *Mohammedan Observer* visited the guesthouse where Webb was staying with the purpose of transcribing the Calcutta lecture, which probably appeared afterward in that journal.[17] In Bombay, the *Bombay Gazette* and *Times of India* followed the same procedure for his lecture there and gave him the galleys, which he spent the greater part of a day proofreading.[18] Hassan Ali oversaw the printing of Webb's lectures in Hyderabad at a press in Secunderabad.[19] A local judge took it upon himself to cover the expenses of printing and provided Webb with one hundred and twenty-five copies for personal use.[20] Webb would package as many printed copies of his lectures as he could and post them to America.[21]

The Calcutta Lecture

Webb's first official lecture was in Rangoon, where he delivered "The Faith of Islam," similar in title and possibly content to his later Bombay lecture,

"Islam." "The Faith of Islam" was not published, however, and the Rangoon press took no note of it.[22] Webb's Calcutta address of October 16, 1892, which was given in a less than suitable venue because of a last-minute withdrawal of government permission, was first published in the *Mohammedan Observer* and was eventually reprinted in Lahore in 1893 under the title "The Lecture Delivered in Calcutta."[23] It was roughly the same length as Webb's other Oriental lectures.

Webb began the lecture by affirming his American identity: "We Americans are accredited with a desire to talk about ourselves and our great country. I shall have nothing to say about my country; but it would be necessary to say something about myself." The lecture focused on six themes common to Webb's presentations: his conversion, the meaning of religion, humanity's inherent need of religion, the esoteric and exoteric dimensions of religion, the inadequacy of institutional Christianity, the spiritual poverty of materialism and material science, and Islam's legacy as reflected in the civilization of medieval Muslim Spain.[24]

Most of Webb's discussion of religion and theology, which makes up a substantial part of the Calcutta lecture, is not repeated in his subsequent lectures or writings. He cited Herbert Spencer's observation that "religious ideas of one kind or another are almost universal" and concurred with Spencer that religion per se must be as "normal as any other [human] faculty" and ultimately "conducive to human welfare." Stressing Islam's fidelity to the primordial legacy of the human religious experience, Webb argued that Islam constituted living proof of the truths underlying all religions. He stressed the need for Europeans and Americans to overcome their erroneous views of "Oriental religions as if they were entirely different and distinct in their essence and purpose from Christianity and its numerous progeny." The dichotomy between the exoteric and esoteric was, he contended, natural to all religions, although more conspicuous in the Oriental religions than in "Western Christianity, notwithstanding Jesus' teaching, "unto you it is given to know the mysteries of the kingdom of heaven but unto them that are without, all things are done in parables." Webb assailed as "absurd" such Christian dogmas as the Trinity, and he insisted again that one of Christianity's greatest failings was neglect of its esoteric dimension, which had created a "Procrustes' bed" allowing for only "one presentation of religion" which could never be "suited equally to all classes and castes of men."[25]

Webb's Calcutta lecture developed the theme of the blindness of material science, which had the power to describe physical life precisely but could not discern life's secret or understand the world of the spirit. Although this was one of Webb's favorite themes, he developed it in Calcutta in a special way, emphasizing the antithetical nature of matter and spirit, the former always being "the enemy of spiritual perception." To be receptive to their inherent spiritual dimension, humans had to "dematerialize" themselves to "obtain the seeing eye and hearing ear in respect of divine things." This loss of materiality did not mean separating the soul from the body but purifying both body and soul "from engrossment in the things of sense." Purification taps the latent spiritual potential of human beings and allows them to gain "full access to stores of knowledge laid upon [the] soul and [attain] cognition alike of God and of the universe, and for [such] it is said 'there is nothing hid which shall not be revealed.'" Webb asserted that such purification of body and soul constituted the very spirit of Islam, although, in essence, it was to be found in "every religious system the world has ever known."[26]

For Webb the late nineteenth century was a time of "all-embracing research, exhaustive analysis and unsparing criticism." Thus, he described it as an age in which "no religious system can endure unless it appeals to the intellectual as well as the devotional side of man's nature," an aspect that, Webb contended, was missing from "orthodox Christianity." He judged "orthodox Christianity" to be in perpetual conflict with "rapidly advancing materialistic science" and predicted it would necessarily lose its hold upon "the minds of men capable of candid, unprejudicial thought and research." Christianity required doctrinal purification to remove "the soul-destroying reason-enchaining error and superstition" that had been fostered over centuries, altering the original beauty of Christ's teachings, which, for Webb and in accord with standard Islamic doctrine, had been identical to "true Mohammedanism." Webb averred that "the principles of Mohammedanism [were] such as any intelligent Christian [could] fully and heartily adopt without doing violence to any of the doctrines taught by Jesus." Moreover, Islam had proven itself a powerful civilizing force, engendering "incentives to a universal brotherhood of humanity and the guide to the light of everlasting truth." "The principles of Mohammedanism" led "to all that is purest, holiest and loftiest in the human character; and those who follow them humbly and faithfully will surely find that paradise wherein is perfect rest, perfect peace and perfect love."[27]

Islam

Webb presented a lecture called "Islam" in Bombay on November 10, 1892. It appears in *The Three Lectures* and was published separately in Bombay and in Lahore a year later. All versions are virtually identical, with only slight changes in wording, although a multitude of mistakes appear in the Lahore edition. Published under the auspices of Budruddin Kur, the Bombay and Lahore editions have the added advantage of including facsimiles of three early letters between Kur and Webb. The Lahore edition is also prefaced with an exhortation by Quilliam delivered to his Liverpool Muslim community.[28]

"Islam" focused on Webb's conversion narrative with recurrent polemics on the doctrinal corruption of "so-called Christianity," although Webb added that Islam had suffered similarly from the interpolations of its scholars. He

championed the integrity of the Prophet of Islam by looking at various aspects
of his biography and referred to Islam's esoteric dimension, insisting that the
Sufis had remained closest and most faithful to the original Prophetic legacy.[29]

"Islam" differed from Webb's Calcutta address by concentrating on the
tenets and ritual practices of the Islamic faith and treating the "bug-bear"
polygamy, which he had avoided until that time. Webb called attention to the
fundamental articles of Islamic faith, "the six heads of orthodox Mohammedanism." Webb mistook "belief in the Koran" for belief in all the revealed
books and insisted that Islamic belief in "predestination" did not "deprive
man of his character as a free agent."[30] Webb called the "five pillars" the five
"articles of religious practice." In Bombay and elsewhere, he omitted the first
pillar, the declaration of faith, and put ritual ablution in its place.[31] In closing,
Webb summed up his assessment of the Islamic faith:

> The essence of the true faith of Islam is resignation to the will of God,
> and its corner-stone is prayer. It teaches universal fraternity, uni-
> versal charity, universal love, and universal benevolence, and requires
> purity of mind, purity of action, purity of speech and perfect physical
> cleanliness. It is the simplest and most elevating form of religion
> known to man. It has not paid priesthood, nor elaborate ceremonial,
> admits no vicarious atonement, nor relieves its followers of any of the
> responsibility for their sins. It recognizes but one God, the Father of
> all things, the divine spirit that dwells in all the manifestations of
> nature.[32]

Philosophic Islam

"Philosophic Islam," Webb's best-attended Indian lecture, was delivered in
Hyderabad on November 25, 1892. Webb used the term "philosophy" generically here and elsewhere for the wisdom implicit in a religion's inner
teaching, and not in reference to classical philosophy. Philosophic Islam, for
Webb, referred to certain aspects of the Islamic scriptural teaching, especially
its insistence that nature bears witness to God's perfection. The lecture was
similar to Webb's presentation in Calcutta, focusing on the effects of material
science and materialism on the religious mood of the time and their intrinsic
methodological inability to discover spiritual truth. Philosophic Islam returned to the issue of polygamy but added the institution of gender segregation (purdah), which Webb had not treated before:

> I know very little of the practical application of the purdah system or
> of polygamy in the East, and, therefore, cannot say whether they are
> practiced in the true Islamic spirit or not. If they are not applied
> properly and justly they cannot produce good results; but in my

humble opinion the purdah system and polygamy, rationally and intelligently engrafted upon our social system, are the only possible remedies for the evils with which it is afflicted to-day. Prostitution, marital infidelity, drunkenness and kindred vices are prevalent from one end of the vast country to the other. Orthodox Christianity and orthodox Christian laws have fought in vain against these evils for a hundred years, and still they have steadily increased. Now, I believe that Islam and Islamic laws should have an opportunity to try and rid our social system of the monsters of sin that are preying upon it.[33]

"Philosophic Islam" broached the topic of Webb's proposed American Mission (the funding committee was intent on securing the financial backing of the Nizam of Hyderabad) and the lecture addressed the misgivings of some Indian Muslims Webb had encountered who feared that Islam would repel a "progressive and intelligent" people like Americans. He argued that it was precisely those forward-looking qualities in Americans that would attract them to Islam, if it were properly presented and understood.[34]

Webb thought that modern materialistic philosophy might ultimately be of use in bringing Westerners to Islam. He understood the critical spirit of modern thought as having brought humanity "direct and positive benefit" and created the possibility of new spiritual growth. At the same time, materialistic philosophy had exposed humanity to a hazard potentially greater than its benefits: the danger of effacing forever the universal religious truths and moral values without which humanity could not survive. It had torn down the edifice of spirituality with "little or no hope of rebuilding." Skepticism and doubt had become the "legitimate offspring of advanced materialistic education and civilization," and "the simple, childlike faith" of the past had been "blighted by the cruel frosts of atheism and agnosticism or frozen to death by our Western nineteenth century civilization."[35]

"Philosophic Islam" explored at length the limitations of modern science for disclosing the ultimate nature of reality or arriving at spiritual truth. Science could describe and unlock the material secrets of the physical universe but never discover the meaning of life. The latter was the province of "higher science," the primordial knowledge of the "mysteries of life and death" as revealed through the prophets.[36] To illustrate the limitations of scientific methodology, Webb invoked the analogy of the screwdriver and the gimlet (a pointed awl-like instrument):

Now what would you think of a man who tried to take a screw out of a piece of hard wood with a gimlet and insisted upon it that the thing couldn't be done because the tool wouldn't fit into the slot of the screw? Wouldn't you quite naturally and properly call him an idiot and tell him to go and get a screw-driver? Now modern science has found that its gimlet will not turn the screw of spiritual dynamics and therefore declares that it cannot be turned. Now what rather surprises me is that the sceptic clings so tenaciously to that gimlet when there is a screw-driver so near at hand.... Every true prophet the world has ever known has pointed out the way to the solution of the problems of life and death and every sceptic and materialist has stubbornly and foolishly persisted in ignoring it and following the path which leads directly away from it. He clings to the gimlet and refuses to take the screw-driver when it is offered to him.[37]

In the lecture, Webb revisited the theme of humanity's universal "religious instinct" and the phenomenon of spiritual atrophy, which, he insisted, governed the "intellectual faculties" as well as bodily ones. Natural spiritual gifts, he argued, could be lost just as they could be nurtured and developed to perfection. One's spiritual potential could be developed until the "higher faculties of our nature" came "to dominate our whole being," but this required a life of sound spirituality based on "the cultivation of fraternal love, perfect cleanliness of mind and body, and devotion to God."[38]

The Better Way

Webb delivered "The Better Way" in Madras on December 11, 1892. It was immediately after this speech, as mentioned in chapter 6, that Colonel Henry Steel Olcott of the Theosophical Society leaned over to congratulate Webb on being a "devilish good speaker."[39] The lecture's title reflected its primary theme: that Islam is a superior "system of salvation." Thus, it constitutes "the better way" because it embodies uncorrupted, primordial truth, "handed down to man from age to age, by the chosen Prophets of God":

Because it *is* that eternal truth. Because it is the only system that will satisfy the longings of the soul for a higher existence. Because it is the only system known to man which is strictly in harmony with reason and science. Because it is free from degrading superstitions, and appeals directly to human rationality and intelligence. Because it makes every man individually responsible for every act he commits and every thought he thinks, and does not encourage him to sin by teaching him a vicarious atonement. Because it is elevating and refining in its tendencies, and develops the higher, nobler elements of humanity when it is faithfully, wisely and intelligently followed.[40]

Antichurch polemic was prominent in the speech. Webb presented Islamic ritual as both a vehicle to salvation and a cornerstone of a sound public order by instilling social values like equality and fraternity, while inspiring a dynamic spiritual life through the proper balance of the esoteric and exoteric dimensions of religion. In reaction to the common nineteenth-century Western prejudice that Islam was an entirely outward faith, lacking a powerful inner dimension, Webb answered that the faith offered a "deeper more philosophical aspect than is apparent at first glance." Yet its chief beauty was exactly to be found in its outward dimension, so perfectly adapted "to the spiritual needs of all classes of humanity, from the humblest laborer to the most advanced thinker and man of letters."[41]

"The Better Way" culminated in a call to support for the American Mission, since "the better way" was hidden from the American people by their ignorance of Islam and lack of access to sound knowledge about it: "It is the plain and unmistakable duty of every Mussulman who loves and reveres the memory of our grand Prophet to use his earnest efforts to assist in planting that monument—Islam—upon the soil of every nation." He alluded to Quilliam's mission and the "firm foothold" it had established in Britain, which inspired Webb to hope that Islam would soon be established "in liberal progressive America," where "the masses of people [were] waiting to receive it."[42]

Mission Journals

Tocqueville observed with regard to early-nineteenth-century America: "The only historical monuments of the United States are newspapers. If a number comes to be missing, the chain of time is almost broken: present and past are no longer joined."[43] The statement remains apt for Webb's Islamic journals, which were the most credible achievement of his mission and are today an endangered monument to the early history of Islam in the United States. At present, more than half of the issues are missing, breaking "the chain of time" and severing the present from the past. Until recently, the New York Public Library was probably the only institution to have a full set of the *Moslem World*, but it was lost a few years ago.[44] The St. Louis Public Library has the journal in its listings, but it was mistakenly catalogued and bound, so that the library has only two issues of the *Moslem World* in its collection, though all issues of the *Moslem World and Voice of Islam*, which ran from 1895 till 1896, are present. Because of their age and the poor quality of the paper, all issues of the journals are in very poor condition, and it is hardly possible to turn a page without fear of its crumbling to pieces.[45]

In style and content, the journals differ greatly from Webb's lectures and other writings. Webb is completely at home in the journal genre. His work is of good quality, even by today's standards, and the materials he presents provide insight into his character and outlook, creating an excellent complement to his other writings. Much of the content of the *Moslem World* and subsequent

Moslem World and Voice of Islam is made up of short, untitled features and tidbits of information in block paragraphs, what the journalistic world calls "FOBs" (literally, "front of the book"), although there are also articles of various lengths. The *Voice of Islam* may well have been similar in content and structure to the later *Moslem World and Voice of Islam*, but it was edited by Mary Nafeesa Keep, and so its style may have differed from Webb's. Since no copies of the *Voice of Islam* have yet been discovered, it is impossible to say.

Webb had a taste for poetry and filled his journals with selections from American poets like Whitman and "the fireside poet," James Russell Lowell. Some poems were written especially for the *Moslem World* by converts or sympathizers. Others were reproduced in translation, such as Victor Hugo's French poem on Muhammad, "The Death of the Prophet," translated by Teresa Viele. Generally Webb's journals began and ended with poetry or English translations of Qur'anic passages, and there were also frequent excerpts, often lengthy, from English renditions of the Persian masters Sa'di and Rumi.[46]

The Moslem World

The *Moslem World* in its original form was published for less than a year. Its introductory installment appeared on May 12, 1893, and the series likely ran as a monthly until November, totaling seven issues, according to most sources.[47] Webb insisted that he had kept the *Moslem World* alive, despite lack of funds, until eight numbers had been issued.[48] Thus, there may have been a December issue, which has not come to light. The journal contained sixteen to seventeen relatively large folio pages, not counting additional advertisement leafs. Feature articles and translations made up the bulk of subject matter, although there were dozens of FOBs as well. Webb filled his journals with advertisements, and in the *Moslem World* these often took up entire pages.

Cover pages portrayed examples of Islamic architecture with brief commentaries. The October edition shows the Pearl Mosque of India with the comments of someone named Taylor: "It is a sanctuary so pure and stainless, revealing so exalted a spirit of worship that I am humbled as a Christian to think that our noble religion has never inspired its architects to surpass this temple to God and Mohammed."[49] Webb gave frequent expression in the journal to his lasting fascination with Islamic art and architecture. "Our Prophet's Tomb" was given a full column with an elaborate description of Muhammad's burial place in the central mosque of Medina and the graves of his two closest Companions, Abu Bakr and Umar, next to him.[50] Another edition printed a poem (without illustrations) by George Croly on the majesty of the Alhambra in Granada.[51]

The *New York Times* acknowledged the *Moslem World* as a journal worthy of note:

FIGURE 8.1. The Front Cover of the *Moslem World* (1893) Showing the Pearl Mosque

It is a well-printed paper of sixteen pages, and as it has as yet scarcely any advertising patronage, except the announcements of American dealers in Oriental carpets, it is [not] evident that it will be capable, in the course of a year, of absorbing a very handsome sum of money. Its literary contents consist, for the most part, of the praise of Islam, and set forth in some detail why it is preferable to Christianity. These arguments are not especially cogent, it must be said, from a Christian point of view, but there is no question of the uniqueness of the publication, and it may, perhaps, attain a success of curiosity which will mitigate the assessment of its enterprising Asiatic projectors.[52]

Webb printed sympathetic reactions to the *Moslem World* from faraway places like Norton, Kansas, where the editor of the *Liberator* welcomed Webb's journal with the words: "While it is advocating the Mohammedan religion it also teaches the necessity of living higher lives. No man can read it and be made worse, and he who follows its teachings will surely be made better. We wish there were more such journals throughout the country."[53]

Webb advertised the paper as "the only Mohammedan journal published in America," and Nyang rightly hails it as "the first Muslim periodical published in the United States."[54] The journal proclaimed itself a "magazine devoted to the interests of the American Islamic Propaganda" with the objective of spreading "the light of Islam in America."[55] Osman thought highly of the *Moslem World,* contending that Webb "never minced his words" and wrote "trenchantly and nobly" in defense of "a maligned and misunderstood Islam."[56] Webb assured readers that the *Moslem World* would provide them with "a general exposition of the Islamic religion" and noteworthy "contributions from the most learned Mussulmans of Turkey, Egypt, and India." His vigorous promotion read:

> Every student of Oriental Religions
>> SHOULD READ IT,
> Every independent thinker
>> SHOULD READ IT,
> Every investigator of spiritual philosophy
>> SHOULD READ IT,
> Mussulmans, Unitarians and Non-Sectarians
>> SHOULD READ IT,
> Religionists of all Sects and Creeds
>> SHOULD READ IT,
> Every truthseeker
>> SHOULD READ IT,
> In short, everybody
>> SHOULD READ IT.
>> 10 Cents for single copies.[57]

Conversion was one of the major themes in all Webb's journals, despite his repeated claims in the press that he did not aim to proselytize. He set aside three pages in the *Moslem World* for an article titled "The Evidences of Islam" by Hajee Abdulla Browne, essentially an invitation to conversion.[58] Most reports of conversion emanated from British India but often pertained to Western converts, British, French, and Spanish, who had embraced Islam there.[59] He noted the spread of Islam among Indian Hindus and around the world.[60] Webb announced the conversion of a "young Japanese" Muslim and foresaw a bright future for Islam in that land.[61] He contended that Islam was spreading rapidly in China and aired the story "rumored about two years ago that the Queen [Victoria] had become a convert to Islam," based on her preferential treatment of Hafiz Abdul Kareem, a secretary and personal attendant, which included building him a private mosque within yards of Balmoral Castle.[62]

The *Moslem World* frequently raised issues related to gender. Webb argued that the status of women in Islam was superior to their status in Western societies of the time, and he reported a number of items from the American press that he felt reflected poorly on the status of American women.[63] He quoted a Muslim lecturer in Britain:

In England, until lately, a wife's property was that of her husband and
what was his was his own. No such iniquity ever existed in Islam.
In case of marriage, in addition to the mutual consent, there is another condition, viz. [namely]: dowry, which is a debt upon the husband which, unless the wife forgives, can never be disputed. Marriage
is by mutual consent but the dissolution of it depends only on the
husband who must pay the dowry if he dissolves the marriage. A divorce without a just cause renders man hateful in the sight of God.[64]

Webb disapproved of a movement afoot at Wesleyan College in Middletown,
Connecticut, to exclude women from higher education.[65] He spoke favorably
about steps taken toward women's suffrage in the South, a matter, he believed,
which would "interest all the thinking women and many thinking men in the
country."[66]

As a rule, Webb let women speak for themselves. It was his most effective
technique regarding polygamy and gender segregation in traditional Muslim
societies. He printed an article by Esmeralda Cervantes titled "The Women of
Turkey," and she spoke on the topic at the Chicago World's Fair.[67] He reprinted an extensive interview with Sarah Parker, "the well-known Oriental
traveler, journalist, and lecturer," that had run in the *New York Mercury*.
Parker spoke from personal experience and noted that she had entertained
typical Victorian biases before traveling to the Muslim world, where she
discovered "true refinement" such as she had never believed possible. She
found the "true position of women" in the Muslim world one of its "least
understood" aspects and noted that, although plural marriages were lawful in
Islam:

Yet women have so much influence over men there that more than
one wife is an exception. The Mohammedan lady governs her own
home; the whole internal management is hers, and the members of
Mohammedan families are obedient, forgiving, not selfish—and
overflowing with hospitality. They are consulted on all matters of
business, politics and social questions, and they own their own property and manage it as pleases them during life and dispose of it as
they wish at death. Their movements are free, going about veiled....
It would be hard to think these women were unhappy.[68]

Webb prided himself in being a "liberal American," and he often invoked
liberalism in contrast to what he perceived to be bigoted and unjust in the
society around him. He disparaged Oxford for its treatment of the Romantic
poet Percy Bysshe Shelley, whom it expelled in 1811 as a "rebel against God
and collegiate authority," a "poet of atheism," and the "apostle of anarchy."
Webb noted that Oxford reversed its position in a ceremony honoring Shelley

during the summer of 1893, where the head of the university declared: "Truly, like the heathen of old, we burn what once we adored, and we adore what once we burned."[69] Webb defended Oscar Wilde:

> For rank Phariseeism there is nothing in history to compare with the sanctimonious ostracism of Oscar Wilde. Just think of it! Theatres withdraw his name from their play-bills and libraries throw his books out of window. Wilde was once called a pretty fair specimen of a Church-Christian, too. If his books and plays were not vicious and degrading before, how can they be so now that his private immoralities have been exposed?[70]

Webb eulogized Thomas Henry Huxley, proclaiming him a champion of truth:

> All lovers of truth should hold his memory in reverence, for he was ever active and fearless in his exposure of the fallacies and superstitions of a religious system, the natural tendency of which is to enchain and paralyze the intellect and reasoning powers and hold mankind in a thralldom of abject submission to clerical authority. To this extent he was of inestimable service to Islam, although he never openly advocated its great truth.[71]

Webb made frequent references to Colonel Robert Green Ingersoll, who stood at the center of the great controversy in Victorian America between science and the church.[72] Webb admired Ingersoll's "sturdy, uncompromising devotion to what he believes is the truth" and his "positive antagonism to superstitions and delusions."[73] He defended Ingersoll against a rabbi who attacked him for his lack of sympathy with the Bible:

> If there was ever a man upon earth who has read the Bible intelligently and understandingly, Col. Robert G. Ingersoll has done so, but we will agree with the Rabbi, that he has never had much sympathy with it. That requires the sort of blind unreasoning belief that Col. Ingersoll is incapable of. We, of course, cannot endorse wholly his declaration of principles but we are quite sure that he has a deeper, more intelligent and comprehensive knowledge of the Bible than 999 out of every one thousand of his Church-Christian critics.[74]

Webb defended Ingersoll against the "intolerance of Church-Christians" in Hoboken, New Jersey, who had attempted to prevent Ingersoll from expressing his opinion about the Bible. Webb suggested that Ingersoll's adversaries would never tolerate behavior like their own if it came from Muslims: "If a Mussulman community should try to prevent a Church-Christian missionary from abusing the Koran, what a howl would arise all along the church-line!"[75]

The Voice of Islam

Ferris writes that Webb's Moslem World Publishing Company issued "at least twenty-six volumes of the *Voice of Islam* and *The Moslem World: Dedicated to the American Islamic Propaganda* between 1893 and 1895."[76] Although Ferris confused the *Moslem World* of 1893 with the *Moslem World and Voice of Islam*, which came out later, there is no question that Webb also issued a separate publication titled the *Voice of Islam*. It was initially intended to be a weekly, but Webb's later references to it indicate that only a limited number of editions of the *Voice of Islam* ever appeared. Not surprisingly, the American Propaganda lacked the means to publish it on the scale originally proposed.

Webb mentioned the *Voice of Islam* in his January 15, 1894, correspondence with the Ottoman embassy in Washington.[77] In 1894, the *New York Times* mentioned the paper by name in conjunction with Nafeesa Keep noting that she was its editor, which indicates that the *Voice of Islam* ran through 1893 till possibly as late as July 1894.[78] During the first four months of 1895, the *Moslem World and Voice of Islam* offered for sale back issues of the *Voice of Islam* at 3 cents a copy, postage included.[79]

The *Moslem World and Voice of Islam*

The *Moslem World and Voice of Islam* was a monthly and first appeared in January 1895 as a temporary replacement for the two earlier journals combined in its title. It was a scaled-down version of the *Moslem World*, presumably following the format of the *Voice of Islam*, since both the *Voice of Islam* and the combined journals sold for 3 cents including postage.[80] A four-page paper, the *Moslem World and Voice of Islam* was dominated by FOBs but contained occasional articles like those that made up the greater part of the *Moslem World*. Webb acknowledged that the new paper was not on a par with the *Moslem World*, and he urged readers to give him the financial backing that would allow him to expand it to a size that would be "more widely read and more influential."[81]

Like its predecessors, the *Moslem World and Voice of Islam*'s purpose was "to spread the light of Islamic truth in the United States and to assist in uniting under a common brotherhood all who accept the Moslem faith, intelligently, honestly, and unselfishly and sincerely."[82] It came at a time when the American Islamic Propaganda was in the process of taking on the name of the American Moslem Brotherhood, which carried distinct missionary implications. It is not surprising that conversion was a more prominent theme in the new journal than in the *Moslem World*. Success at conversion was clearly an Ottoman concern, and Webb opened the first issue of the *Moslem World and Voice of Islam* on a suitable note: "We think that the American people are becoming more serious every day as they realize the corrupt social and political conditions into which we have drifted. There is not the slightest doubt of their becoming Moslems in the near future—and good Moslems, too."[83]

As before, there were ample reports of British and European converts to Islam in British India.[84] Webb noted that a "Church-Christian priest" had recently converted to Islam in Bombay and taken the name Abdul Kadir.[85] He spoke of a Parsee youth who had made the decision to embrace Islam, although his family punished him severely for it.[86] Webb made general pronouncements about the spread of Islam in America, England, Africa, and China, where the Muslim population, according to Webb, had more than doubled during the last twenty-five years.[87]

Webb contended that the Unitarians and Universalists were on the verge of conversion and commended in particular the Unitarian minister Reverend J. T. Sunderland, founder and editor of the *Unitarian*, whose wife had spoken in Webb's favor at the World's Parliament of Religions. "Mr. Sunderland," Webb declared, "is one of the broad-minded intelligent Unitarians who are practically Mussulmans. It is only a question of a short time, we believe, when this class of Unitarians will fully realize the practical utility of organizing under the banner of Islam."[88] Regarding the Unitarians and Universalists in general, Webb asserted:

There are hundreds, possibly thousands, of Unitarians and Universalists in the United States who, since the commencement of our
Islamic propaganda in this country two years ago, have given assent
to the truths taught by Mohammed (peace be upon him) and yet they
shrink from making the fact known among their friends.[89]

Webb argued that there were "thousands of presumably well-educated persons in this blessed country" who were simply "afraid to read Islamic literature." He had met no less than twenty-five who "frankly admitted the fact and said they feared they might lose faith in the religion of their ancestors. We have met many more who ignored the subject entirely and strutted grandly on—proud of their ignorance and credulity."[90]

Webb sent out "quite a number" of the first three issues of the *Moslem World and Voice of Islam* "to our Oriental brothers as sample copies, free of charge" to demonstrate that the paper was back and to seek their support.[91] "Fraternal greetings" and a "vast number of letters of sympathy and congratulation" were "showered" on Webb with the publication's appearance. He regretted not being able to print them all in the paper's columns but declared:

We desire to thank our loyal brothers for their expressions of fraternal
love and confidence and assure them of our firm belief that the Almighty God who knows all hearts will ever make the truth triumphant. A perfect trust in God and unwavering reliance upon the

teachings of our Holy Prophet will carry us safely through any
storm that may descend upon us.[92]

The *Mohammedan Observer* of Calcutta wrote:

> We are happy to learn that M'd Alexander Russell Webb's mission is
> not a failure, and he has not abandoned it, but on the contrary, is
> working at it as vigorously as ever, and will continue so to do, so long
> as life and health are left to him.[93]

The *Madras Mohammedan* echoed the same sentiments, concluding that
"truth must prevail, no matter how numerous its enemies."[94] Letters of support came from fifteen Muslims of Mauritius.[95] "The good Shaikh Yussuf bin
Abdulla Ebrahim of Busreh, Arabia" not only encouraged Webb to continue
his work but also gave "generous assistance."[96] A "Brother S. Moosa" from
the "Moslem community at Hong Kong, China" wrote: "We Moslems here all
join in wishing you success in your labors for the progress of Islam."[97] An
anonymous Indian schoolteacher counseled Webb:

> In the end I only remark that as you are sincere in your efforts God
> will bless you and yours. Every great man has to face difficulties
> and so you must encounter and conquer them. You can well imagine
> the case of your Holy Prophet, whom you have so graphically de-
> scribed in your "Islam in America;" how he was beset with danger,
> yet did not despair—did not give up the cause he had taken up until
> he was successful. You are revealing the Truth unto those who
> have not been told of it before. They will certainly hate you, dislike
> you and do everything in their power to harm you. But at last you will
> succeed. Have God on your side and let the whole world turn against
> you. The Koran says: "Truth came and Untruth disappeared; and
> Untruth must disappear." In the history of the spread of Islam in
> America your name will stand in the first place. May the blessing of
> Allah be upon you and your family.[98]

Another "Indian Mussulman brother" wrote: "Despair not; pearls are often
unstrung that they may be put in better order."[99] S. R. Shepherd of Leavenworth,
Kansas, who had been an enthusiastic supporter of the *Moslem World* and a
contributor to it, wrote to Webb regarding the *Moslem World and Voice of Islam*:

> I welcome your little missionary journal and desire to have my name
> entered on the list. I grant courteous hospitality to all religions and
> extend the right hand of fellowship and fraternity to all men of
> whatever race or religion, but particularly and more cordially to those
> who, by spiritual unfoldment, have attained the royal purple degree
> of universal love and toleration.[100]

Appeals for financial backing run through the *Moslem World and Voice of Islam* from beginning to end. Webb still aspired to build an indigenous foundation for his movement, independent of outside support. He told his readers that it was "the sacred duty of every true Mussulman to help our little journal grow until it becomes what the old *Moslem World* was: viz. [namely], one of the most attractive and instructive publications in the United States":

> We desire to issue a twenty-page monthly and a four-page weekly to
> dispel the dense clouds of ignorance that prevail in this country
> concerning Islam and its grand Prophet but we cannot do so until
> this small journal becomes self-supporting and we have a substantial
> publication fund to draw upon. Help us to spread Islam throughout
> the length and breadth of this land.[101]

There is no indication that he received any money for it from his original Indian backers, whom, in fact, he indicted in the journal's first issue for their failure to stand behind him.[102] He was, of course, seeking Ottoman help for his publications as early as January 1894, and it is likely that they helped finance the *Moslem World and Voice of Islam* either wholly or in part. The Ottoman connection is borne out by the paper's enthusiasm for Turkish concerns. In contrast to the *Moslem World*, there are several acclamations of Sultan Abd al-Hamid II and defense of the Turks on the Armenian question.[103] Two pro-Turkish pamphlets, *The Armenian Troubles* and *A Few Facts about Turkey*, which Webb anonymously edited appeared concurrently with the paper. Webb not only had the finances to produce and advertise the booklets in his journal but was able to send them free, postage included, to anyone who requested them, a clear sign of Ottoman financial backing.[104]

Toward the end of 1895, Webb announced to his readers that support for the paper had been inadequate to allow for an expanded version the following year.[105] The announcement caused confusion among readers, many of whom understood Webb as planning to discontinue the paper, to which he responded:

> We have never entertained this idea and will continue to publish it
> (Insha-Allah), even if we do not enlarge it now, as long as we are able
> to do so. We recognize in it a very important factor in our work
> of introducing Islam in this country and our earnest efforts shall
> be devoted to its continued improvement. We entered upon this
> noble work determined to succeed in spite of all the obstacles
> thrown in our way by wicked schemers and fanatical religion-
> ists, and we are availing ourselves of the best means at hand to bring
> about success. We consider our journal one of them. In our efforts we
> are constantly reminded of the words of the poet:

> If thou canst plan a noble deed,
> And never flag till it succeed,
> Though in the strife thy heart should bleed,
> Whatever obstacles control,
> Thine hour will come—go on, true soul,
> Thou'lt win the prize, thou'lt reach the goal.[106]

Nevertheless, with the onset of 1896, Webb announced that the *Moslem World and Voice of Islam* had been published at a loss and urgently required support to continue.[107] The paper discontinued the following month.

Books and Booklets

Islam in America

Webb published *Islam in America* in April 1893, shortly after the inception of his mission and hoped to follow it up with "larger and more complete works." All of Webb's books are short, and *Islam in America*, at seventy-one pages of length, is no exception, but it probably stands out as the best summary of Webb's thought.[108] The proposed larger works never came to fruition, leaving *Islam in America*, as Melton observes, Webb's "major apology."[109] Webb thought highly of the work and advertised it in glowing terms:

> This is positively the first work of its kind ever printed in the English language and should be in the hands of Every Honest Seeker after Truth who is capable of considering without prejudice a religious system which is the guide of life of nearly Three Hundred Millions of the Human Race.[110]

The book is still readily available in the United States and Great Britain, indicating that it enjoyed wide dissemination.[111]

For the content of *Islam in America*, Webb borrowed heavily from *The Three Lectures*, and there is hardly anything in the former which was not in the latter.[112] He began *Islam in America* by lauding the "almost universal disposition among liberal-minded Americans, to know more of the Oriental religions" and break away from "soul-destroying religious superstitions" in the search to develop "an independent, fearless spirit of thought and investigation, which is gradually becoming the aggressive and relentless enemy of the mental slavery of creeds." He claimed somewhat implausibly, given his preoccupation with conversion in the mission journals, that his purpose in writing the book was neither to "destroy nor weaken any creed or system of theology, nor to make proselytes for Islam, but to arouse and encourage among English-speaking Christians a spirit of calm, persistent and unprejudiced investigation to be applied to their own as well as other systems of religion."[113]

Webb said that he and his mission had met with widespread interest in the United States, especially through correspondence, reflecting an honest desire among "broad-minded Americans" to learn about the Islamic faith.[114]

In his Oriental lectures, Webb hardly made mention of Islamic law per se, although he made frequent reference to Islam's exoteric dimension. *Islam in America* claimed, however, that "the Islamic laws" are "an outgrowth of this [religious] system, as well as of the social and climatic conditions prevalent in the East for ages, and which cannot be said to belong to the religion itself."[115] He added new points about marriage in Islam, such as its being a "civil, not a religious contract" and insisted, as in the journals, that "the rights of the wife are more fully protected and guaranteed than those of the average European or American wife." He refuted the common Western misconception that Islam sees women as spiritually inferior to men, lacking souls, or incapable of entering paradise.[116] He also treated in some detail a number of controversial topics like slavery, concubinage, and jihad.[117]

Webb included brief references to his "protracted sojourn among the Mussulmans of the East."[118] Although he spoke hesitantly of purdah in India, he confidently declared in *Islam in America* that it was not "a part of the Mohammedan system" but, rather, "a custom borrowed from the Hindus and other Eastern peoples, who practiced it long before Mohammed was born":

> During the Prophet's life, as well as in the reign of the early Caliphs, the Arabian women were perfectly free to go about as they pleased, and a woman could travel alone in any part of the country by day or night, without being subjected to assault or insult. The idea of seclusion arose from a misconception of the following passage of the Koran: "And speak to the believing women, that they refrain their eyes and observe continence; and that they display not their ornaments except to their husbands or their fathers, or their sons or their husband's sons." The question of abolishing the purdah is being seriously considered by the more advanced Mussulmans of India; and in some parts of Turkey, Egypt and Arabia it is not practiced at all.[119]

Among Webb's new material in *Islam in America* were extensive citations from "the learned Imam Al Gazzali, than whom there is no higher human authority" in Islam after prophecy. Webb cited a lengthy theological credo by al-Ghazali on the Islamic conception of God and repeated it later in the *Moslem World and Voice of Islam*.[120]

A Guide to Namaz

Webb wrote *A Guide to Namaz* at the height of his mission in 1893 to teach Islamic prayer ritual and procedures for ablutions and bathing. In India, the

Islamic prayer ritual is called *namāz*, a Persian word that Webb encountered among Indian Muslims and mistakenly believed to be Arabic.[121] The twenty-seven page booklet, the shortest of Webb's monographs, contained sketches to illustrate movements and postures. It reflects Webb's fundamental concern with the exoteric dimension of Islam and his conviction that it and not the esoteric aspect of the faith, which he valued more highly, was the foremost objective of his Islamic mission and something uniquely suitable to all classes and types of people. Webb stated explicitly in the booklet that he was presenting the teachings of "orthodox Mohammedanism," and he made a point of prefacing his discussion of ritual with a statement of Islamic articles of faith, regarding which all "orthodox Mussulmans" were united.[122] Because of its fundamental concern with "orthodox" exoteric Islamic ritual, *A Guide to Namaz* confirms Webb's public declarations that his mission would make orthodox Islamic morality and practice its fundamental concern. By the same token, the book clearly rebuts Dannin's misapprehension that Webb's attachment to Islam was solely esoteric and that he had no interest in the religion's exoteric, outward dimensions as reflected in mainstream Islamic orthodoxy.[123]

Webb opened the book in a missionary voice, declaring Islam to be the "True Faith." He suggested that Islamic prayer ritual would be of general interest to the public and that familiarity with it would help to "soften or break down" the barriers of "bitter prejudice and intolerance that now shut out the truth from the eyes of the masses of educated Americans." He also prepared the booklet with American and English converts in mind, since the rituals it treated were essential obligations for them to learn:

> It is not exaggeration to say that there is not more than one Church-Christian in half a million who has any just and proper conception of the Islamic system of religion or knows how and when and where the Mussulman prays; what his prayer means, what his daily religious practices are or how the system he follows is arranged. In writing this book I have had two objects in view. The first, is to supply American and English converts to Islam with a complete and explicit guide to prayer; the second, is to educate honest, fair-minded, thoughtful people to a better knowledge and appreciation of the leading doctrine, or cornerstone of the Islamic system.[124]

Webb averred that many "intelligent Americans" had asked him how one became a "Mussulman" after "they become convinced of the truth of the Unity of God and the inspiration of our Holy Prophet (Peace be with him)." He emphasized that conversion to Islam was without formalities, contrary to the assumptions of most Americans: "They are unaware, of course, that in declaring their belief in these truths they are already Mussulmans and fully entitled to membership in the grand Moslem Brotherhood."[125]

A Guide to Namaz reflects attention to accurate terminology regarding Islam and Muslims, a concern that also appears in the *Moslem World and Voice of Islam*.[126] Webb noted that "Mohammedan, Moslem, and Mussulman are synonymous" but added that Muslims generally preferred to be called "Mussulmans" instead of "Mohammedans." "Islam," a word he had rarely used up to then, meant "resignation to the will of God, or aspiration to the higher divine principle that exists within every man":

> We may carry this expression of the Islamic idea further and say that a Mussulman, Moslem, Mohammadan [sic] or Follower of Islam is one who not only believes in the Unity of God and the inspiration of Mohammed, but who endeavors earnestly and honestly, from daylight to the hour when he closes his eyes in sleep, in every thought and act of his life, to cultivate his higher spiritual nature and bring his soul nearer to that divine spirit which is a part or accompaniment of his spiritual nature. Perfect purity of thought, word and deed, the deepest fraternal love, and the exercise of all the virtues must be the active elements of every true Mussulman's daily life.[127]

A Few Facts about Turkey

The pro-Turkish booklets *A Few Facts about Turkey under the Reign of Abdul Hamid II* and *The Armenian Troubles and Where the Responsibility Lies* were published anonymously. Although they were Webb's handiwork, neither publication was an original composition by Webb; rather, both were editorial compilations of materials Webb selected from various sources.[128] They were unquestioning in their support of the Turks and relentless in their condemnation of the Armenians, especially American missionaries and naturalized Armenian Americans whom Webb portrayed as principal fomenters of the trouble. Anonymity was obviously aimed at concealing Webb's direct involvement in the works. It gave the books greater credibility and served to conceal Webb's Ottoman support (a matter the Ottoman embassy preferred to keep clandestine) since the pamphlets clearly served Turkish interests. Webb liked the Turks and was always inclined toward them. In return, he enjoyed their favor, and the pro-Turkish pamphlets undoubtedly increased his official good standing with the Ottoman government and were probably a major reason for his appointment as Honorary Turkish Consul-General to New York in 1901 and official trip to Turkey, where he was decorated and given the honorary title Bey.

A Few Facts about Turkey was published in early 1895, since Webb first advertised it in the May issue of the *Moslem World and Voice of Islam*.[129] Like its companion piece, *The Armenian Troubles* appeared in early 1896 and addressed the mounting Armenian crisis in the Ottoman Empire. Allegations of Turkish massacres, some of which Webb acknowledged in the second pamphlet, had become the burning issue of the day, similar in magnitude to the Arab-Israeli crisis now.

What became of the Turkish Armenians in the two decades between 1895 and 1915 and the role of Turkish authorities in the matter remain as hotly contested today as ever. Historians, prominent people around the world, Armenians, and many Turks now insist that relevant sections of the Ottoman Archives and other historical resources be opened to the public so that the truth can finally be verified. The Armenian issue remains a sensitive topic among Armenians and in Turkey, especially among nationalists, to the extent that prominent Turkish writers and intellectuals who have dared to broach the issue honestly have been imprisoned, turning the Armenian question into a matter of free speech as well as a long-neglected problem of human rights.

Armenians constituted one of the oldest and most important Christian minorities in the Ottoman Empire, which, for centuries, ruled all Armenian regions in Anatolia, the Caucasus, and Central Asia. During these centuries, the Armenians were well-integrated into the Ottoman Empire, enjoyed extensive liberties, and were generally regarded as Turkey's most loyal Christian subjects. This state of affairs changed radically in the nineteenth century. In 1828, major Russian victories forced the Ottomans to cede large parts of Eastern Armenia to the Russian Empire. As the Russians, British, French, and Austro-Hungarian Hapsburgs vied for influence in Turkish realms, the substantial Armenian populations that remained within the Ottoman heartlands were converted into a political fulcrum for direct leverage in internal Turkish affairs. Christian missionaries also became deeply entangled in the controversy. From the Turkish standpoint, the Armenian question was unmistakably political. Sanctimonious Western demands for Armenian self-determination were seen as perilous attempts to destabilize the Ottoman Empire, already known as "the sick man of Europe." Armenian insurgency movements employed terrorist tactics, took many innocent Muslim lives, and were, to a considerable extent, instigated and backed by foreign interests. From the Turkish standpoint, defeating the Armenian insurgency was a vital matter of national security. The period from 1895 till 1896, covered in the pamphlets, was one of the earliest episodes of the ever evolving crisis, and the Turkish response provoked allegations of repression and massacre. The worst, however, was yet to come, and it is the massacres that allegedly took place in 1915 during World War I that have been called the first genocide of the modern age.[130]

Nothing Webb did under the auspices of the American Islamic Propaganda raises thornier questions than the Armenian pamphlets, given the enormity of the Armenian question and the allegations of genocide later associated with it. Webb's overtly partisan endorsement of the official Turkish line and his equally strong prejudice against the Armenians, including the dissemination of anti-Armenian racist slurs, are immeasurably graver than the racist epithets in his diary.

Turkish influence is unmistakable in the workings of the American Islamic Propaganda during 1895 and 1896. There is no doubt that the pro-Ottoman pamphlets reflect the depth that influence had reached and demonstrate the degree to which Webb's Turkish patrons were willing to exploit him and his movement for political gain, while relegating the "religious" dimension of his undertaking to a much lower status. The Armenian pamphlets diverted Webb's American Islamic Propaganda from its original goal and converted the American Propaganda into an exercise in propaganda in the twentieth-century sense of the word.

At the same time, Webb was hardly an unwilling participant. He seems clearly to have believed in what he was doing by editing the pamphlets, and probably never regretted having done so. He never disavowed the Turks and proudly accepted the honors Sultan Abd al-Hamid bestowed upon him in 1901. Webb's movement had never been totally apolitical and often went on record in support of Muslim interests abroad against the colonial aspirations of Western powers. It is valid, however, to question the extent to which the politicization of Webb's movement under the aegis of Sultan Abd al-Hamid and the Ottoman cause might have ultimately have caused Webb to abandon his Islamic mission. Webb apparently terminated his American Moslem Brotherhood work imme-diately after the second pamphlet's appearance, which may not have been merely a matter of coincidence. Webb and his family endured financial hardship for at least the last two years of the mission, and it seems unlikely that continued financial deprivation alone can account for Webb's abrupt termination of his movement early in 1896, when his journal continued to speak of his enthusiasm for his mission. The political turn that the American Moslem Brotherhood had taken in support of Ottoman policy, however, was not consistent with Webb's original vision. It is plausible that Webb ultimately became as disillusioned with his Turkish patrons as he had been, years before, with his Indian sponsors. In that light, the movement ceased to merit in Webb's eyes or those of his family the immense sacrifices they had been willing to make until that time.

There is great similarity between A Few Facts about Turkey and the somewhat later Armenian Troubles. Both works focused on the alleged role of recently nat-uralized Armenian Americans in the crisis, and the latter booklet repeated ex-tensive portions of the former. The Moslem World and Voice of Islam became an outlet for the expression of similar sentiment by others. In December 1895 and in February 1896, Webb published in his paper two lengthy poems by Cora Wilburn of Marchfield Hills, Massachusetts—"In Defence of the Right" and "To His Imperial Majesty, Sultan Abdul Hamid II"—that were written especially for the journal and replete with references to matters mentioned in the pamphlets, such as the sultan's protection of Jews in the face of Europe's indifference toward them.[131]

Webb gave A Few Facts about Turkey good marks, pronouncing it "prob-ably the most important and interesting work on Turkish affairs, given to

English readers in the present century."[132] It could not "fail to have a potent influence upon honest public opinion, relative to the Armenian question" and showed the progressiveness of the sultan's reign:

> No lover of truth and fair-play, who has even a faint suspicion of the wicked misrepresentations of Turkey and her sovereign that have been circulated for years by Armenian conspirators and bigoted, intolerant Church-Christian missionaries, can read the book without wondering how the Sublime Porte could have been so grossly maligned by American newspapers and Church-Christians without a single protest from honest men and women.... The broad tolerance and liberality displayed by His Imperial Majesty toward the Church-Christians who invade the country and, not infrequently, are insolent, presumptuous and insulting to those who do not follow their religion, shows what a noble spirit of forbearance he must possess. The book also deals fully and fairly with the Armenian agitation and justly arraigns fanatical Church-Christian missionaries for their active efforts to create trouble in the Turkish domain. "Let American missionaries and their Board," writes the author, "realize that it is not their duty and mission to help in securing the freedom and independence of any nationality in Turkey or to countenance secret societies, or to accuse the Turkish government of massacres that have not and cannot have any existence in reality." The main purpose of the book is not to show how Church-Christian missionaries have flagrantly abused the privileges freely given them in the Turkish Dominions and have aided and encouraged conspiracies against the government, but to give the plain, unvarnished truth concerning the progress made and the civilization attained under the reign of Abdul Hamid II; his perfect freedom from religious intolerance and his deep interest in the welfare and prosperity of the people. We earnestly hope that this book will find its way into the hands of every fair-minded, truth-loving American.[133]

A Few Facts about Turkey focused on modern technological development in Turkey, a matter of great concern to Victorians in their evaluation of themselves and others as chief indicators of progress. Webb drew attention to extensive railway development, the expansion of harbors and ports, the intensification of industry and manufactures. He noted the initiative of Ottoman Chambers of Commerce throughout the empire, the development of agriculture and forestry, river and canal improvements, banking, and educational reform. He drew attention to public works like the creation of municipal gardens, zoological and botanical gardens, and the spread of gas lighting.

Webb's pamphlet sought to create the impression that Turkey enjoyed substantial economic resources and was regaining its fiscal strength. It described

Constantinople as surely "one of the first commercial centers of the entire world."[134] The Turkish national debt was in the process of being repaid by virtue of the "miraculous settlement" of 1881 due to "the wisdom of its author, the Sultan Abdul Hamid." The booklet insisted that the "syndicates of the financial establishments of London, Paris, Vienna, and Berlin," which held most Ottoman bonds, welcomed heartily the Sultan's consolidation of the public debt.[135]

A Few Facts about Turkey emphasized the potential military strength of the Ottomans to protect their interests against attack. Both topics, the economy and the military, were linked implicitly to the Armenian crisis, attempting to make clear that Western intervention would be unlikely to succeed. The pamphlet painted a picture of modern Turkey reminiscent of the invincible Ottomans of old, insisting that the Turks could still "defy all attacks:"[136]

> The Ottoman infantry has from all time been renowned for its power
> of resistance and impetuosity in attack. In an assault upon the en-
> emy at the point of the bayonet, the Ottoman infantry is like a human
> avalanche, of which the tremendous impulse can be checked only
> by a much superior force. In defending a place, a redoubt, the Turk-
> ish foot-soldier is always at his post, firm as a rock.[137]

It added that the Ottoman navy had been reorganized, thanks to the sultan's "foresight and tenacity," and it enumerated the types of ships and new vessels at its disposal, some of which were so "superb" that Turkish naval construction could "rival other maritime powers."[138]

The last fifteen pages of the booklet were devoted to "the Armenian agitation." It maintained that the Armenian minority had profited greatly under the present regime and cited the sultan's "innumerable encouragements" to them in education in particular, insisting that he "distribute[s] his generosity from his purse to all subjects regardless of their religion," for "all his subjects, sons of the same country, are absolutely equal."[139] It indicted American missionaries working in collaboration with Armenians who had become U.S. citizens only, it alleged, in order to return to Turkey and resume separatist activities under the aegis of American citizenship. The pamphlet recommended that the United States adopt a policy regarding naturalized citizens like that of Great Britain, which revoked the citizenship of naturalized Britons if they returned to their native lands to live.[140]

The Armenian Troubles

Webb announced publication of The Armenian Troubles in January 1896 and contended that "in a rank and evidently thoughtful manner, it lays bare the plots of the Armenian revolutionists and shows the animus of the agitation against Turkey." As with A Few Facts about Turkey, Webb promised to deliver it free of charge, postage included, to anyone who desired a copy, a clear indication, given Webb's poverty at the time, that much if not all of his budget was coming from the Turks.[141] *The Armenian Troubles* was composed from five different articles, all of which had appeared in the New York press, written by Americans and Europeans who lived in Turkey, where, Webb insisted, "impartial and correct information was accessible."[142] Webb contended that his only wish in presenting the pamphlet was "to impart to his readers a true and thorough knowledge of the present Armenian troubles," despite an atmosphere that had become charged with invective and "polluted with falsehoods and exaggerations."[143]

The Armenian Troubles focused on the severest period of the 1890s crisis, when certain allegations of Turkish atrocities were admitted to be fact.[144] The pamphlet portrayed the crisis as purely political, directing the brunt of its argument against the Armenian revolutionary committees, but also playing on contemporary racial bias by ranking the Turks over the "certainly much inferior" Armenians.[145] The pamphlet began with the frank admission that "troubles" existed: "Turkey has never denied that serious disturbances have taken place at the district of Sassoun. What it has denied is the accusation that there was a premeditated massacre; and yet this is the absurd basis upon which is built the whole Armenian agitation, both in America and Europe."[146] Given the fact that it is a later pamphlet and new information had come to light, the language of the second pamphlet differed somewhat from *A Few Facts about Turkey*, which hesitated to acknowledge that strife had broken out: "Evidently there have been troubles at Sassoun, which will be investigated, the firm wish of the Sultan being to treat all his subjects with justice, and to punish, according to law, all guilty parties."[147]

The Armenian Troubles contended that the pro-Armenian positions being fostered in the United States were, in reality, "erroneous and even anti-American," because they bolstered the colonial interests of other states, most notably Great Britain.[148] It faulted the American press for its "lack of attention to proper proof for accusations," compounded by the "boldness and fanaticism of not a few American clergymen, who try to impart a religious and fanatical tendency to a question that is, and ought to remain, a political one."[149]

Finally, the pamphlet impugned the American record on minorities, which made its position on Armenian rights appear bigoted. Webb cited "a remarkable letter published by Mrs. S. L. Baldwin, in the New York *Tribune*," which called to mind the massacre of Chinese immigrants within the United States working for the Union Pacific Railroad in 1885: "More Chinese were killed, shot down, burned alive, in one awful hour, that day in September in Rock Spring, Wyoming, than were English and Americans killed in China in twenty-five years." Though Chinese authorities had, she contended, arrested and executed persons responsible for attacks on Americans and Europeans, no one had been arrested or punished in Wyoming for the massacre of the

Chinese.[150] Similarly, in *A Few Facts about Turkey*, Webb argued that American missionaries should devote "all their energies and good intentions on American Indians or on American Negroes," instead of going to Turkey "to educate in a certain fashion, and to convert, if possible, Christian Armenians to Protestantism." He observed that American missionaries would never accept foreign involvement "to educate and convert our Indians, for example," although they regarded it as their right to intervene in Turkey.[151]

The Turkish pamphlets exemplify Webb's Victorian faith in the printed word and its potential to shift public perceptions. The same confidence is reflected in the American Islamic Propaganda as a whole, from its official name to the content it produced. Webb clearly believed that his newspapers and books had the potential to sway public opinion about Islam. As we have seen, though, he never lost sight of the effectiveness of direct personal relations in shifting perceptions, especially in the form of parlor talks and public lectures. The next chapter takes us back to 1893 and the beginnings of Webb's Islamic work in America. It shows him not as a writer and editor but as a speaker at the time of his greatest moment in the public eye and one of the most celebrated events of the nineteenth century, the First World's Parliament of Religions. Webb did not underestimate the value of his Parliament lectures in furthering his mission, yet he felt it imperative to print them independently along with a personal account of the Parliament. Dwindling financial resources never permitted him to do so, although the speeches were preserved in various other sources. No other product of Webb's tongue or pen enjoyed wider public exposure than his Parliament speeches.

9

Chicago World's Fair and First Parliament of Religions

World Fairs were a hallmark of the Victorian Age and a vital element in the historical development of the United States. The 1893 Chicago World's Fair ranked among the greatest and most important of them all and is widely regarded as a watershed in American cultural history.[1] During Webb's lifetime, more than twenty World Fairs were held in the United States, Great Britain, France, and elsewhere. The first World's Fair was held in London in 1851, when Webb was a child. The French Eiffel Tower is a vestige of the 1889 Paris Centennial, which, taking place on the eve of the Chicago World's Fair, was seen as its natural rival and had to be outdone.[2]

Host nations and cities solicited investment and active participation from around the world. In theme and outlook, Victorian World Fairs were optimistic and utopian, bringing to life romantic notions of the past and idealized visions of the future. World Fairs allowed the masses to enter directly into the exotic fantasy of other eras, cultures, and civilizations, while showcasing the dominant ideologies of the time. They were marketplaces for futuristic ideas and newfangled theories, and they highlighted technological development and scientific invention. Many attending the Chicago World's Fair saw the automobile for the first time and were introduced to an array of new grocery items ranging from Juicy Fruit Gum and Shredded Wheat to Aunt Jemima pancake mix.[3] At the St. Louis World's Fair of 1904, Earnest (Anas) Hamawi, a young Arab-American pastry vendor belonging to the first wave of Syrian-Lebanese immigrants, introduced ice-cream cones. He went on to establish the St. Louis-based Cornucopia Waffle Company and Missouri Ice Cream Cone Company.[4]

Muslims were among the many international guests brought together in the World Fairs. Substantial numbers of Muslims from North Africa and the Middle East took part in the 1876 Philadelphia Centennial of the American Revolution, making it the first public event of note on American soil that brought Muslims and Americans together on a large scale.[5] The inscription on the Egyptian pavilion proclaimed: "The Oldest People of the World Send Their Morning Greetings to the Youngest Nation." The American public stood in awe at the marvelous contents of more than 140 crates of historical artifacts, which Egypt had sent to display at the fair and afterward donated to the American people. The Ottomans sent troupes of merchants with their Oriental wares, and Morocco set up a replica of a "Moorish village."[6]

At the Chicago World's Fair, Jamal Effendi, a member of the Ottoman delegation, opened the grand occasion by facing east and performing the Islamic call to prayer. The *Chicago Tribune* noted that he raised his hands and "chanted prayers to Allah," while Muslims in the audience responded by repeating each refrain to themselves and making what sounded to the reporter like "loud Amen[s] in old fashioned Methodist style."[7] Delegations from Muslim lands, especially the Ottoman Empire, presented striking displays of their histories and cultures in Hyde Park along the Midway Plaisance: a handsome, roseate mosque with a gleaming white minaret, splendid models of Islamic cities and Oriental bazaars, simulations of centers of religious learning, and other highly regarded feats of architecture.[8]

The Chicago World's Fair, the biggest in history, was meant to establish the city's status as a world-class metropolis and a viable contender with New York.[9] From across the nation and around the world, Chicago recruited the best architects available in what some called the greatest meeting of artists since the Renaissance. Pavilions and lesser buildings took up more than five million square feet, twice as much as the greatest expositions of the past. With more than a thousand acres, the fairgrounds took in more than three times as much land as any previous fair.[10] Costs for the grounds and buildings alone amounted to $20 million, an astronomical sum at the time.[11]

The Chicago World's Fair was the greatest tourist attraction of the nineteenth century. Almost half the total population of the United States at the time visited the fair from all quarters of the country. Thousands of others came from more than seventy foreign lands.[12] Recorded in countless drawings and photographs, the fair was the talk of the time and captivated the imagination of the American people. It emerged as a leading theme in national literature and a shining symbol of America's promised greatness.[13]

In an effort to ease the traumatic memories and lingering images of the Great Fire of 1871, Chicago used the fair to emblazon a new icon of the city onto the nation's imagination: a phoenix rising from its ashes, the logo of newly founded Harper's College, later to become the University of Chicago.[14] The fair would also transform the popular picture of Chicago as a "gritty frontier city on the make" into that of a sophisticated metropolis that had finally arrived. As Janet Abu-Lughod writes in a recent study: "The [cultural] hub of the universe had been transferred from Boston to Chicago."[15]

In preparation for Lake Michigan's debut as "the queen of the inland lakes," the swamps and marshes along it were drained, and the scrublands and dunes were developed. "Beautification" programs augmented Chicago's network of city parks and engineered the city's future urban development. Park development drove up nearby real estate values and put Chicago's parks on a par with New York. At the same time, the new park system cordoned off Chicago's slums, magnifying prosperous areas while concealing the poor and hiding the city's most glaring social ills from sight. In this manner, the fair's groundwork exaggerated patterns of social cleavage within Chicago, turning it into a "dual city" of haves and have-nots and solidifying its bifurcation, as Abu-Lughod says, "into two sharply contrasting parts: an elegant façade and a deeply shadowed backstage."[16]

When the fair finally opened, the entire world seemed captivated by Chicago's new "elegant façade." In an inaugural address, Cardinal H. E. Gibbons christened Chicago *Thaumatopolis*, "the city of wonders and miracles."[17] An English clergyman, Dr. Alfred Momerie, a deputy to the Parliament of Religions, exclaimed: "I have seen all the great exhibitions of Europe during the last fifteen years, and I can safely say that the World's Columbian Exposition [the Chicago World's Fair] is greater than all of them put together."[18] A London editorial titled "Do Not Miss the Fair!" said: "If the visitor can only be a single day at the Fair, or a single night, it is worth any sacrifice to enjoy this alone. And if it were to be a question between the daytime or the illumination at night, we would advise the latter; for surely no eyes now opened on this world are likely ever again to behold any sight so nobly beautiful."[19] Dharmapala, a Ceylonese (Sri Lankan) delegate in the Parliament, said, "All the joys of heaven are in Chicago." An English participant responded: "I wish I were sure that all the joys of Chicago are to be in heaven."[20]

Oasis of Fantasy

To win the right to host the fair, Chicago outbid New York, Washington, and St. Louis in a campaign so fierce and so long-winded that Chicago earned the nickname, "The Windy City."[21] After winning the bid, it spared no efforts to make the event a consummate triumph. Congress granted approval in 1888, and the Chicago press was filled with unconcealed glee, applauding congressional endorsement as the city's greatest triumph.[22] New York editorials, oozing with jealousy, expressed skepticism that such a feat could succeed in the Midwest.[23] Over the next four years, Chicago applied itself diligently to preparation.[24] Planners declared that it would be "the greatest fair in history," surpassing all previous world fairs, even the Paris Exposition of 1889.[25] Officially designated the Fourth Columbian Centennial Exposition, the fair's original deadline was naturally 1892 to correspond with Columbus's discovery of the New World in 1492. Given the grandiose scale of preparations, Chicago did, in fact, prove unable to meet the deadline but was allotted an additional year. Other American towns and cities went ahead with their local centennials in 1892, turning the Chicago celebrations of 1893 into an exclusive affair.[26]

The Chicago World's Fair opened on May 1, 1893, unveiling "an oasis of fantasy and fable" that endured for six months.[27] The fair's nucleus was near Lake Michigan on Chicago's South Side, centered on what is today the Museum of Science and Industry. The fairgrounds extended westward through Hyde Park along the Midway Plaisance.[28] The World's Parliament of Religions convened in September at the climax of the great centennial summer.[29] The Parliament and all other congresses associated with the fair were held separately in downtown Chicago at the Memorial Art Palace, known today as the Art Institute of Chicago Museum.[30]

The pavilions surrounding the Museum of Science and Industry were called "the White City" by virtue of their gleaming neoclassical stonework and colonnaded exteriors. The White City was the fair's "great Mecca." Such grandeur and beauty seemed to transform it into "sacred space." Some christened it a "Celestial City" and others a "New Jerusalem on earth."[31] "I have stood upon the seven hills of Rome," Chicago Mayor Carter Harrison declared in his address to the nation's mayors. "I have been in Athens, but no imagination could recall any of those ruins and make me compare them to the White City."[32] In one of the most ambitious experiments in electricity the world had seen, Chicago illuminated the White City with electric lights, winning it another soubriquet as the "City of Lights" and making nocturnal outings at the fair even more popular and highly acclaimed than daytime visits.[33]

The Bazaar of Nations was the most popular part of the fair. Stretching an entire twelve blocks beyond the White City along the Midway Plaisance, the Bazaar of Nations was filled with exotic buildings from faraway lands and whole villages of "natives" in local costume, presenting "a mile long avenue of amusements and ethnological exhibitions."[34] Its exhibitions followed an implicit hierarchy from the "civilized" to the "barbarous." Just as the White City proclaimed the United States as "the fulfillment of universal history," the Bazaar of Nations created the impression that America was "the finest flower of human culture," while illustrating the superiority of the world's "more highly evolved" nations. Its "march of progress" began with full-scale replicas of European villages and specimens of the quaint folk traditions of Europe. Then came the Turks, Egyptians, Hindus, and the Chinese, followed by "barbarous" peoples like the Malays, the Dahomeyan Africans, and Native Americans.[35]

The genteel "racist consensus" that dominated the fair assigned African Americans no ranking at all. Despite repeated petitions, they were denied permission to set up any meaningful exhibitions demonstrating "the progress of their race," although racist exhibits patently insulting to blacks were authorized.[36] African Americans were allowed to attend the fair, and several noted black leaders took part in its various congresses. Among them were Ida B. Wells, an outspoken African American champion of human rights, and Frederick Douglass, who published a joint protest against the fair's racist agenda titled *The Reason Why the Colored American Is Not in the World's Columbian Exposition*. Douglass proclaimed that African Americans had hoped to tell the world that "progress and enlightenment have banished barbarism and race hate from the United States" and that "the souls of Negroes are held to be precious in the sight of God, as are the souls of white men." But, "morally speaking," Douglass asserted, such proclamations were impossible. The flaunted symbol of the White City, which in the eyes of the fair's planners was a proclamation of America's providential greatness, was for African Americans nothing more than "a whitened sepulcher."[37]

FIGURE 9.1. Ibrahim Hakky Bey, Commissioner General of the Ottoman Empire at the Chicago World's Fair

Unlike African Americans, Muslims from abroad were offered favorable circumstances to participate in the fair and showed, in return, a "most lively interest" in it. Their contributions were prominent and ranked among the most popular of all. Out of the almost thirty nations officially invited to the fair, the Ottoman Empire was among the first to give a positive response to the fair, although their reaction to the World's Parliament of Religion, which it hosted, was unsupportive. Sultan Abd al-Hamid II appointed Ibrahim Hakky Bey as the Ottoman Empire's commissioner general to the fair. Hakky Bey was a highly decorated young government servant, educated in diplomacy and experienced in the foreign service. He was fluent in English, French, and German and often served as Sultan Abd al-Hamid's personal interpreter on special missions.[38]

The interior of the Ottoman mosque in the Midway Plaisance was lit by chandeliers and richly laid out in Oriental carpets. There were regular calls for daily prayers, and "all Mohammedans at the Exposition worshiped there during their sojourn in Chicago." Americans, "unfamiliar with the Mohammedan religious rites," found the mosque of great interest. Within its vicinity were several large Oriental markets, in which merchants occupied stalls similar to those in their native lands and sold abundant quantities of "rugs, shawls, embroideries, jewelry, and every imaginable ornament used in the decoration of the person." One of the larger buildings housed a theater at which sword contests, dance presentations, and musical performances were on display almost every hour of the day and night. At some distance from the mosque, the Ottomans staged their own highly successful version of an Oriental "Buffalo Bill's Wild West Show," featuring superb horsemen and sharpshooters. There were Oriental refreshment stands, which dispensed exotic types of food and drink. The Bazaar of Nations included Turkish, Tunisian, and Algerian villages and a recurrent "wedding procession" in the streets of Cairo. Several "brawny Turks" offered expensive rides in sedan chairs through the Oriental "casbahs" but could hardly compete with the less costly donkey and camel rides, which were all the rage.[39]

To the shock of all, the Chicago World's Fair ended abruptly in a twilight of gloom. On October 28, Patrick Eugene Pendergast shot and killed Chicago Mayor Carter H. Harrison at his residence on Ashland Boulevard. Pendergast, who had been active in Harrison's election campaign, harbored resentment for Harrison because of his failure after the victory to secure for Pendergast the political appointment he felt was his due. Harrison was one of the promethean forces behind the fair's success, and earlier in the day he had delivered one of his most forceful speeches on the significance of the fair, which he intended to keep open for at least another year.[40] Instead, the fair was hastily closed the next day,, and all flags were lowered to half-mast. What had been slated as a "day of jubilee" became a day of mourning. Remaining festivities were cancelled, including a reenactment of Columbus's landing (on the shores of Lake Michigan), fireworks, and concerts.[41]

FIGURE 9.2. Royal Ottoman Summer Cottage at the Chicago World's Fair

John Henry Barrows, chairman of the World's Parliament of Religions, and a chorus of Chicago preachers expressed their horror: "A great shadow has come over our pride and our rejoicing." P. S. Henson, a Baptist minister, declared the ending "a dreadful finale to the great Exposition."[42] Rabbi Emil G. Hirsch, a well-known reformed Jew from New York embodying the spirit of its liberal Jewish intelligentsia and a prominent participant in the parliament, noted that a "black cloud of horror and grief" had eclipsed the smile of the sun that "had hung over Chicago during the Columbian summer." He asked rhetorically, Had it all been "a dream, unreal, destined to vanish into thin air?"[43]

The fair's opulent festivities masked much deeper problems in American society at large. Economic depression had set in during the summer.[44] By autumn, the ranks of Chicago's unemployed had risen to an estimated two hundred thousand, prompting "armies of unemployed men" to swarm the streets. An upsurge of social unrest overtook the city and was exacerbated by an outbreak of smallpox two days before the fair officially closed.[45] Although Mayor Harrison had been on the verge of persuading Congress to extend the life of the White City another year, his assassination removed all hope that the fair would continue.[46] Once abandoned, the fairgrounds deteriorated quickly. By New Year, the vacant buildings of the White City were, in the words of the

FIGURE 9.3. Chicago World's Fair Bazaar of Nations on the Midway
Plaisance/"Streets of Cairo" Showing Wedding Procession Group

Chicago Tribune, "swarming with tramps." On the night of January 8, 1894,
fire broke out, quickly gutting almost all remaining buildings.[47]

The First World's Parliament of Religions

The First World's Parliament of Religions was one of the most promising
events of the Victorian era. Organizationally, it was a branch of the Chicago
World's Fair and constituted one of its many secondary congresses. Webb's
participation in the parliament marked his moment of maximum public exposure, while also offering him the opportunity to establish valuable contacts
for future work. The parliament ran for seventeen days, commencing on
September 10 and concluding on September 27, 1893. Though numbered
among the fair's nearly fifty special congresses, the parliament was, without
question, the "capstone of the congresses and the whole Exposition." The Art
Palace, where the parliament convened, provided a central location near the

shores of Lake Michigan, since Chicago's newly completed system of subways and elevated trains were within walking distance.[48] Nearness to the Illinois Central Railroad and Navy Pier, congested at the time with steamers, meant that the parliament's speakers were continually interrupted by the screech of whistles and the blasting of horns.[49]

Charles Carroll Bonney originated the idea of the parliament and was its presiding chairman.[50] Bonney was a Protestant of eclectic background and owed much of his liberal outlook to the mysticism of Emanuel Swedenborg. Bonney maintained that his Swedenborgian theology allowed him to accommodate Islam as part of God's universal dispensation: "The Mahometan religion was permitted by the Divine Providence of the Lord for the extirpation of idolatries in countries where Christianity would not be received. In that religion there is something out of both the Testaments of the Word; teaching that the Lord came into the world; that he was the greatest prophet, the wisest of all, and the Son of God."[51]

John Henry Barrows, general chairman, and Jenkin Lloyd Jones, secretary, worked under Bonney and were responsible for organization and administration. Both were churchmen, but they embodied diametrically opposed religious perspectives, which created a "schism" that ran through the entire American delegation at the Parliament. Barrows was a "New School" Presbyterian. He was forward-looking and committed to the liberalization of Christian creeds. At the same time, he was committed to a missionary perspective and believed that salvation was possible only through Christ. Barrows looked forward to the eventual "Christian conquest of Asia."[52] He had tremendous drive, was devoted to hard work, and was capable of great generosity, which helped the Parliament immensely to achieve its main goals, but he often "combined generosity with arrogance."[53] The French clergyman Bonet-Maury compared Barrows to Columbus, a man "who not only had radically new ideas but was willing to fight for them."[54]

Jenkin Lloyd Jones was a religious liberal and belonged to the Midwestern Unity Movement. Webb held Jones to be "an intensely earnest and honest man who seeks the truth with the determination to find it."[55] Jones described himself as a theist who, in Richard Seager's words, held that "common ethical aspirations and humanistic religion, not the affirmation of theism or of supernatural religious propositions," constituted the true basis of meaningful religious fellowship.[56] One of Jones's lectures was titled "Seven Great Teachers of Religion," and he identified these "great teachers" as Moses, Zoroaster, Confucius, Buddha, Socrates, Jesus, and Muhammad. Like Webb and the Theosophists, Jones espoused the underlying unity of their teachings and proudly declared: "The Lovers of Light are One."[57]

Bonney charged Barrows and his organizational staff with the highly idealistic task of working "to unite all Religion against irreligion" on the basis of the Golden Rule. They were to design a worldwide assembly in which the "common aims" of the world's religions and the "common grounds of union" among them could be set forth.[58] Bonney set out "to secure from leading scholars representing Brahman, Buddhist, Confucian, Parsee, Mohammedan, Jewish, and other Faiths, and from representatives of the various Churches of Christendom, full and accurate statements of the spiritual and other effects of the Religions which they hold, upon the Literature, Art, Commerce, and Government and Social Life of the peoples among whom these Faiths have prevailed."[59] The committee sent more than ten thousand solicitations to scholars and religious figures around the world. An Advisory Council of three thousand "religious personalities" was put together to execute parliament goals and included such luminaries as Max Müller, a renowned British scholar of comparative religion and philology; Edwin Arnold, a scholar of Buddhism; Sir Alfred Lord Tennyson, the British poet laureate; and John Greenleaf Whittier, the American "muse of freedom and of every virtue." Tennyson and Whittier had looked forward to attending, but they died before the parliament commenced. Tennyson, according to Walter Houghton's account of the parliament, had hoped to "gladden" its assembly "with, perhaps, his last earthly song."[60]

The parliament's delegates represented an array of religious traditions and came from all over the world, making it possible for the Art Palace to host many of the most illustrious personages of the nineteenth century. Although unable to attend, Max Müller sent a paper and remarked that there were few events that he regretted missing as much as the World's Parliament of Religions: "Who would have thought that what had been announced as an auxiliary to a world's fair could have become the most important part of that immense undertaking?" In his estimation, the parliament was not just "the greatest success of the past year" but "one of the most memorable events in the history of the world."[61]

FIGURE 9.4. First World's Parliament of Religions/Opening Session in the Hall of Columbus September 10, 1893 (Webb Not Shown)

Although the parliament solicited participants from several diverse ethnic and racial backgrounds, it excluded representatives of Native American religions and the Mormon faith.[62] The Mormon hierarchy had revoked the doctrine of plural marriages three years earlier, but the issue of polygamy remained a burning one and provided the grounds upon which Barrows repeatedly rejected Mormon petitions for inclusion. According to Barrows, there were a number of "stormy meetings" centering on polygamy with regard to Mormon participation. Elder B. H. Roberts, a Mormon spokesman, finally registered a formal protest against Bonney and Barrows, accusing them of capitulation to the "fear of public sentiment:" "Gentlemen, where you should have been lions you have been hares; where foxes, geese. Turn which way you will and you will be confronted by the facts which proclaim that you have shrunk before the fear of public sentiment within your churches, all unmindful of that greater public sentiment outside of your churches which demands generous, open, and fair treatment, even for Mormons in such a gathering as your parliament."[63]

Non-Christian participation in the Parliament ran up against a number of obstacles. Bonney found it hard to meet the aims he had set for himself regarding active non-Christian involvement. Barrows observed that there were "real and formidable difficulties" with the non-Christian delegations, which ended up being "less complete and imposing" than had been wished. Muslim participation was regarded as particularly inadequate, and Barrows deplored that there were no official delegates from Islam's native lands.[64] Bonet-Maury also lamented the insufficiency of a Muslim scholarly presence at the parliament.[65]

The blame for minimal Muslim participation in the parliament was pinned on the Ottoman sultan, Abd al-Hamid II. His great interest in the exposition contrasted sharply with his reaction to the parliament. Barrows wrote, "It was with little surprise that the Chairman [Charles Bonney] learned how decided was the opposition of the Sultan of Turkey to the proposed Conference, an opposition very embarrassing to the leaders of the Greek and Armenian Churches in the Turkish Empire."[66] Richard Seager suggests that Abd al-Hamid's antagonism toward the parliament may explain the absence of scholarly, world-class Muslim delegates like Ameer Ali. [67]

The exact nature of the sultan's opposition to the Parliament is unclear. The Armenian question and official Turkish convictions that American missionaries were behind the trouble were undoubtedly major factors. It is doubtful that he opposed the parliament out of purely exclusivist concerns. His nation's robust participation in the Chicago World's Fair demonstrated his concern that Islam be represented there in the best of lights. Moreover, there were at the exposition's secondary committees and even the parliament a number of European women and Ottoman Christians of Armenian and other backgrounds who unequivocally presented pro-Ottoman and pro-Islamic points of view.

Herant Mesrob Kiretchijian, a young Ottoman delegate of Armenian Christian stock, proudly began his address to the parliament by comparing Chicago to his native Constantinople (Istanbul) and making a positive allusion to Webb's mission:

> Again, it is a great honor to stand before any religious body in the world and represent the greatest religious city of the world— Constantinople. We have had there a religious parliament for four hundred years, and we have survived it. (Laughter) You are certainly like Constantinople to-day, when you have a minaret in the Midway Plaisance and actually the gospel of Mohammed has begun to be preached to you. (Laughter) I wish to assure you that it is not going to stop, and I believe you will be especially interested in the young men of the Orient because you may look upon them as the outcome after four hundred years, such as you, very likely, will become in the future. (Laughter and applause)[68]

Parliament proceedings were recorded in numerous journals and reports, officially and privately. Barrows stated that one of the parliament's major objectives had been "to set forth, for permanent record to be published to the world, an accurate and authoritative account of the present condition and outlook of Religion among the leading nations of the earth."[69] His official edition of the proceedings attempted to fulfill that objective and proved extremely popular. Bonet-Maury, who wrote a useful summary in French, interpreted the popularity of Barrows's edition as an indication that the parliament had been an astounding success.[70]

Barrows freely exercised the prerogative to edit his "official account" and alerted readers at the outset that he hoped to make the parliament records "even more valuable" by having them "rigorously condensed" and "carefully pruned." He excluded materials not "bearing directly on the topics of comparative religion" in order to separate the gold from the dross.[71] In some cases, his "careful pruning" amounted to the lopping off of whole trees, especially when materials did not meet his approval, as was the case with Fannie Barrier Williams, a brilliant African American, who indicted the church for supporting slavery.[72] Webb's two addresses at the parliament were not spared Barrow's editorial shears either.[73] Barrows also excluded Webb's biography from the extensive list of speaker notes, although he included several others who delivered only minor presentations.[74]

Jenkin Lloyd Jones prepared a summary of the parliament titled *A Chorus of Faith*. In size, it hardly compares to Barrows's edition but offers a valuable alternative. Jones faulted Barrows for "doctrinal bias" in his "official record." For Jones, the parliament's greatness rested in the fact that it worked to remove obstacles of gender and sectarian difference. He opposed the Christocentric focus that Barrows stamped on his record and preferred the

Parliament's "homocentric" perspective instead: "Not the supernatural Christ, but the natural soul of man was the center around which the Parliament moved."[75] Jones gave three times as much attention to Webb as he did to George Washburn, president of Robert College in Istanbul and another official speaker on Islam at the parliament. Barrows, on the other hand, showed definite preference for Washburn and gave the full text of his presentation, while submitting Webb's to extensive editing. Jones endorsed Webb's assertion that "in Islam caste lines [were] broken down" and esteemed Webb's focus on the fraternal spirit of Islam. Jones made no mention at all of George Post, one of the Parliament's most discordant voices with regard to Islam.[76]

Additional accounts were written of the parliament. Walter Raleigh Houghton's version, titled *Neely's History of the Parliament of Religions*, condensed some materials but still showed a commendable concern for accuracy. John W. Postgate, its principal compiler, stated in the frontispiece: "The speeches, papers, and essays reported in this volume are largely from my stenographic notes, and from manuscripts secured from authors. In some instances it has been necessary to condense, but the essential features of all addresses have been carefully retained, making a thorough and comprehensive report of the great World's Parliament of Religions."[77] Webb directed his readers to *Neely's History*, which he believed to be "positively the best and most complete report of the proceedings of the great Parliament of Religions."[78]

Defining Moment in American Culture

The *Chicago Tribune* called the parliament "a peaceful gathering of the warring creeds."[79] Many Christians hailed it as the "Chicago Pentecost" with the hope that it would spread "the new spirit of human fraternity" in the modern age.[80] Bonney mistakenly foretold that the Chicago Pentecost would make the quickly approaching twentieth century the beginning of a universal millennium of peace.[81] The "manifold wonders" of nineteenth-century progress would descend "at last from the luminous mountains of thought to the fertile fields of action, and [enter] upon the [peaceful] conquest of the world." There would be no more war:

> Henceforth, the "decisive battles of the world" will be fought on moral fields and on intellectual heights. The artillery of argument will take the place of the shot and shell hurled by the mighty guns of modern war. The piercing bayonet of perception and the conquering sword of truth will take the place of the weapons of steel which soldier and captain bear. The fame of a great general will become less attractive than that of a great statesman, or orator, or poet, or artist, or scientist, or teacher. The laboratory of the chemist, the workshop of the architect, the field of the engineer or scientific investigator, the

study of the author, and the institution of learning will more and more attract the rising genius of mankind.[82]

Paul Carus, an influential scholar of Buddhism and a person toward whom Webb felt a strong affinity, invoked the Pentecost metaphor as he declared the parliament one of the greatest events in history:

> The Parliament of Religions is undoubtedly the most noteworthy event of modern times. What are the World's Fair and its magnificent splendor in comparison with it? Or what the German Army Bill, the Irish Home Rule Bill in England and its drastic episodes in the House of Parliament, or a change of party in the United States? It is evident that from its date we shall have to begin a new era in the evolution of man's religious life. Whether or not the Parliament of Religions be repeated, whether or not its work will be continued, the fact remains that this congress at Chicago will exert a lasting influence upon the religious intelligence of mankind.[83]

Others shared Carus's sentiment. Barrows hoped the parliament would give American universities a strong incentive to study comparative religion and follow the precedent of establishing similar interfaith assemblies around the world.[84] Bonet-Maury ranked the Parliament of Religions as one of the glowing accomplishments of the American Republic, inspired by the precedent of the gathering of faiths at the French Centennial of 1889.[85] Houghton compared the parliament to the great ecumenical councils in church history: "In the twenty councils of the Christian church, from the year 325 A.D. to the great ecumenical council of 1870, no such sight has been vouchsafed to mortal eyes!"[86] He acknowledged the interfaith precedent at Paris during the French centennial but regarded it as only a "rehearsal" for the Chicago parliament: "Whether genuine or in disguise, [the French Centennial] indicated an indifferent gathering of Christians and heathen to enjoy a feast of humanity, not an earnest attempt at searching diligently for the highest truth."[87]

At the time of the parliament, the Protestant missionary spirit was at its height. Christians of a missionary bent harbored hopes that the Chicago Pentecost would prove forever the superiority of their faith and win humanity's conversion.[88] For many like Rev. George T. Candlin, a missionary to China, who appeared at the Parliament in ethnic Chinese dress with a Manchu hat and moustache, the parliament was to be followed by universal conversion to Christianity: "As a missionary I anticipate that this parliament will make a new era of missionary enterprise and missionary hope.... [T]his is Pentecost, and behind is the conversion of the world."[89]

Some missionary-minded Christians imbibed little of the parliament's pluralistic spirit and protested that Christians had shamed their faith by sharing a platform with other religions. The archbishop of Canterbury was among those who opposed the parliament on the belief that accommodation of Christian sectarians and non-Christian faiths was an unwarranted affront to the church's exclusive claim to truth. He wrote to the parliament committee:

> I do not understand how that religion [Christianity] can be regarded as a member of the Parliament of Religions without assuming the equality of the other intended members and the parity of their positions and claims. Then again, your general program assumes that the Church of Rome is the Catholic [i.e., truly universal] Church, and treats the Protestant Episcopal Church of America as outside the Catholic Church, I presume the Church of England would be similarly classified: and that view of our position is untenable.[90]

One of the official delegates, Rev. Joseph Cook of Boston, was rudely outspoken and blatantly unaccommodating. His antics drew more attention than those of anyone else at the parliament.[91] Cook stood six feet tall, weighed three hundred pounds, and commanded a large following. At the drop of a hat, he would shout his disapproval or thunder his agreement. The *Chicago Tribune* reported: "At one moment the expression on his face [had] been more eloquent than words in condemning what was being spoken on the platform. At the next he would be waving a white handkerchief high above his head and leading the applause."[92] When he stood at the podium, it would shake and totter with the blows of his "sturdy New England fists." He would "tramp to and fro" across the stage, stomping his "heavy feet" and making the floor tremble "with the weight of [his] three hundred pounds of orthodoxy," spewing forth "a torrent of denunciations with a face red with the vehemence of his utterance."[93]

Cook and his followers never missed a session, nor did they leave their points of view a matter of public doubt.[94] Webb like many others looked upon Cook as the parliament's chief nemesis. Cook's conduct, according to Webb, constituted the only truly "inharmonious and disagreeable feature of the Parliament."[95] Charitable Christians saw Cook as "narrow, dogmatic, uncharitable, and discourteous." Insisting that he humiliated "liberal and tolerant Christians" by sounding the first discordant note in the Parliament, they regretted that "the first manifestation of bigotry and ill-will" had come not from "a Pagan, Mohammedan, or Jew" but from their own quarter.[96]

Despite discordant voices, popular sentiment regarding the parliament was immensely positive. Over the seventeen days of its existence, the parliament attracted nearly one hundred and fifty thousand visitors, an average of about nine thousand people a day. Two large auditoriums were at the Parliament's disposal: the Hall of Columbus and the adjacent Hall of Washington. A number of smaller rooms served as venues for minor meetings and special committees. Major official presentations were delivered in the Hall of Columbus, which could accommodate an audience of four thousand. As soon as its doors swung open, crowds rushed into the hall, quickly filling it to capacity and sitting expectantly until the lectures began. Given the frequent overflow crowds, the most well-liked presentations were often repeated in the Hall of Washington.[97]

Parliament lectures were open to the general public. In the estimation of Bonet-Maury, the audiences represented a broad cross-section of genders, denominations, nationalities, and social classes. The majority, in his estimation, however, were women and members of the Chicago working classes. The eager throngs that welcomed the parliament bore witness to the intellectual curiosity and spiritual thirst of Victorian America. They were "persistent and intelligent," and their level of participation was consistently enthusiastic and thoughtful. In Houghton's words: "If some came not to worship, none dared to scoff, and few wandered away to sneer!"[98]

Parliament audiences, in Bonet-Maury's view, tended to applaud both the most orthodox doctrines and the most radical theses, while reserving their most fervent applause for speakers who "expressed elevated moral ideas, grand and sublime religious ideas, and the sentiments of human fraternity."[99] He contended that "a sentiment of sympathy always electrified the hall," and only on two or three occasions were there "volleys of antipathy."[100] The *Chicago Tribune* noted, however, a distinct bias in the audience: "To a careful observer it has become easy to tell in what direction the sympathies of the more demonstrative auditors lean. When an orator who advocates the faith in which they believe is presented they show at once their approval by almost frantic applause. When a speaker who tells of the glories of another faith is on the platform they are ominously silent."[101] The *Inter Ocean*, a prominent Chicago newspaper, noted, however, that "the good points of the foreign religions" never failed to receive enthusiastic response, and the paper added that if the Christian religion were to win "any fresh laurels in this parliament over all competitors it will not be because of prejudice in its favor on the part of the jurors who sit in Columbus hall, but because it has by its practical results established its claim to fully meet the needs of man."[102]

The parliament was "America's first serious encounter" with the religions of the East, and, as a rule, the public gave them a hearty welcome. Although virtually unknown before the parliament, Swami Vivekananda was inundated by an uproar of applause when, in his turban and ochre robes, he rose to speak and greeted the audience with the words, "Sisters and Brothers of America." Vivekananda proved to be the most charismatic Asian representative, but other representatives of the Oriental faiths shared the same favor, which continued to follow them after the parliament. This approval was reflected in the press, which created a stir throughout America with its glowing reports and sympathetic editorials.[103]

The "Asiatics" who spoke at the Parliament belonged to the young generation and voiced the aspirations of the "New Asia." Having been exposed since childhood to colonial schools, they enjoyed full mastery of English and intimate knowledge of the ideals and realities of Western civilization. They arrived in Chicago "steeled by almost one hundred years of struggle versus missionaries" and were more than able to hold their ground against the "presumptive spirit" of their missionary adversaries. The parliament culminated in "the greater glory of the Oriental religions." America discovered "to its surprise" that "the heathen were both appealing and intelligent," a revelation that pleased many and disconcerted others. It intensified Victorian America's spiritual crisis and reinforced the sense, already clear in the minds of people like Webb that "the old truths of the nineteenth century were beginning to crumble."[104]

Although the parliament had bitter critics and aroused considerable controversy—especially among conservative Christians—many contemporaries regarded it as an extraordinary success and the dawn of a new age. Houghton declared the event "completely without parallel."[105] Jones averred that it had "unsected and unsexed" humanity, that is, removed traditional barriers based on sectarian affiliation and gender.[106] Rabbi Emil Hirsch likened it to "an Oriental flower that fades but keeps its powerful aroma" or "a star that, although dead, still sends its light and cheer and glory to distant planets."[107] The parliament stood in a class by itself, a "one-of-a-kind" event, not likely ever to be repeated. It stood out like "a punctuation mark in American cultural history," signaling the climax of nineteenth-century liberalism and idealism and a "hail and farewell" to the old America "dominated by agrarian economy and rural values."[108]

The parliament was, in short, a salute to the new America about to emerge. Having donned the mantle of pluralism and cosmopolitanism, it declared the nation ready to lead the world as an emerging economic, political, and cultural force. "After the Parliament," Seager states, "the radically pluralistic nature of religious truth began to be acknowledged as an irreducible fact of life" in America. The parliament was the nation's "rite of passage" from an earlier atmosphere of toleration that rarely extended beyond Protestant denominations to the cosmopolitan pluralism that would develop during the course of the twentieth century. In the decades following the parliament, two non-Protestant Western faiths—Catholics and Jews—were the first beneficiaries of the new pluralism and corresponding breakdown of Protestant hegemony.[109]

Official Discourse on Islam

Compared to other faiths, Islam received modest attention at the First World's Parliament of Religions. Seager notes the relatively little space allotted to Islam in contrast to Buddhism and Hinduism, and, as mentioned above, Bonet-Maury lamented the lack of a Muslim scholarly presence at the parliament.[110] Originally, the organizing committee extended invitations to Sayyed Ameer

Ali, the distinguished Indian jurist and writer, and Sayyed Ali Belghrami, the famed Indian linguist and translator.[111] For reasons that are not clear, neither chose to accept, and no one equaling their caliber could be found. In his reply to Bonney, Ameer Ali praised the idea of the parliament as "marking an epoch in the history of religious development" but politely declined attendance. Neither Ali nor Belghrami agreed to send papers to be read in absentia.[112]

No Muslim from the traditional Islamic world was found to speak on behalf of Islam or submit a presentation in absentia, and the parliament seems to have selected Webb and J. Sanua Abou Naddara, an Egyptian Jew living in Paris in exile, by default. Because of their lack of academic credentials, Bonet-Maury asserted that neither of them was a true delegate. Webb's two presentations constituted the lengthiest statements on Islam at the parliament, while Abou Naddara submitted a short paper to be read in his absence. Despite Islam's lackluster presence at the parliament, there were a notable number of papers on the faith and its peoples. Two missionaries working within the Ottoman Empire, George Washburn and George Post, spoke on Islam's behalf, and there were several other relevant papers and references in the Parliament and related congresses.

J. Sanua (or Sanna) Abou Naddara, an Arab Jew, was widely known by his nickname, "Abou Naddara," meaning "the man with the glasses." His full name was Jacob Sanua or, in Arabic, Ya'qûb ibn Râfâ'îl Sanû' al-Mûsawî. He belonged to an old and distinguished Egyptian family and had studied in Egypt and Italy. Abou Naddara attained considerable fame as a journalist and writer of short stories and plays and was a master of languages, fluent in Arabic, Hebrew, Italian, French, English, and German and acquainted with Spanish and Greek. He helped establish the modern theater in Cairo and published a popular newspaper in his name, *Abou Naddara* (classical Arabic: *Abū Naẓẓāra*). The paper was outspoken in its criticism of the Egyptian government, which led to his banishment to France, where he continued to publish the paper. Abou Naddara's Jewish background did not prevent him from developing close links with the Muslim intelligentsia of Egypt and the Ottoman Empire, and he was a special friend of Jamal al-Din al-Afghani and Muhammad 'Abduh, the most renowned Muslim modernists of the period.[113]

Abou Naddara's "letter to the Parliament" was titled "The Koran and Other Scriptures" and reflected his characteristically open-minded and pro-Islamic point of view.[114] Barrows submitted Abou Naddara's contribution to radical editing, altering the original structure, cutting out more than four hundred words from the introduction, and leaving only a handful of Qur'anic citations in praise of learning, women, and other matters but without Abou Naddara's commentary or their original context.[115] Abou Naddara made no reference to his Jewish background, although he acknowledged that he was no "Mohammedan priest" and described himself as a "deist" and a "very faithful believer in God and a sincere admirer of all those who make Him known to men, and celebrate His sublime work." He emphasized that the Qur'an was "tolerant, human, and moral," and had been a "mercy upon slaves." Muhammad and his followers were not "as some supposed them to be, adversaries of instruction: nay, they [were] great friends of knowledge."[116]

George Washburn, president of Robert College (today Istanbul's Boğaziçi University), held a doctorate of divinity from the Andover Theological Seminary and, academically, was the parliament's most qualified speaker on Islam.[117] A regular contributor to *The Contemporary Review* and a number of other notable American and English periodicals, he had been among the parliament's earliest supporters and wrote to Bonney, "It will be something to bring together Catholics, Jews, and Protestants of different denominations, but the Congress should also include representatives of the Eastern Churches, Mohammedans, and the Indian and Chinese Religions." He added, "The Holy Spirit leads men of the most diverse faiths to the knowledge of our common Father." Washburn defended the parliament against those who held that it would harm the Christian mission, contending that "the Master has been wounded in the house of his friends" and that it created the impression that "one religion was as good as another." Washburn responded that there could be "no better exhibition of the power of Christianity and the confidence of Christians in their faith" than the World's Parliament of Religions.[118]

On September 15, 1893, five days prior to Webb's initial appearance, Washburn gave his presentation, called "Points of Contact and Contrast between Christianity and Mohammedanism."[119] He asserted at the outset that his intention was neither to attack Islam nor to defend it but as impartially as possible to compare and contrast it with Christianity. Kenten Druyvesteyn accurately evaluates the presentation as "very learned and non-polemical," while Seager calls it "the most extended and intelligent discussion of the [Islamic] tradition" at the parliament.[120] Washburn emphasized that Muslims were not monolithic and had as many different interpretations of their faith as Christians have of theirs.[121]

Although generally objective and favorable in his approach, Washburn entertained no reservations about Christianity's compatibility with modern civilization and its superiority over Islam in that regard. He made no direct reference to Webb but appears to have had a sufficiently good idea of the content of Webb's presentation for the following week, since he frequently undercut in advance the force of Webb's arguments. By casting doubt on the modernist interpretations of Ameer Ali, he also impugned one of Webb's principal sources, whose work had even inspired the title of his first lecture:

> There are *nominal* Mohammedans who are theists, and others who are pantheists of the Spinoza type. There are also some small sects who are rationalists, but after the fashion of old English Deism rather than of the modern rationalism. The Deistic rationalism is represented in the most interesting work of Justice Ameer Ali, *The*

Spirit of Islâm. He speaks of Mohammed as Xenophon did of
Socrates, and he reveres Christ also, but he denies that there is any-
thing supernatural in the inspiration or lives of either, and claims
that the Hanife and the other Imams corrupted Islâm as he thinks
Paul the apostle did Christianity; but this book does not represent
Mohammedanism any more that Renan's "Life of Jesus" represents
Christianity. These small rationalistic sects are looked upon by all
orthodox Moslems as heretics of the worst description.[122]

In reference to Ameer Ali's biography of Muhammad, Washburn reflected
disparagingly: "If Moslems generally believed in such a prophet as is described in the *Spirit of Islam*, it would greatly modify the tone of Mohammedan
life."[123]

The content and tone of Washburn's address were generally accurate and
favorable toward Islam. Relying on the popular twelfth-century "catechism"
(*Al-'Aqā'id*) of 'Umar Najm al-Dîn al-Nasafî, Washburn spoke well of Islamic
theology: "In truth there is no conceivable perfection which the Moslem
would neglect to attribute to God."[124] He noted that Muslims believed in
Christ's "miraculous birth, his miracles, his moral perfection, and his mission
as an inspired prophet or teacher," although they rejected the Crucifixion and
believed that "the Jews crucified one like him in his place." The chief doctrinal difference between Muslims and Christians was in the Islamic denial of
the dogmas of the Trinity and Incarnation—which, Washburn observed, were
in Muslim eyes "not only blasphemous but absurd and incomprehensible"—
and the common Muslim belief that "this heresy originated with Paul."[125]
Washburn spoke admirably of Islamic ethics:

> The Moslem code of morals is much nearer the Christian than is
> generally supposed on either side, although it is really more Jewish
> than Christian. The truth is, that we judge each other harshly and
> unfairly by those who do not live up to the demands of their religion,
> instead of comparing the pious Moslem with the consistent
> Christian.[126]

Islam's moral code, he emphasized, imposed on every Muslim "an indispensable obligation . . . to practice virtue and avoid vice, *i.e.*, all that is contrary
to religion, law, humanity, good manners, and the duties of society. He ought
especially to guard against deception, lying, slander and abuse of his neigh-
bor."[127] While noting the popular Islamic belief in Prophetic intercession and
that "the sinning Muslim goes to hell for a time" and then to Paradise,
Washburn emphasized: "Still, we need to repeat, the Moslem does not look
upon sin as a light thing." He stressed that the religion enjoined "honesty in
business; modesty or decency in behavior; fraternity between all Moslems;
benevolence and kindness toward all creatures. It forbids gambling, music, the

making or possessing of images, the drinking of intoxicating liquors, the taking of God's name in vain, and all false oaths."[128]

Washburn held Islam's Sufi mystics in high regard and contended that their "conceptions of pure spiritual religion seem[ed] to rival those of the Christian mystics." He criticized popular Sufism, however, for dealing in "magic, sorcery, and purely physical means of attaining a state of ecstasy; but others are neither pantheists nor theosophists, and seek to attain a unity of spirit with a supreme, personal God by spiritual means." He recited to the assembly an English translation of a Sufi mystical poem by the Ottoman Lady, Shareef Hanum, which is fully cited in the official accounts of his lecture.[129]

For all of Islam's favorable points of contact with Christianity, Washburn averred in the end that Christianity was superior and the two faiths were irreconcilable:

> While there is a broad, common ground of belief and sympathy,
> while we may confidently believe as Christians that God is leading
> many pious Moslems by the influence of the Holy Spirit, and saving
> them through the atonement of Jesus Christ, in spite of what we
> believe to be errors in doctrine, these two religions are still mutually
> exclusive and irreconcilable.[130]

He concluded: "This is not the place to discuss the probable future of these two great and aggressive religions, but there is one fact bearing upon this point which comes within the scope of this paper. Christianity is essentially progressive, while Mohammedanism is unprogressive and stationary." He added: "If progress is to continue to be the watchword of civilization, the faith which is to dominate this civilization must also be progressive."[131]

By declaring "unchecked progress" the hallmark of superior religion, Washburn's definition of Islam excluded the possibility of the religion's making any serious contribution to modern civilization and sentenced it to remain a stationary monolith of the past.[132] Paul Carus never hesitated to find fault with Washburn's static image of Islam in contrast to Webb's insistence on the religion's universal spirit. Carus pointed to Washburn's failure to recognize that many of his indictments regarding Islam could be made equally of Christianity: "Dr. Washburn's quotation of the Koran reminds us of similar passages in the New Testament; the old orthodoxy of the Moslems, however, is giving way to broader views. *Tout comme chez nous!* [everything (with them) is just like it is with us]."[133]

There was nothing original about Washburn's presentation, which merely reiterated standard Victorian views of Islam—albeit more favorably than many of his contemporaries—and its presumed stagnancy and opposition to progress. Carus's views, on the other hand, were remarkably ahead of their time, although it should be noted that the Muslim Modernist Movement, (1840–1940), which insisted on Islam's compatibility with Victorian standards of progress, had prominent spokespersons throughout the Muslim world at the time. Abou Naddara was connected to the movement, and Webb's primary mentors—Sir Sayyed Ahmad Khan, Ameer Ali, and Cheragh Ali—were also among its leading thinkers.[134]

George R. Post, the second missionary to present on Islam, was the president of the Syrian Protestant College of Beirut, Lebanon, which would later become the American University of Beirut. His training was in physiology, zoology, and botany, not theological studies.[135] Post's presentation, "The Ethics of Islam," was delivered one day after Webb's second address and is often taken as a refutation of him.[136] In terms of structure and content, however, Post's lecture appears to have been originally written as a rebuttal of Abou Naddara's paper. Webb did, however, take Post's criticisms as a personal attack on himself. Since Webb had left the parliament by that time, he later reported that, with the exception of Cook, "the Church-Christian delegates" refrained from replying to Webb in person but waited until he left the parliament before "they began to vilify and slander and abuse Islam and its advocate."[137] Even Barrows was not impressed with Post's presentation and "pruned" more than a thousand words from it, including his faint praise of the Prophet of Islam: "Mohammed was magnanimous—he had many great and noble qualities, of which I would like to speak at another time."[138]

Post was less forgiving than Washburn and sought to demonstrate "the moral defects" of Islam's ethical system by using selective quotations from Islamic scripture.[139] He stepped up to the speaker's platform holding a thick black copy of the Qur'an:

> I hold in my hand a book which is never touched by 200,000,000
> of the human race with unwashed hands, a book which is never
> carried below the waist, a book which is never laid upon the floor,
> a book every word of which to these 200,000,000 of the human race
> is considered the direct word of God, which came down from heaven.
> I propose without note or comment to read to you a few words of
> the sacred book, and you may make your own comments upon them
> afterward.

He began with the verse: "O Prophet, attack the infidel with arms," more accurately rendered as: "O Prophet, strive against the atheists and hypocrites and be harsh toward them" (9:73).[140]

Webb contended that Post's misrepresentation of Islam sprang primarily from his reliance on Sale's translation of the Qur'an while taking its verses out of context: "If he had any disposition to be honest and just he would not state as facts his own prejudiced conclusions instead of trying to ascertain the truth. There is no translation of the Holy Koran in English that is not grossly inaccurate and untruthful."[141] Webb repeatedly insisted on the inadequacy of available translations of the Qur'an, although it is not clear what authority he based his assessment on. Having no knowledge of Arabic himself, Webb was unable to base his judgment on a personal reading of the original. The theme of the deficiency of existing English translations of the Qur'an was common in the Muslim literature of the time, however, and Webb had probably encountered it in his readings as well as having heard it mentioned by his Muslim acquaintances in India and elsewhere.

The *Pro-Ottoman Chorus*

In addition to the relatively few official presentations on Islam in the parliament, a number of men and women spoke on Islam and Muslims or made noteworthy references to them at subsidiary exposition congresses or occasional addresses under the parliament's auspices. It is noteworthy that pro-Ottoman sentiment predominated in these extra-parliamentary presentations. Esmeralda Cervantes, for example, who, in Webb's words, was a "distinguished delegate and member of the board of lady jurors for the exposition," presented a paper, "The Women of Turkey," at an auxiliary congress in the Palace of Art in July 1893.[142] She expressed deep affection for Islam and Ottoman society and regretted that the parliament had given no place to Turkish women either "in person or by representation." Cervantes defended the position of women in Islam and insisted that "the Mohammedan religion is not an obstacle to woman's development."[143] Webb was clearly impressed with her and drew on her work in subsequent issues of his journal. In 1895, he advertised her book, *Education and Literature of Women of Turkey*.[144]

Herant Kiretchijian, the young pro-Ottoman Armenian from Istanbul, spoke the evening following Webb's presentation. He was a graduate of Robert College, where Washburn was the president. Kiretchijian was "engaged in journalistic and mercantile work" and served as the treasurer for Turkey's Protestant National Council. With an Ottoman fez and tassel, clean-shaven cheeks, a full Oriental moustache turned up at the ends, and a Western-cut suit and tie, Kiretchijian looked the part of the new reform-minded generation of Young Ottomans, whom he was proud to represent.[145] Humorous, upbeat, and filled with favorable references to Islam, his address, "A Voice from the Young Men of the Orient," invoked applause and laughter. The upcoming generation of Ottomans, he asserted, took abiding interest in the parliament and hoped it would provide the foundation for a true "brotherhood of man."[146]

Teresa Viele, whom Webb described as a "delegate from Turkey," expressed great sympathy for Islam, although there is no evidence that she was a Muslim. She delivered her presentation, "Turkey and the Religion of Islam," at the Woman's Branch of the Congress on September 25, four days after Webb's second speech. Viele spoke at length on the relation of "the Turkish government and the sultan to the religion of Islam, and also the practical operation of that religion as it affects the Turkish people." Like Cervantes, she argued that Islam was not an impediment to the development of women but enjoined evenhandedness for both genders. She argued that Islamic teachings in Turkey were responsible for the "good care bestowed" on boys and girls alike.[147] Interestingly, Abou Naddara, with his own Ottoman connections, insisted on many of the same points regarding women and the education of children.[148] Webb was positively impressed by Viele and, as mentioned earlier, later printed her translation of a French poem about Muhammad by Victor Hugo called "The Death of the Prophet."[149]

Christophore Jibara—"Archimandrite [lesser bishop] of the Apostolic and Patriarchal Throne of the Orthodox Church in Syria and the whole East"—addressed the Parliament four days after Webb's last speech.[150] He hailed from the Ottoman realms of Syria, and religious figures of his stature were officially appointed and had close ties with Ottoman authorities. Jibara's speech, "Unity of Faith and Harmony of Religions," was perhaps the parliament's most explicitly favorable presentation on Islam. Webb later advertised Jibara's published treatise with essentially the same title, *Unity in Faiths and Harmony in Religions.*[151] Jibara declared before the Parliament that his research over the preceding seventeen years exemplified the "universal spirit" of the parliament in calling for full reconciliation between Christians and Muslims:

> I think and believe that when the gospels and the Koran, which are
> really one, are reconciled, and the two great peoples, Christians
> and Mohammedans, are also reconciled, the whole world will come
> into unity and all differences fade away.... Asking the mem-
> bers of the parliament, in the name of God, to study with reverence
> this vital question on the harmony of religions, I hope the time will
> come when these two great peoples, Christian and Mohammedan,
> the greatest, the strongest, the brightest, and the richest among all the
> nations of the earth, may unite in one faith, serving one God.[152]

Jibara acknowledged that Muslim social realities were far removed from Islamic ideals and revealed that his brother and his professor, "a most saintly man," had been killed in sectarian violence. "Still," he continued: "I stand here and tell you that the Koran is an inspired book." He asserted that Christians could understand the Gospels correctly only by referring them to the Qur'an. Christianity, he contended, had embodied the true teachings of Christ only during its first three centuries, "before the development of heresies," and the Qur'anic inspiration embodied the original understanding of Christ in the early church. It was, therefore, essential to a sound reading of the Gospel:

> I assure you also that by the Koran, we can understand the gos-
> pel better, and without the Koran it is impossible to understand it
> correctly. It is for that I believe that God has preserved the Koran

and also preserved Islam because it has come to correct the doctrines and dogmas of the Christians. There is no difference in the books themselves—the gospel and the Koran. It is only in the understanding of the people in their reading of the Bible and the gospels and the Koran.[153]

In addition to the pro-Ottoman voices—Cervantes, Kiretchijian, Viele, and Jibara—there were a number of other noteworthy references to Islam at the parliament, some more favorable than others. J. Estlin Carpenter addressed the assembly four days before Webb and underscored the parliament's pluralistic outlook by citing an apocryphal statement of the Prophet, which was actually a faulty paraphrase of a Qur'anic verse: "Every nation has a creator of the heavens to which they turn in prayer. It is God who turneth them toward it. Hasten then emulously after good wheresoever ye be. God will one day bring you all together."[154] Professor M. S. Terry spoke on "the Mohammedan Bible" and contended: "As a volume of sacred literature the Koran is deficient in those elements of originality and independence which are noticeable in the sacred books of the other great religions of the world. Its crowning glory is its glowing Arabic diction."[155]

Dr. Eliza Sunderland of the University of Michigan spoke five days before Webb and spoke favorably of Webb and his mission. Her paper, "Lessons from the Study of Comparative Religion," emphasized the importance of "hierology," the emerging field of comparative religion.[156] Contrary to Terry's view of "the Mohammedan Bible," Sunderland welcomed Webb's mission, alluded favorably to the Qur'an and, in characteristic Victorian fashion, praised Islam for its moral system, which she deemed "the strongest in the world" in combating "drunkenness and games of chance."[157] She was frequently interrupted with ovations. The audience approved her endorsement of Islam as "the greatest total abstinence society in this world," and her allegations that the church had failed to deal adequately with drinking and gambling were also applauded. Alluding to Webb's mission, Sunderland suggested, again with her audience's sanction, that it would be useful "if the Mohammedans should establish several good living missions right here in Chicago." The *Inter Ocean* wrote that her remarks "created some amusement at the expense of Mayor Harrison," especially when she recommended that Muslim missionaries be allowed to "preach their temperance doctrines in the saloon quarters."[158]

The "Yankee Mohammedan" Expounds His Faith

Webb addressed the Parliament on Wednesday morning and Thursday afternoon, September 20 and 21, 1893.[159] Although it was a cold morning, the cooling ventilator in Columbus Hall was turned on full blast, prompting the *Inter Ocean* to observe the suitability of Webb's warm, red fez for the day.[160]

Leaks had sprung in the roof of the newly constructed Art Palace, and water remaining from a severe thunderstorm Tuesday night continually dripped from the ceiling the next morning, forcing some in Webb's audience to open their umbrellas while he spoke. As soon as the previous speaker had finished and the doors of the hall were swung open, there was "a big inrush to hear the Yankee Mohammedan Russell Alexander Webb [sic] expound the spirit of Islam."[161]

John Henry Barrows chaired Webb's first session.[162] Rabbi Emil Hirsch presided over the second and gave Webb a hearty welcome, while expressing his own enduring interest in Islam as a Jew.[163] Webb's speeches stayed within parliament guidelines, and he hardly left untouched the several topics that delegates had been asked to address: universal belief in God, the fraternity of mankind, the future life, and the relation of religion to social problems.[164] Thematically, both of Webb's Chicago speeches were similar to his Indian lectures and the mission statement in his booklet *Islam in America*. Toning down his rhetoric against "Church-Christianity" and materialism, Webb made frequent references to America's endemic social ills—the industrial slums, for example—and his conviction that Islam offered a viable solution to such problems. He stressed the theme of Islamic fraternity but avoided emphasizing Islam as a superior path of salvation as he had in earlier speeches and writings.

Speaking on behalf of the Muslim masses, Webb self-assuredly conveyed their greetings to his American audience, informing them of "millions of Mussulmans in India, Turkey, and Egypt, who are looking to this Parliament of Religions with the deepest, the fondest hope."[165] As Seira Shalton notes, "Webb assumed the responsibility of becoming Islam's spokesperson in America and a liaison to the rest of the Islamic world."[166] This was undoubtedly the image that Webb, who called himself an "American of the Americans," sought to create for himself at the parliament.

His speeches focused on the need for open-mindedness and the free examination of religious truth: "The day of blind belief has passed away," he said to applause. "Intelligent humanity wants a reason for every belief, and I say that spirit is commendable and should be encouraged wherever it goes, and that it is one of the prominent features of the spirit of Islam." The comment was welcomed by applause.[167] Webb sought common ground with his listeners by expressing his confidence that their spiritual aspirations and religious questions were the same:

> I take it that we all desire to know the truth, and that we are willing
> to have our attention called to the fact if we make a mistake in our
> estimate of our neighbor's religion. That was the sentiment that pos-
> sessed me ten years ago, when I began the study of the Oriental re-
> ligions, and I hope that it largely influences the minds of all who
> hear me to-day.[168]

He repeatedly emphasized that Islam was the most misunderstood of religions, emphasizing that he had once shared the same misconceptions as other Americans but never doubted that they, like him, would ultimately give it a fair hearing:

> I carried with me for years the same errors that thousands of Americans carry with them to-day. Those errors have grown into history; false history has influenced your opinion of Islam. It influenced my opinion of Islam and when I began, ten years ago, to study the Oriental religions, I threw Islam aside as altogether too corrupt for consideration.[169]

Despite the inclement weather, a large crowd filled Columbus Hall to hear Webb's first speech, "The Spirit of Islam."[170] Webb referred to Sayyed Ameer Ali's biography of Muhammad during the speech, asserting that it was one of the few biographical and historical works that treated the subject fairly and reflected "in any sense the spirit of Islam."[171] Barrows left Webb's first speech nearly intact, although he removed about forty words that touched on polygamy, Muslim acceptance of Jesus, the reality of Islamic brotherhood, and Webb's closing remarks.[172]

Webb's second speech was titled "The Influence of Social Condition" in *Neely's History*, though Barrows rendered it, "The Influence of Islâm on Social Conditions." The former title is more consistent with the paper's content because it emphasized the importance of understanding how "social conditions" and historical contexts often distorted religions, Islam included. The presentation touched on certain social problems but was not primarily concerned with how Islam as a religion would treat them.[173] Barrows gave the second speech a good "pruning" by lopping off the first one thousand words, in which Webb, consistent with the paper's theme, asked his audience not to judge Islam or any religion by the deportment of its ignorant followers. Barrows also deleted several hundred words in which Webb argued that Muslim social problems should be judged by analogy with American social problems, such as those of the industrial slum. In these deleted sections, Webb addressed the inadequacy of English-language materials on Islam and described Islam's legacy as a powerful force of civilization in Muslim Spain.[174] Barrows provided the reader instead with Washburn's insistence that the intellectual achievements of medieval Cordova and Baghdad were not the work of "Arab or orthodox Mohammedan scholars and thinkers" but "Jews, using Moslem auspices and enjoying the favor of princes whose Moslem orthodoxy was very uncertain."[175]

Though Barrows took great liberty in editing Webb's speeches, Jenkin Lloyd Jones was impressed with Webb's presentations and emphasized his concluding remarks, deleted in Barrows, which emphasized the common theological ground that all Muslims, Jews, and Christians shared:

We Mussulmans firmly believe that the teaching of Moses, Abraham, Jesus, and Mohammed were substantially the same; that the followers of each truly inspired prophet have always corrupted and added, more or less, to the system he taught, and have drifted into materialistic forms and ceremonies; that the true spirit has often been sacrificed to what may, perhaps, be called the weak conceptions of fallible humanity.[176]

"The Spirit of Islam," which Webb began with an impromptu reference to polygamy, was one of the most controversial presentations in the Parliament, although both of his speeches evoked a wide spectrum of responses. Bonet-Maury accused Webb of painting a "seductive" picture of Islam. He did not find the speech's enthusiasm for Islam surprising, since Webb, in Bonet-Maury's eyes, was a neophyte with little true knowledge of his adopted religion.[177] Carus noted a similar reaction from an Armenian Christian, Mina Tchéraz, who remarked "sarcastically that real Mohammedanism was quite different from the Islam represented by Mr. Webb." Carus countered:

This may be true, but Mr. Webb might return the compliment and say that true Christianity as it showed itself in deeds such as the Crusades, is quite different from the ideal which its admirers claim it to be. Similar objections, that the policy of Christian nations showed very little the love and meekness of Jesus, were indeed made by Mr. Hirai, a Buddhist of Japan. We Christians have reason enough to be charitable in judging others.[178]

Carus continued to praise Webb's presentations: "Even Mohammedanism, generally supposed to be the most authoritative of all religions, appeared mild and rational as explained by Mohammed Alexander Russell Webb. Mr. Webb said: 'The day of blind belief has passed away. Intelligent humanity wants a reason for every belief, and I say that that spirit is commendable and should be encouraged, and it is one of the prominent features of the spirit of Islam.'"[179] Seager ventures to state that "Webb's two papers were designed to be a corrective to common misconceptions about Islam and must be considered the most authoritative statement about the Islamic tradition at the Parliament."[180]

The subject of polygamy had not been part of the original version of Webb's first speech. He had planned instead to treat the topic briefly the following day. Since Barrows chaired the first session, it is quite possible that Barrows himself prompted Webb to begin his speech by addressing the issue of polygamy. After rising to his feet to speak, Webb began somewhat tongue-in-cheek:

But today I have been requested to make a statement very briefly, in regard to something that is considered universally a part and parcel of the Islamic system. There are thousands and thousands of people who seem to be in mortal terror that the curse of polygamy is to be

inflicted upon them at once.... Now, I want to say to you, honestly
and fairly, that polygamy never was and is not part of the Islamic
system. To engraft polygamy upon our social system in the condition
in which it is today would be a curse. There are parts of the east
where it is practiced. There are conditions under which it is beneficial. (Cries of "No"; hisses; and slight applause). But we must first
understand what it really means to the Mussulman, not what it means
to the American. I say that a pureminded man can be a polyga-
mist and be a perfect and true Christian [sic]. (Cries of "No," "No",
hisses and groans), but he must not be a sensualist. When it is
understood what the Mussulman means by polygamy, what he
means by taking two or three wives, any man who is honest and
faithful and pure minded will say, "God speed him." (Cries of "No",
"Shame", hisses and applause.) Now, I don't intend to go into this
subject.[181]

Webb's contention that polygamy was not "part and parcel of the Islamic
system" was consistent with similar statements of his about plural marriage,
which many Americans believed to be the highest form of marriage in Islam
and an obligatory article of the faith.[182] In the aftermath of Webb's "defense
of polygamy" at the parliament, the *Chicago Tribune* printed a cartoon of a
buxom middle-aged matron sitting on the back of a prostrate and struggling
Webb in turban and Arabian robe with sandals flying from his feet, as she
beat him mercilessly with her uplifted parasol. The caption read: "Mohammed Webb's defense of polygamy not well received at the Congress of
Religions."[183] Given the controversy that erupted over Webb's words on polygamy, he was apparently disappointed with his presentation, feeling that it
had been misconstrued.[184]

Shalton contends that Webb "encountered a hostile reception," and some
contemporary witnesses felt that the outbreak of hisses and cries almost de-
terred Webb from continuing his speech.[185] One account noted that, although
the audience was "eminently liberal," "ex-Consul Webb, who claims to be a
convert to Mohammedanism," was "so vigorously" hissed when he tried to
speak a "good word for polygamy" that he had to change his topic at once. The
report insisted that Webb had not broached a "religious question but rather a
question of ethics:" "The moral sense of two continents unites in condemning
polygamy as a crime against society, and on that ground the subject should be
ruled out of all meetings of religious congresses."[186] Webb was not a supporter
of polygamy, although he argued that Westerners were ignorant of how it was
actually practiced in the Muslim world and that their categorical condemnation
of it was self-righteous and hypocritical in view of the problems that surrounded
the marital and sexual practices of their own societies. What is, however, especially important to note is that Webb did not broach the topic in violation of

Parliament protocol, but rather it may well have been Barrows himself—the chairman of Parliament itself and Webb's session in particular—who asked him to begin his speech by commenting on the highly controversial topic.

The Inter Ocean concurred that Webb "deserved the rebuke he received," since he had raised a sensitive matter "peculiar to [his religious] tradition," while other delegates had been careful to avoid such issues, including "child widows and caste in India and married priesthood in orthodoxy."[187] The same paper added, however, that Webb's audience was "intelligent, sympathetic, quick to appreciate and applaud." His "mild defense of polygamy in the opening part of his address came near making things lively, but as he got on to speak of the good qualities of Mohammed he won sympathy."[188] As the speech proceeded, Webb was able to establish a rapport with his audience, gaining its approval by reference to his own initial ignorance of Islam and antipathy toward it and his subsequent spiritual quest, which finally led him to embrace it:

> But when I came to go beneath the surface, to know what Islam
> really is, to know who and what the prophet of Arabia was, I changed
> my belief very materially, and I am proud to say that I am now a
> Mussulman (applause).[189]

Barrows regarded the audience's hostility toward Webb's defense of polygamy as a solitary incident at the Parliament, an outburst of emotion that he, the session chairman, could not control. The statement left mute the issue of who it was that had asked Webb to address the issue of polygamy in the first place. The audience's response, Barrows stated, was not the repudiation of a "doctrinal statement" but of what was taken as an attack on "a fundamental principle of social morality." Like others, Barrows noted that the audience listened patiently and appreciatively, once Webb returned "to a more appropriate line of discourse."[190]

Bonet-Maury contended that the whistles and shouts of "shame" in response to Webb's defense of polygamy were "so spontaneous and of such a unanimity" that they forced Webb to leave the subject quickly and to understand that public opinion had rejected polygamy on principle as a fundamental contradiction to the essentials of social morality.[191]

Webb blamed much of the chaos on Rev. Joseph Cook, who immediately stood up in protest but was derided by others as momentary pandemonium reigned in Columbus Hall. In a later review of the parliament, Rev. George Dana Boardman remarked: "We listened to each other with profound respect, as becomes men made in the image of God." Webb countered: "Mr. Boardman was evidently not present when the Moslem delegate was interrupted, while speaking, and grossly insulted by a Church-Christian preacher from Boston named Cook. Cook was hissed for his brutal and ungentlemanly conduct, but he failed to notice it."[192]

Clay Lancaster, a contemporary researcher on the parliament, remarks that its audience responded to Webb's comments on polygamy as if "they had never heard of David and Solomon."[193] A contemporary journal, the *San Francisco Argonaut*, made a similar observation in Webb's defense:

> As for polygamy, Mohammed Webb need not plead the examples of the Old Testament and the silence of the New. He can triumphantly show that his prophet (who never pretended to be more than a man) lived for twenty-four years the faithful husband of one wife, who was much older than himself, and did not make imitation of his subsequent laxness obligatory upon his followers.[194]

The paper noted that the "Mohammedan harem" was, in the majority of cases, "nothing more noxious than a sort of Old Ladies' Home, where the charitable Mussulman immures in comfort the widows of his brothers, his superannuated aunts, and other needy female connections." It concluded:

> Occasionally, of course, for the sake of variety or other reason, a good-looking young woman is installed; but this, we fancy, will hardly shock unbearably the moral sensibilities of the wealthy Christian populations of New York, Chicago, and San Francisco, where, we understand, practical polygamy and even polyandry, are not altogether unknown.[195]

The Parliament through Webb's Eyes

Having returned to Chicago after two decades of absence, Webb found a city that appeared totally transformed when he arrived to participate in the Parliament of Religions. The former boom town on the shores of Lake Michigan which he encountered in 1869 and where he met his first wife had receded into a bygone era, and the new showcase city on hand must have indeed seemed "a phoenix risen from the ashes" of the Great Fire of 1871. Webb took pride in attending the parliament as an indigenous American spokesman of his faith. He later reprinted the words of an Indian Muslim who had declared with reference to Quilliam and Webb: "In England Englishmen represent and spread Islam and at the Religious Parliament not an alien, but an American of Americans represented Islam."[196]

There was widespread interest in Webb's generation for copies of the parliament's proceedings. Given Webb's recognition of the centrality of the printed word and his possession of a printing press, he desired to publish his own record of his speeches and general parliament proceedings, even if only in pamphlet form. But he found himself lacking the means to do so:[197]

> We have received a number of requests for a report, in pamphlet
> form, of our two addresses on Islamic doctrines and customs deliv-
> ered before the World's Parliament of Religions at Chicago, in Sep-
> tember, 1893. Those addresses have been preserved only in the
> official and newspaper reports of the proceedings of the Parliament,
> and, in view of the widespread desire to have them in cheap form, we
> have decided to print them for general circulation if some of our
> Moslem brothers will assume the necessary expense.... [W]e will
> compile the addresses with an introduction and print them in one
> pamphlet.[198]

In the absence of his own account of the proceedings, Webb directed
his readers to Walter Raleigh Houghton's *Neely's History of the Parliament of
Religions*.[199]

Webb frequently expressed his feeling about "the great Parliament of Religions," which he believed to be "one of the most notable gatherings of the
century."[200] He was convinced it would have a lasting effect on the nation: "No
event of the century has sown such seeds of tolerance and fraternity."
It had "achieved results which will leave their effects upon the religious systems
of the world for many years to come." In Webb's view, two "grand results" of the
Parliament overshadowed all others. It had established "a kindlier feeling on
the part of broad-minded Church-Christians toward the religionists of the East,"
and it had "spread abroad a healthy, thoughtful spirit of investigation."[201]

Consistent with his aversion toward organized religion and official
"Church-Christianity," Webb contended that the parliament had unwittingly
struck organized religion "a blow that it will feel to its dying day," and he
presumed that the parliament had hastened "the dawn of the day when Islam
will be the universal faith."[202] When a number of Chicago churches commemorated the parliament in 1895, Webb remarked: "This very Parliament of
Religions was the severest blow that Church-Christianity has had in a century.
It would seem more rational if the promoters of the event would try to forget
that it ever occurred."[203]

A former colleague at the *Missouri Republican*, who encountered Webb
at the Parliament by chance, recalled that he "cut a pretty wide swath among
the great religious leaders at the Congress."[204] As a noteworthy matter of
historical coincidence, Webb shared the parliament platform with the earliest
proponents of America's earliest Buddhist and Hindu missions and probably
met in Chicago the pioneers of the American Baha'i movement, one of whom,
Anton Haddad, later assisted him in New York.[205] Of the diverse relationships
Webb fostered in Chicago, the Ottoman connection would prove the most
valuable and lasting. His links with the pro-Ottoman speakers Esmeralda
Cervantes, Theresa Viele, and Christophore Jibara provided Webb with useful
sources for future materials and articles.

Webb declared that, with a few egregious exceptions: "Good-will and cordial fellowship seemed to prevail generally [at the parliament], and there was a manifest disposition to accord to every speaker the right to present his religious beliefs without any hindrance whatever." The results were "most beneficial to the cause of truth and universal tolerance," and, in the end, one of the parliament's "grand results," towering above its occasional skirmishes, was "a healthy, thoughtful spirit of investigation."[206] He acknowledged the "kindlier feelings on the part of broad-minded Church-Christians toward the religionists of the East" and took pleasure in the fact that "whenever a representative of an Oriental religion had the platform, he was applauded heartily by the audience and encouraged to feel that he was among friends."[207]

Though some Christians displayed "kindlier feelings" toward Webb and the representatives of other non-Western religions, others clearly harbored sterner sentiments. He reflected on the sermon of Rev. Morgan Dix in Manhattan, who "strongly condemned" the recent parliament because it did not fulfill his millennial expectations of convincing representatives of the Oriental religions of Christianity's superiority.[208] Webb suspected missionary motives and had personal misgivings that the parliament's planners had followed a hidden agenda of laying a "trap" for the "Asiatics," though he credited the Orientals with the astuteness to see through it easily. Webb cited as proof that his misgivings were justified an official parliament statement specifying its goal of presenting "Church-Christianity to the best advantage." He observed: "The paragraph did not say so in so many words, but implied that if the Asiatic delegates would come, and see, and hear eminent Church-Christian speakers, they would become so awed and impressed that they would be converted, and return home to preach Church-Christianity."[209]

Webb's strongest objection was to the Reverend Cook, the embodiment of everything Webb found repellent in Church-Christianity. Persons like Cook, in Webb's estimation, would prove its undoing: "The class of fanatics of the Joe Cook stamp who inflicted their presence upon the Parliament did more to hasten the downfall of Church-Christianity than anything known within the past-decade." Webb objected not so much to Cook's "disgracefully intolerant conduct" toward him as toward the Oriental delegates: "the bigoted and fanatical Boston preacher" with "a few of his friends" had not only insulted and abused the Eastern delegates but made "a pestiferous nuisance of himself whenever an opportunity offered."[210] "Joe Cook, the Boston preacher," Webb declared, "is in favor of a universal religion, but it must be *his* kind of religion. Nothing else will fit the bill."[211] Cook's presence and conduct constituted the only "inharmonious and disagreeable feature of the Parliament." Webb suggested: "What this country really needs is one more Parliament of Religions, with Joe Cook and his friends counted out."[212]

A longtime student and admirer of Eastern traditions, Webb welcomed the Oriental presence at the Parliament, although he felt it fell short of what was deserved. "It would have been very much better if the Oriental systems had been more largely and more effectively represented," he said.[213] He identified with the Oriental camp and admired both the courage of its members and their demeanor: "It has been plainly shown that the Oriental systems have been grossly misrepresented, and that Church-Christianity's claims to superiority are not as valid and complete as they have been heretofore considered."[214] He admired the liberal spirit and presence of mind of the Eastern delegations: "One of the good results of the Parliament of Religions was the comparison of the broad, liberal and tolerant conduct of the representatives of the Oriental religions with the extreme intolerance, bigotry and brutality of some of the orthodox Church-Christian representatives."[215] Webb had no doubt that "fair-minded Church-Christians" who attended the Parliament left it with "a much higher opinion of Islam, Buddhism, Hinduism and Brahminism [sic] than they had before."[216]

In Webb's view, many "Church-Christians" came to the parliament convinced of the exclusive truth of their message but left in a state of doubt. "This very doubt," he asserted, would "lead them to break the chains that have bound them to a delusion, and encourage them to seek for the truth."

> It is undoubtedly true that all the honest, fair-minded Church-
> Christians who attended entertain a much higher opinion of Islam,
> Buddhism, Hinduism and Brahminism [sic] than they had before.
> Instead of regarding the representatives of the Oriental reli-
> gions as deluded "heathen" and intolerant fanatics, thousands of
> Church-Christians, in the vast audiences attending the Parliament,
> became deeply impressed by the intelligence and earnestness of the
> former.[217]

He insisted that people like Cook and his followers "gained nothing from the Parliament" and were incapable of rethinking old positions. But he said that "the better class of Church-Christians, those who have within them some of that spirit of tolerance, fraternal love, kindness and humility so clearly taught and exemplified by Jesus of Nazareth, as well as by our Prophet, have reaped benefits incalculable."[218]

Webb returned to New York after his moment of prominence at the parliament to open his opulent Twentieth Street headquarters, an event that Webb must have seen at the time as a fitting culmination to the parliament and the prominence it had given to non-Western religions. But the new headquarters would prove to be an illusory moment of greatness. Within weeks the World's Fair would end abruptly in tragedy. As for Webb, he would face massive budgetary problems before year's end, which would make it impossible to maintain his new headquarters. By midsummer 1894, his fledgling movement would be brought to its knees, leading to its ultimate failure in 1896.

10

Mission Runs Aground
and Webb's Final Years

Webb's participation in the Parliament of Religions was the high point of his American Islamic Propaganda. He returned to Manhattan for the October 6 grand opening of the mission's new headquarters on Twentieth Street, but only months later the mission was in financial trouble. From the beginning, according to Webb, support from abroad had fallen short of expectations. The final installment arrived from India on November 16, 1893, bringing the total sum for the first year to $3,000, $10,000 less than had been promised.[1] Only with the greatest difficulty did he succeed in keeping his Twentieth Street offices open after January 1894, and he finally had to close them six months later.[2] In desperation, Webb turned to the Ottoman Embassy in Washington and wrote to the Ottoman ambassador, Alexander Mavroyani Bey, asking him to visit the New York headquarters and observe its operations for himself. Mavroyani declined but invited Webb to visit him in Washington instead. Webb did so and gave a favorable impression of himself and the mission, leading Mavroyani to commend him officially to Ottoman authorities as a "sincere, honorable, and hardworking man."[3]

Mavroyani never ceased to hold a high opinion of Webb over the subsequent months and advocated his cause in Istanbul. He requested a financial report on the mission and included it in his official request for assistance. Webb informed Mavroyani that Hajee Abdulla Arab and the Indian support group had failed to keep their commitments and that the mission urgently required a monthly outlay of $837 in order to continue publication of the *Moslem World*. Mavroyani filed a petition on Webb's behalf with the Ottoman Ministry of Foreign Affairs on December 21, 1893. He argued that it would be in the best interest of the Ottomans to support Webb's work, drawing attention to the fact that Webb had a record of writing favorably about the Turks.

Mavroyani advised that the assistance be clandestine in order to avoid political repercussions. He proposed that Webb be granted a monthly sum of 25,000 Ottoman *kuruş*, equal at the time to U.S. $1,100.[4] The matter was presented to Sultan Abd al-Hamid II for approval on January 15, 1894, but unspecified misgivings made the sultan vacillate.[5] Webb received a lesser sum, $500, toward the end of March 1894 through a certain Mukhtar Pasha, possibly serving as a covert channel.[6]

Mavroyani's proposal remained before the Ottoman bureaucracy for consideration well into the summer of 1894. On June 15, 1894, Webb wrote again to Mavroyani informing him that continued publication of the *Voice of Islam* at a rate of one thousand copies a month would require $18 for production and $17 for distribution (a sum of $35 a month). Webb added that subscriptions and advertisements for the *Voice of Islam* had been insufficient to defray expenses and that he and his associates had been paying outstanding expenses from their own pockets.[7]

Webb required a monthly budget of $837 for the *Moslem World* and only $35 for *The Voice of Islam*. The discrepancy seems reasonable, since the *Moslem World* was a major operation and the backbone of the American Islamic Propaganda, while the *Voice of Islam* was essentially a circular. The *Moslem World* was almost four times larger than the *Voice of Islam*, richer in content, and presumably required a more extensive and costly distribution.

Five days later Webb wrote Mavroyani again, this time in a somber vein, conveying growing pessimism about the future of the mission. He expressed a loss of confidence that Islam would spread in America or become the world religion, claiming that he no longer expected help from Muslims but from God alone.[8] He lamented the sizable debts the mission had incurred and complained that his conversion to Islam had caused him personal damage, including the loss of old friends, some of whom had become enemies, and he feared that his family's future had been destroyed. If Muslims truly loved their religion, Webb insisted, they would not have failed to support his work. He asserted that if they would only extend adequate financial support, he would continue to devote himself to the mission full time. Mavroyani interpreted Webb's complaint as implying that the sultan, as "the protector of Islam," should come to Webb's aid, and Mavroyani urged the sultan to do so.[9]

The Nafeesa Keep Incident

The Ottoman bureaucracy was still reviewing Mavroyani's proposal to rescue Webb's mission when, on July 14, 1894, the *New York Times* broke a story that Nafeesa Keep, a member of Webb's staff, had accused Webb of financial wrongdoing.[10] The news probably did not take Mavroyani Bey by surprise. Nafeesa Mary Keep, who was at the center of the controversy, had written to him earlier to complain of Webb's alleged misconduct and, according to her story, received word from him to take her grievance to the Turkish Consulate in New York.[11] Keep, a convert like Webb, worked as editor of the *Voice of Islam* and secretary of the Moslem World Publishing Company and was clearly well-informed of the mission's internal workings.[12] The *New York Times* apparently doubted her commitment to her newly adopted faith, asking her if she believed in "the Mohammedan religion." Keep replied to the reporter: "I believe in it more than I do in Christianity. But I judge of a religion by its fruits, and Webb is the rottenest fruit that I ever knew to drop from any kind of a tree." The reporter queried whether she might not now return to Christianity, to which she retorted: "No. Decidedly not. I would adopt a happy medium and become a follower of 'Bob' Ingersoll."[13] She was referring to prominent free-thinker and agnostic Colonel Robert G. Ingersoll.

Two days earlier, on the morning of July 12, 1894, Nafeesa Keep locked herself up in the Twenty-Third Street headquarters, the only offices that remained, and refused access to Webb, business manager Harry Jerome Lewis, assistant librarian R. Othman White, and other staff members. Webb tried to enter through the assistance of two policemen, but they declined to force their way in, since Keep had attached a sign on the front door reading: "Forcible entrance or an attempt at forcible entrance will be prosecuted by law under the law providing protection from breach of peace." Keep allowed the reporter into the offices for interviews after reassurance that he would not help Webb to enter. A group of sympathetic artists living on the floor above supplied Keep with food, which they lowered in baskets from a window.[14]

Keep's statements to the *New York Times* conform to the general financial picture that Webb mentioned in his earlier appeal to Mavroyani Bey. She explained that Webb's mission had been facing great financial obstacles and kept its publications going only with great difficulty. She protested that Webb had borrowed large sums of money "right and left," which he could not repay. She and other mission associates had spent money out of their own pockets to keep the project afloat. Keep claimed that the mission owed her $150 for back pay and other expenditures on the mission's behalf. In addition to bitterness over personal monetary losses, she was convinced that Webb had misappropriated considerable amounts of money by using it for personal gain through real estate instead of mission ends.[15]

In Keep's assessment, Webb's mismanagement had made it impossible for the mission to survive. "The storm," she said, had "been gathering for some time." She had "often remonstrated about useless expenditures" and charged that Webb had failed to keep proper accounts of the money he had received from "the East." She contended that the mission books were in her possession and would prove her case by showing that $12,000 had been received payable to Webb from March till December 1893. More damningly, she accused Webb of using $600 to purchase a farm in Ulster Park, New York, and noted that she had written letters of complaint to Webb and to his wife clarifying what had to be done to reach a just settlement.[16] Keep "did not wish to have poor people in the East give their money for nothing" and would "hold the fort" until Webb turned management of "the magazines" over to her "so that she could run them as she believed they ought to be run."[17]

Keep produced for the *New York Times* a circular that Webb had written to "the Moslems of the Orient," asking for money to support his cause:

I have given up all my worldly advantages and find myself without the means of support. God has not allowed me nor my family to suffer. This vast country, four times larger than all India, is buried in the darkness of materialism, and many of its people are nominally following that false system known as Christianity. Yet there are many thousands of honest, earnest souls who are sincerely seeking for the light of truth. Send me all you can spare from your own money and then urge your brother Mussulmans to do the same. If you can send 1 rupee or 1 piaster it will help us. If you can send me 100, 500, or 1,000, so much the better for you and for Islam. The Christians spend millions of dollars every year to spread their false religion in the Orient; why cannot the Mussulmans spend a few thousand to spread the true faith here? There was a time when Islam was the glory of the world; it can be made the religion of the whole world if each Mussulman in the East will do his duty to God and him-self. Help me to plant the standard of Islam in the United States of America, and millions of Americans will clasp your hands in fraternal love.[18]

Keep protested that Webb had "bled India dry" and warned that he was "now turning his attention to the dominions of the Sultan of Turkey." She declared that she would remain locked up in the headquarters and allow Webb and his associates no entrance until either he resigned or "the Turkish Minister in Washington" renounced Webb's support.[19] Keep's charges did come to Mavroyani's attention, but the latter did not question Webb's denial of them and persevered in standing by him. Mavroyani's dispatches to the Turkish Ministry of Foreign Affairs continued to urge official support for Webb and maintained that the charges against him were groundless.[20]

Keep resolved to visit the Turkish Consul in Manhattan, as she contended Mavroyani had directed her to do, and "explain to him what a fraud Mohammed Webb is."[21] She made her way to the Turkish Consulate on July 16, 1894. Finding the consul absent, she spoke instead to the vice consul, Ismael Bey, alleging to him that Webb had proclaimed "that the Sultan of Turkey had commissioned him to preach the Mohammedan religion in this country and secure converts for the faith." She contended that Webb had been using the sultan's name to collect subscriptions from "the faithful." Ismael Bey responded that the Turkish government had nothing to do with Webb or his mission and that "the Sultan had not authorized him to use his name in any way." The *New York Times* related that Keep was "delighted when she heard this news, and she left the Consul's office in a happy frame of mind," though no less determined than before to carry on the fight until the end and to take legal action against Webb to stop him from obtaining more money.[22] After visiting the Turkish Consulate, Nafeesa Keep received no further attention from the press. Whether she ever pressed charges is unclear, but one of Webb's obituaries intimates that he became "tangled up in some sort of litigation over some property details."[23]

The Nawab of Basoda

More than a year later, the story of Webb's alleged financial culpability was revived in the New York press. Muhammad Umar Ali Khan, the wealthy nawab of Basoda in India—among thousands of Muslims in colonial India with the *nawāb* title (although described in the *New York Times* as the "ruling Prince of India")—arrived in New York on a visit to the United States and stayed at the exclusive Astor House.[24] The nawab claimed that he represented Webb's Indian financial backers and desired to examine Webb's work on their behalf. Though he failed to locate Webb, the nawab accused him in the press of squandering nearly $150,000, part of which he had received in India and the remainder in bills of exchange (personal money orders). With "a sore trouble oppressing his heart" as he departed for England, the nawab regretted not having seen Webb or discovering any evidence of the fruits of his "American Propaganda of Islam."[25]

According to the nawab, Webb had visited "a number of wealthy Mohammedan gentlemen of India" during his Oriental tour, advocating "the conversion of the New World to the faith of Islam." Webb's hosts had "supplied him plentifully with money, and rich and poor alike were influenced by the promise held out to them of the proposed spreading of the true faith among the great people across the water. High and low, the exalted and the humble, fell victims to Mr. Webb's glowing oratory and all subscribed." The nawab mentioned Abdulla Arab as one of Webb's chief sponsors and contended that Arab had contributed £5,000 [$25,000][26] to Webb's mission. When asked if he had also donated, the nawab stated that he had demurred, desiring first to see "proofs of [Webb's] faithfulness":

> He was to build a mosque in America and staff a newspaper to dis-
> seminate the true faith. Had he done so, I should gladly have
> aided him. Could he show that he has conscientiously applied the
> money received by him for the Propaganda, he could have had as
> much more as he wanted. But I see no mosque, no newspaper,
> nothing. He went away on his mission and nothing has been
> heard from him or his work. We do not know where he is nor
> what he is doing. Now I feel that the prospect so brilliantly
> painted for us is false. The faith has not been spread. I cannot find
> out how the money given for this grand missionary work has
> been spent.[27]

Though Webb was nowhere to be found, John Lant of Tarrytown-on-the Hudson, one of Webb's former mission associates, was among those who frequented the nawab during his stay in New York. Lant informed the nawab that "he, too, had been converted to Islam, but that he was disgusted with Webb, who . . . owed him £600 [$3,000] for services rendered in connection with the spread of the light of Islam." In the words of the *New York Times*, Lant hinted "delicately" that the nawab "might very properly repay this sum," although the nawab's Scottish translator and assistant would have no part of it. Lant presented the nawab with a copy of a lecture he had presented on Islam and an advertisement for a new journal, the *American Moslem*, which Lant was publishing in Tarrytown. He expressed his desire to accompany the nawab on his journey to England, "at the Nawab's expense," the *Times* was careful to note, "in order to help along the cause of Islam in London and elsewhere." Again, the nawab's secretary "would have nothing of it," but Lant kept pressing his case hopefully until the end.[28]

After the nawab's departure, the *New York Times* reporter turned his attention to Lant but found him "very shy" when asked to comment on his Islamic faith or line of work: "He seemed anxious to get away, as though his train was waiting." Lant insisted: "Really, I don't care to say anything now for publication." The reporter queried further: "Are you a Mohammedan?" Lant replied: "Oh yes. But I'd sooner say nothing now. When the time comes I'll make a long statement, but not now." When asked if his *American Moslem* was still being published, Lant "look[ed] about wearily" and stammered: "Well, now, really, you know. I don't want to talk." The reporter inquired further about Webb, causing Lant to "look distressed" until he "muttered something about not caring to say anything about the ex-Consul, and then hurried away."[29]

Penniless in Ulster Park

To his credit, the *New York Times* reporter set out to speak to Webb in person in Ulster Park after the nawab's visit. Arriving by train on Thanksgiving morning and not knowing Webb's residence, he asked local residents about Webb. The reporter intended to see for himself the "fine estate in Ulster County" and the "great real estate speculation" that "the prophet of the Prophet" and "the Apostle" of Islam in America had allegedly procured from mission proceeds "after hoodwinking the Indian Moslems."[30]

Ulster Park lies in the Catskills about eighty miles north of New York City and today is little more than a tiny, isolated post office along the train tracks. It seems not to have been much more developed in Webb's time. When the reporter got off the train, he found "nothing in sight but a desolate-looking railroad station and a few houses, not over half a dozen, lying widely apart and seeming sadly in want of paint. Not a sign of life anywhere."[31] The sunshine added some cheer, but "the disappearance of the train down the track made one feel homesick and forsaken."

Pondering over Ulster Park in "gloomy weather," the reporter observed, "It would seem a most likely place to drive a man to suicide when the sky is low, with a shifty wind sending the snowflakes about." He concluded, "Mohammed Alexander Russell Webb's great real estate speculation was certainly not promising."[32]

The reporter asked the station agent where he could find Webb and was told that he lived about two miles away but that getting there would require a buggy: "You can't walk it. That road's the roughest thing anybody ever saw. When it's warm it's about nine feet deep in mud, and when it's frozen like it is this morning, it has got more humps to a mile than any piece of roadway in New-York." The reporter directed his questions about Webb, the "apostle of Mohammedanism," to some of the village locals, but the station agent intervened, stating that Webb "never talks religion, never. We wouldn't know what he is if it hadn't been for the newspapers writing so much about him."

Having come to the Catskills to discover "the American Mecca of the Mussulman," the reporter asked the foremost question on his mind: "Does [Webb] own all this place around here?" "The agent opened his eyes wide, and after a moment said: 'Own all this? No, of course not. All he owns is a little bit of a place, ten or twelve acres, about two miles or so out from here." The reporter followed up his question: "Didn't he found Ulster Park, or buy it?" The station agent demanded: "Say, what put that into your head? He came here two years ago, and Ulster Park was here long before that." The reporter continued: "He's rich, isn't he?" The agent replied: "Not that I know of. If he is, he keeps it mighty quiet. He is a good fellow, sociable, and mighty smart, but I don't think he's rich." The reporter inquired what made the station agent conclude that Webb was smart: "Well, he's been an editor several times, hasn't he, and a Consul? I guess a man's got to be pretty smart to be an editor. He gets stacks of letters and goes to New-York about once a month, or so."

While a buggy was being hitched for him outside, the reporter questioned further about Webb: "Got a fine place, hasn't he?" The agent hesitated: "Well, now, I can't say that he has. Just a little bit of ground and the plainest house you ever saw." Still, the reporter "conjured up a vision of an old-fashioned Colonial mansion." Before setting out, the reporter socialized with "the male population of Ulster Park" at the saloon. Despite Webb's "queer religion," all of them knew Webb and "seemed to think him a pretty good sort of a fellow."

After setting out in the buggy with a local driver, who "turned out [to be] the village wit," the reporter found "the station agent's prophecy as to the rocky nature of the road [to be] more than borne out. There seemed no good reason why the buggy should hold together. The road, rising steadily, wound, or rather shot, in and out, among the stoniest-looking farm land one could hope to see. It seemed to be principally stone fences with patches of earth in between." The reporter remarked to the driver: "Pretty hard soil to cultivate, isn't it?" The driver grinned: "Well, kind o'. The only good thing about it is there isn't much of it." They passed a few houses "showing every indication of poverty," each with a "hard weather-beaten look, and the people in and out about them look[ing] as poor as the soil."

Finally, the buggy arrived at a house "on the side of a bleak, desolate hill, in the rockiest part of Ulster County, where the stones are so deep in the fields that they 'reach clear to China,'" and the driver pointed: "That's Webb's," to which the reporter replied incredulously: "Not that?" The driver retorted: "Yep, that's the place." Instead of the "home of a 'gentleman farmer'" that he had envisioned, the reporter found "a miserable house, without step, stoop, or porch, set in the middle of a rough, uneven patch of ground that was fenced off from the road by a few strands of wire that dragged most wearily." It was "built of plain boards, a story and a half high, with a wing, if such a thing could be called a wing, or kitchen." Although "large enough," the house was "utterly shapeless, like a long, narrow wooden box with a peaked top." The only redeeming feature was that the house was neatly painted white.

Webb's property impressed the reporter as the "picture of poverty and desolation" with no "sign of garden or lawn—just a hilly, lumpy rough yard that ran back 100 feet or so until it lost itself in a clump of woods at the back":

Three goats were roaming disconsolately about, nibbling hun-
grily at the spare grass that cropped up here and there between
the rocks. Across the road was a crazy-looking, narrow two-story barn,
as ill shaped as the house, and lacking the slightest suggestion of
paint. In a shaky lean-to stood a sort of buggy that looked much
the worse for wear. Nothing about the place looked prosperous....

[T]he sunshine served only to accentuate the grotesque ugli-
ness of the house, barn, and grounds. It brought out the crooked
lines of the house and barn, both of which seemed abnormally out
of plumb. It was a picture of poverty and desolation.

The reporter approached and knocked sharply at the door, "which opened
directly into the yard." A "rather neat-looking Irish girl" opened the door and,
upon his inquiry, informed him that Webb was at home and asked him to step
into the parlor.[33] It was "literally a step" into the parlor, which had "a low-
ceiled roof, with crooked walls that threatened any moment to tumble in
and smother you." In a corner under the stairs, there were "some well-filled
bookshelves":

For the rest, it was a poor, cheap-looking parlor, with furniture that
was sadly worn and shabby, and no ornaments to speak of, except a
few trophies that had evidently seen the Orient, as shown by their
queer shapes. But everything in the room was neat, and the musty
smell so often found in farm houses was absent. A cheap carpet of a
bright pattern lent an air of cheerfulness to the place, which was
heightened still further by an upright piano that stood against one
side of the wall. But there was no suggestion of luxury, hardly comfort. The parlor was such a one as one might find in most farmhouses,
where the people have been in touch with city life in the poorer
class of flats in New York.

After a few minutes, "a little girl of seven or eight," no doubt, Webb's daughter
Nala, "put her head in the door and said: 'If you want to see papa, he says you
are to come to his office.'"

Webb's office was located at the top of the shabby two-storied barn across
the road, "which the apostle of the Propaganda of Islam in America had fitted
up as his workshop." As the reporter approached, a "tall, broad-shouldered,
heavily-built man of perhaps forty-eight or forty-nine" appeared at the top of
the landing on the outside of the barn that led up to the office.

The reporter called out: "Mr. Webb?" "That's my name," Webb replied
"in a deep and not unmusical voice." The reporter was surprised to find Webb
looking like "a well-fed country store-keeper, but with a handsome and intelligent face withal," although it seemed "almost ludicrous" that there was
nothing about him, in the reporter's eyes, "suggesting Islam, India, and the
Orient." Webb wore "a frock coat of some checked brown and white material,
with a vest to match, and a pair of white and gray trousers. A negligee shirt of
red and white, a pair of heavy boots, and a close-fitting cap with a small peak."
"Everything was well worn, and seemed in keeping with the barn and house."

Webb welcomed the reporter into his office. Like the house, it was "scrupulously neat." Webb's office was divided by "a blue silk and satin banner

hanging on a screen or rough boards." The divider and "a number of pictures cut from illustrated papers and showing scenes of India" were "the only indication of Moslem or Orientalism [sic]" that the reporter could find. There was a "big old-fashioned cylinder stove that burned great logs of wood" and "threw out an agreeable warmth."

There was a pine bench along one of the walls, where "a lot of papers in single wrappers" were spread out next to "a book containing a list of names." Webb explained: "I am just getting my paper ready for the mails." He added with a smile: "I am my own mailing clerk." The paper was the *Moslem World and Voice of Islam*, and the reporter asked in surprise: "Then you still get your paper out?" Webb replied: "Certainly—sadly reduced in size, but still it is a paper. It is published monthly. Let me give you a copy." Webb handed him "a neatly printed little paper of four pages, with three columns on each page."

The reporter noted that "the apostle of Islam" showed no surprise at his visit. "I am used to it," Webb added:

> Somebody is always coming up, until in the village they all sus-
> pect that I have robbed the Government, or something of that sort,
> and the detectives are after me. My enemies down in New-York see to
> that. Only a few days ago a Post Office Inspector came up here to
> investigate a charge made against me that I was using the mails for
> swindling purposes.

After settling down, the reporter asked Webb about the nawab's recent accusations. "The Nawab of Basoda was very anxious to see you, Mr. Webb. He said that you had received between £40,000 [$200,000] and £50,000 [$250,000] from the Mohammedans of India, and that you had never accounted for any of it." Webb replied: "Why didn't he come up here, so that I might have shown him all about the money? Or why didn't he send me word to come and see him. I will see him now. I will go to-morrow." The reporter informed Webb that the nawab had embarked just the day before, to which Webb retorted: "Of course. That's the way they do—wait until the last moment, then make this sort of statements, and before I can answer them, or show them the facts, they go away. That's the way it was with another Indian nawab who stopped at the Waldorf. I got a telegram from him on a Sunday, and the next day he went away."

The reporter inquired: "Is it true that you received all this money, £40,000 [$200,000] to £50,000 [$250,000]?" Webb replied:

> Certainly not. Nothing like such an absurd sum. There have been
> spent in this Propaganda, speaking roughly about $20,000. Of this a
> considerable sum was earned here in various ways, by subscrip-
> tions, advertisements, &c [etc.]. The rest was sent me from India.

I have the cable notices in the house, and you can figure it out for yourself. I was just about making up my report.

The reporter asked about the £5,000 [$25,000] that Arab was said to have given Webb. He replied:

> He gave me no such sum. Abdulla Arab came to me in Manila and induced me to give up my Consulship, which I could have held as long as I wanted. Acting on behalf of himself and a number of other wealthy Mussulmans, he made a contract with me to undertake the work of bringing a knowledge of the Mohammedan religion to America. At his invitation I went to India to lecture. I never personally received a rupee. I refused to take money in person, and turned all offerings over to Abdulla Arab. Neither the Nizam of Hyderabad nor any other Indian gave me a penny. When I had finished in India I came over here. They were to send the money after me as fast as I needed it. I brought $500 with me for my own and my family's expenses. In the contract they made with me I was guaranteed a proper maintenance for my family and myself, and I was absolutely assured $13,000 for the first year, $10,000 for the second, and $10,000 for the third to carry on the work.

It is notable that Webb made no mention of Nafeesa Keep in his lengthy complaints to the press over the failure of his mission. He did protest, however, that the press itself contributed to wrecking his project from the outset by exaggerating the funding he received: "It was reported as soon as I landed in America that I had millions at my command to convert Americans; and at once sharks began to flock to me from all directions. When they found they couldn't bleed me they ruined me." Webb identified Lant as a leading "shark" and major antagonist in New York:

> This man has served, as I have since learned, several terms in prison. When I found who he was and what he was after, I turned him out of my office in New-York. Then he printed an alleged Moslem paper attacking me, and circulated it all over India. He joined forces with a half caste named Hamud Snow, whom I happened to have offended unwittingly in India. Snow is now in prison for attempted murder. He was formerly editor of a paper over there, and with Lant at this end and Snow at the other I was maligned most outrageously. This is how the fifty-thousand-pound story started. These people printed in their papers that I had received that much money, and so the impression that I really did got fixed in India and traveled back here. They also poisoned the minds of Abdulla Arab and his associates, and they broke their contract with me, leaving me

absolutely without funds. The only source of support I have now is a single Moslem in India who knows all the circumstances. He is not a rich man, but he has told me he will give me half of all he has until I can get on my feet again, and the trouble that has been made is cleared away.

The reporter inquired: "Then you have not given up the Propaganda?" Webb replied:

No, of course not. I am going into literary work that will help me out, and fresh aid will come from India again sooner or later. In the meantime we will get out our paper, and do what we can. My boy and I do all the work, and we manage to eke things out by raising a little something here on the place.

The reporter asked: "Why did you come up here in this out-of-the-way place of desolation?" Webb explained: "Because we could not stay in the city. We had no means. We had to get out where rent and expenses ceased. My wife bought this place for $1,000, paying $900, all she had, down."

He inquired of Webb further if he had attempted to convert the locals to Islam. Webb answered: "No. We can only hope for converts among thinking people, to begin with. The people here are not educated to think." The reporter then asked, "Have you made any converts at all?" Webb responded: "I have never tried. I did not start out to make converts. I was only to prepare the way at first by starting people to thinking. The preaching missionaries were to follow."

Assessing the Failure

During the initial stages of the American Mission, Webb expressed boundless confidence that it would succeed: "I honestly believe that within five years we will have a Moslem brotherhood in America very strong numerically and composed of just as earnest and faithful Mussulmans as the world has ever seen."[34] Webb's relatively short-lived experiment fell drastically short of his predictions, beginning in February 1893 and lasting until February 1896. The mission maintained its headquarters in Manhattan through 1893 and the first half of 1894. Webb probably acquired his house in Ulster Park and moved his family there toward the end of 1893, where he edited his newly consolidated journal, the *Moslem World and Voice of Islam*, and published the two pro-Ottoman pamphlets, *A Few Facts about Turkey* and *The Armenian Troubles*.[35] As indicated earlier, Webb's American Islamic Propaganda presumably ended abruptly after these last two publications, which he assembled and edited in Ulster Park.

There are various, often radically opposed interpretations of the collapse of Webb's mission. The first sees it as a failure of patronage, probably compounded by less than brilliant management. In this view, Webb's Indian patrons failed to provide him with the backing they promised, and, although the Ottomans apparently came to his aid, it was too little, too late. There is sufficient indication of Webb's diligence, but never in his life does he appear to have been especially practical or fitted for management. A second explanation, that of Keep and Webb's other antagonists, combines allegations of financial and administrative shortcomings with misconduct. It presumes that Webb, in addition to being an unwise administrator, misappropriated for personal gain the funding he received, which led to internal division in the mission and ultimately alienated its Indian sponsors. A third analysis focuses on the hostility of Victorian American society and the incompatibility of Webb's mission with its time and place.

Emory Tunison suggested that the mission's collapse resulted from public indifference and inadequate financial support.[36] Marc Ferris gives two primary reasons: internal strife and the fact that "few Americans were receptive to Webb's message."[37] Shalton holds that Webb failed and quickly faded from the American collective consciousness because of the "Islamophobia" which dominated Victorian America as a result of "anti-Islamic propaganda" from Christian missionaries, bringing "American intolerance of Islam" to a pinnacle.[38] "The social climate of nineteenth-century America," she asserts, "was not conducive to open Muslim communities," and any American who renounced traditional religion and the established lifestyle of the dominant culture would, like Webb, "have been ostracized from their own society."[39]

Webb attributed the collapse of the American Islamic Propaganda to a failure of patronage, which he ultimately laid at the feet of Hajee Abdulla Arab, instigated by "numerous vicious falsehoods and misrepresentations" concerning him and his work by "persons who have pretended to be converts of Islam, in order to better their worldly conditions."[40] His claim that he never received "a rupee" in India, refused to take money in person, and turned over all funds to Arab matches the picture portrayed in his diary: Webb generally paid for his own travel and personal expenses during the tour with the exception of accommodations, which, as a rule, were provided by his hosts. Webb gave an extensive account of his side of the story in the *Moslem World and Voice of Islam*:

> As there are thousands of English-speaking Mussulmans in the
> Orient who have never fairly understood why the publication of *The
> Moslem World* was discontinued, and as numerous vicious falsehoods
> and misrepresentations concerning me and my work have been cir-
> culated there by persons who have pretended to be converts of Islam,
> in order to better their worldly conditions, it seems proper, at this

time, to explain briefly the character of my contract with Hajee Abdulla Arab Sahib, of Jeddah, Arabia, under which I was given the management of The Moslem World Co.'s affairs. This contract was signed at the American Consulate in Manila, the capital city of the Philippine Islands, in the presence of an upright, honorable witness from Bombay, India. The portion of it which refers to finances reads as follows: "We agree to advance $13,500 for the American Propaganda, for the establishment and maintenance of its publication department and lecture course for one year and, if necessary, $10,000 for each of two subsequent years for the maintenance of the same. We also agree to provide for the proper maintenance of yourself and family." After this contract was signed, the expression: "We also agree to provide for the proper maintenance of yourself and family," was modified by mutual agreement, in the presence of the witness referred to, and I consented to accept a regular salary of $200 per month, to begin on the day of my retirement from the U.S. Consular Service, *i.e.*, the 6th of Sept. 1892. Hajee Abdulla Arab also made the proposition, in the presence of the witness, and it was mutually agreed that this contract should run for five years instead of three.

I arrived in America on the 16th of February, 1893, and as Hajee Abdullah had failed to send $2,000 which he had promised to send me by telegraph, I was compelled to wait until the first of April in order to begin operations. The total amount paid to me by Hajee Abdulla Arab was $10,243.01, which included the amount paid for my passage and incidental expenses from Bombay to New York. The last sum I received from Hajee Abdulla Arab under this contract, came on the 16th of November, 1893, more than a year ago. The sum total received from him for the support of *The Moslem World*, exclusive of my salary, was $3,256.99 *less* than he agreed to furnish the first year. The total amount of subscriptions received was $518.97.

The journal was kept alive by careful management until eight numbers had been issued, and I found myself compelled to stop its publication. But from loans and contributions from others than Hajee Abdulla Arab I should have been compelled to close my New York offices on the first of January, 1894. I managed, however, in the face of most harassing conditions, to keep them open until about the 1st of June last, when they were closed permanently. Notwithstanding Hajee Abdulla's failure to comply with the terms of his contract, and in spite of the vigorous, persistent and utterly unprincipled efforts of our enemies to destroy our mission, I have been able, with God's help, to continue the good work undertaken for Islam, and the results have fully equaled my expectations. God put it into the minds of faithful Mussulmans to come to my relief when help was most

needed, and if He spares my life, I will perform, to the best of
my ability, all I promised to do under my contract with Hajee
Abdulla Arab. God knoweth the hearts of all men and will judge us
both.

> Peace be with you and with all who follow the true path.
>
> Your Brother,
>
> MD. ALEXANDER RUSSELL WEBB.[41]

Thus, in the end, Webb placed the onus for financial failure squarely on
the shoulders of Arab, although protesting against "false American Moslems," who, in their desire to acquire money, had undertaken to ruin him and
his mission:

> Since we began our efforts in the United States, nearly two years ago,
> we have encountered hundreds of people, male and female, who have
> schemed and lied vigorously in order to gain the confidence of the
> Oriental Mussulmans and thus reap a profit. There are three persons,
> of whom we know now, who are actually engaged in this nefari-
> ous work. We would, therefore, advise our Oriental brothers to care-
> fully investigate the character of those who manifest a desire to receive
> money and merchandise, in America, without offering ample secu-
> rity for the fulfillment of their promises.[42]

Hassan Ali's opinion concurred with Webb's view that the mission failed
due to inadequate funding, and Ali claimed that he had foreseen the outcome
from the beginning: "It happened just as I had said. The Muslims of India did
promise donations, but the collections were few." Ali asserted that Arab exerted himself to collect the donations but met with notable success only in
Rangoon and Hyderabad. Arab raised an inadequate sum at best, and more
than half of it came out of his own pocket.[43]

Although Ali spoke of Arab as a saintly person, he also regarded him as
overly enthusiastic and unrealistic about his ability to provide Webb the
funding he had promised. After some initial success in raising funds in
Hyderabad, Arab, against Ali's advice, had rushed to telegram Webb from
Bombay, prematurely asking him to resign his diplomatic post and take on
the mission.[44] According to Ottoman records, Arab gave Webb reason to
believe that he would visit him in New York.[45] But Arab's trip never materialized, although, in retrospect, it would have been much more prudent and
critical to the mission's success than his initial visit to Manila in 1892.

The full story of Webb's alleged misappropriation of funds, the records of
his actual holdings in Ulster Park, and any litigation that might have been
brought against him have yet to be searched out and fully examined.[46] At
present, the accusations against him by Nafeesa Keep, the nawab of Basoda,
and others appear unfair in the light of conflicting evidence, especially the

failure of the mission's patrons to fund it adequately. Although Tunison apparently had no knowledge of the years in Ulster Park, he was convinced that Webb's "unmistakable fervor and persistence" for his mission could "have been inspired only by sure conviction."[47] Webb's dogged determination to endure poverty in Ulster Park and the shame of a nationwide scandal in order to bring the mission back to life was not only indicative of fervor, persistence, and sure conviction but, without fear of exaggeration, may also be called heroic by the common standards of human endeavor.

Internal strife was certainly an element in the mission's disruption. It generated a public scandal and fostered rumors that undercut Webb's remaining support. From Webb's point of view, even that discord grew out of the issue of promised finances and especially the false expectations that the press created by reports of Webb's unlimited funding, rousing the unwanted interests of the "sharks," as Webb called them. Keep's own supposition that Webb had "bled India dry" hinted at her fixation with the mission's alleged wealth and reflected her belief that Webb had access to resources far in excess of the $150 owed her.

The failure of Webb's patronage and his inability to establish an indigenous economic base may also have reflected the economics of the time. Webb's mission coincided not only with unfavorable market conditions in India, but also with economic depression in the United States. On June 27, 1893, just shortly after Webb launched his mission, the stock market crashed, triggering the greatest depression of the Victorian period, which lasted until 1897.[48] At the time, the Indian economy was still overwhelmingly agrarian. As the crown jewel of Britain's colonial possessions, India was its most resource-laden colony, and India's integration into Britain's colonial economy meant that it was influenced by world economic trends and felt the pressures of the global economic downturn after 1885 and throughout most of the 1890s. British taxes were heavy and unforgiving, and Britain neglected to take steps to protect emerging Indian trade, industry, and manufacturing.[49] Thus, economic circumstances certainly were not auspicious and probably conspired against Webb's Indian support group, despite Ali's firm belief that well-to-do Indian Muslims had the means to support their frivolous interests and simply lacked the sincerity to come to Webb's aid.[50]

There is probably truth to allegations about Webb's managerial shortcomings. Failure of the mission was not the first nor last time a Webb enterprise went bankrupt. Within a few years after the mission's failure, he would take over the Rutherford News but, in the aftermath of the paper's insolvency, he was remembered in Rutherford as a good editor and "interesting gentleman" who, for all his insight into spiritual truth, "was not sufficiently versed in the unrevealing method of conducting a newspaper without cash" to keep the paper running.[51] One of Keep's key objections was, of course, that Webb was inept at management, and he does not appear to have

attempted to run his mission on a tight budget commensurate with un-
certainties surrounding his foreign support, not to mention the dim economic
prospects of the period. The mission's opulent Twentieth Street headquarters
created an immense overhead: a four-storied rental property with abundant
facilities and a generously furnished public lecture room, which, however,
proved to be of little utility in the end. The October grand opening, shortly
after Webb's return from the Parliament of Religions, came when the depression was already three months old. Yet Webb seems to have entertained
no fear of financial breakdown, and he proceeded with the implementation of
plans as though no economic trouble was in the air.

As for "Islamophobia" causing the mission's failure, the term is more
applicable today than it was in Victorian America. Though Webb spoke of
hostility toward him, his mission, and his religion, he never regarded it as a
serious obstacle or intractable reality. On the contrary, he maintained that
many Americans, especially Unitarians and Universalists, looked upon his
work with favor and occasionally acknowledged to him privately their belief in
the soundness of Islamic theology, although they feared the consequences of
making public admissions. Webb remarked in exasperation:

> The true man is not a slave to public opinion but has the courage to
> express his honest convictions, no matter whether it ostracizes him
> from "good society" or not. The time will come when it will re-
> quire no courage for an American to declare himself a Mussulman—
> it *does* require it now.[52]

For the most part, the negative responses that Webb encountered were the
result of ignorance and misinformation rather than a deeply embedded fear or
hatred of Islam, and Webb's publications are replete with positive responses
from Americans throughout the nation, although in terms of numbers they
represented a very small minority. As for himself, Webb believed that he
belonged to a new generation of Americans that was in the process of transition from the religious narrow-mindedness of the past and was open to other
faiths and philosophies. He claimed to have kept careful watch as a journalist
over "the course of religious thought" in America for many years and to have
seen "the masses of intelligent people drifting away from the Christian
churches and forming themselves into free-thought societies, ethical culture
societies, non-sectarian societies and numerous other organizations the purpose of which [was] to seek religious truth." "Beside these," he added, "there
are the Spiritualists, the Theosophists, and an infinite number of other smaller
bodies which follow no religious system. Then, too, there are the Unitarians,
who, I am satisfied, will adopt Islam when they really know what it is."[53]

Webb was probably not wholly mistaken in his optimistic reading of Victorian America. His mission got off to a promising start and enjoyed a rea-
sonably good reception among the American people—certainly one that would

have been adequate to build on if he had received the means to continue his work. Webb testified amply to the scores of enthusiastic welcomes Americans had given him. Webb stated in *Islam in America*: "During the past six weeks I have received numerous letters from various parts of the United States asking me for literature giving a faithful reflection of the Islamic religion."[54] He concluded:

> These letters have convinced me that there is a widespread and
> honest desire among broad-minded Americans to know the truth,
> and have induced me to give this work to the public, in advance of
> larger and more complete works, which will be published later on.
> If this effort results in prompting a few persons to loosen, even tem-
> porarily, the chains that bind them to the church, and to give the
> Islamic doctrines fair, unprejudiced and honest investigation, I
> shall feel amply repaid for the time and labor I have given to it.[55]

Despite the hostility that Webb encountered among certain circles of Americans, especially those committed to a missionary agenda of their own, it is worthy of note that his most implacable opponents did not seem to find his faith or mission inherently discordant with American culture or an intolerable addition to its pluralistic religious landscape. His enemies may have personally found Islam to be distasteful, but they did not attack Webb or his message as anti-American. The press found the thought of a "Yankee Mohammedan" humorous, but, for all that, Webb remained a "Yankee" in their eyes.

Webb's Life in Perspective

Looking back on Webb's life, he had witnessed the passing away and the advent of two different worlds as the result of new and powerful industrial forces. As a child, he traveled by horse and carriage, watched sailboats on the Hudson, and probably listened to the yarns of old whalers on the Hudson waterfront. He saw the "iron horse" supplant earlier modes of transportation and become "the most conspicuous machine of the age" and his own principal means of travel during the epic period of the American railroad. He and his family took the transcontinental railway, completed in 1869, to San Francisco, where they set out by sea to the Philippines.[56]

Webb saw the "horseless carriage" introduced at the Chicago World's Fair in 1893, and, during the last decades of his life, cars competed with trains. The year of Webb's death, Henry Ford's "Model T" became an object of national mania. Nearly 2 million cars and more than two hundred thousand trucks were manufactured in the United States that year.[57] Newspapers were teaching Americans how to pronounce the word "Chevrolet" (a St. Louis advertisement read "Say 'Chev-ro-lay'") and carried ads for deluxe cars that were guaranteed to reach a sensational maximum speed of "one hundred miles an hour."[58]

Webb witnessed the birth of modern aviation. In 1903, Orville and Wilbur Wright manned the Kitty Hawk, and military biplanes became formidable weapons in the "Great War."[59]

The last fifty years of Webb's life marked one of the most critical phases in American modernization. Telegraphs and typewriters became essential, speed of communication surged, and innovation accelerated. By the 1890s, the telephone had become virtually ubiquitous and could be found even in rural areas, linking farms to cities. On January 25, 1915, Alexander Graham Bell inaugurated America's first transcontinental phone service, linking coast to coast.[60]

Industrialization brought new types of art and entertainment. Phonographs, nickelodeons, and motion pictures—unimaginable during Webb's childhood—had become commonplace by the end of his life. Old-style photography had recorded the Civil War and introduced photojournalism. By the turn of the century, inexpensive film and individual cameras became common. Webb became familiar with the Kodak Brownie, selling at the astoundingly low price of $1.

By 1900, only vaudeville could compete in popularity with "moving pictures." Opera houses of the Gilded Age were converted into movie theaters, which sprang up across the country by the thousands. When Queen Victoria died in 1901, her funeral was filmed and shown in theaters throughout the country.[61] By the time of Webb's death, Americans were engulfed in the "dizzying sense of acceleration" of modern life. Jazz and ragtime put to music the exuberance and "nervous hurry" of the times.[62]

Racially, the last decades of Webb's life constituted one of the lowest points of American history. In 1896 with its ruling on *Plessy v. Ferguson*, the Supreme Court legally established racial segregation as the standard of American race relations for generations to come. Within two years, *Williams v. Mississippi* upheld the complete disenfranchisement of Southern blacks by overturning any last remnants of the Reconstruction policies that had given them the right to vote after the Civil War.[63] Many whites, among them prominent educators, feared the "degeneration" of whites through racial mixture with "undesirable," non-Nordic European elements. Although the Statue of Liberty, the universal symbol of America's egalitarian spirit and openness to immigrants, was completed in 1886, in that same year Josiah Strong published his bestseller *Our Country*, "extolling undiluted Anglo-Saxon racial and religious purity."[64] The period before Webb's death was one of rampant racism and fear of new immigrants, called by some an era of "the most intense racial xenophobia in American history," which peaked during World War I.

On January 1, 1915, D. W. Griffith released his film *The Birth of a Nation*, which premiered under the title *The Clansman*. The film eulogized the Ku Klux Klan and advocated white supremacy, emphasizing the dogma that blacks could never be assimilated into white society. The film was also blatantly anti-Jewish and anti-Catholic. The film was an immediate box-office sensation on both sides of the Mason-Dixon Line.

The year before Webb died, a popular abridgement appeared of Arthur Gobineau's *The Inequality of the Races*. In 1916, Madison Grant published *The Passing of the Great Race*, "the summa of American anti-immigrant works," which forewarned the disappearance of America's Nordic population, "the white man par excellence."[65]

Thomas Hardy foresaw the advent of the twentieth century—which would herald the end of the Victorian Era—as "an age of wonders and horrors." Webb did not see much of it but lived long enough to catch a glimpse of Hardy's prediction. It was said that the century did not really begin on New Year's Eve 1900 but with the loss of the "unsinkable" Titanic in 1912, followed two years later by "the Great War."[66] Webb, an old and wizened man, must have felt his contemporaries' horror and astonishment at both events. He died during the presidency of Woodrow Wilson, two years after the outbreak of the First World War, at a time when the United States had not yet entered hostilities, and the general outlook was dismal.

Mohammed Webb Bey: The Final Years

After four or five years in Ulster Park, Webb moved with his family to Rutherford, New Jersey, in 1898 and spent the remaining eighteen years of his life there.[67] The Depression of 1893, which enveloped his mission, ended in 1897, and by the time Webb moved to New Jersey, the national economy had taken a turn for the better. In New Jersey, Webb often worked locally or commuted to New York City, which during his last years had entered its "golden age," beginning with the consolidation of the city's boroughs into "Greater New York" in 1898 and lasting until the end of World War II.[68]

Webb and his family appear in the 1900 New Jersey Census, which listed him as a journalist renting a home but owning no property at the time. Ella was a homemaker; Russell Lorenzo Webb was twenty-one, single, and working as a bank cashier. Webb's two natural daughters, Mary and Nala, were still young and unmarried. There was an Irish live-in maid, Nellie Hins, twenty-one and single, who had only recently immigrated to the United States.[69] Webb's adopted daughter, Bessie, had married eight years earlier, while Webb was on his Oriental tour. Webb does not appear in the 1910 Census. His son, Russell, does appear, however, and was listed as married to a woman from New York State named Grace, with a daughter of eight named Rhoda. He owned a house and was listed as the manager of a mercantile agency.[70]

Upon coming to Rutherford, Webb returned to daily journalism, working as editor for the *Rutherford News*, a Democratic weekly. By 1898, he was the paper's proprietor. The *Rutherford American* heralded Webb's purchase of the *Rutherford News*, describing him as "a gentleman of education, experience and ability, who has an excellent chance to make a good newspaper and valuable ally for Democracy." Webb also contributed a "fashionable 'Commuters' Column'" to the paper, which "made quite a journalistic hit in Rutherford and vicinity."[71]

Webb remained at the *Rutherford News* for about three years—roughly until the time of his appointment as Honorary Ottoman Consul General in 1901—but ultimately sold it in a merger to the *Bergen County Herald* of Hackensack, after which he continued on as editor of the new paper for another six months.[72] A local newspaper historian, writing years later, described Webb as "the most interesting gentleman ever connected with the newspaper press of Bergen County," noting his diplomatic service and the fact that he was "an American Mohammedan." The *Rutherford News* had been foundering when Webb bought it and was no better off when he sold it. Eugene Bird, a local Rutherford historian writing about Webb years after his death, noted his remarkable lack of managerial skills.[73] There is no mention of Webb's involvement in journalism after 1901. During his last years and at the time of his death, he was head of the sales department of the Martindale Mercantile Agency of New York City and would commute to Manhattan from Rutherford.[74]

The most notable occurrence of Webb's final years was his appointment as Honorary Turkish Consul General in New York shortly after the turn of the century.[75] At present nothing is known about the nature of Webb's appointment other than its honorific title. Without doubt, it was the culmination of his long and generally positive connection with the Ottomans and constitutes further evidence that they did not believe the earlier allegations against Webb. Relevant documents in the Ottoman Archives have not been made public at the time of this writing, but they should soon reveal the details of the appointment.

With respect to the Ottoman consulship, Tunison stated that Sultan Abd al-Hamid II appointed Webb as "Honorary Turkish Consul of New York" in 1900 as a "reward for, and an appropriate climax to his tireless efforts" in the service of Islam. He added that the sultan commended Webb for "plans to build a mosque in America and obtain grounds for a Moslem cemetery."[76] The *New York Times* reported Webb's appointment on September 30, 1901: "The State Department was notified that the Sultan of Turkey had appointed Alexander R. Webb Honorary Consul General of the Turkish Government at New York." It added that the appointment was "permanent" and that the sultan had conferred upon Webb the Medal of Merit.[77] Webb's obituary in the *Rutherford Republican* added that Webb was given the honorific title of "Bey" (Sir), an apposite title for his diplomatic position.[78] According to Osman, who relied in part on Webb's daughter Mary ("Mrs. [Garrabant R.] Alyea"), Webb's consular appointment preceded his journey to Turkey in 1901, where he received his title and medals of honor. Mary Webb showed Osman the official correspondence on the letterhead of "the Turkish Legation in Washington" commending her father for his many services. Osman stated that Alexander Russell

FIGURE 10.1. Mohammed Alexander Russell Webb Bey/Honorary Consul General of the Ottoman Empire at New York (1901)/Showing the Ottoman Medal of Merit and the Medal of the Third Order of Mejidi

Webb journeyed to Turkey in 1901 and was received by the sultan himself in Istanbul, where he was given the title of "Bey" and decorated with the Third Order of Mejidi and the Ottoman Medal of Merit. She averred that Webb was the only American ever to receive the distinction.[79] The photograph of Webb on the title page of Tunison's article shows him with an Ottoman fez and wearing on his lapel two medals of honor—undoubtedly the ones Osman mentioned.[80]

In 1902, Webb presented a public lecture with photographs in Rutherford titled "Constantinople and Turkish Home Life" based on his recent trip to Turkey. Nala Webb played the "Sultan's Grand March" on the piano, and two ushers wore Turkish fezes. The article reported that Webb himself, the "Honorary Turkish Consul-General at New York," appeared in "Turkish garb" but the article was quick to note that behind the "resounding title reposed the pleasing personality of Mr. A. R. Webb, former Editor of the 'Rutherford News.'"[81]

In Marc Ferris's view, Webb spent the last years of his life in "relative obscurity" interrupted only by his 1901 appointment by the sultan of Turkey as Honorary Consul General of the Turkish government in New York.[82] Though Webb lacked his earlier notoriety of the 1890s after coming to New Jersey, his final years were hardly obscure. Webb's move to New Jersey and his return to mainstream journalism marked his return to politics. The *Rutherford News* was a Democratic newspaper, and New Jersey Democrats hoped the paper would become a more effective voice for the party under Webb's editorship. The *Rutherford Republican* described him as "an ardent Democrat [who] took an active part in the work of his party while a resident in Rutherford," noting that he was the president of the Bergen County Democratic Club.[83] Webb's activity in New Jersey politics appears to have been primarily at the local level, although his career was not without broader regional and national dimensions.

In 1898, shortly after his arrival in Rutherford, the Bergen County Delegation of the Eighth District Democratic Congressional Convention in Hackensack put up his name for nomination to U.S. Congress. Webb withdrew his name, however, in favor of another nominee, William Hughes.[84] Webb was elected to the Rutherford Board of Education in 1902 and served a three-year term until 1905. During the same period, from 1903 until 1904, he served simultaneously as Rutherford district clerk. He was reelected to the board of education for a second term from 1905 till 1908 but did not run again after that.[85] Webb served as foreman of the Bergen County Grand Jury for four months in 1912 and was also president of the Rutherford Campaign Club.[86]

Webb suffered from diabetes for many years and died of the disease at his home on Sunday, October 1, 1916, at the age of seventy. He had returned from the Martindale Mercantile Agency in New York City the previous day and complained of illness upon his return. His condition worsened during the night, and he died the following morning.[87] The *Rutherford Republican* wrote: "Mr. Webb had passed through a prominent career. He was an ardent Democrat and took an active part in the work of his party, while a resident in Rutherford, and possessed many warm, personal and social friends aside from politics."[88]

Webb was buried in the Hillside Cemetery outside Rutherford in what is today the township of Lyndhurst.[89] His wife, Bessie, and Nala were later interred next to him. Webb maintained his Theosophical connections until the last and was an enthusiastic member of the Knights of Pythias, a nonsectarian society devoted to peace and mutual understanding; he served as "chancellor of the order" at the organization's Rutherford Lodge. Members of the Knights of Pythias served as his pallbearers.[90] In the absence of a local Muslim community, Webb's funeral services were conducted in private and by Rev. Elizabeth Padgham of the local Unitarian Church, a member of the denomination that Webb always regarded as the most compatible with Islamic teachings. It is worthy of note that Reverend Padgham, a woman, had become a member of the clergy at a time when such attainments for women were unheard. Her eulogy of Webb was described as "most impressive," although no record of it was preserved.[91]

Webb did not regard his Theosophical interests or Unitarian inclination as antithetical to his Islamic religious affiliation. Thus, the eclectic nature of his burial does not contradict Tunison's assertion that Webb remained "a devout Muslim to the end."[92] Eugene Bird, the local historian, still remembered Webb years later as "an American Mohammedan."[93] In the same vein, Osman maintained that Webb kept his Islamic faith until his death and that his affiliations and sympathies were never secret. "We have been assured," she declared in her memorial lecture, basing herself on Mary Webb, "that Mohammed Webb died a Muslim." She continued: "I have been touched by the sight of his last photograph, taken shortly before he passed away, a likeness that displays his shining, resigned face, crowned with snowy hair, as he stands in the midst of his family, his beard still uncut in the shaven America of 1916."[94]

There is an Arabic saying, al-nâdir laysa lahu hukm: "General rules do not apply to exceptional things."[95] Webb was an exceptional person, although his life, for all its distinctiveness, was not a total exception to the rule. For it cannot be fully understood outside its Mid-Atlantic cultural context and the particularities of the Victorian period. Webb's background instilled in him a spirit of religious individualism and nonconformity. The post–Civil War Victorian period not only fostered a sense of skepticism in him and many of his contemporaries regarding traditional religion, but also provided unprecedented access for him and others to knowledge about non-Western religious traditions and an inspiration to learn more about them.

Webb's choice of Islam was atypical of Victorian Americans. What is particularly remarkable about Webb, however, was not so much his choosing Islam but the way he did it and his fortitude to stand by his faith the remainder of his life, despite the bitter experience of his mission failure and the absence of supporting Muslim communities. Doubtless his affection for the Turks and their reciprocation by bestowing official honors upon him helped buttress Webb's faith during his last years and reinforced his positive sense of identification with the world Muslim community abroad. At the local level, however, Webb's lifelong association with Theosophy societies, the Unitarian Church, and other religious groups in which he found a kindred spiritual openness helped him to compensate psychologically and spiritually for the lack of an indigenous Muslim community.

Webb's life transpired "in the middle of it all," and to tell his story is to relive one of the most important periods of the American experience. Although Webb was largely forgotten after his death, historians have renewed his memory in recent decades. For the large and growing Muslim population of the United States, Webb may soon regain his place in the middle of it all, although no longer standing there alone but with a large contingent of other notable figures in American Islam who, like Webb, were long forgotten after their deaths. Webb was not alone among the early representatives of Islam in America in his struggle to persevere in his religion in the absence of a supporting community. Like his precursors and successors, Webb provides the American Muslim community today not only with a sense of the importance of community, but also with a deeper sense of identity and historical continuity.

Conclusion: Webb's Legacy

Footfalls echo in the memory
Down the passage which we did not take
Towards the door we never opened
Into the rose-garden.

—T. S. Eliot, "Burnt Norton,"
Four Quartets

The story of Mohammed Alexander Russell Webb is a story of what
might have been. Nadirah Florence Ives Osman concluded her speech
commemorating him in 1944 by saying: "He did what he could. Today, he remains for us, like an embedded monument, that we can
search and find, as we brush aside, with our hands, the dust and sand
of his generation."[1] Half a century earlier, when Webb's mission was
being launched, Hassan Ali had said, "We could not have found a
better man." Although overstatement is typical of such rhetorical
statements, Ali's words were, if anything, understated.[2]

Webb's legacy is valuable for the future of American pluralism
and the emerging self-definition of its large and growing Muslim
community. Sulayman Nyang articulated Webb's importance for the
American Muslim community's future by defining Webb as the
prototype of a "Webbian tradition" within American Islam, one that
is "color-blind," addresses itself "to the plight of all people in the
world," and is disposed to balance religious identity with American
culture, creating a sense of self that is at once genuinely American
and truly Islamic.[3] As a historical generalization, Nyang's Webbian
tradition may be somewhat problematic, although it is useful as

a sociological concept and future ideal. Webb was not completely color-blind. He did, however, express concern for the plight of the poor and oppressed, and he certainly saw Islam as eminently compatible with an American identity.

Our historical knowledge of Webb and his generation does not allow us, as yet, to trace any indigenous Muslim American community or movement directly to his name. Writing twenty years after Webb's death but without reference to him, G. H. Bousquet asserted that "the aspects of Moslem religious influence in the United States [were] manifold, but none of them seriously affected the religious aspect of American life."[4] Muslim American converts like Emory Tunison and Nadirah Osman would have disagreed and were proud to identify themselves as part of a living Webbian tradition; others like them would, no doubt, have felt the same at the various Webb commemorations held in and before 1943.[5]

It is likely that Webb's mission influenced, to some degree, subsequent efforts to establish Islam in America by inspiring early Muslim immigrants in New York to organize themselves and make their faith known.[6] During Webb's lifetime, he cultivated useful contacts with several immigrants whose names appear in his journals and of whom Emin Nabakoff, "the Russian Mussulman," was the most prominent. Webb probably supported New York's little-studied International Moslem Union, which was formed in 1895, most likely with the help of local Muslim immigrants and itinerant businessmen.[7] In March 1895, Webb welcomed the union to the fold of "the American Moslem Brotherhood," hoping that it would "promulgate the truths of Islam." He also took note of several similar organizations in New York, asserting, correctly or incorrectly, that their existence spoke "volumes in favor of our American Islamic Propaganda, commenced in this country less than two years ago."[8] When the Arab World—an Arab-American journal—took note of Webb by publishing Tunison's article on him in 1945, it demonstrated the emerging immigrant Muslim community's genuine interest in Webb.

But for decades, Webb and his work were largely forgotten. Only the development of scholarly interest in American Islam toward the close of the twentieth century rescued his memory from oblivion and began the process of brushing away the "dust and sand of his generation." Hopefully, the present work will constitute a sound beginning for the full account of the Webb story to finally be told. A Muslim in Victorian America is neither an ending nor the last word. There yet remains much "dust and sand" to be removed from the "embedded monument" before Webb becomes fully a part of the American collective consciousness. Academically, extensive materials pertinent to his story still lie hidden or lost in missing journals and neglected archives.

When the final word is in, Webb's "embedded monument" will not be one of an idealized human being. Whatever else Webb may have been, he was very human and had the strengths and weaknesses, virtues and blemishes inherent in human beings. His true story does not diminish his humanity or undo its potential for edification. Idealized narratives are not only unacceptable to honest people and for sound historical methodology but make up the substance of fable and ideology, providing little good in the real world. When such idealized narratives disembody their subjects—even legitimate heroes— from the reality they lived, they only serve to mislead, disempower, and immobilize because they present fictional figures that cannot be emulated or learned from.

All the same, the real Webb had many outstanding characteristics. Although never at a lack for self-esteem, he was not self-important, nor did he see himself as preeminent over others. As a rule, he took a fairly evenhanded view of himself as "an American of the Americans" and had little difficulty associating with others, almost invariably winning their admiration.[9] Though he was well-connected and probably would have ranked himself somewhere in the upper middle class, Webb did not belong to America's financial elite; in fact, he was hardly ever financially sucessful. He did not regard himself as either the most intelligent or the best educated of Americans but placed himself somewhere in between:[10]

> I am not vain enough to believe that I am the only American in this vast and progressive country capable of comprehending the system taught by the inspired Prophet of Arabia, and of appreciating its beauty and perfection. Nor do I believe that I am so deficient mentally as to accept, as truth, a religion which no one else in this country would be foolish enough to accept. But whether those who do accept it are wise or foolish in the estimation of their fellow men, I feel quite confident that at least a few may be benefited by my experience.[11]

In its broad strokes, Webb's psychological profile was the product of nineteenth-century New York, with its variegated landscape of "uncompromising religious dreams," borne of the Second Great Awakening and the "democratization" of American religion. This background instilled in him a profound sense of self and a birthright of religious liberty. It became his second nature and created within him ample psychological space for Islam or any other faith he should choose to follow. Nineteenth-century New York not only generated a multitude of religious ideas, many of them nonconformist and radical, but fostered broad social tolerance to go along with them. This social background inculcated in Webb an unquestioned attachment to his American birthright to interpret his adopted faith in a manner he found reasonable and personally acceptable. His family background in nineteenth-century American journalism reinforced his Mid-Atlantic regional cultural proclivities in conjunction with national ideals of enterprise and individual freedom.

Webb's ability as a convert to Islam to work virtually alone showed tremendous personal strength. That fortitude must have been largely due to his cultural formation. Almost without exception, converts are psychologically dependent on communities that they can belong to, and a convert's attachment to the adopted community is as vital a part of conversion as the content of the adopted faith itself. Webb had no such community, indigenous or otherwise, although he did try to pioneer the creation of one. His ability to adopt Islam, call others to it, and continue to identify with it despite the failure of his mission in the absence of a supporting faith community reflects Webb's resilient cultural formation, on the one hand, just as it is a tribute to Islam's holding power as a universal faith, on the other.

In all that he did, Webb was unmistakably Victorian. Even in going against the Victorian mainstream, he proceeded to do so in a Victorian way. His conception of the American Mission appealed to Victorian expectations of what was proper, especially regarding morality and social reform. Webb's disillusion with traditional religion and his spiritual search were products of the Victorian ethos of the post–Civil War period. This outlook included widespread skepticism of traditional Christianity, often accompanied by a new openness to non-Christian religious traditions, especially those of the East. Webb's American Islamic Mission simulated the colonial Muslim world in its reaction against the inroads of Western missionaries, which had driven Muslims to create their own missionary movements along the lines of Christian missions. Webb felt the same deep antipathy toward the missionary movements, and his Islamic mission in America was, to a great extent, an institutional and psychological reversal of the Christian missionary phenomenon in an American context.

Webb's story was the outcome of his complex relationship to the wide-ranging historical possibilities of the Victorian world in America and abroad. One of the most noteworthy facets of that relationship was Webb's indebtedness to the Modernist Movement of Islam (1840–1940), which played a central role in his conversion and imparted most of his principal ideas about the Islamic faith. The Muslim modernists rejected earlier traditionalist perspectives on reform and consciously adopted "modern" values such as "rationality, science, constitutionalism, and certain forms of human equality."[12] Sayyed Ahmad Khan, Ameer Ali, and Cheragh Ali—Webb's chief mentors and primary sources for Islam—were the most outstanding representatives of the Modernist Movement in British India. When Webb made the astonishing choice of adopting Islam, he accepted, for the most part, Islam as understood by the Aligarh Movement, and his indebtedness to Sayyed Ahmad Khan, Ameer Ali, and Cheragh Ali runs through the entirety of his work.[13]

Islamic modernism took different perspectives on Sufism, some regarding it favorably, and others abhorring it as the paramount reason for Islam's decline.[14] Webb found little in the modernism of Muslim India to encourage his penchant for Sufism, and, by adopting Sufism and making it a central part of his Islamic vision, Webb diverged from his mentors. Webb's attitude toward Sufism undoubtedly owed much to Theosophy and its conception of the esoteric and exoteric dimensions of faith at the heart of all world religions. But Webb's incorporation of Sufism as the central part of Islam is a good example of his native ability to take interpretative control over his adopted faith, independent of the Islamic modernists. Webb's mission circles were likewise predicated upon a similar commitment to individual freedom of mind, inviting converts and sympathizers, men and women, to use their minds and not requiring anyone to believe what they could not rationally accept as sound.

The struggle to establish interpretative mastery and cultural ownership in religious traditions has constituted a major source of tension among competing religious establishments in America ever since Old World denominations began arriving in the New World. The First and Second Great Awakenings and the "democratization" of American religion were examples of this phenomenon. Non-Western faiths presented an even greater challenge. To their credit, Buddhist and Hindu movements in America often recognized that the key to their success on American soil hinged on responding correctly to the question of whether religious directives were to be made in America by Americans or to emanate from India.[15] Within the mainstream Muslim communities of North America, the long-standing tensions between foreign-based and foreign-educated religious leadership and their local communities have been great and divisive.[16] The issue of indigenous religious authority also arose in the early Baha'i community of America and virtually tore it apart. From the movement's introduction in America during the 1890s and until the first decades of the twentieth century, American converts to Baha'ism had generally sought to preserve their spiritual autonomy. Many of them, including George Ibrahim Kheiralla, their first leader, rebelled against the attempts of Baha'i central authority in Lebanon to control their American mission.[17] Similar problems faced the Ahmadiyya Movement in America, especially among its African American followers, who often expressed discontent over the failure of Ahmadiyya headquarters in the Indian Punjab to fathom American realities and relate to them appropriately.[18]

Although of a disposition to interpret his personal religious beliefs himself, Webb's mission was closely linked with the East from the beginning. Had his mission succeeded, resolving the issue of indigenous and nonindigenous religious authority would, at some point, have become a crucial concern. Webb's journals welcomed the possibility of foreign teachers joining his mission in New York at some future time, which he spoke of as his mission's second stage. Although he prepared an entire floor of the Moslem World Building for the teachers, they never came, and it is not clear if Webb foresaw the problem that their arrival was likely to create. In 1892, Quilliam objected to opinions Webb had expressed in the Indian press about the utility of foreign teachers of Islam in Britain and America. Quilliam foresaw that their presence might lead to failure.[19]

Webb experienced firsthand the predicament of conflicting claims to religious authority in his relationship with Hassan Ali, who insisted, against

Webb's wishes, on being his mentor and frequently annoyed Webb with his fussiness about minute details. Webb's resistance to Hassan Ali's mentorship was, of course, not just an issue of taking religious interpretative control but also a function of Ali's infringement on Webb's perceived prerogative as a white man of considerable social eminence. In addition to cultural background, Webb's age and social status reinforced the independence of his judgment and enabled him to insist upon it among others. His espousal of Anglo-Saxon racial ascendancy also conferred on him, in his grasp of things, an aura of implicit authority and a natural inclination to be "progressive."

In his conversion to Islam, Webb generally conformed to the standard pattern of other Western converts to the faith. His cultural background was an essential contributing factor, but even it might not have been sufficient without the profound cultural shift that took place in Victorian America after the Civil War, modifying traditional American attitudes toward inherited Christian traditions and fostering new and vibrant interests in exotic religious and philosophical traditions, especially those of the Orient.

It is notable that Webb's adoption of Islam did not conflict with his sense of himself as an American. One might even argue that it empowered his sense of himself as an American, by enriching it with a living attachment to the Muslim East and the Ottoman Turks. In this matter, Webb's religious and psychological profile contrasts with that of many Muslim immigrants to the United States. For a number of them, Islam constitutes their greatest cultural and psychological vulnerability, putting them on the defensive in an alien land in what may appear to them as a hopeless cultural battle. Many early immigrants abandoned Islam altogether or "reinterpreted it" so completely that it ceased to be itself and became little more than a species of Unitarian Christianity.[20] Webb too had a strong affinity for Unitarians but thought of them in very different terms. Instead of him becoming like them, he was convinced they would ultimately become like him. In India, he informed his Muslim listeners of his confidence that Unitarians would "adopt Islam when they really know what it is."[21]

For Webb, Islam was not a psychological or cultural impediment, despite the hurdles he and his family confronted because of their espousal of it. Islam did not threaten his self-image as an American but affirmed it, creating a self-confident and optimistic religious vision. Webb refused to surrender his common sense or his own judgment to the authority of others who had no understanding of him or his people. Webb's circles, open to converts and sympathizers, men and women alike, were, in principle, predicated on the same ideal that no one in or outside of Islam should be required to believe what he could not rationally accept. Through Webb's circles, he sought to extend the principle of interpretative control to each follower. Unlike many twentieth-century American converts, Webb's conversion to Islam did not put him in a bind with himself and his American identity, causing him to forsake his heritage and commit cultural apostasy. On the contrary, Webb found in

Islam the very fulfillment of the American ideals he believed in. He did not see himself as standing "apart from or superior to his fellow Americans after his acceptance of Islam." Rather, he kept living as an American and was comfortable with that identity, feeling no alienation from surrounding society or seeking to alienate it from himself.[22]

Though Webb's attitudes on race, class, gender, and the church often clashed with what is generally acceptable today, they were common among white Victorians, both liberal and conservative. Webb identified himself consistently and unequivocally as a "liberal progressive" Democrat in opposition to "the spirit of Puritanism and fanaticism" and did not believe there to be any inconsistency between his liberalism and his social views.[23] Webb's private view of Hassan Ali is the most illiberal view in his diary, but does not represent blanket racial condemnation of nonwhites or Eastern peoples in general. Webb admitted willingly the preeminence of Asians in spiritual matters and valued the legacy of their great civilizations of the past. He relied almost entirely on Indian Muslims such as Ameer and Cheragh Ali for his understanding of Islam and had sought his diplomatic post in the Orient in the hope of discovering there the religious truth that he believed to be their unique heritage.

Webb's liberalism in religion found expression in Theosophy and an abiding curiosity in Oriental religions, which long preceded his adoption of Islam and, in fact, was an essential part of the path that brought him to discover his adopted faith. He also felt that the success of his Islamic mission in the United States required the combination of the spirit of indigenous liberalism and broad-mindedness with a similar spirit among the "educated, broad-minded liberal Moslems" of the East.[24] Webb felt at harmony with those Christian theologies, especially the Unitarian, that he regarded as open-minded and liberal. His attitude toward Christians who, in his view, were not tolerant of others was never magnanimous. He believed that the church, with its historical record of intolerance, was a threat to American civil liberties. He remarked: "The freedom of this country is not in half as much danger from the influx of foreigners, as it is from that spirit of selfishness, bigotry and intolerance, that was such a prominent feature of Church Christianity a few centuries ago."[25] Because of such convictions, Webb did not regard his illiberal attitude toward Church-Christianity as violating his liberal principles. Similar feelings about the church were characteristic of Theosophists and many rank-and-file Christians, and Webb's stance on the church was well-developed long before his entrance into Islam.

Webb's animosity toward organized religion lay at the base of many of his actions, including his journey to Islam and the mission work he adopted afterward. Shalton analyzes Webb's antichurch rhetoric as his "passion for Islam as a recent convert," noting, however, that it must surely have reduced his potential audience by alienating many who might otherwise have been inclined to listen.[26] Based on her thesis of Victorian Islamophobia, she regards Webb's verbal assaults on Church-Christianity as a "defense mechanism," by which he offset the hostility that Christians showed him, his faith, and his mission.[27] Victorian America was neither monolithically nor even generally Islamophobic, and Webb had no difficulty finding Americans who were very interested in hearing his message. His rhetoric against the church was not atypical of his time; it may even have gained him as many listeners as it lost. Webb's cultural and psychological defense mechanisms were firmly in place as an adolescent and were a bequest he owed to his formative period. After he adopted Islam, and even in the context of his greatest crises, he showed little indication of having lost his self-assurance or of being in need of defense mechanisms other than the ones he already had.

Webb assumed his Islamic identity as naturally as he had adopted Theosophy and Buddhism before or, for that matter, would have embraced and advocated any other faith that met his approval. Even as an elderly man, he felt no need to hide his faith from others or to justify himself for having chosen it. During the Oriental tour, he readily engaged others in discussions about Islam, including the U.S. consul in Calcutta, with whom he spoke forthrightly about his faith, finding a way to get the consul to "melt" despite his initial coldness.

Webb directed his thoughts on the church toward the institution, certain dogmas like the Trinity, and policies like the missionary movement. His response seems at times to have been dictated by a counteractive psychology, and it was probably in this sense that he frequently asserted that Islam, not Christianity, would ultimately prove to be the universal faith, a virtual polar reversal of the opposite claim by the missionaries. In his treatment of Church-Christianity, Webb was often guilty of a double standard not unlike the one he criticized in Church-Christians. In speeches and writings, Webb ignored the "very queer specimens" of Muslims whom he had encountered in the East, and he painted an idealized picture of Muslim fraternity. He entertained hateful thoughts of Hassan Ali but described him glowingly in public. Webb attributed the ascendance of the West to Anglo-Saxon progressiveness, following closely the Ingersoll thesis that Christian morality "does not make men good" but rather that "good men have given Christianity the good reputation that it has."[28] But when it came to Muslims, Webb excused Islam, attributing Muslim social decay to deficiencies of race and climate while lamenting their fall from past glory.

Webb was quick to commend Christians who were broad-minded and committed to the welfare of others, but he held that the worthy ideals and social objectives of Christianity could be fully realized only through Islamic faith and practice.[29] His hostility toward Church-Christianity did not imply rejection of Christ's original message. In a characteristically Islamic vein, he spoke of Christ as God's "meek and lowly" prophet and as a chosen instrument for human guidance whose message confirmed the earlier messages of Abraham and Moses and the later revelation of Muhammad.[30] Webb won hearty applause at the Parliament of Religions when he stated:

> A man said to me in New York the other day, "Must I give up Jesus and the Bible if I become a Mohammedan?" No! no! There is no Mussulman on earth who does not recognize the inspiration of Jesus (applause). The system is one that has been taught by Moses, by Abraham, by Jesus, by Mohammed, by every inspired man the world has ever known. You need not give up Jesus, but assert your manhood. Go to God.[31]

In some ways, the script for the World's Parliament of Religions had been set a century earlier at the Third Columbian Centennial of 1792, which was held in New York and Baltimore. Those who envisioned the earlier post-revolutionary event included prominent religious figures, thinkers, and poets who embodied the spirit of the American Revolution and the European Enlightenment. To them, the youthful Republic was the greatest social experiment in history, and they foresaw that America would someday become the meeting ground of the world's great faiths under the aegis of toleration and religious freedom. As Seager relates, Jeremy Belknap, a Congregationalist minister and one of the "visionaries" of the Third Columbian Centennial, foresaw that the "scattered tribes" of humanity would ultimately come together in the new Republic, where the "Jew, the Mahometan, the Gentoos [Hindus], and the Disciples of Confucius" would join in "various experiments of happiness."[32] It took generations before America achieved a more genuine pluralism and succeeded in incorporating Jews and Catholics into American society. Webb welcomed religious pluralism enthusiastically and played his own role in America's gradual evolution toward it.[33]

Hassan Ali praised Webb as a "proper Muslim" (pucca Mussulman) [sic], one who knew Islam's true spirit and was neither overly rationalistic nor dry, but worthy of Islam's "sacred treasure" as reflected in spiritual masters like al-Ghazali and Rumi. Webb's heart, Ali contended, was filled with the love of God and his prophet.[34] It was the spirit of Islam, rather than its aberrations, that won Webb's allegiance. In this regard, he truly constitutes an "embedded monument" from the past for the future. Perhaps, his legacy may once again play a role in furthering and protecting an even more pluralistic America, one eager to extend its hand to the world at large and its own growing Muslim community at home in the spirit Webb invoked more than a century ago when he addressed the Muslims of India: "I want to take your hand and carry it across the sea to be seized in an earnest, fraternal grasp by the people of America."[35]

Notes

ABBREVIATIONS

"Dispatches"   "Dispatches from United States Consuls in Manila,
               Philippine Islands 1817–1899"
EI   *Encyclopedia of Islam*
MW   *Moslem World*
MWVI   *Moslem World and Voice of Islam*
OA   Ottoman Archives

CHAPTER I

1. *The Inter Ocean*, 21 September 1893.

2. Houghton, *Neely's History*, 460, 464; Barrows, *The World's Parliament of Religions*, 2: 989–990, 996.

3. Webb, "A Letter," *The Allahabad Review*, July 1892: 77.

4. "Mr. Webb on Turkish Life"; Haberly, *Newspapers*, 11. Webb's lecture was described as pleasing from beginning to end. He presented his audience with several "stereopticon pictures" of Turkey: "[Webb] described humorously the famous dogs of Constantinople, told how they give a fire-alarm in the city and how the fire-men turn out; pictured the Turkish horse car, and told of some of the famous sites of interest with which Constantinople abounds. Altogether, the lecture, by a man in thorough sympathy with his subject, was interesting and of educational value."

5. Haberly, *Newspapers*, 11; and Bird, "The Press of Bergen County," 203.

6. Naipaul consigns Webb to the "white Muslim line-up" of famous converts. Somehow, Naipaul transposed Webb's death date from 1916 to 1961 and says of him that he was "born in 1846 and died at the age of 115

in 1961," attributing to him by this mistake, as Bunker notes, an "immensely long life in Islamic missionary work." See Bunker, *Bits and Pieces*, 282; Naipaul, *Among the Believers*, 115–116.

7. Fishburn, *The Fatherhood of God*, 41.

8. See *MWVI*, February and March 1895: 4.

9. Maass, *The Gingerbread Age*, 9–10.

10. Regarding *Frank Leslie's Illustrated*, see Schlereth, *Victorian America*, 185.

11. Stiletto, "Face Studies: Alexander Russell Webb," *Frank Leslie's Illustrated Weekly*, 30 March 1893: 204.

12. Stanton-Hope, *Arabian Adventurer*, 94.

13. "Asked to Turn Moslems"; "To Preach Moslemism." An 1887 sketch of Webb appears in the *Missouri Republican*, showing him much thinner and sporting a closely cut beard. See "Got a Consulship."

14. "Muhammad Webb's Mission."

15. Tunison, "Mohammed Alexander Russell Webb," 14; Lancaster, *The Incredible World's Parliament of Religions*, 16.

16. Maass, *The Gingerbread Age*, 22, 28.

17. He had to buy a pair in India and "was duly robbed, of course—eye-glasses which sell in the States for 75¢ and $1.00, they asked 12 R's for or about $5.50—generously consented to sell them to me for 10 R's or about $4.75—original cost about 40¢." See Webb Diary, 29 October 1892.

18. Maass, *The Gingerbread Age*, 22, 28.

19. Osman, "The Story" (1944), 8.

20. Tunison, "Mohammed Alexander Russell Webb," 14.

21. Seager, *The Dawn of Religious Pluralism*, photographs and sketches between 270 and 271.

22. *Inter Ocean*, 21 September 1893. A Webb obituary described him as presiding over a number of sessions at the parliament and wearing, in one of them, a "gorgeous turban." Although containing many details, the obituary was also filled with inaccuracies. See "*Republic* Reviews Alex Webb's Life."

23. "Interview of a Correspondent," in Webb, *Lectures on Islam*, 29.

24. "A Bit of History," *MW*, October 1893: 7.

25. Turner, *Islam*, 65.

26. "Muhammad Webb's Mission," 1.

27. "Asked to Turn Moslems."

28. Webb Diary, 26 November 1892.

29. Ibid., 30 November 1892.

30. See *History of Columbia County*, 51–55, 73–74, 82–83, 92–94.

31. See McMullin, *Hudson Revisited*, 9–9; Webb, *Claverack*, 41–42, 66, 69.

32. *History of Columbia County*, 201.

33. Based on a June 2002 interview with Mary Howell, Columbia County historian. A historical marker at Catskill's Uncle Sam Bridge states that Samuel Wilson lived there from 1817 till 1822 and provisioned the U.S. Army with supplies. The initials "U.S." were stamped on his supplies, and it is said that soldiers jokingly linked the initials to his name, "Uncle Sam." The historical validity of the matter is

open to question, but the account, according to Mary Howell, is generally accepted in the region.

34. *History of Columbia County*, 10–14.

35. Ibid., 128.

36. Twain, *Tom Sawyer Abroad*, 98.

37. Zelinsky, *Cultural Geography*, 23.

38. McMullin, *Hudson Revisited*, 8–10.

39. Tocqueville, *Democracy in America*, 1: 245, 288; 2:445–446, 445n.

40. See Allison, *The Crescent Obscured*, xiv–xvii; Obeidat, "Washington Irving," 27–36. Irving followed in the footsteps of Thomas Carlyle, whose work, *The Hero as Prophet* (1841), was a relatively favorable account of Muhammad and admired by Webb. Irving probably knew Gustav Weil's *Mohammed der Prophet* (1844) and Simon Ockley's *History of the Saracens* (1847), also a remarkably objective work for the age.

41. See Marty, *Pilgrims*, 219.

42. Whitman, *Leaves of Grass*, 48, 44, 43, 29.

43. Muhammad, "Muslims," 195.

44. Tunison, "Mohammed Alexander Russell Webb," 13; Osman, "The Story" (1944), 6. Osman titled her presentation on Webb "The Story of the First American Convert to Islam."

45. See Austin, *African Muslims*, 3–5 13–14, 51–61, 65–78; and Diouf, *Servants of Allah*, 39–40, 46–47, 60, 77, 203.

46. Khan, "Mohammed Alexander Russell Webb," 1.

47. Hamdani, "Canada's Muslims," 98; follow-up information through a friend from his personal conversation with Hamdani.

48. Arnold, *The Preaching of Islam* (1896 edition), 465 n. 1.

49. Garcin de Tassy, *La langue et la littérature hindoustanies* (1875), 91–92. The issue of the *Indian Mail* treating Norman is dated 25 May 1875.

50. Muhammad, "Muslims," 198. Despite Muhammad's allusion to Norman, he still recognizes Webb as initiating "the earliest organization to attempt directly the conversion of Americans to Islam." This assertion may prove true, but, for the present, its validity depends on Norman's full identification and an assessment of his mission. Two years after the appearance of Muhammad's article, Melton mistakenly recognized Webb as America's first Islamic convert (Melton, "Webb, Muhammad Alexander Russel"). *The Encyclopedia of American Religious History* ventured to say with some circumspection that Webb was "generally regarded as the first American convert to Islam," although it amended the assertion by referring to him as "the first European American convert to Islam" (1: 344 and 2: 781). In 1997, Turner joined the litany of depicting Webb as "the first known American convert to Islam," also attributing to him the establishment of "the first Islamic mission in the United States" (Turner, *Islam*, 64).

51. *MWVI*, September 1895: 2.

52. Ibid., October 1895, 3.

53. Shalton, "Mohammed Alexander Russell Webb," 21–22.

54. Seager, *The Dawn*, 248.

55. See Nyang, *Islam*, 103, 112; Shalton, "Mohammed Alexander Russell Webb," 14.

56. Turner, *Islam*, 64.

57. Smith, *Islam*, 189–190; Ferris, "Immigrant Muslim Communities," 210.

58. Smith, *Islam*, 189–190.

59. Nyang, *Islam*, 109. The Syrian and Lebanese Muslim immigrants of Cedar Rapids, Iowa, built the "mother mosque" in 1922. It deserves distinction not because it was indisputably the oldest mosque in the United States—although it is certainly among the oldest—but because it continues to flourish today.

60. Hermansen, "Roads to Mecca," 187 and n. 157.

61. Smith, *Islam*, 189–190.

62. Melton, "Webb, Muhammad Alexander Russel."

63. Zwemer's *Moslem World*, according to its early imprints, was established "since 1911." For the articles, see Aijian, "The Mohammedans in the United States," 30–35; Holmes, "Islam in America," 262–266; Crabites, "American Negro Mohammedans," 272–284; Bousquet, "Moslem Religious Influences in the United States," 40–44; and Braden, "Islam in America," 309–317.

64. At the time, Steinway Hall, a well-known concert hall, was located in Manhattan at 109 West Fifty-Seventh Street. In 1955, it was sold to Metropolitan Life (Jackson, *The Encyclopedia of New York*, 1121).

65. Muhammad, "Muslims," 199.

66. After the death its founder, Mirza Ghulam Ahmad, in 1908, the Ahmadiyya movement, which took its name from him, split into two branches: the Lahoris and the Qadianis. The former group was the more moderate and sought to reconcile itself with mainstream Islam. It discarded a number of beliefs regarding the movement's founder—such as his having been a prophet or messiah—and was content with calling him a "centennial renewer" [*mujaddid*] of the Islamic faith. See Friedmann, *Prophecy Continuous*, 16, 22, 150.

67. Osman, "The Story" (1944), 7–8.

68. Such initiative is sometimes referred to by the awkward sociological expression "voluntaryism," as opposed to "voluntarism." It refers to a distinctive American religious social psychology that grew out of the constitutional principle of denying state contributions to religious institutions and requiring them to rely on member support. It led to voluntary individual initiative and a spirit of religious competitiveness not just in the establishment of faith communities but in the interpretation and propagation of religion as well. See Marty, *Religion and Republic*, 44; and Poston, *Islamic Da'wah*, 184.

CHAPTER 2

1. The Victorian age is generally broken down into three periods: early, middle, and late. The early Victorian period is sometimes dated as early as 1820 or 1830 and lasted until midcentury. The mid-Victorian period is dated from 1850 till 1870, and the late Victorian period was from 1870 till 1900, although some date the late Victorian period till 1914 and the outbreak of World War I. During the second and third decades of the nineteenth century, years before Queen Victorian's reign, the essentials of the Victorian worldview were already widely propagated in sermons, literature, and newspapers. The classical Victorian worldview coalesced during the middle

Victorian period. During the late period, this world view came to permeate Protestant middle-class culture. See Schlereth, *Victorian America*, xi–xii; May, *Great Expectations*, 17; Fishburn, *The Fatherhood of God*, 18, 23; Maass, *The Gingerbread Age*, 7; Rose, *Victorian America*, 7 n. 9; Tweed, *The American Encounter*, xxiii.

2. Morgan, *Victorian Culture*, xi; Maass, *The Gingerbread Age*, 7.

3. *History of Columbia County*, 99.

4. Schlereth, *Victorian America*, xi.

5. Fishburn, *The Fatherhood of God*, 33.

6. Noll, *The Old Religion*, 129.

7. Fishburn, *The Fatherhood of God*, 97; Abu-Lughod, *New York, Chicago, Los Angeles*, 103. Chicago's ten-story Home Insurance Building (1885) is generally acknowledged as the "forerunner of the modern skyscraper."

8. *History of Columbia County*, 170.

9. Ibid., 22.

10. Ibid., 153–155; McMullin, *Hudson Revisited*, 1–2.

11. The Napoleonic wars around the turn of the eighteenth century brought Hudson lasting economic harm. In 1806, Britain declared all ports from Brest in France to the Elbe River in Germany under blockade. Napoleon retaliated by placing the British Isles under embargo, which led to an even more stringent British response against all French ports. Ships violating the blockades were seized and condemned, and Hudson lost many vessels as a result. Hudson merchants whose ships escaped seizure found their profits stifled all the same. The final blow came from President Jefferson's embargo of December 1807. One wealthy Hudson sea merchant declared bitterly that "the ship of state had been turned out of her course and yawned about by a lubberly helmsman, until the voyage was ruined and the owners half broken." The War of 1812 increased Hudson's maritime losses. By war's end in 1815, Hudson had lost its former economic prestige. The Bank of Hudson failed in 1819, and the city's population declined sharply. See *History of Columbia County*, 157, 160–163; McMullin, *Hudson Revisited*, 3–4.

12. *History of Columbia County*, 159, 162–165; McMullin, *Hudson Revisited*, 4.

13. *History of Columbia County*, 132–134; McMullin, *Hudson Revisited*, 4.

14. Zelinsky, *Cultural Geography*, 9.

15. See ibid., 117. American English was a product of pan-British culture. It worked the various accents and speech levels of colonists into regional forms.

16. Marty, *Pilgrims*, 53.

17. Elazar, "The American Cultural Matrix," 13–42.

18. Zelinsky, *Cultural Geography*, 114, 117.

19. Marty, *Pilgrims*, 66.

20. See Zelinsky, *Cultural Geography*, 20.

21. *History of Columbia County*, 154, 162, 181; McMullin, *Hudson Revisited*, 2, 7.

22. *History of Columbia County*, 182–189, 197.

23. McMullin, *Hudson Revisited*, 8–9; and based on June 2002 interview with Mary Howell, Columbia County historian.

24. The First Presbyterian Church still stands at Fourth and Warren Streets. Webb mentioned his conversion to the Episcopalian Church in an 1892 interview ("Interview of a Correspondent," 30) and married Ella, his second wife, in an Episcopalian church.

25. Tocqueville, *Democracy in America*, 2: 405–406.

26. See Menand, *The Metaphysical Club*, 80–81; Marty, *Pilgrims*, 138, 169–170; Olmstead, *History of Religion*, 192; LeBeau, *Religion in America*, 46–52, 87. Jonathan Edwards of Boston was the principle figure of the First Great Awakening, which is roughly dated from 1720–1750. His spirit engulfed the thirteen colonies and filled them with "pietistic rapture." Both the First Awakening and the American Revolution were major forces in breaking down religious barriers and Old World socioeconomic hierarchies and promoting the "democratization" and greater unification of American religious consciousness. The Second Great Awakening was akin to the First Awakening but more subdued. Its spirit permeated the newly independent United States and spread beyond into the frontier, where tent revivals and camp meetings became standard cultural institutions. The Second Awakening brought the process of democratizing Old World Christianity to its completion and led to the massive absorption of a popular Protestant spirituality into American culture, stripping away what remained of the traditional formalities and hierarchies of European Christianity.

27. Marty, *Pilgrims*, 190–191.

28. Ibid.

29. Zelinsky, *Cultural Geography*, 117, 127.

30. See Zelinsky, *Cultural Geography*, 117, 127; Menand, *The Metaphysical Club*, 81; Littell, *From State Church*, 98–99, 101.

31. Noll, *The Old Religion*, 100.

32. *History of Columbia County*, 182–189, 197; Webb, *Islam in America*, 11; Webb, "Islam," 24. Regarding the history and social geography of American denominations, see Marty, *Pilgrims*, 109, 124, 138, 169–170; LeBeau, *Religion in America*, 42–44; Zelinsky, *Cultural Geography*, 9. Congregationalists predominated in New England, which later became a center of Unitarianism. Episcopalians dominated the Old South but were hospitable to most major Protestant denominations except the more radical ones.

33. *History of Columbia County*, 182.

34. Ibid.

35. See ibid., 307–310; Olmstead, *History of Religion*, 339; Marty, *Pilgrims*, 191–192; LeBeau, *Religion in America*, 121–123.

36. See *History of Columbia County*, 307, 310; Olmstead, *History of Religion*, 339; Marty, *Pilgrims*, 191–192.

37. Olmstead, *History of Religion*, 339; LeBeau, *Religion in America*, 121–123.

38. Olmstead, *History of Religion*, 339; LeBeau, *Religion in America*, 121–123.

39. *History of Columbia County*, 309; Marty, *Pilgrims*, 191–192.

40. Marty and Marty, *When True Simplicity Is Gained*, inset page.

41. Olmstead, *History of Religion*, 335.

42. Marty, *Pilgrims*, 198–199, 201; LeBeau, *Religion in America*, 156.

43. Marty, *Pilgrims*, 204–205.

44. Ibid., 203–205.

45. On July 12, 1843, Smith received a revelation commanding him to reinstitute the Old Testament covenant of plural marriage "or be damned by God," although *The Book of Mormon* itself had condemned the practice. Although Brigham Young has

been regarded as instituting plural marriage, there is now strong evidence that Smith introduced the practice and enforced it as a test the loyalty of his closest associates. See Marty, *Pilgrims*, 203, 208; LeBeau, *Religion in America*, 156–157.

46. Z[wemer], "Mormonism," 436; compare LeBeau, *Religion in America*, 155. Zwemer reviewed a similar work by John Quincy Adams—not to be confused with the American president by that name—which appeared in 1916, titled *The Birth of Mormonism*. Zwemer asserted: "Here this monstrous system is traced to its origin namely, Yankee cunning and deceit among a superstitious people. It is a sordid, well nigh incredible story, without one redeeming feature. That such a deception was played in the nineteenth century and among a community which at least was far in advance of the Arabs in the seventh century throws considerable light on the origin of Islam" (Z[wemer], "The Birth of Mormonism," 95).

47. Olmstead, *History of Religion*, 343–344; Noll, *The Old Religion*, 100.

48. Olmstead, *History of Religion*, 344.

49. See ibid., 344–345; Marty, *Pilgrims*, 321–322; Noll, *The Old Religion*, 101; Rosten, *Religions of America*, 619.

50. Littell, *From State Church*, 101.

51. Olmstead, *History of Religion*, 342–343; Marty, *Pilgrims*, 193–195; LeBeau, *Religion in America*, 124–126.

52. Marty, *Pilgrims*, 195.

53. Olmstead, *History of Religion*, 342–343; Marty, *Pilgrims*, 193–195; LeBeau, *Religion in America*, 124–126.

54. Welter, "A Century of Protestant Anti-Catholicism," 43.

55. Tocqueville, *Democracy in America*, 1: 302–303, 335–336.

56. Welter, "A Century of Protestant Anti-Catholicism," 43; Abu-Lughod, *New York, Chicago, and Los Angeles*, 63, 71.

57. *History of Columbia County*, 220.

58. Interview with Mary J. Howell, Columbia County historian, June 2002; and *History of Columbia County*, 270–271.

59. *History of Columbia County*, 169.

60. Ibid., 46; McMullin, *Hudson Revisited*, 4.

61. *History of Columbia County*, 136; Abu-Lughod, *New York, Chicago, Los Angeles*, 83.

62. Based on June 2002 interview with Mary Howell, Columbia County historian. Compare McMullin, *Hudson Revisited*, 14.

63. Based on June 2002 interview with Mary Howell, Columbia County historian; McMullin, *Hudson Revisited*, 14.

64. *History of Columbia County*, 56.

65. McMullin, *Hudson Revisited*, 12. The school was named after the renowned English educator Joseph Lancaster and, following his monitorial system, used proficient older students to teach the younger ones. There were adult teachers for large classes. Lancaster immigrated to the United States in 1818 and died in New York City twenty years later.

66. *History of Columbia County*, 191–193, see n. 193; also based on June 2002 interview with Mary Howell, Columbia County historian.

67. Based on information from Mary Howell, Columbia County historian.

68. Ibid. For early nineteenth-century usages of "bushwhacker," see *The Oxford English Dictionary*, 2: 694.

69. See Hart, *A History of the St. Louis Globe-Democrat*, 97.

70. See Olmstead, *History of Religion*, 371–373; Menand, *The Metaphysical Club*, 14. The Missouri Compromise authorized Missouri's admission to the Union as a slave state on condition that slavery be banned from the remainder of the Louisiana Purchase north of the Mason-Dixon Line, the latitude demarcating Pennsylvania from Maryland. Most of the newly acquired territories were south of the line.

71. Gunn, *New World Metaphysics*, 217; Olmstead, *History of Religion*, 372.

72. Olmstead, *History of Religion*, 372–373.

73. Menand, *The Metaphysical Club*, 28.

74. Olmstead, *History of Religion*, 366.

75. Tocqueville, *Democracy in America*, 1: 329–330.

76. Ibid., 1: 339.

77. See Abu-Lughod, *New York, Chicago, Los Angeles*, 83; *History of Columbia County*, 46; McMullin, *Hudson Revisited*, 4.

78. *History of Columbia County*, 82–83.

79. "A. H. [sic] Webb, Former St. Louisan Dies." The obituary contains many other inaccuracies, including errors in Webb's name. The Columbia County register of Civil War veterans makes no mention of Webb (*History of Columbia County*, 417–436). The following databases were checked for Webb's Civil War records but turned up nothing: *NYS Civil War Soldier Database*; *National Archives*; *New York Public Library: Ask Librarians Online*; *New York Civil War Records*; *U. S. Archives and Records Administration*.

80. Gunn, *New World Metaphysics*, 258.

81. See Olmstead, *History of Religion*, 375; Marty, *Pilgrims*, 245; LeBeau, *Religion in America*, 174–181. Not all churches were divided. The Congregationalists and Unitarians remained united but had insubstantial followings in the South to begin with. Episcopalians and Roman Catholics had congregations on both sides of the Mason-Dixon Line—Maryland and Louisiana in particular had substantial Catholic populations—but neither church divided over the issue of slavery. Both were socially conservative and had strong cross-regional or international ecclesiastic ties and interests. Episcopalian and Catholic soldiers fought in both armies, but their churches did not actively promote the violence.

82. Olmstead, *History of Religion*, 385, 397–398; Noll, *The Old Religion*, 110–111.

83. Noll, *The Old Religion*, 109; Olmstead, *History of Religion*, 385; LeBeau, *Religion in America*, 181–185; Menand, *The Metaphysical Club*, 201.

84. Olmstead, *History of Religion*, 385.

85. Marty, *Pilgrims*, 223; LeBeau, *Religion in America*, 163, 166–169, 170–174.

86. Marty, *Pilgrims*, 223–224.

87. Gunn, *New World Metaphysics*, 258; Marty, *Pilgrims*, 224; LeBeau, *Religion in America*, 180.

88. Menand, *The Metaphysical Club*, 201, ix–x.

89. Rose, *Victorian America*, 126–128, 146; Fishburn, *The Fatherhood of God*, 25.

90. Rose, *Victorian America*, 149–153, 163, 166.

91. Osman, "The Story," (1944), 6.

92. Truesdell, *Descendants*, paragraph 1187. Truesdell states that Alexander Nelson Webb was "proprietor of the 'Hudson Daily Star' . . . for 35 years." Osman also states this; Osman, "The Story" (1944), 6.

93. See Truesdell, *Descendants*, paragraph 1187.

94. Lant, *The Hudson Directory* (1870), 101, 127; and June 2002 interview with Mary Howell, Columbia County historian. See *History of Columbia County*, 156; McMullin, *Hudson Revisited*, 2. The print shop was at 327 Warren. Neither the Webb home nor the print shop appears to stand today.

95. McDannell, *The Christian Home*, 8.

96. Schlereth, *Victorian America*, 71–73; Fishburn, *The Fatherhood of God*, 11–12. Domestics generally received payment "in kind": room and board. Occasionally, they were given used clothing and monetary wages. They were segregated in sparsely furnished areas of the house, such as the attic or kitchen.

97. *New York 1850 Census Index, Columbia County*, role 491. In the *New York 1860 Census Index, Columbia County*, role 738 he is listed as an independent printer. He is cited again in Lant, *The Hudson Directory* (1870), 101, 127.

98. *New York 1860 Census Index, Columbia County*, role 738. Fifteen years later, the assessed value of Hudson, New York was $5,102,280 (*History of Columbia County*, 207). Just to indicate the value of the amount almost twenty years earlier, in 1841, the state of New York had borrowed the sum of $5,000 to build and furnish three schoolhouses (McMullin, *Hudson Revisited*, 12).

99. There is some discrepancy about Webb's date of birth. Three different birthdays are given for Webb: 9, 18, and 20 November 1846. But 20 November has the strongest support. It occurs in Webb's official testimony to the State Department in 1887. The *Missouri Republican* gave the same date in its announcement of Webb's appointment to the consulship, as did Ali in his preface. Both the newspaper article and preface were written in close association with Webb. See "Dispatches," 4 October 1887; "Got a Consulship"; and Ali, "Preface," 3.

100. Nineteenth-century America witnessed the retreat of the large family. By midcentury, the average birthrate had declined to slightly less than six children in the family. See McDannell, *The Christian Home*, 8.

101. Truesdell gives Webb's younger brother's name as Hubert, but census records give the name as Herbert (See Truesdell, *Descendants*, paragraph 1187). The *Unionville Republican* makes several references to the younger brother but only by his initials. The 1850 New York Census of 1850 mentions three children: Edward (10), Alexander (4), and Henry (1) (*New York 1850 Census Index, Columbia County*, role 491). In the 1860 census, five children are mentioned, but only Edward and Alexander: Edward C. (19), Alex R. (14), Herbert N. (7), Carrie E. (5), and Anna M. (1) (*New York 1860 Census Index, Columbia County*, role 738). Willie Bunker was born in 1861 after the 1860 census but would not be likely to appear in it, because of time lags in gathering and printing information. Another indication that several siblings died early is Osman's account of Webb's family following him to Missouri, which mentioned only two sisters and three brothers ("The Story" [1944], 6).

102. He is mentioned as the editor of the two editions in Lant, *The Hudson Directory* (1870), 101, 127. The 1850 census cites his profession as "editor" (*New York 1850 Census Index, Columbia County*, role 491). In the 1860 census, his profession

is given as "printer" (*New York 1860 Census Index, Columbia County*, role 738). Osman states that Alexander Nelson Webb owned the *Hudson Daily Star* for thirty-five years. Truesdell repeats the same claim (Osman, "The Story" [1944], 6; and Truesdell, *Descendants*, paragraph 1187).

103. *History of Columbia County*, 119; Lant, *The Hudson Directory* (1870), 101, 127. Newspaper names are a problem because they changed so often. To avoid confusion, I restrict myself to later, standard names of papers, even though they may be anachronistic. A. N. Webb's initial daily was called the *Daily Morning Star*. A year later, it was christened the *Daily Evening Star*. It was only somewhat later that it became known as the *Hudson Daily Star*, a name it kept for decades. Hudson's principal newspaper today, the *Register-Star*, is a direct descendant of Alexander Nelson Webb's paper.

104. Bellah, "The Protestant Structure," 18.

105. McMullin, *Hudson Revisited*, 14.

106. From June 19, 2002 interview in Hudson, New York, with Mary Howell, Columbia County historian. The full title was *The Rural Repository: A Semi-Monthly Journal Embellished with Engravings*, W. B. Stoddard, ed. and proprietor (Hudson, New York), and Ms. Howell showed me several old copies of the journal.

107. Webb, *Claverack*, 69; Rammelkamp, *Pulitzer's Post-Dispatch*, vii.

108. Tocqueville, *Democracy in America*, 1: 198, 290.

109. Ibid., 2: 494.

110. See *History of Columbia County*, 49.

111. Ibid., 119.

112. Ali, "Preface," 3; Tunison, "Mohammed Alexander Russell Webb," 15; Grebsonal, "The Mohammedan Propagandist," 204.

113. Today, Glendale is only a post office and a handful of houses. The Glendale Home School would have been located outside of Stockbridge at 3 Williamsville Road, where "the Little Red House" is located today, dating from 1820–1840; house site, "Chesterwood," 4 Williamsville Road. *The History of Berkshire County*, 1: 589; and based on personal communication, July 2002, from Joshua D. Hall, intern at the Stockbridge Historical Collection in the Stockbridge, Massachusetts, public library. Existent records often merely mention "schools" without further detail. Mary Howell, Columbia County historian, suggested during a June 2002 interview that Great Barrington, Massachusetts, might hold records on the Glendale Home School.

114. *Claverack Academy and Hudson River Institute Register 1855–1865*; and Osman, "The Story" (1944), 6. See also *History of Columbia County*, 243; Webb, *Claverack*, 38; Saunders, "Remembering Claverack," 62, 69–70.

115. Ali, "Preface," 3; and Tunison, "Mohammed Alexander Russell Webb," 15. Grebsonal states in general that Webb received his education in the public schools of Hudson and at private schools in Massachusetts and New York ("The Mohammedan Propagandist," 204).

116. *History of Columbia County*, 243; Saunders, "Remembering Claverack," 62.

117. Rose, *Victorian America*, 94.

118. Tocqueville, *Democracy in America*, 1: 51.

119. Schlereth, *Victorian America*, 247–252.

120. Ibid., 64.

121. I have found no trace of Webb's early writings. Grebsonal, "The Mohammedan Propagandist," 204; Osman, "The Story" (1944), 6; and Tunison, "Mohammed Alexander Russell Webb, First American Muslim," 16.

122. Saunders, "Remembering Claverack," 61–65.

123. Ibid., 69.

124. *Claverack Academy and Hudson River Institute Register 1855–1865; Hudson River Institute, September 11, 1865–1885;* Saunders, "Remembering Claverack," 59–71.

125. Saunders, "Remembering Claverack," 66–69.

126. See *History of Columbia County,* 242; Webb, *Claverack,* 37–38; Saunders, "Remembering Claverack," 59.

127. Saunders, "Remembering Claverack," 66, 72–73.

128. See *Hudson River Institute, September 11, 1865–1885,* registry for January 1864; Saunders, "Remembering Claverack," 68.

129. Ibid., 66–69. There was a "lovers' lane" on the banks of Claverack Creek. Students were not allowed to meet there but often did anyway. A school poem commemorated its lovers' lane: "For, on the old red bridge, full oft, / A man and maid would whisper soft, / Sweet sentiments that have a part / In blending two into one heart."

130. Webb, *Claverack,* 38; Saunders, "Remembering Claverack," 61.

131. Saunders, "Remembering Claverack," 65.

132. Members of Claverack's Dutch Reformed church and other "prominent residents of the area" initiated the college in 1777 as the Washington Seminary, named after General George Washington. Its main buildings stood just south of the Old Dutch Reformed church. *History of Columbia County,* 243; Webb, *Claverack,* 38; Saunders, "Remembering Claverack," 64; and based on visit to Claverack, June 2002.

CHAPTER 3

1. Olmstead, *History of Religion,* 397–398; Noll, *The Old Religion in a New World,* 95–96, 110–111; Menand, *The Metaphysical Club,* 80.

2. Menand, *The Metaphysical Club,* x, 80; Olmstead, *History of Religion,* 397–398; Noll, *The Old Religion,* 110–111.

3. Olmstead, *History of Religion,* 397–398; Noll, *The Old Religion,* 110–111; Menand, *The Metaphysical Club,* 80.

4. Hermansen, "Roads to Mecca," 187 n. 157. She notes that Webb, unlike some others, did not write a single comprehensive testimony of his conversion.

5. DeCaro, *On the Side of My People,* 36.

6. Books like *The Adventures of Tom Sawyer* (1876) and *The Adventures of Huck Finn* (1885) set forth appealing images of American boyhood that appealed to Webb's contemporaries. Webb's image of himself suits Twain's style as opposed to the "model boy" of whom Twain spoke drolly in *Life on the Mississippi* as "the admiration of all mothers and the detestation of all their sons." Such a "model boy" was exemplified in *Little Lord Fountleroy* (1886) but hardly captured the Victorian imagination as the ideal image of boyhood.

7. Webb, "Islam," 24; Webb, *Islam in America,* 11.

8. Osman, "The Story" (1944), 6.

9. Webb, *Islam in America*, 11.

10. "Interview of a Correspondent," in Webb, *Lectures on Islam*, 31.

11. Webb, *Islam in America*, 11.

12. Rose, *Victorian America*, 22.

13. Based on visit to Hudson, June 2002.

14. Webb, "Islam," 24; Webb, *Islam in America*, 11–12.

15. Webb, *Islam in America*, 12.

16. Ibid.

17. Ibid.

18. The doctrine of the Immaculate Conception declares that the Virgin Mary was born free from Original Sin by virtue of her mother's "immaculate conception" of her. The dogma had roots in the Middle Ages and was upheld by notable churchmen like Duns Scotus and the Franciscan Order. St. Thomas Aquinas and the Dominicans, on the other hand, opposed it as heresy. See Turmel, "Immaculate Conception," in *The Encyclopedia of Religion and Ethics*, 7: 165–167.

19. Webb, "Islam," 24; Webb, *Islam in America*, 11.

20. Webb, *Islam in America*, 12.

21. Webb, "Philosophic Islam," 40.

22. "Interview of a Correspondent," in Webb, *Lectures on Islam*, 30.

23. Ibid.

24. Webb, "Islam," 24; Webb, *Islam in America*, 12.

25. "Interview of a Correspondent," in Webb, *Lectures on Islam*, 30.

26. Tunison, "Mohammed Alexander Russell Webb," 15.

27. Webb, *Islam in America*, 12; Webb, "Islam," 24; Ali, "Preface," 4.

28. Webb, *Islam in America*, 12; Webb, "Islam," 24; Ali, "Preface," 4.

29. "Interview of a Correspondent," in Webb, *Lectures on Islam*, 31–32.

30. Webb, "Two Remarkable Phenomena," 250.

31. Ibid., 249.

32. Ibid., 250.

33. Ibid., 248.

34. Webb, "Islam," 25.

35. "Interview of a Correspondent," in Webb, *Lectures on Islam*, 31–32.

36. See Bulwer-Lytton, *Zanoni*. The novel was set around the time of the French Revolution and ended with the death of Robespierre, who was proclaimed by his enemies to be "Mahomet." *Zanoni* was predicated on the belief in spiritual guides. Its central figures, Zanoni and Mejnour, were both masters of the unseen, belonging to the same "mystic order." Both were of obscure, probably Middle Eastern background, which was especially clear in the case of the "mystic Mejnour." His name sounds like a corruption of the fictional Majnūn of *Majnūn wa Laylā*, a central image in Sufism: "So sunburned and swarthy were [Mejnour's] hues, that he must apparently, have derived his origin among the races of the farthest East. His forehead was lofty, and his eyes so penetrating, yet so calm in their gaze." Zanoni stood for idealism and the contemplation of the Ideal, while Mejnour represented authentic science and the contemplation of the Real. The theme of the Supreme Being and humanity's need of him ran throughout the book and was exemplified in Zanoni and Mejnour. The notion that a profound level of esoteric truth underlies the exoteric

teaching of religion was also essential to the book, as well as the contention that "atheistic philosophy," the denial of the hereafter, and morality based wholly on a concern for humanity were socially destructive in addition to being philosophically and theologically misconstrued. Zanoni declared, "Oh, when shall men learn, at last, that if the Great Religion inculcates so rigidly the necessity of FAITH, it is not alone that FAITH leads to the world to be; but that without faith there is no excellence in this [world]."

37. Webb, "Islam," 24.

38. Webb, "Two Remarkable Phenomena," 250.

39. Webb, "The Better Way," 22; Webb, "Progressive Mohammedanism," 156–157; Webb, "A Letter"; *MWVI*, February 1896: 2.

40. Olmstead, *History of Religion*, 523.

41. Webb, "Progressive Mohammedanism," 156–157; Webb, *Islam in America*, 7.

42. Rose, *Victorian America*, 50–51.

43. Saunders, "Remembering Claverack College," 65.

44. Rose, *Victorian America*, 18; compare Tweed, *The American Encounter*, 51.

45. Olmstead, *History of Religion*, 345.

46. "*Republic* Reviews Alex Webb's Life." I was unable to identify Cordingly.

47. See, for example, *MW*, October 1893, inset page, where Webb advertises a number of books on Theosophy and the occult such as *The Life and Doctrines of Jacob Boehme*, *The History of the Rosicrucians*, *The History of Magic*, *The Missing Link of Modern Spiritualism*, *The Tarot of the Bohemians*, and so forth.

48. Pool, *Studies*, 400.

49. See *Muslim India and Islamic Review*, June 1913: 161–163; August 1913: inside back cover; *Islamic Review and Muslim India*, January 1914: 7–9, 16–20; July 1914: 271–272.

50. "Annie Besant on Islam," 504–510.

51. Tweed, *The American Encounter*, 51–53; Jackson, *Vedanta*, 97–100.

52. Tweed, *The American Encounter*, 34, 92.

53. Jackson, *Vedanta*, 50.

54. Tweed, *The American Encounter*, 1–2, 8; Jackson, *Vendanta*, 9.

55. Tweed, *The American Encounter*, 40.

56. *MW*, October 1893: 13.

57. Tweed, *The American Encounter*, 1–2, 8; Jackson, *Vedanta*, 9.

58. Jackson, *Vedanta*, v.

59. Jackson, *Vedanta*, 100, xii; see also Tweed, *The American Encounter*, 95; Seager, *The World's Parliament*, 13. See Webb's indebtedness to Sir Sayyed Ahmad Khan, founder of the Aligarh Movement, in Webb, "Sectarian Exclusiveness," 177.

60. "Republic Reviews Alex Webb's Life."

61. Webb, "Islam," 24; Grebsonal, "The Mohammedan Propagandist," 204; Osman, "The Story" (1944), 8; Tunison, "Mohammed Alexander Russell Webb," 15–16. Tunison stated that Webb "inquired after Eastern religions and philosophies" in 1881, although later in the article, he specified 1883 as the time when Webb's Oriental interests began.

62. Webb, "Islam," 24.

63. *MWVI*, April 1895: 2; see also *MWVI*, November 1895: 2.

64. Webb, "Islam," 24; Webb, *Islam in America*, 13.

65. Webb, *Islam in America*, 12. Compare Ali, "Preface," 4; Osman, "The Story" (1944), 7.

66. Webb Diary, 10 December 1892; Cranston, HPB, 426.

67. Webb, "Two Remarkable Phenomena," 249.

68. Osman, "The Story" (1944), 7.

69. Webb, "Letter to Mirza Ghulam Ahmad."

70. Mills, *One Hundred Years of Theosophy*, xi–xii.

71. Tweed, *The American Encounter*, 51–53.

72. Olmstead, *History of Religion*, 523.

73. Jackson, *Vedanta*, 9.

74. See *Encyclopedia of American Religious History*, 2: 781.

75. "Muhammad Webb's Mission."

76. Khan, "Mohammed Alexander Russell Webb," 6–7. Khan cites *The Path* (July 1893), the Theosophical Society's official journal, regarding a conversation that Judge had with Webb: "The conversion to the religion of the Prophet Mohammed of Alexander Russell Webb, F.T.S., and his establishing in New York a paper devoted to Islamism, together with his lectures on the subject, have caused a great deal of attention to be given to Mohammedanism. Bro. Webb is still a member of the Society, with an interest in its progress, and this is another illustration of the broadness of our platform."

77. Khan, "Mohammed Alexander Russell Webb," 7.

78. "Republic Reviews Alex Webb's Life."

79. See Hadji Erinn, "Regarding Islamism," *The Path*, July 1892. Among Judge's other pseudonyms were "An American Mystic" and "Eusebio Urban." See Mills, *One Hundred Years of Theosophy*, 8.

80. Grebsonal, "The Mohammedan Propagandist," 204–205.

81. "*Republic* Reviews Alex Webb's Life."

82. The belief in a *Mujaddid* (Renewer), appearing at the onset of each Islamic century—consequentially a "Centennial Renewer"—is a long-standing Islamic belief. It was not controversial in itself, although a particular person's claim to it might be.

83. Rippin, *Muslims*, 2: 33.

84. Lavan, *The Ahmadiyah*, 11–12, 26.

85. Ahmad, *Mujaddid-e Azam*, 157.

86. See Nyang, *Islam*, 105. I believe the reference is to John A. Dowie, although he is referred to in the book as Joseph Dowie.

87. Webb, "Letter to Mirza Ghulam Ahmad."

88. Mirza Ahmad, *Shahna-e Haqq*, 372–373, 439–444.

89. Easton Avenue was a major thoroughfare at the time and should not be confused with the smaller street that goes by that name today. It was renamed Dr. Martin Luther King Drive in accordance with Ordinance 56174. The 1886 St. Louis Directory gives 3019 Easton Avenue as Webb's address, while the 3021 Easton address does not appear in the directory until the following year. There is no reason to doubt that Webb was living at 3021 Easton at the time he wrote the letter, because there was a considerable time lag between the collection and publication of directory information

(*Gould's St. Louis Directory* [1887], 1240). From roughly 1884 or 1885, he had been living next door to that address at 3019 Easton Avenue (ibid. [1885], 1210; [1886], 1231).

90. Ali, "Preface," 4; Ahmadiyya Anjuman, *Alexander Russell Webb*.

91. See, for example, Ahmad, *Mujaddid-e Azam*, 159–161.

92. Smith, *Islam*, 189.

93. Dannin, *Black Pilgrimage*, 44.

94. Webb is reported to have said: "There were twelve years of the life of Christ of which there was no record but [Webb] knew where they had been spent, though the Catholic Church did not." A young reporter from Yonkers "jumped up and begged Mr. Webb to tell him about it." The *New York Herald* reported that Webb at first said he was unwilling to speak further on the matter but went on to say that "Moslems claim that Christ was in India studying Buddhism during those years." See "Asked to Turn Moslems."

95. Muhammad Ali, a Lahori Ahmadiyya leader, was one of the most important figures in the Woking Mosque outside London and a major contributor to the *Islamic Review* from the time of its inception in 1913 until Muhammad Ali's death. The *Islamic Review* made extensive references to Western converts to Islam, featuring Lord Headley in particular and dozens of other British, American, and Continental converts. It was typical of the journal to write obituaries in honor of prominent Muslims, especially Western converts, yet there was no obituary of Webb in 1916 or subsequent years. Given Muhammad Ali's prominence at the *Islamic Review*, lack of a Webb obituary indicates that whatever relationship existed between Muhammad Ali and Webb, it must not have been especially close. Despite Osman's report of Muhammad Ali's indebtedness to Webb for helping him revise his translation of the Qur'an, when the translation was first advertised in the *Islamic Review* there was mention of Ali's six years of long labor but no reference to Webb's assistance. See "An English Translation of the Holy Quran," *Islamic Review and Muslim India*, October 1915: 496.

96. *Moslem Sunrise*, October 1921: 25.

97. Weller, "The Contribution of the Ahmadiyya."

98. Mirza Ahmad, *Shahna-e Haqq*, 342–343.

99. Webb, "Letter to Mirza Ghulam Ahmad."

100. Ibid.

101. Ibid.

102. Ibid.

103. Ibid. Curiously, Webb also stated in the letter that he had taken vows of celibacy for life, although married with three children. Perhaps Webb's celibacy was a remnant of his commitment to Buddhist teaching, but I have no idea.

104. Ibid.

105. Mirza Ahmad, "Letter to Alex. R. Webb, 4 April 1887."

106. His correspondence with Kur would express the same interest in undertaking an Islamic mission in America.

107. Webb, "Letter to Mirza Ghulam Ahmad."

108. Ibid.

109. Ibid.

110. "Interview of a Correspondent," in Webb, *Lectures on Islam*, 31.

111. "Muhammad Webb's Mission."

112. Tunison, "Mohammed Alexander Russell Webb," 16.

113. Ali, "Preface," 4; Osman, "The Story" (1944), 7.

114. Ali, "Preface," 5. Ella had three children by Webb and a daughter, Elizabeth, by an earlier marriage. If the statement is precise, it may indicate that Beth did not embrace Webb's new faith.

115. Osman, "The Story" (1944), 7.

116. Grebsonal, "The Mohammedan Propagandist," 204.

117. Tunison, "Mohammed Alexander Russell Webb," 16.

118. See Poston, *Islamic Da'wah*, 147–156; compare Wohlrab-Sahr, *Konversion zum Islam*, 84, 365; Allievi, *I nuovi musulmani*, 48.

119. Webb, "Islam," 25.

120. Ibid., 32.

121. Ibid., 27.

122. See Poston, *Islamic Da'wah*, 176–179.

123. Webb, "The Lecture Delivered in Calcutta," 22–24.

124. Tweed, *The American Encounter*, 92.

125. See Menand, *The Metaphysical Club*, 80–81; Rose, *Victorian America*, 8; Tweed, *The American Encounter*, 93.

126. Tweed, *The American Encounter*, 92.

127. Menand, *The Metaphysical Club*, 201.

128. Rose, *Victorian America*, xi, 4, 13, 20, 27.

129. Fishburn, *The Fatherhood of God*, 18.

130. Tweed, *The American Encounter*, 77; Jackson, *Vedanta*, 97–100.

131. Rose, *Victorian America*, 4.

132. Tweed, *The American Encounter*, 47.

133. Ibid., 43.

134. Ibid., 43–46.

135. Ibid., 94.

136. Jackson, *Vedanta*, 4.

137. Tweed, *The American Encounter*, 53.

138. Jackson, *Vedanta*, 97–99.

139. Ibid.

140. Tweed, *The American Encounter*, 23.

141. See Arnold, *The Preaching of Islam* (1896), 465 n. 1; Garcin de Tassy, *La langue et littérature hindoustanies*, 92.

142. *MWVI*, January 1896: 2.

143. *MWVI*, October 1895: 1; Murad, "The Great Dive," 23–31; Stanton-Hope, *Arabian Adventurer*, 114–115.

144. Cunliffe, "A Moslem Prayer," *MW*, November 1893: 11. The book is advertised in the same issue, page ii.

145. *MWVI*, April 1895: 2.

146. See, for example, John Yehya-en-Nasr Parkinson, a British convert and active contributor to the *Islamic Review* until his death in 1919 (Parkinson, "The Liverpool Movement," *Islamic Review and Muslim India*, May 1914: 166: "In Memoriam," *Islamic Review and Muslim India*, April 1919: 151). Dr. Ameen Neville Whywant was

another prominent convert and frequent contributor to the *Islamic Review* on mysticism and psychology (see the *Islamic Review and Muslim India*, October 1915: inset).

147. Matar, *Islam in Britain*, 72 n. 62.

148. See ibid.; Pool, *Studies*, xiii–xiv; Orchard, *Liverpool's Legion*, 563; Iyilik, "The Unveiling," 1. Most sources state that Quilliam had been on a visit to Morocco. Orchard contended that he had been in Algeria "for his health's sake."

149. Pool, *Studies*, 395.

150. Matar, *Islam in Britain*, 72 n. 62; Pool, *Studies*, xiii–xiv; Iyilik, "The Unveiling," 1.

151. Parkinson, "The Liverpool Movement," 166–167.

152. Arnold, *The Preaching of Islam* (1896), 369–370; Iyilik, "The Unveiling," 1.

153. Pool, *Studies*, 404.

154. Arnold, *The Preaching of Islam* (1896), 369–370; Iyilik, "The unveiling," 1.

155. "William Henry Quilliam," 1.

156. Parkinson, "The Liverpool Movement," 168.

157. Ibid.

158. "William Henry Quilliam," 1.

159. *MWVI*, October 1895: 3.

160. Ibid., May 1895: 4.

161. *MW*, November 1893: 9.

162. The statement in parenthesis is part of the original quotation and constitutes an early objection to the use of "Mohammedanism" for Islam. "Mohammedanism" did not offend most early converts or Muslims of the period, but, as the twentieth century proceeded, the term and its derivative "Mohammedan" fell into almost universal disrepute.

163. *MW*, October 1893: 17; ibid., November 1893: inset page.

164. See *MWVI*, October 1895: 3; ibid., May 1895: 3.

165. Browne, "The Evidences of Islam," *MW*, November 1893: 1–3.

166. See *MWVI*, January 1895: 4; ibid., February 1895: 2.

167. *MW*, October 1893: 8.

168. Browne, "The Evidences of Islam," *MW*, November 1893: 1–3.

169. *MW*, October 1893: 17; ibid., November 1893: inset page.

170. Ibid.

171. *MWVI*, February 1895: 2.

172. Ibid., May 1895: 3.

173. Ibid., August 1895: 3.

174. Ibid., September 1895: 3.

175. Regarding the dates of Headley's conversion, see the *Islamic Review*, August 1923: 314; the *Islamic Review and Muslim India*, January 1914: inset, which gave his name as Saif-ur-Rahman Shaikh Rahmatullah Farooq. See Headley, "What Is Dogma?" *Islamic Review and Muslim India*, November 1914: 490.

176. *Islamic Review*, August 1923: 314.

177. *Islamic Review and Muslim India*, January 1914: inset and 1, 5.

178. Headley, "What Is Dogma?" *Islamic Review and Muslim India*, November 1914: 490.

179. Weitbrecht, "A Moslem Mission," *MW*, April 1914: 195–196, 201.

180. "Lord Headley on Islam in the West," *Islamic Review*, February 1923: 47–51.

181. *Islamic Review*, June–July 1923: 269.

182. Ibid., April–May 1925: 176.

183. Ibid., 174–176.

184. Hermansen, "Roads to Mecca," 59–60; Wolfe, *One Thousand Roads*, 406–408.

185. Hermansen, "Roads to Mecca," 80; Wolfe, *One Thousand Roads*, 406–408.

186. See Murad, "Marmaduke Pickthall," 23–31. He embraced Islam in 1914 and worked in close association with the Woking Mosque and contributed articles to the *Islamic Review*. He was a prolific writer of fiction and nonfiction, especially about the Muslim world, and his work, *The Meaning of the Glorious Quran*, which first appeared in 1930, has influenced generations of English-speaking Muslims and non-Muslims. See Murad, "Marmaduke Pickthall," and Clark, *Marmaduke Pickthall*; see also Pickthall, "The Prophet's Gratitude." The *Islamic Review* proudly announced the conversion in 1922 of Pickthall's wife, Muriel, who, it took care to note, "[had] now of her own free volition embraced the faith (see the *Islamic Review*, January 1922: 43).

187. Guénon was among the most influential French converts to Islam in modern times. He embraced the faith "unobstrusively" in 1912, a year before Lord Headley. Guénon's writings positioned the exoteric aspects of world religions against the "unique and primordial tradition of which estoericism alone is the depository." He did not share Webb's infatuation with Theosophy, however, and he thought Madame Blavatsky to be a fraud and Theosophy a "counterinitiatory snare." For Guénon, the spiritual search—however valid it might be within various traditions—required "adherence to [a particular] tradition and orthodoxy." See Johnson, *Initiates of Theosophical Masters*, 5; Rocher and Cherqaoui, *D'une foi l'autre*, 12 n. 2. Weiss became a Muslim in 1926 and became the most widely recognized Western Muslim convert thinker in the modern world. See Asad, *The Road to Mecca*.

CHAPTER 4

1. Interview in Hudson with Mary Howell, Columbia County historian, June 2002.

2. May, *Great Expectations*, 22.

3. See Saunders, "Remembering Claverack College," 69; Osman, "The Story" (1944), 6.

4. "Got a Consulship"; "*Republic* Reviews Alex Webb's Life." In 1893, both Grebsonal and the *New York Times* asserted that Webb was also associated with Chicago newspapers, although neither indicated the newspapers by name or gave the date when the associations occurred. There is no other evidence of Webb's involvement in journalism during his Chicago years or later during his career in Missouri journalism. See Grebsonal, "The Mohammedan Propagandist," 204; "Muhammad Webb's Mission,"

5. Rose, *Victorian America*, 94.

6. Abu-Lughod, *New York, Chicago, Los Angeles*, 106.

7. "Got a Consulship." The partnership included jewelers William A. and Charles K. Giles and James L. Rowe (*Edward's Annual Director* [1870], 333).

8. Lucian W. Conger was born in New York on July 23, 1823, and died in Unionville on October 9, 1902. He appears in the 1860 Illinois census as a resident and merchant of Oneida, Illinois. His wife, Elizabeth, born in Rhode Island, and his eight-year-old daughter, Laura, and other children, all born in Illinois, also appear. Conger's real estate was worth $2,500, and his personal estate was valued at $3,000. See Phillips, *Putnam County Cemeteries*, 174, and *Illinois Census 1860*, 493. Conger appears with his wife in the 1880 Unionville census as a farmer. *Missouri Census 1880*, image 0249.

9. At the time, Chicago addresses did not use the directional designations East and West or North and South. "*Republic* Reviews Alex Webb's Life." See also "Obituary: Alexander R. Webb"; and Osman, "The Story" (1944), 6. The partnership is given mistakenly as "Cooper & Webb" in "Got a Consulship." *Merchant's Chicago Census Report* (1871), 1156, cites him as "A. Webb, a jeweler born in New York." Webb does not appear in the 1869 Chicago Directory, because of the lag time required to become registered and published in such directories (*Edward's Annual Directory* [1869]). Webb first appears in the 1870 edition as an associate of "Congon & Webb," which is a misspelling for Conger & Webb; no Congons appear in the 1870 directory. The correct spelling is given under L. W. Conger's entry, which describes Conger and Webb as "watchmakers and jewelers" (177).

10. The 1870 census listed L. W. Conger as owning real estate worth $12,500 and a personal estate of $15,000. Webb lived at the Conger residence with his bride but possessed no property or any personal estate worthy of note.

11. See Osman, "The Story" (1944), 6; and "Got a Consulship."

12. "*Republic* Reviews Alex Webb's Life."

13. "Married," *Chicago Tribune*, 6 May 1870; *1870 Cook County Census*; *Illinois 1870 Census*, 22; and Fink, *Index*, "Webb/Conger." Laura was born in Illinois, presumably in the town of Oneida in Knox County, on August 23, 1852. The couple were married at Lucian Conger's residence by Rev. Dr. William H. Ryder. The announcement asked that no cards be sent. Fink mistakenly gives the date of May 6 for the marriage, but his information was taken from the *Chicago Tribune*.

14. The following databases contained no record of Laura C. Conger's death: *Chicago Tribune Historical Archives*; *Obituary Collection*; *Family Search Database*; *Heritage Quest*; *Historical New York Times*; *America's Obituaries and Death Notices*. Though the fire destroyed Chicago's vital statistics for years prior to 1871, attempts were made to restore them as much as possible from references in the city's newspapers and other documents. None of the recovered records provides evidence of Laura Conger's death from sickness or childbirth or any other cause, nor has any evidence appeared since then of her death or divorce. She is absent from her family's records in Unionville, Missouri.

15. Forest Avenue in Webb's time is not to be confused with Forest Avenue in Chicago today. At the time of the Chicago Fire, Forest Avenue ran north-south and was a few blocks east of Indiana Avenue. The Webb residence would have been south of Thirty-First Street. The fire did not burn farther south than Twelfth Avenue. See *Gaylord and McDonald Maps*, "Fire Limits in Chicago in the 1870s" and "Progress of the Chicago Fire of 1871."

16. See *Gaylord and McDonald Maps*, "Fire Limits in Chicago in the 1870s" and "Progress of the Chicago Fire of 1871."

17. *The Fire Edition*, 57, 158. He does not appear in *The New Chicago Directory* (1872).

18. The 1873 Chicago directory mentions an "Alexander R. Webb & Co." as the proprietor of a billiard hall at 758 Michigan Avenue, and there is no reason to doubt that the reference is to Webb himself, although no other information corroborates his connection with billiard halls. Webb's ownership of such a business would have been consistent with his versatility in exploring different lines of work. More tellingly, no "Alexander R. Webb" appears in later Chicago directories, increasing the likelihood that the reference was to him, since he was definitely in Unionville, Missouri, by the beginning of 1874. Had the reference been to another person by the same name, it would be reasonable to expect it to have reappeared in subsequent years. See *Edward's New Chicago Directory* (1873), 975, 1177–1178; *1874–1875, The Lakeside Annual Directory*, 2: 1131; and *1875–1876, The Lakeside Annual Directory*, 1022.

19. "Got a Consulship"; "Muhammad Webb's Mission"; "Obituary: Alexander R. Webb"; and Osman, "The Story" (1944), 6.

20. Rose, *Victorian America*, 94.

21. Webb, "Salutatory." Several sources date Webb's entrance into Missouri newspaper work in 1873 (Grebsonal, "The Mohammedan Propagandist," 204); "Obituary: Alexander R. Webb"; "Alexander H. Webb"; Tunison, "Mohammed Alexander Russell Webb," 15; "Got a Consulship"). Unionville's own obituary set Webb's period in the town from 1875 till 1876 ("*Republic* Reviews Alex Webb's Life"). Note that some sources mistakenly cite the *Unionville Republican* as the *Missouri Republican* (Grebsonal, "The Mohammedan Propagandist," 204; Osman, "The Story" (1944), 6). Dannin construes that Webb came to Missouri before 1872 to work in small-town newspapers owned by his father and gives 1872 as the date of Webb's conversion to Islam. See Dannin, *Black Pilgrimage*, 43.

22. *Unionville Republican*, 25 December 1873: 2.

23. Ibid., 177. See Fishburn, *The Fatherhood of God*, 17, 23.

24. Mrs. Edward C. Webb was elected the president of the local temperance society in 1878, indicating that Edward was living in Unionville prior to that time (*History of Adair [County]*, 515).

25. Alexander Nelson Webb died on March 1, 1877, shortly after Alexander Russell Webb moved to St. Louis. He probably had a significant estate at the time of his death. The New York census of 1870 put his personal estate at $10,000, although the Webb family real estate, valued at $6,000, was listed under his wife's name (see *New York Census 1870*). His heirs were his wife; his sons, Edward, Alexander R., Herbert, and William; and his daughters, Caroline and Annie. The written will, #945, filed March 10, 1877, is on record. Phillips, *Putnam County Estate Records*, 123. See also Osman, "The Story" (1944), 6; Truesdell, *Descendants and Ancestors*, paragraph 1187.

26. *Unionville Republican*, 8 January 1874: 1.

27. *History of Adair [County]*, 563.

28. Taken from historical landmark at Unionville courthouse, June 2002.

29. Webb, "Salutatory."

30. Rammelkamp, *Pulitzer's Post-Dispatch*, 45.

31. Zelinsky, *The Cultural Geography of the United States*, 117.

32. Ibid., 33, 10.

33. The image of "Jim Crow" is taken from a black folk song, "Jump, Jim Crow." Jim Crow was a handsome and assertive Southern black. Gunn, *New World Metaphysics*, 223.

34. Balkin, "History Lesson," 45–46.

35. Ibid.

36. "Got a Consulship."

37. Only in the election of 1860 on the eve of the Civil War did Columbia County vote Republican, allowing President Abraham Lincoln to take the county by a slim margin. When Lincoln ran again in 1864, the county voted against him. In 1868, after the war, Columbia County voted against President Ulysses S. Grant and, one may infer, "the Grantist" policies that underlay the Reconstruction and Radical Republicanism. *History of Columbia County*, 56.

38. *History of Adair [County]*, 564.

39. Webb, "Salutatory."

40. *Unionville Republican*, 25 December 1873: 2.

41. Osman, "The Story" (1944), 6.

42. Tunison, "Mohammed Alexander Russell Webb," 15.

43. "*Republic* Reviews Alex Webb's Life."

44. L. W. Conger and H. D. Marshall founded the Putnam County Bank in 1874. Since Webb arrived on the first day of that year, it is reasonable to assume that the bank was founded somewhat later that year. In 1879, Marshall purchased the bank, and it changed its name to Marshall's National Bank (*History of Adair [County]*, 516.)

45. *History of Adair [County]*, 564; cf. *Unionville Republican*, 25 December 1873: 2; ibid., 8 December 1873: 1.

46. Clarence La Fayette Conger was born June 16, 1855, in Illinois and died in Unionville on October 24, 1925. See Lemen, *Putnam County Cemeteries*, 174; *Illinois 1870 Census*, 22.

47. *Unionville Republican*, 9 March 1876: 2; *History of Adair [County]*, 564. See *Merchant's Chicago Census* (1871), 227.

48. "Announcement," *Unionville Republican*, 23 March 1876: 2.

49. Ibid., 8 January 1874: 1.

50. Ibid., 9 March 1876: 1.

51. Ibid., 23 March 1876: 2.

52. Webb Brothers, "Campaign Republican," ibid., 20 July 1876: 2.

53. *History of Adair [County]*, 564.

54. *History of Columbia County*, 74.

55. For this and preceding references, see "Business Notice," *Unionville Republican*, 3 May 1877: 2.

56. *History of Adair [County]*, 564.

57. Phillips gives his date of death as January 1, 1884, and reports the will as being filed two years later on March 15, 1886. The information in the local history appears more accurate. See Phillips, *Putnam County Estate Records*, 123; and *History of Adair [County]*, 564.

58. Ibid.

59. Logan, *Old Saint Jo*, pp. 129, 131–132, 136–137, 140, 158.

60. Ibid.

61. Ibid.

62. Olmstead, *History of Religion in the United States*, 401.

63. Federal troops occupied St. Joseph in August 1861 and held it throughout the war. Local sentiment remained unabashedly secessionist, creating a spirit of despondency among resident unionists. In September 1861, Confederates poured into the city and disarmed every unionist who could not escape to Kansas. Federal troops regained control before mid-September. See *St. Joseph Gazette*, 13 June 1877: 2; and Logan, *Old Saint Jo*, 95–97, 100–104, 116, 130.

64. See Taft, *Missouri Newspapers*, 141. In Webb's time, newspaper writing was generally anonymous because of the grave dangers that editors and writers ran. Consequently, it is very difficult—with some notable exceptions in Unionville—to determine exactly what Webb wrote during his newspaper career. Regarding Jesse James, see *The Heritage of Buchanan County*, 237. James was a year younger than Webb and hailed from Clay County, just southeast of St. Joseph. The James Gang was at its most violent around the time of Webb's residence in St. Joseph. Only a year before, in 1875, Pinkerton detectives had bombed James's stepfather's house. They had intended to kill Jesse but accidentally killed his nine-year-old half-brother and blew off his mother's arm, pushing the James brothers to further extremes. In 1881, James attempted to settle down in St. Joseph under the alias of Thomas Howard, but a former associate shot and killed him there in his home in 1882 for the reward money. See Logan, *Old Saint Jo*, 150; Logan, *History of Buchanan County*, 205; White, "The Press," 371.

65. "Got a Consulship"; Grebsonal, "The Mohammedan Propagandist," 204; "Alexander R. Webb Dies: Former U.S. Consul"; Osman, "The Story" (1944), 6. The *St. Joseph Gazette* was established in 1845 from what remained or could be recovered from the vestiges of the Mormon press of Independence, Missouri, which an angry mob had destroyed during the state's anti-Mormon disruptions. *History of Buchanan County*, 459; Rutt, *History of Buchanan County*, 193; Logan, *Old Saint Jo*, 28.

66. Logan, *Old Saint Jo*, 95, 126. Because of its Confederate sympathies, the *St. Joseph Gazette* was closed in 1861. Its publisher left St. Joseph and joined the Confederate Army. Its other proprietors followed suit and "laid away the pen and went to the front to do battle for the South with the sword." When the paper opened again in June 1868, it still belonged to its ex-Confederate proprietors. Ownership changed in 1873, but the *St. Joseph Gazette* remained pro-Democratic and anti-Reconstructionist during the time Webb worked for it and for a considerable time afterward. Even after Webb left the paper, the *St. Joseph Gazette* focused on news from Virginia, South Carolina, Louisiana, and other parts of the South. It mocked "Louisiana Radicals," scoffed at New York preachers, and thankfully observed that the Army and Navy had been unable to block the inauguration of an anti-Reconstructionist governor in Louisiana. See the *St. Joseph Gazette*, 2 January 1877: 2; Logan, *Old Saint Jo*, 95; and Rutt, *History of Buchanan County*, 193; *History of Buchanan County* (1881 edition), 460.

67. *Ballenger and Hoyes* (1876), 322; (1877), 326; (1878), 320.

68. *Newspapers in Missouri*, 2: 685.

69. "*Republic* Reviews Alex Webb's Life."

70. "Muhammad Webb's Mission"; and Ali, "Preface," 3. An obituary gives the paper's name as the *St. Joseph Day Gazette*. See "Obituary: Alexander R. Webb"; Tunison, "Mohammed Alexander Russell Webb," 15.

71. "Alexander H. Webb."

72. Grebsonal, "The Mohammedan Propagandist," 204; Ali, "Preface," 3; Osman, "The Story" (1944), 6.

73. Osman, "The Story" (1944), 6. Field appears only in the St. Joseph directory of 1876. See *Ballenger and Hoyes* (1876), 126; (1877), 127; (1878), 126, 298.

74. Field wrote "Lovers' Lane Saint Jo" in London in 1890 to console his wife's loneliness, whom he had courted in the city (Logan, *Old Saint Jo*, 256):

> "LOVERS' LANE SAINT JO"
> Saint Jo, Buchanan County,
> Is leagues and leagues away;
> And I sit in the gloom of this rented room,
> And pine to be there today.
> Yes, with London fog around me
> And the bustling to and fro,
> I am fretting to be across the sea
> In Lovers' Lane, Saint Jo.
> Let us sit awhile, beloved,
> And dream of the good old days,
> Of the kindly shade which the maples made
> Round the staunch by squeaky chaise;
> With your head upon my shoulder,
> And my arm about you so,
> Though exiles, we shall seem to be
> In Lovers' Lane, Saint Jo.

75. Field also wrote children's poems, although he did not like being called a children's poet. "Wynken, Blynken, and Nod" was, perhaps, his most famous (Logan, *Old Saint Jo*, 255):

> "LITTLE BOY BLUE"
> The little toy dog is covered with dust,
> But sturdy and staunch he stands,
> And the little toy soldier is red with rust,
> And his musket moulds in his hands.
> Ay, faithful to Little Boy Blue they stand,
> Each in the same old place,
> Awaiting the touch of a little hand,
> And the smile of a little face,
> And they wonder, as waiting these long years through,
> In the dust of that little chair,
> What has become of our Little Boy Blue
> Since he kissed them and put them there.

76. Ibid., 254–255.

77. A few months after Field joined the *Times-Journal*, the *St. Joseph Gazette* wrote: "We are glad to see that honors crown the brow of Eugene Field of the St. Louis 'Journal.' He was unanimously elected Assistant Chief Clerk of the House by the Republican Caucus. We knew after his last New Year's address, written for the *Gazette*, that some good fortune would happen to him" (6 January 1877: 1). Field joined the *Kansas City Times* in 1880 and the *Denver Tribune* as editor in 1881. In 1883, Fields joined the *Chicago Morning News*, where he wrote his famous daily column, "Sharps and Flats." Field's career peaked in 1889. Then his health suddenly began to deteriorate, making his last six years a constant struggle with illness. He died in his sleep of heart failure on November 6, 1895. See Logan, *Old Saint Jo*, 251, 255–257.

78. Officially, the case *Scott v. Sandford* began in Missouri in 1846. Dred Scott had traveled with his Missouri master to the free states of Illinois and Wisconsin, which prompted Scott to claim freedom on the ground that his master had invalidated his slave status by taking him to states where slavery was not legitimate. The Supreme Court's decision against him in 1857 was looked upon as a major victory for the South, but it polarized the country and became a harbinger of war. See Logan, *Old Saint Jo*, 249–250.

79. See Taft, *Missouri Newspapers*, 132; White, "The Press," 371–372; Steven, *One Hundred Years of the St. Louis Republic*, 16; Armstrong, "Beginnings of the Modern Newspaper," 3–4.

80. Rammelkamp, *Pulitzer's Post-Dispatch*, 20, 25, 237.

81. Ibid. St. Louis population statistics for 1870 were fraudulently inflated and created the "great illusion" of the city's meteoric growth. The 1880 federal census dealt the city a humiliating blow by showing that it was not as large as projected and had been greatly outdistanced by Chicago.

82. Magnan, *Streets of St. Louis*, 57; and Rammelkamp, *Pulitzer's Post-Dispatch*, 268.

83. Easton Avenue was one of St. Louis's main thoroughfares at the time. It was renamed Dr. Martin Luther King Drive in accordance with Ordinance 56174. The city assessor assured me that street numbers had not changed, and upon visiting the area where the house had been, I found a large grassy lot with trees. Magnan, *Streets of St. Louis*, 57. Webb is first listed in the St. Louis directory in 1878 and 1879 as living at 1719 Cass Ave. (*Gould's St. Louis Directory* [1878], 959; and [1879], 1008). The 1880 directory lists him for the first time as living at 1218 Madison with his wife, Ella, although they were married in 1877 (1073). In the 1877 directory—probably prior to her marriage to Webb, since the directory reflected data collected of the previous year—Ella G. Hotchkiss is listed as living at 1218 Madison. She moved to Page Avenue the following year, and then to 1717½ Cass Avenue, where she appears in the 1879 directory. Webb is listed that year just next door at 1719 Cass. Presumably, the Webbs moved back to 1218 Madison in 1879 (*United States City Directories, 1861–1881*, St. Louis, reel 10, 437; *Gould's St. Louis Directory* [1877], 464; [1878], 452; [1879], 488, 1008). They are listed as living at the same address from 1880 until 1885. (See *Gould's St. Louis Directory* [1880], 1073; [1881], 1161; [1882], 1192–1193; [1883], 1141; [1885], 1151). The 1885–1886 and 1886–1887 St. Louis directories show the Webbs as having moved to 3019 Easton Ave. ([1885], 1210; [1886], 1231). Webb's final residence in St. Louis was next door at 3021 Easton, where he is listed in the 1887–1888

directory (1240). According to an 1875 topographical survey of St. Louis taken from observations in a hot-air balloon, Webb's address would have been at the intersection of Easton and Garrison, which appears to have been a prosperous neighborhood at the time. (See Dry, *Pictorial St. Louis*, plate 72; Magnan and Magnan, *The Streets of St. Louis*, 200; Magnan, *Streets of St. Louis*, 35, 61; and information from Dusty Reese and Tom Gruenenfelder of the St. Louis assessor's archives, June 2002.)

84. Mark Twain's "Old Times on the Mississippi" first appeared as an article in 1875 and in book form, as *Life on the Mississippi*, in 1883. Rammelkamp, *Pulitzer's Post-Dispatch*, 28.

85. Rammelkamp, *Pulitzer's Post-Dispatch*, 20.

86. Magnan, *Streets of St. Louis*, 57; and Rammelkamp, *Pulitzer's Post-Dispatch*, 268. St. Louis's initial experiment with electric lighting was during the period from 1878 to 1881.

87. Rammelkamp, *Pulitzer's Post-Dispatch*, 20, 23–25.

88. Hart, *A History of the St. Louis Globe-Democrat*, 113.

89. From a personal visit, June 2002. The monument is in Forest Park and was built in 1914.

90. Steven, *One Hundred Years of the St. Louis Republic*, 15–16; Rammelkamp, *Pulitzer's Post-Dispatch*, 33.

91. See "Got a Consulship." A laborer named Alexander Webb appears in the 1876 and 1877 directories but is another person. *United States City Directories, 1861–1881, St. Louis, Missouri*, reel 9, 916; *Gould's St. Louis Directory* (1877). Webb appears in the 1878 Gould's directory, 959.

92. Phillips, *Putnam County Estate Records*, 123.

93. The English servant, Mary Higgs, was 31. The black servant, Rosette Robinson, was 24. See *1880 Missouri Census of the City of St. Louis*, role 729, house # 1218.

94. *Index of Male Marriage Records 1871–1881* (St. Louis), "St–Z," 229 and 18: 77. Ella's maiden name is not given. The marriage license gives Ella the title "Mrs.," indicating that she had been previously married.

95. *Index of Male Marriage Records 1871–1881* (St. Louis), "St–Z," 229 and 18:77. Webb and his wife were married by Rector Abiel Leonard at the Grace Church of St. Louis, presumably the Grace Episcopal Church, since it was the only St. Louis church by that name in 1877. See Schild, *Houses of God*, 79. Truesdell states that Webb married "Ellen" ("about whom the records know hardly anything") in 1887 and that they had two daughters and one son (Truesdell, *Descendants*, paragraph 2562).

96. The Missouri census and Ella's tombstone epitaph indicate that she was about the same age as Webb but give no exact indication of date of birth (*1880 Missouri Census of the City of St. Louis*, role 729, house # 1218 and based on personal visit to the grave site in the Hillside Cemetery, Lindhurst, New Jersey, January 2001). Ella's tombstone states that she was born in 1846. The New Jersey Census of 1900, however, gives her birth as December 1848. It notes that she was born in Ohio and that her father was born in England and her mother in Pennsylvania. See *(U.S. Census) Twelfth Census of Population 1900: New Jersey, Bergen County, Rutherford Burrough, Vol. 5*.

97. See Schlereth, *Victorian America*, 280; Rose, *Victorian America*, 154.

98. The 1880 census registers Ella as Webb's wife and a schoolteacher, noting that she was born in Ohio (*1880 Missouri Census of the City of St. Louis*), role 729, house # 1218). Ella appears in the St. Louis directories from 1877 to 1879 as Ella G. Hotchkiss, a teacher. She first appears as Ella Webb in 1879 and is still listed as a teacher. In 1878, she is registered as teaching at Everett School (*United States City Directories, 1861–1881, St. Louis, Missouri, 1877*, reel 10, 437; *Gould's St. Louis Directory* [1877], 464; [1878], 452; and [1879], 488, 1008). She does not appear in the 1880 directory, indicating that the birth of her son in May 1879 obliged her to stay at home that year. She appears again as a teacher the following year and continues to be listed as such over the next five years until the birth of her daughter Mary in May of 1885. After Mary's birth, she probably did not return to work for the remainder of the family's stay in St. Louis (*Gould's St. Louis Directory* [1880], 1073; [1881], 1161; [1882], 1192–1193; [1883], 1141; [1884], 1151; [1885], 1210; [1886], 1231; and [1887], 1240).

99. Based on visit to the Hillside Cemetery, Lindhurst, New Jersey, January 2001. Webb; his wife; youngest child, Nala; and adopted daughter, Elizabeth, are buried next to each other. Webb's tombstone reads, "Alex R. Webb (1846–1916)." His wife's reads, "Ella G. Webb (1846–1920)." Nala's reads, "Nala W. Fries (1888–1919)," and Elizabeth's reads "Elizabeth F. H. Hallam (1870–1954)." The Missouri Census of 1880 gives Elizabeth's age as ten. See *1880 Missouri Census of the City of St. Louis*, role 729, house # 1218; Schlereth, *Victorian America*, 280; and Rose, *Victorian America*, 154.

100. Russell Lorenzo Webb's age is given in the Missouri Census of 1880 as one year old. No other children are mentioned at the time; see *1880 Missouri Census of the City of St. Louis*, role 729, house # 1218. The New Jersey Census of 1900 confirms this information and gives R. L. Webb's birth date as May 1879 in Missouri. Mary's birthdate is given in the New Jersey Census of 1900. See *[U.S. Census:] Twelfth Census of Population 1900: New Jersey, Bergen County, Rutherford Burrough*, Vol. 5. Mary C. Webb married Garrabant R. Alyea of Rutherford, New Jersey, on April 10, 1915. She graduated from high school in 1903 and attended Reid Institute in New York in 1904. Mary worked as an assistant kindergarten teacher in December of 1904 at a salary of $400 a year and became a kindergarten teacher in 1910. She stopped teaching in Rutherford in June 1915, after marrying Garrabant R. Alyea on April 10, 1915. The Rev. Elizabeth Padgham of the Church of Our Father performed the marriage in a private service. Mary was said to have been "a musician of rare ability." See Bunker, *Bits and Pieces*, 282.

101. "Dispatches" (2 January 1890) lists the Webb family in Manila as follows: Alex. R. Webb, born Hudson, N.Y.; Ella G. Webb, born Cincinnati, Ohio; B. F. H. Webb, born St. Louis, Mo.; R. L. Webb, born St. Louis, Mo.; Mary C. Webb, born St. Louis, Mo.; and Nala D. Webb, born in Manila. Nala's date of birth is given in the U.S. Census of 1900 for New Jersey (*Twelfth Census of Population 1900: New Jersey, Bergen County, Rutherford Burrough*, Vol. 5). Nala died in her early thirties. She married C. C. Fries of Louisburg, Pennsylvania. "Obituary: Alexander R. Webb"; and Tunison, "Mohammed Alexander Russell Webb," 18.

102. Webb Diary, 29 August 1892.

103. *Gould's St. Louis Directory* (1878), 959.

104. The *St. Joseph Gazette*'s president was F. M. Tufts, and the editor in chief was S. A. Gilbert. Eugene Field is not mentioned either, although the paper held him in great regard, and he was regarded as one of the promising upcoming journalists of the time. See *Ballenger and Hoyes* (1876), 322; (1877), 326; (1878), 320.

105. White, "The Press," 371.

106. From Keith Zimmer and Noel Holobeck of the St. Louis Area Studies Center at the St. Louis Public Library during a personal visit, June 2002.

107. Taft, *Missouri Newspapers*, 132.

108. Muhammad, "Muslims," 198.

109. "*Republic* Reviews Alex Webb's Life." It states that Webb "drifted to St. Louis after St. Joseph and worked on either the old *Journal* or *The Dispatch* for a very short time." See also "Obituary: Alexander R. Webb"; "Alexander H. [sic] Webb"; and Tunison, "Mohammed Alexander Russell Webb," 15. Webb's obituary in the *St. Louis Post-Dispatch* mentions that he worked for "several St. Louis papers" but makes no mention of his working for the *Post-Dispatch* ("Alexander R. Webb Dies: Former U.S. Consul"). The *Evening Dispatch* used that name from 1864 to January 10, 1878, when it became the *Evening Post*. Toward year's end, the paper took on the compound title of the *St. Louis Evening Post and Dispatch* and, on 8 March 1879, was finally christened the *St. Louis Post-Dispatch*. Anachronisms and confusions regarding newspaper names are common in the old city directories because of the lag between gathering information and getting it published. See *Newspapers in Missouri*, 2: 685, 719.

110. It was called the *Daily Journal* at the time. See *Gould's St. Louis Directory* (1878), 959; and (1879), 1008.

111. Rammelkamp, *Pulitzer's Post-Dispatch*, 8, 41–44, 207–209, 239.

112. Ibid., vii, 207.

113. See *Newspapers in Missouri*, 2: 703. The *Times-Journal* began as a weekly in St. Louis in 1857 called the *Journal*. It became a daily in 1869, and it changed its name to the *Daily Journal* in 1876. Two years later, it incorporated with the city's *Daily Times* and became the *Times-Journal* (*Newspapers in Missouri*, 2: 702–703, 713). Some accounts state that Webb worked at "the old *Journal*," a reference to the *Daily Journal* before its incorporation into the *Times-Journal* ("*Republic* Reviews Alex Webb's Life"). Others cite the *Times-Journal* without referencing the *Journal*. Most biographical reports make no mention of either ("Obituary: Alexander R. Webb"; "Alexander H. [sic] Webb"). Ali asserts that Webb worked as associate editor for the *Morning Journal*, and Webb's *New York Times* obituary also refers to the paper by that name ("Preface," 3; "Alexander H. Webb"). There was, however, no newspaper in St. Louis by that name at the time. The reference is almost certainly to the *Times-Journal* at the time that it was called the *Daily Journal* and indicates the paper's morning edition of the paper (see *Newspapers in Missouri*, 2: 530).

114. *Gould's St. Louis Directory* (1878), 305, and (1879), 335. Field last appears in the 1879 directory. Another Eugene Field is listed as an agent of the Blue Lines but was someone else and had been listed in the 1879 directory next to Field, the "editorial writer." See ibid. (1880), 353; (1881), 373; and (1882), 328.

115. Webb first appears as an employee of the *St. Louis Globe-Democrat* in the 1880 directory, indicating that he had established himself at the paper a year earlier (*Gould's*

St. Louis Directory [1880], 1073). See also "Alexander H. [*sic*] Webb"; and Tunison, "Mohammed Alexander Russell Webb," 15. The *Globe-Democrat* was a daily, formed through a merger between the *St. Louis Daily Globe* and the *St. Louis Democrat* in 1872. Like many other American newspapers of the time, it continued to run a weekly edition until 1876. Webb's association with it—as with the *St. Joseph Gazette*—was with the daily edition. Although a daily, it maintained a weekly edition until 1876. The *Globe-Democrat* was discontinued in 1986 (*Newspapers in Missouri*, 2: 711).

116. Hart, *A History of the St. Louis Globe-Democrat*, 155.

117. Rammelkamp, *Pulitzer's Post-Dispatch*, 36–37; Hart, *A History of the St. Louis Globe-Democrat*, 155.

118. Hart, *A History of the St. Louis Globe-Democrat*, 116–118. The *St. Louis Globe-Democratic* ran from 1875 till 1986. See *Newspapers in Missouri*, 2: 711.

119. Rammelkamp, *Pulitzer's Post-Dispatch*, 36–37; and Hart, *A History of the St. Louis Globe-Democrat*, 155. "Little Mack" was suicidal and, after an unsuccessful attempt the day of his death, succeeded in a second attempt that night. He died in 1896 at the age of fifty-four. See Hart, *A History of the St. Louis Globe-Democrat*, 155.

120. *Gould's St. Louis Directory* (1881), 1161; "Got a Consulship"; "*Republic* Reviews Alex Webb's Life."

121. *Gould's St. Louis Directory* (1882), 1192–1193.

122. "*Republic* Reviews Alex Webb's Life."

123. Ibid.

124. Ibid.

125. Hyde and Conard, *Encyclopedia of the History of St. Louis*, 3: 1525. The journal changed owners in 1884. "Dramatic" was dropped from its title, and it became "a general local and sporting paper."

126. *Gould's St. Louis Directory* (1883), 1141; and "Got a Consulship."

127. "*Republic* Reviews Alex Webb's Life."

128. *Gould's St. Louis Directory* (1884), 1151; (1885), 1210; (1886), 1231; and (1887), 1240. Cf. Tunison, "Mohammed Alexander Russell Webb," 15; Ali, "Preface," 3; Grebsonal, "The Mohammedan Propagandist," 204; "Obituary: Alexander R. Webb"; "*Republic* Reviews Alex Webb's Life"; "Alexander H. Webb"; Osman, "The Story" (1944), 6.

129. On the newspaper's centennial in 1908, it numbered among roughly one hundred American newspapers that had been in existence for more than a century (*Century Club of American Newspapers*, 2). It was first called the *Missouri Gazette and Public Advertiser*. It became a national newspaper in 1822 and took the name the *Missouri Republican*. In 1822, it became a national weekly. Its daily edition began in 1869, but the weekly edition continued until 1888. From 1875 until 1888—the period Webb worked at the paper—it was actually known as the *St. Louis Republican*. It then took the name the *St. Louis Republic*, which it kept until 1919. The paper's high point came during Reconstruction from 1865 till 1877. It was St. Louis's leading newspaper during the mid-1870s and continued well into the twentieth century, when, in 1975, it was absorbed by the *St. Louis Globe-Democrat*. See Hyde and Conard, *Encyclopedia of the History of St. Louis*, 1: 1631; Hart, *A History of the St. Louis Globe-Democrat*, 116–118; *Missouri Republican*, 26 September 1887: 1; *Newspapers in Missouri*, 1: 507–508, 2: 722;

Rammelkamp, *Pulitzer's Post-Dispatch*, 32; and Armstrong, "Beginnings of the Modern Newspaper," 2.

130. Steven, *One Hundred Years of the St. Louis Republic*, 15–16; and Rammelkamp, *Pulitzer's Post-Dispatch*, 32–33.

131. "*Republic* Reviews Alex Webb's Life."

132. Ibid.

133. Ibid.

CHAPTER 5

1. "Dispatches," 4 October 1887, and 1 January 1892.

2. Ibid., 24 October 1887, 10 December 1887, and 1 January 1888.

3. Ibid., 1 June 1888. Cowan registered similar complaints against the Spanish, who refused to recognize him for a long time and compelled him to write the American ambassador in Madrid to expedite matters. See ibid., 5 September 1892, 15 February 1893, and 1 March 1893.

4. On one occasion, Webb protested Spanish treatment of a group of "naturalists" from the University of Michigan. See ibid., 22 September 1888.

5. Seager, *The World's Parliament of Religions*, 157; Dannin, *Black Pilgrimage*, 44.

6. "A. H. Webb, Former St. Louisan Dies"; "Obituary Notes," *Editor and Publisher*, 7 October 1916: 34; and "Alexander H. Webb."

7. Dannin, *Black Pilgrimage*, 44.

8. Grebsonal, "The Mohammedan Propagandist," 204.

9. "To Preach Moslemism."

10. OA, document B.

11. "Dispatches," 26 July 1891.

12. Taft, *Missouri Newspapers*, 143–144.

13. "Got a Consulship."

14. Ibid.

15. Tunison, "Mohammed Alexander Russell Webb," 15; and "Alexander H. Webb."

16. "To Preach Moslemism."

17. "*Republic* Reviews Alex Webb's Life."

18. Rose, *Victorian America*, 119.

19. Rammelkamp, *Pulitzer's Post-Dispatch*, 125.

20. Rose, *Victorian America*, 193–196, 223–224, 228.

21. Osman, "The Story" (1944), 7; "Dispatches," 3 October 1889, 2 January 1890, 4 November 1890, 23 September 1891.

22. "Dispatches," 20 January 1890. A year and a half later, Webb complained again of low pay and high inflation, insisting that Manila was "the most expensive port in the East." See ibid., 26 July 1891.

23. Ibid., 26 July 1891.

24. Ibid., 22 December 1887 and 17 April 1888.

25. Ibid., 26 October 1893.

26. Ibid., 17 April 1888.

27. Ibid., 29 May 1890.

28. Ibid., 26 July 1891.

29. Webb, "A Letter," 77; "Dispatches," 22 June 1892, 7 July 1892.

30. "Dispatches," 19 February 1888.

31. Ella worked as office clerk at intervals during the September quarter of 1890 and the summer and fall of 1891. See ibid., 4 November 1890, 23 September 1891, 1 January 1892.

32. Ibid., 20 January 1890.

33. Ibid., 1 January 1888.

34. Ibid., 20 January 1890.

35. Ibid., 4 November 1890, 23 September 1891.

36. Ibid., 3 October 1889, 4 November 1890, 23 September 1891.

37. Schlereth, *Victorian America*, 185–186.

38. "Dispatches," 26 October 1893.

39. Ibid., 3 October 1889.

40. Ibid., 4 November 1890, 23 September 1891.

41. Ibid. Roll 5 introductory statement.

42. Ibid., 21 May 1888. Webb requested $150 to $200 to prepare and bind the records at a rate of $1.25 a volume.

43. Ibid., 7 June 1888.

44. Ibid., 11 August 1890, 12 October 1887. The uprising began on June 26, 1890. Webb reported that a unit of colonial soldiers had been building a road, when two hundred "natives" ambushed them, killing all but two and arming themselves with the Remington rifles they took from the dead soldiers. They proceeded to attack the soldiers' barracks but were repelled after killing ten more soldiers and an officer. Webb noted that the "natives" were Protestants and did not "feel kindly toward the Spaniards nor toward the Catholic priests, who have been very earnest and persistent in their efforts to convert them from the Protestant faith to the church of Rome," adding that Doane and the other American missionaries had won their confidence and esteem in contrast to the suspicion they felt toward the priests. He elaborated that the Spanish had provoked the attack a few days earlier by sending other "natives who had converted to Catholicism" under the protection of soldiers to erect a Catholic chapel within three feet of the missionary church, which the villagers had regarded as a hostile act intended to block missionary work. The workmen and the four guards were killed first. Then the "natives" ambushed the soldiers building the road in the jungle a short distance away. Webb wrote to U.S. Rear Admiral Belknap, giving him the same information and requesting him to take necessary action "as he may deem proper to protect our interests at Ponape." See ibid., 11 August 1890.

45. Ibid., 5 December 1891.

46. Ibid., 16 April 1888.

47. Ibid., 16 April 1888.

48. Ibid., 20 August 1889.

49. Ibid., 5 June 1890.

50. "Dispatches," 9 March 1891, 11 April 1891, 4 January 1892.

51. See Murad, "The Great Dive," 23–24. As the title of his *Moslem World* article indicates, Webb clearly regarded Williamson to be an American, an impression

which Williamson may have encouraged. At the end of the article, Webb refers to Williamson a second time as "an American Mussulman now residing in Arabia." Murad gives Williamson's Muslim name as Hajji Abdullah Fadhil (27). Webb gives it as "Abdallah bin Fadle, the American."

52. Murad, "The Great Dive," 24–25.

53. "Dispatches," 11 August 1890. See note 44 above.

54. Ibid.

55. Stanton-Hope, *Arabian Adventurer*, 94.

56. Ibid.

57. Although Webb was almost certainly a Muslim at the time, Stanton-Hope portrays him as open in his attitude toward drink, a picture that disagrees with Webb's contention in a dispatch of the same year that "we have never indulged in these things and have no inclination to do so" ("Dispatches," 26 July 1891). Webb then "ordered a Filipino boy to mix a John Collins for himself and his guest." At the end of the account, Webb, Williamson, and the English captain who smuggled Williamson out of Manila made congenial farewells in Webb's living room over glasses of whisky and rye (Stanton-Hope, *Arabian Adventurer*, 95, 97).

58. Ibid., 96.

59. Ibid.

60. Murad, "The Great Dive," 24–27; and "Moslem Fraternity: An American Moslem in Arabia," *MWVI*, 1 October 1895: 1.

61. Ibid., 97.

62. See Kur, "To the Editor," 15; "Fall of Islam"; Grebsonal, "The Mohammedan Propagandist," 204; Ali, "Preface," 4; OA, Document B; Tunison, "Mohammed Alexander Russell Webb," 16; Osman, "The Story" (1944), 7; Ahmad, *Mujaddid-e Azam*, 158.

63. See Webb "Letter to the Editor," *Allahabad Review*, July 1891: 109–111; Webb, "Progressive Mohammedanism"; Webb, "Sectarian Exclusiveness"; Webb, "To the Editor," *Allahabad Review*, May 1892: 60; Webb, "A Letter."

64. Grebsonal, "The Mohammedan Propagandist," 204; "Fall of Islam"; Ali, "Preface," 4; OA, Document B.

65. Webb, "To the Editor," *Allahabad Review*, May 1892: 60.

66. According to Kur, the correspondence began in 1890. Webb dated it somewhat later and reported to the *New York Times* that it had begun in August 1891. In the *Allahabad Review*, Webb dated the beginning of Arab's correspondence with him in early 1891. Since Kur's correspondence with Webb well antedated that of Arab, it is likely that the correspondence began in 1890, as Kur indicated. See Kur, "To the Editor," 18; "Fall of Islam"; Webb, "To the Editor," *Allahabad Review*, May 1892: 60; Grebsonal, "The Mohammedan Propagandist," 204; Ali, "Preface," 4; OA, Document B; Ahmad, *Mujaddid-e Azam*, 158. Most sources indicate that Arab came across the Webb-Kur correspondence in the Bombay newspapers, but it is doubtful that such was the case. Arab did not know English well or at all, and Kur's account that he personally brought Webb to Arab's attention appears more likely.

67. Kur, "To the Editor," 18.

68. Ahmad, *Mujaddid-e Azam*, 158–159. Ahmad states explicitly that Arab had no knowledge of English. Webb stated that Arab was "unable to speak English

fluently" and required a translator for the Manila talks with Webb ("To the Editor," *Allahabad Review*, May 1892: 60). Arab must have spoken some English. Webb's diary gives the impression that Webb and Arab had no trouble communicating worthy of note. Webb never complained of being unable to converse with Arab, and when the two met alone at the train station before Webb set out for Agra, they conferred over breakfast about their agenda for the remainder of the tour. The fact that Arab was not proficient in English is indicated by the difficulty he apparently had in preparing a response to accusations regarding the mission's fundraising efforts. Arab and two others "spent the greater part of the forenoon constructing [the] letter." See Webb Diary, 9 December and 16 November 1892.

69. Webb, "To the Editor," *Allahabad Review*, May 1892: 60; Ahmad, *Mujaddid-e Azam*, 158–159; "Fall of Islam." See also Ali, "Preface," 4; Grebsonal, "The Mohammedan Propagandist," 204. Ahmad refers to the translator as a "Eurasian." In his letter to the *Allahabad Review*, Webb spoke of him as "a Mohammedan missionary form Calcutta." Webb mentioned Serajuddin Ahmad in his diary also, noting that he lived in Midapore near Calcutta and was very sick at the time of Webb's visit. Webb noted that the convert was the object of considerable suspicion: "He seems to be a good man but the Moslems here do not like him and tell rather hard stories about him. But I find considerable feeling against the European converts who happen to be here. English sparrows on the esotea." See Webb Diary, 19 October 1892.

70. Webb, "To the Editor," *Allahabad Review*, May 1892: 60.

71. See "To My Oriental Brothers," *MWVI*, January 1895: 3.

72. OA, Document B.

73. "Muhammad Webb's Mission"; "To My Oriental Brothers," *MWVI*, January 1895: 3–4. The Ottoman Archives, based on reports in the *New York Herald*, confirm the five-year provision and Webb's confidence in gaining self-sufficiency at the end of the period (OA, Document B).

74. "Fall of Islam"; "To My Oriental Brothers," *MWVI*, January 1895: 3.

75. "Fall of Islam"; Kur, "To the Editor," 18.

76. "Fall of Islam"; Webb, *Islam in America*, 68–69; Grebsonal, "The Mohammedan Propagandist," 204.

77. Kur, "To the Editor," 18.

78. Ali, "Preface," 5; Osman, "The Story" (1995): 17–18; Ahmad, *Mujaddid-e Azam*, 159.

79. Webb, "A Letter," 77.

80. Osman, "The Story" (1944), 7.

81. "Fall of Islam."

82. Webb, "Letter to Budrudin Abdulla Kur."

83. "To My Oriental Brothers," *MWVI*, January 1895: 3–4. Compare "Fall of Islam."

84. Cranston, *HPB*, 426.

85. Webb, "Letter to Mirza Ghulam Ahmad."

86. Webb, "Letter to Budrudin Abdulla Kur."

87. Webb Diary, 4 September 1892.

88. "Dispatches," 26 July 1891.

89. Ibid.

90. Webb, "A Letter," 77.

91. "Dispatches," 7 July 1892.

92. Webb Diary, 4 September 1892.

93. "Dispatches," 5 September 1892.

94. Ibid.

CHAPTER 6

1. Webb Diary, 3–4 September 1892.

2. See Barrows, *The World's Parliament of Religions*, 1: 630; "A Bit of History," *MW*, October 1893: 7.

3. See "Dispatches," 7 July 1892; Bektashi, "Mohammed Alexander Russell Webb," unnumbered.

4. Ibid., 30 August 1892.

5. Ibid., 2 September 1892.

6. See Osman, "The Story" (1995), 17–18; Ahmad, *Mujaddid-e Azam*, 161; compare Dannin, *Black Pilgrimage*, 43.

7. Based on a personal communication from Timothy Winter, Lecturer at Cambridge University.

8. "Muhammad Webb's Mission"; Grebsonal, "The Mohammedan Propagandist," 204. Ali stated explicitly that the last leg of Webb's tour took him to Lahore. See Ali, "Preface," 5. Webb traveled by sea, and passage through the Suez Canal and Straits of Gibraltar was the most direct route to England and New York. The course was mentioned specifically in the *New York Times* ("Muhammad Webb's Mission"). Quilliam's journals, the *Crescent* and *Islamic World*, made no mention of Webb's visiting Liverpool but did announce his return to America. An article in the *Crescent* said: "Mr Mohammed Webb has arrived in America, and is about to commence the propaganda of our Holy Faith in that continent. We cordially wish him every success" (29 April 1893: 3). There were few if any further references to Webb, which may suggest an element of rivalry between Quilliam and Webb, based on a personal communication with Timothy Winter at Cambridge University.

9. Ibid., 6 September 1892.

10. Ibid., 6 and 21 September 1892.

11. McDannell, *The Christian Home*, 59.

12. Webb Diary, 6, 8, and 9 September 1892.

13. Ibid., 14 September 1892.

14. Ibid.

15. Ibid., 21 September 1892.

16. Ibid., 28 September 1892.

17. Ibid.

18. Ibid.

19. Ibid.

20. Ibid., 30 September 1892.

21. Ibid., 1 October 1892.

22. Ibid., 8 October 1892.

23. Ibid., 12 October 1892.

24. Ibid., 13 October 1892.

25. Ibid., 23 and 25 October 1892.

26. Ibid., 27 October 1892.

27. Ibid., 28 October 1892.

28. Ibid.

29. Ibid., 31 October 1892; Ali, "Preface," 5; "Muhammad Webb' Mission."

30. Webb Diary, 7 November 1892.

31. Ibid., 17 November 1892.

32. Ibid.

33. Ibid., 18 November 1892.

34. Ibid., 20 November 1892.

35. Ibid., 21 November 1892.

36. Ibid.

37. Ibid., 29 November 1892.

38. Ibid., 24 November 1892.

39. Ibid., 6 December 1892.

40. Ibid., 8 December 1892.

41. Ibid., 9 December 1892.

42. Ibid., 10 December 1892.

43. Ibid.

44. Ibid., 11 December 1892.

45. Ibid., 11–12 December 1892.

46. Ibid., 11 December 1892.

47. Ibid.

48. Ibid., 15 December 1892.

49. "Muhammad Webb's Mission."

50. Webb Diary, 16 November 1892.

51. Ibid.

52. See Webb, *Islam: A Lecture*, 7; Webb, *Lectures on Islam*, 18.

53. See Osman, "The Story" (1995), 17–18. Ali avoids making reference to fund-raising (Ali, "Preface," 5).

54. "Interview of a Correspondent," in Webb, *Lectures on Islam*, 33.

55. Webb Diary, 31 October 1892.

56. Ibid., 11 December 1892.

57. "Fall of Islam."

58. See Webb, "Letter to Budrudin Abdulla Kur"; Webb Diary, 28 October 1892.

59. Webb, *Islam in America*, 68–69; "Fall of Islam."

60. Webb Diary, 4, 11, 17 November 1892.

61. Ibid., 1 November 1892.

62. Ibid., 9 November 1892.

63. Ibid., 9–10 November 1892.

64. Ibid., 16–17 November 1892.

65. Webb, "The Better Way," 19; *MW*, November 1893: 9; *MWVI*, April 1895: 3; June 1895: 2.

66. Osman, "The Story" (1995), 18; Ahmad, *Mujaddid-e Azam*, 160.

67. Webb Diary, 7 November 1892.

68. Ibid., 27 November 1892.

69. Ibid., 3 December 1892.

70. Ibid., 8 December 1892.

71. For the second usage, see Webb Diary, 12 December 1892: "Went to my cracker box where I left two oranges and found that one of them had disappeared— niggers who slept in the wash-room must have nipped it."

72. Kennedy, *Nigger*, 4–5.

73. Ibid., 4.

74. Ibid., 7–8.

75. Jones, *Chorus of Faith*, 16.

76. See "Muhammad Webb's Mission," 2.

77. Grebsonal, "The Mohammedan Propagandist," 6. See also Webb, "The Influence of Social Condition" (Houghton), 544.

78. Washington, *Madame Blavatsky's Baboon*, 69; Mills, *One Hundred Years of Theosophy*, xi.

79. Grebsonal, "The Mohammedan Propagandist," 6; Webb, "The Spirit of Islam" (Houghton), 464.

80. Webb, *Islam in America*, 33.

81. "Fraternal Love," *MW*, November 1893: 7.

82. Ibid., October 1893: 12.

83. Ibid., 8.

84. Ibid.

85. "Moulvie Cheragh Ali," *MWVI*, September 1895: 1.

86. Webb Diary, 28 October 1892; see also 31 October.

87. Ibid., 14 September 1892.

88. Ibid., 17 September 1892.

89. Ibid., 14 October 1892.

90. "Interview of a Correspondent," in Webb, *Lectures on Islam*, 31.

91. Webb Diary, 3 November 1892; Webb, *Islam: A Lecture*, 1. Webb spells the consul's name "Ballantyne," although it appears in the lectures as "Ballantine."

92. Webb Diary, 14 November 1892.

93. Ibid., 16 November 1892.

94. Ibid., 15 November 1892.

95. Ibid., 18 November 1892, 28 October 1892.

96. Ibid., 29 October 1892.

97. Ibid., 31 October 1892.

98. Ibid., 11 December 1892.

99. Ibid., 12 December 1892.

100. Ibid.

101. Khoda Baksh was a noted bibliophile and creator of libraries and is buried within the precincts of the library that Webb visited. See "Khuda Baksh," *EI*, 5: 43. Cheragh Ali was a leading member of the Aligarh Movement, a prominent modernist thinker of Muslim India, and a staunch supporter of the reform movement of Syed Ahmad Khan. See Kurzman, *Modernist Islam*, 277.

102. Webb Diary, 24 October 1892.

103. Ibid., 27 November 1892.

104. Ibid., 26 and 27 November 1892; "The Moslem Wars," *MW*, October, 1893: 1–5.

105. Webb Diary, 5 November 1892; see also 24 and 27 November and 5 December 1892.

106. Ibid., 30 November 1892.

107. Ibid., 28 November 1892.

108. Ibid., 1 November 1892.

109. Ibid., 12 December 1892.

110. Ibid., 4 November 1892.

111. Ibid., 22 October 1892.

112. Ibid., 29 November 1892.

113. Ibid., 26 November 1892.

114. Ibid., 21 October 1892.

115. Ibid., 25 October 1892.

116. Ibid., 30 September 1892.

117. Ibid., 28 November 1892.

118. "Muhammad Webb's Mission"; Grebsonal, "The Mohammedan Propagandist," 204.

119. Osman, "The Story," *The Light* (1995): 18; Ahmad, *Mujaddid-e Azam*, 160.

120. Ibid., 14 November 1892.

121. Ibid., 26 November 1892.

122. Ibid., 10 November 1892. There may well have been a sixth lecture in Lahore, although none has come to light.

123. Ibid., 7 October 1892.

124. Ibid., 6 October 1892.

125. Ibid., 14 October 1892; OA, Document B.

126. Webb Diary, 16 October 1892.

127. Ibid., 19 October 1892.

128. Webb, *Islam: A Lecture*, 1; Webb, *Lectures on Islam*, 23.

129. Webb Diary, 10 November 1892.

130. Ibid., 25 November 1892. The Ottoman Archives state that the lecture was delivered at the Grand National Assembly and note that Webb had spoken informally beforehand at the city's principal mosque (OA, Document B).

131. Webb Diary, 25 November 1892; Webb, "Philosophic Islam," 39; "Muhammad Webb's Mission."

132. Webb Diary, 25 November 1892.

133. Webb, "Philosophic Islam," 39; Webb Diary, 25 November 1892.

134. Webb Diary, 11 December 1892. See also Webb, "Islam," 23; "Muhammad Webb's Mission"; Webb, "The Better Way," 7.

135. Webb Diary, 11 December 1892.

136. Ibid.

137. Ibid., 12 December 1892.

138. See ibid., 29 September and 19 October 1892.

139. Ibid., 30 September 1892.

0. Ibid., 29 August 1892.
141. Ibid., 23 September 1892.
142. Ibid., 22 September 1892.
143. Ibid., 12 October 1892.
144. Ibid., 16 September 1892.
145. Ibid., 6 November 1892.
146. Ibid., 10, 12 December 1892.
147. Ibid., 3 November 1892.
148. Ibid., 17 October 1892.
149. Ibid., 11 October 1892.
150. Ibid., 28 September and 12 October 1892.
151. Ibid., 10 December 1892.
152. Ibid., 24 November 1892.
153. Ibid., 12 December 1892.
154. Ibid., 17 November 1892.
155. Ibid., 23 October 1892.
156. Ibid., 4 November 1892.
157. Ibid.
158. OA, Document B.
159. Webb Diary, 13 September 1892.
160. Ibid., 12 November 1892.
161. Ibid., 20 October 1892.
162. I am not sure what the word means, although the handwriting is clear. It may be an abbreviation for artichoke or related to the Spanish "arta," a type of plantain, which Webb would have probably known from Philippines, but this seems unlikely. See Rancés diccionario ilustrado, 53.
163. Webb Diary, 3 October 1892.
164. Ibid., 30 September 1892.
165. Ibid., 17–18 November 1892.
166. Ibid., 5 December 1892.
167. Ibid., 4 December 1892.
168. Ibid., 3 December 1892.
169. Ibid., 29 November 1892.
170. See ibid., 23 September 1892. En route to Rangoon, Webb encountered a German who attempted to strike up a conversation in French, hoping it would prove to be a shared idiom. Webb replied in broken French that he did not speak the language and added: "No. Hablo Español y Ingles" [No, I speak Spanish and English]. Although he picked up a few words of Urdu, Webb knew no Muslim language, and his publications show that he could not distinguish between Arabic and Persian, which often occurred together in Islamic texts from India. He called "namāz" [Persian for "prayer"] "Arabic nomenclature" for the ritual. Webb, A Guide to Namaz, 9; Webb Diary, 4 November 1892.
171. Webb Diary, 27 November 1892.
172. Ibid., 11 December 1892.
173. Ibid., 27, 29 November 1892.
174. Ibid., 4 October 1892.

175. Ibid., 19 October 1892.

176. Ibid., 2 October 1892.

177. Ibid., 13 October 1892.

178. Ibid., 19 October 1892.

179. OA, Document B.

180. Webb Diary, 2 December 1892.

181. OA, Document B.

182. Webb Diary, 2 December 1892.

183. Ibid., 30 November 1892.

184. OA, Document B.

185. Webb Diary, 11 December and 12 November 1892.

186. Ibid., 24 October 1892.

187. Ibid., 23 November, 22 September, 12 October 1892. Both Eliot and Ward were prominent Victorian writers. It is worthy of note that Webb was reading two female authors, although the passage he cited from *Felix Holt* was misogynic: "I can't bear to see you going the way of the foolish women who spoil men's lives. Men can't help loving them and so they make themselves slaves to the petty desires of petty creatures."

188. See ibid., 20 September, 21, 24 October, 2 November, 22 November 1892.

189. Ibid., 25 September, 5 December 1892.

190. Ibid., 13 December 1892.

191. Ibid., 20 November 1892.

192. May, *Great Expectations*, 17.

193. Webb Diary, 25 September 1892.

194. Ibid., 25 September 1892; also 12 October 1892.

195. Ibid., 25 November 1892.

196. Ibid., 30 September, and 1, 5, and 18 October 1892.

197. Ibid., 12 November 1892.

198. Ibid., 3 December 1892.

199. Ibid., 18 October 1892.

200. Ibid., 29 October, 23 November, 1 December 1892.

201. Ibid., 12 December 1892.

202. Ibid., 18 November 1892.

203. Ibid., 26 November 1892.

204. Ibid., 17 October 1892.

205. Ibid., 17 September 1892.

206. Ibid., 11 November 1892.

207. Ibid., 12 November 1892.

208. Ibid., 11 December 1892.

209. Ibid., 8 December 1892.

210. Webb, *Islam in America*, 67.

211. Webb Diary, 4 December 1892.

212. "Muhammad Webb's Mission."

213. Webb, "Letter to Budrudin Abdulla Kur."

214. Webb, "The Better Way," 22.

215. "Interview of a Correspondent," in Webb, *Lectures on Islam*, 32.

216. Webb, "Philosophic Islam," 51.

217. Ibid., 50–51.

218. "Muhammad Webb's Mission"; Grebsonal, "The Mohammedan Propagandist," 204; Tunison, "Mohammed Alexander Russell Webb," 17; Osman, "The Story" (1944), 5.

CHAPTER 7

1. "Muhammad Webb's Mission."

2. *New York Times* and *New York Herald*, February 1893.

3. "To Preach Moslemism"; Tunison, "Mohammed Alexander Russell Webb," 17; compare Osman, "The Story" (1944), 5–6. I was unable to identify Samuel Brown. Jersey City lies west of Manhattan across the Hudson. Although located in New Jersey, it constituted then as today one of the "core areas" of what has become greater metropolitan New York. See Abu-Lughod, *New York, Chicago, Los Angeles*, 192.

4. Webb, "Progressive Mohammedanism," *The Allahabad Review*, November 1891: 158.

5. Webb, "A Letter," *The Allahabad Review*, July 1892: 77–78.

6. Webb, *The Three Lectures*, 39; Webb Diary, 14 September, 14, 31 October, 1, 16 November 1892.

7. Webb, "To the Editor," *The Allahabad Review*, May 1892: 60–61. Compare Kur, "To the Editor," 15–16; Webb to Budrudin Kur [sic], 4 July 1892.

8. Webb, "A Letter," *The Allahabad Review*, July 1892: 78.

9. Webb Diary, 30 September 1892; 2 October 1892.

10. Webb, *Islam in America*, 67–70.

11. *MWVI*, March 1895: 3.

12. *MWVI*, January 1895: 3: see also ibid., February 1895: 3; and May 1895: 3.

13. Webb, "Sectarian Exclusiveness," *The Allahabad Review*, December 1891: 176–177.

14. Webb, "Harmony," *The Allahabad Review*, February 1892: 15.

15. Webb, "To the Editor," *The Allahabad Review*, August 1891: 110.

16. Ibid., January 1895: 4.

17. *MWVI*, March 1895: 3.

18. *MWVI*, April 1895: 2, 4; March 1895: 3; February 1895: 2; June 1895: 2–3.

19. Compare "Lord Headley on Islam in the West," *Islamic Review*, February 1923: 48. Headley remarked in a manner reminiscent of Webb: "I feel sure that if the people of England fully grasped what Islam really is, common sense, and the natural desire we all have to use our reasoning faculties as well as our emotions, would do much to remove the misunderstandings which exist. It is, I think, much to the discredit of certain persons that they have willfully spread abroad incorrect accounts of Muhammad's work and teaching, and have generally misrepresented Islam to Western nations. To show that Islam stands on a firm foundation and is a religion appealing strongly to the intellect as well as to the natural sentiments engrafted in human nature, should now be our closest duty."

20. Holmes observed in the 1920s: "In nearly every country on the globe Moslem missions are to be found with trained missionaries armed with all the paraphernalia of modern Christian missions—tracts, Koranic interpretation after the fashion of

Bible dictionaries (and ably done it is too), newspapers and magazines, societies, mosques and enquiry rooms together with instruction in Arabic for converts." From its inception, Islam, like Christianity, was a missionary religion, but systematically organized missions with publications and newspapers were not part of its tradition. The Muslims of British India were the most successful in the creation of the new missions, and the Ahmadiyya, who emerged in the Punjab, are an example of an Indian-based Islamic missionary society deeply influenced by Christian missionary models. Outside of British India, Muslims in Egypt and Turkey also attempted to form Islamic missions on Christian models but were not as successful. See Arnold, *The Preaching of Islam*, 443–444; Holmes, "*Islam in America*," 262; and Case, "The Aligarh Era," 73–74.

21. See *MW*, October 1893: inset; Webb, *Islam in America*, cover sheet; Tunison, "Mohammed Alexander Russell Webb," 17; Osman, "The Story" (1944), 5–6.

22. The bookstore, in Dannin's view, served "the cosmopolitan citizens of Manhattan's midtown import-export business" and was called Orientalis, possibly a misspelling of Orientalia or later modification of it. It became "a focal point for the transmission of mystical thought in turn-of-the-century America" and a "magnet for theosophists and iconoclasts of all persuasions." Dannin presumes that Webb's bookstore became Weiser's Bookstore during the 1980s. See Dannin, *Black Pilgrimage*, 43–44.

23. "For the Faith of Islam"; *MW*, October 1893, inset; Webb, *Islam in America*, 80; Webb, *A Guide to Namaz*, inset page; Tunison, "Mohammed Alexander Russell Webb," 17; Osman, "The Story" (1944), 5.

24. See "To My Oriental Brothers," *MWVI*, January 1895: 4.

25. "Mrs. Keep Visits the Consul."

26. "Nafeesa Keep Breakfasts."

27. See *MWVI*, January 1895 till February 1896.

28. See *MW*, October 1893: 9.

29. Maass, *The Gingerbread Age*, 14.

30. Eraslan, "Muhammed A. R. Webb'in," 86.

31. OA, Document B; Osman, "The Story" (1944), 6–7.

32. Eraslan, "Muhammed A. R. Webb'in," 86.

33. Webb, "Philosophic Islam," 52. See also "Muhammad Webb's Mission."

34. Pool, *Studies in Mohammedanism*, 397.

35. "For the Faith of Islam"; "Headquarters Opened," *MW*, October 1893: 9; Osman, "The Story" (1944), 5–6.

36. Pool, *Studies in Mohammedanism*, xiv.

37. "Our Lecture Room," *MW*, November 1893: 11.

38. Osman, "The Story" (1944), 5–6.

39. "For the Faith of Islam"; Osman, "The Story" (1944), 5–6.

40. "Our Lecture Room," *MW*, November 1893: 11.

41. Osman, "The Story" (1944), 6.

42. "For the Faith of Islam." See also Osman, "The Story" (1944), 6. Ferris gives Emin Nabakoff's anglicized name as Erwin ("Immigrant Muslim Communities," 210).

43. "Headquarters Opened," *MW*, October 1893: 9.

44. "Muhammad Webb's Mission."

45. Melton, "Webb, Muhammad Alexander Russell," 304; Bektashi, "Mohammed Alexander Russell Webb," unnumbered.

46. "Muhammad Webb's Mission." See Osman, "The Story" (1944), 5; Ali, "Preface," 5. Ferris observes that Webb's selection of Manhattan distinguished his mission from those of later New York Muslim immigrants and converts, who were centered in Brooklyn and Queens, "far from Manhattan's glitter." Although Webb did, in fact, establish a branch in Brooklyn, it must be remembered that, at the time of his mission, New York City and Manhattan were synonymous, and the ethnic and social composition of Greater New York was very different than it became a few years later during the era of the later immigrants. See Ferris, "Immigrant Muslim Communities," 209; Abu-Lughod, New York, Chicago, Los Angeles, 74; OA, Document B.

47. "Fall of Islam." Webb wrote in May 1892 that the idea of an American mission had been in his mind for almost three years. See Webb, "To the Editor," Allahabad Review, May 1892: 61.

48. See Webb, "To the Editor," Allahabad Review, July 1891: 109–110: Webb, "Progressive Mohammedanism"; Webb, "Sectarian Exclusiveness"; Webb, "To the Editor," Allahabad Review, May 1892: 60–61.

49. Ali, "Preface," 3.

50. Webb, "The Better Way," 22.

51. Webb, "Progressive Mohammedanism"; Webb, "Sectarian Exclusiveness"; Webb, "To the Editor," Allahabad Review, May 1892: 60–61; Webb, "Philosophic Islam," 50.

52. Ibid.

53. "Fall of Islam."

54. "Muhammad Webb's Mission."

55. Ibid.; Osman, "The Story" (1944), 5–6; "Fall of Islam."

56. "Fall of Islam."

57. Webb, The Three Lectures, advertisement on back page.

58. Webb, "The Better Way," 9–10.

59. Ibid., 8; Grebsonal, "The Mohammedan Propagandist," 6.

60. Webb, Islam in America, 9.

61. Webb, "The Better Way," 8.

62. Ibid., 8–9.

63. Webb, "Philosophic Islam," 52.

64. Ibid., 51–52.

65. See Webb, "Sectarian Exclusiveness," 177; "Interview of a Correspondent," in Webb, Lectures on Islam, 32; "Muhammad Webb's Mission."

66. Webb, Islam in America, 9. Some Muslim scholars of India regarded the use of English as promotion of British interests in colonial India. Shah 'Abd al-'Aziz, the son of Shah Wali-Allah of Delhi and mentor of Sir Sayyid Ahmad Khan, took such a position during the generation before Webb, declaring it "abhorrent and, therefore, improper to learn English for the promotion of better relations with Englishmen, or to serve them in the capacity of munshis, servants, or soldiers." See Case, "The Aligarh Era," 16.

67. Webb, The Three Lectures, advertisement on back page.

68. Khan, "Mohammed Alexander Russell Webb," 41.
69. Osman, "The Story" (1944), 5, 7–8.
70. "To Preach Moslemism."
71. See *MWVI*, June 1895: 3. Webb wrote: "Sales's translation of the Holy Koran is probably the most inaccurate of all the English translations, and yet it is the most popular in this country. There is, really, no good translation in English. To satisfy the many calls for an English translation, we have taken a small supply of Sale's (without the preliminary discourse) in three styles of binding, which we will send, postage paid, for 75 cents, $1.00 and 1.50" *MWVI*, May 1895: 2.
72. Eraslan, "Muhammed A. R. Webb'in," 88.
73. Osman, "The Story" (1944), 5, 7–8.
74. Ibid., 7–8.
75. *MWVI*, April 1895: 3.
76. Ibid., October 1895: 2.
77. "Fall of Islam." See "To Preach Moslemism"; Webb, *Islam in America*, 67.
78. "For the Faith of Islam."
79. Webb, *Islam in America*, 7.
80. *The Inter Ocean*, 21 September 1893.
81. See "To Preach Moslemism"; and Webb, *Islam in America*, 67.
82. Webb, "The Better Way," 10.
83. "Muhammad Webb's Mission,"
84. Webb, *Islam in America*, 28.
85. Webb, "The Spirit of Islam" (Barrows), 2: 990; (Houghton), 460.
86. Webb, "The Better Way," 10.
87. "Muhammad Webb's Mission."
88. Quoted from the *San Francisco Argonaut* in *MW*, October 1893: 7.
89. Barrows, *The World's Parliament of Religions*, 1: 630.
90. "Fall of Islam."
91. "Muhammad Webb's Mission."
92. "To Preach Moslemism."
93. Quoted in *MW*, October 1893: 7.
94. "The Islamic Propaganda."
95. Quoted in *MW*, October 1893: 8.
96. *MW*, October 1893: 8.
97. See "Muhammad Webb's Mission"; "To Preach Moslemism."
98. Muhammad, "Muslims," 199.
99. Rammelkamp, *Pulitzer's Post-Dispatch*, 20.
100. Schlereth, *Victorian America*, 121–124.
101. "Asked to Turn Moslems."
102. Jersey City lies west of Manhattan across the Hudson. Although falling within the borders of New Jersey, it constituted in Webb's time as today one of the "core areas" of greater metropolitan New York. See Abu-Lughod, *New York, Chicago, Los Angeles*, 192.
103. "Asked to Turn Moslems." Sickles's residence is given as 49 West 119th St.
104. See "Muhammad Webb's Mission"; "To Preach Moslemism." For Paul Dana, see Sullivan, *The History of New York*, "Paul Dana"; for Frank Hatton, Klos,

"Frank Hatton"; for John Russell Young, Klos, "John Russell Young"; for Charles Insley Pardee, "Lotos Leaves"; and for Paul Du Chaillu, "Paul Belloni Du Chaillu."

105. See *Republic* Reviews Alex Webb's Life." The obituary is notoriously inaccurate but is not without credibility in some matters. It contended that Webb came to St. Louis immediately after the Parliament and stayed there for several weeks. It is clear from the *Moslem World* and other sources that Webb returned to New York shortly after the Parliament, since he delivered public lectures there beginning eight days after his last Chicago presentation. See "Headquarters Opened," *MW*, October 1893: 9.

106. See "Headquarters Opened," *MW*, October 1893: 9; Osman, "The Story" (1944), 6.

107. *MWVI*, April 1895: 3.

108. See "Headquarters Opened," *MW*, October 1893: 9; Osman, "The Story" (1944), 6.

109. "Headquarters Opened," *MW*, October 1893: 9; Osman, "The Story" (1944), 6.

110. *MW*, October 1893: inset; Tunison, "Mohammed Alexander Russell Webb," 17; Osman, "The Story" (1944), 7.

111. *MW*, November 1893: 8–9.

112. Eraslan, "Muhammed A. R. Webb'in," 88.

113. OA, Document A.

114. *MW*, October 1893: inset page. The engagements were as follows: Ohio: Ashtabula, Cincinnati, Coshocton; South Carolina: Charleston; Indiana: Indianapolis; Michigan: Caro; Illinois: Chicago, Streator, Litchfield, Chester; Iowa: Fort Madison, Des Moines, Cherokee, Ida Grove, Chester; Nebraska: Plattsmouth; Missouri: St. Charles, St. Louis, Poplar Bluff, Kansas City, Cape Girardeau, Joplin; Arkansas: Hold for Ft. Smith [this appears tentative]; Kansas: Harper, Columbus, Fort Scott, Chetopa, Oswego; Pennsylvania: Coatesville, Williamsport; Connecticut: Stafford Springs; Maryland: Baltimore; North Carolina: Tarboro; South Carolina: Columbia; Alabama: Montgomery, Eufaula; Tenn.: Chattanooga, Lebanon; Miss.: Jackson, Natchez, Greenville; Kentucky: Lawrenceburg, Georgetown; and Texas: Henderson.

115. *MW*, November 1893: 9. The release stated that "Mr. Webb expects (Insha-Allah) to go to Rochester, N.Y., to lecture on the 27th inst. [i.e., the present month], and from thence to Chicago, St. Louis, St. Joseph, Kansas City, Grand Rapids and Ann Arbor, Mich." It added that he had openings for February and March and would "accept invitations to lecture, free of charge except for his traveling expenses."

116. *MWVI*, January 1895: 4. The following month, Webb continued to advertise his lectures, informing readers that there were "still a few open dates in March and April of this year." See *MWVI*, February 1895: 4.

117. "For the Faith of Islam." See Osman, "The Story" (1944), 5–6.

118. "Interview of a Correspondent," in Webb, *Lectures on Islam*, 32.

119. See Pool, *Studies in Mohammedanism*, xiii–xiv, 394–404.

120. "The American Moslem Institute," *MWVI*, January 1895: 4.

121. Ryan, *H. P. Blavatsky*, chap. 18.

122. "Muhammad Webb's Mission."

123. Osman, "The Story" (1944), 6.

124. OA, Document B. The name of the California town is not clear. The transliteration of the Ottoman script reads as "*Pô'e Balô'da Qâlîfôrniyâ'da*": "in Pô'e Balô in California," which appears most likely a reference to Pueblo. Other towns also come to mind but are less likely: Palo Alto, San Pablo, Montebello, and Dos Palos. Pueblo, Palo Alto, and San Pablo are all in the Bay Area. Dos Pallos lies about fifty miles southeast of San Jose, and Montebello is in Los Angeles.

125. *MWVI*, November 1895: 2.

126. Turner, *Islam*, 65.

127. Muhammad, "Muslims in the United States," 199.

128. Osman, "The Story" (1944), 6.

129. Ibid.

130. Ibid.

131. OA, Document B.

132. Osman, "The Story" (1944), 6.

133. *MWVI*, April 1895: 2.

134. Ibid., June 1895: 2.

135. Ibid., March 1895: 3.

136. See ibid., October 1895: 2; November 1895: 3; February 1896: 2; January 1896: 2.

137. "The True Faith," *MWVI*, January 1895: 1.

CHAPTER 8

1. See "Special Notice," *MWVI*, October 1895: 2. Regarding the primacy of the printed word in the mission's conception, see also "Muhammad Webb's Mission," Poston assumes mistakenly that Webb's mission relied exclusively on the printed word, avoiding direct contact with the public (*Islamic Da'wah*, 135).

2. *MWVI*, January 1896: 3.

3. "Interview of a Correspondent," in Webb, *Lectures on Islam*, 32.

4. Noll, *The Old Religion*, 101.

5. Mills, *One Hundred Years of Theosophy*, 1–2, 8; Tweed, *The American Encounter*, 40; Marty, *The Infidel*, 75.

6. See Osman, "The Story" (1944), 5.

7. See "Not a Blessing to Asiatics," *MW*, November 1893: 17; *MWVI*, February 1895: 2, and July 1895: 2.

8. Harvard confirmed that the books had been received as a gift from Webb.

9. See Nyang, *Islam in the United States*, 103–105, 112.

10. See Webb, *The Three Lectures*, 7, 10, 21, 24, 26, 32–33, and 40.

11. See Khan, "Mohammed Alexander Russell Webb," 17.

12. Webb, "The Better Way," 7.

13. See Webb, *The Three Lectures*, 7, 10, 21, 24, 26, 32–33, and 40.

14. Khan, "Mohammed Alexander Russell Webb," 10–11, and n. 21.

15. See Ali, "Preface," 5, and frontispiece.

16. Webb, *The Three Lectures; Islam: A Lecture;* and *Lectures on Islam*.

17. See Webb Diary, 19 October 1892.

18. Ibid., 14 November 1892.

NOTES TO PAGES 184–193

19. Ibid., 26 November 1892.

20. See, for example, ibid., 3 December 1892.

21. See ibid.

22. Ibid., 6 and 7 October 1892.

23. See ibid., 19 October 1892; Webb, *Lectures on Islam*, 19–29.

24. Webb, *Lectures on Islam*, 19, 21–22.

25. Ibid., 21–24. The "procrustean bed" is a well-known image from Greek mythology. The giant Procrustes forced travelers to sleep in one of two beds of unequal length. He would stretch their legs to fit the longer bed or cut them off to fit the shorter one.

26. Ibid., 25.

27. Ibid., 26, 29.

28. Webb, *The Three Lectures*, 25; "Islam" (Bombay); Webb, *Lectures on Islam*.

29. Webb, *The Three Lectures*, 26.

30. Ibid. The six articles are belief in God, his prophets, the revealed books, the angels, the last judgment, and divine foreordination.

31. Ibid., 27. The five pillars are the declaration of faith, ritual prayer, alms, fasting, and pilgrimage.

32. Ibid., 38.

33. Webb, "Philosophic Islam," 51.

34. Ibid., 50–51.

35. Ibid., 40.

36. Ibid., 41–44.

37. Ibid., 46–47.

38. Ibid., 48–50.

39. Webb Diary, 11 December 1892.

40. Webb, "The Better Way," 9–10.

41. Ibid., 13.

42. Ibid., 8, 21–22.

43. Tocqueville, *Democracy in America*, 1: 198.

44. Based on personal visit to the collection, January 2001.

45. See Khan, "Mohammed Alexander Russell Webb," 11–12, nn. 22 and 23.

46. "The Death of the Prophet," *MW*, November 1893: 4.

47. Tunison, "Mohammed Alexander Russell Webb," 17; Osman, "The Story" (1944), 5; and Bektashi, "Mohammed Alexander Russell Webb," unnumbered.

48. "To My Oriental Brothers," *MWVI*, January 1895: 4.

49. "Our Illustration," *MW*, October 1893: 1.

50. "Our Prophet's Tomb," *MW*, October 1893: 11.

51. "The Alhamra," *MW*, November 1893: 11.

52. "The Islamic Propaganda."

53. "News Notes," *MW*, November 1893: 12.

54. Nyang, *Islam*, 103.

55. See *MW*, October and November 1893: 1.

56. See Osman, "The Story" (1944), 5.

57. See Webb, *The Three Lectures*, advertisement on back cover. Daily newspapers around the time sold for 5 cents a copy but were generally about four

pages long. See Hyde and Conard, *Encyclopedia of the History of St. Louis*, 1: 1631.

58. Browne, "The Evidences of Islam," *MW*, November 1893: 1–3.

59. See *MW*, October 1893: 13, 15; and November 1893: 8–9, 12, 17.

60. Ibid., November 1893: 16.

61. "Islam in Japan," *MW*, November 1893: 13.

62. "News Notes," *MW*, November 1893: 12.

63. See "What Is Feminine Progress?" *MW*, November 1893: 8.

64. *MWVI*, February 1895: 1.

65. *MW*, November 1893: 8.

66. *MWVI*, March 1895: 3.

67. *MW*, October 1893: 5.

68. Ibid., 16.

69. "The Revenge of Genius," *MW*, November 1893: 10.

70. *MWVI*, May 1895: 2.

71. Ibid., November 1895: 3.

72. Ingersoll toured the United States, lecturing on biblical inaccuracies and contradictions. "Why I Am an Agnostic," his most popular lecture, preached his version of "practical atheism," which left open the questions of God's existence and life after death. Ingersoll was also an epicure and hosted lavish dinners, arguing that the objectionable elements in Christian dogma were the result of "coarse food." See Melton, *Religious Leaders*, 268; Marty, *The Infidel*, 137–143, 148; Fishburn, *The Fatherhood of God*, 4; Rose, *Victorian America*, 127; and Tweed, *The American Encounter*, 61.

73. "Always Truthful," *MW*, October 1893: 12.

74. *MWVI*, February 1895: 3.

75. Ibid., April 1895: 2.

76. Ferris, "Immigrant Muslim Communities," 210.

77. Eraslan, "Muhammed A. R. Webb'in," 87–88.

78. "Muhammed Webb Locked Out," *New York Times*, 14 July 1894: 5.

79. *MWVI*, January, February, March, and April 1895: 4.

80. *MWVI*, October 1895: 2.

81. Ibid.

82. "Our Plans," *MWVI*, January 1895: 2.

83. *MWVI*, January 1895: 2–3.

84. See ibid., May 1895: 2; June 1895: 2; July 1895: 2; September 1895: 2; November 1895: 1; and February 1896: 1.

85. Ibid., February 1895: 1.

86. Ibid., 2.

87. Ibid., September 1895: 2.

88. Ibid., February 1895: 2.

89. Ibid., April 1895: 3.

90. Ibid., March 1895: 3.

91. Ibid., February 1895: 2. Webb clarified that he would continue to send the paper gratis to "poor Mussulmans, who cannot afford to pay for them, and to exchanges."

92. Ibid., March 1895: 3.

93. Ibid.

94. Ibid., April 1895: 3.

95. Ibid., February 1895: 3.

96. Ibid., July 1895: 2.

97. Ibid.

98. Ibid., March 1895: 3.

99. Ibid., April 1895: 2. See also September 1895: 2; October 1895: 3.

100. Ibid., April 1895: 2.

101. Ibid., February 1895: 3. The issue of old subscriptions was an important concern. Webb received many letters from India inquiring whether old subscriptions to the *Moslem World* would be honored for copies of the *Moslem World and Voice of Islam*, to which Webb responded that subscribers to the old journal would receive the *Moslem World and Voice of Islam* "for a period which will reimburse them for the amount of their unfulfilled subscription, or they may take the amount in books, from out Book List." See *MWVI*, June 1895: 2.

102. "To My Oriental Brothers," *MWVI*, January 1895: 3–4.

103. Sultan Abd al-Hamid II assumed the Ottoman throne on September 1, 1876, and ruled until the Young Turks deposed him on April 28, 1909. Intelligent and hardworking, he was among the most approachable of Ottoman sultans. He blended his absolutism with a modernist, pan-Islamic ideology with the hopes that it would revive his empire. Unlike earlier Ottoman sultans, Abd al-Hamid sought to expand the central powers of the sultan at the expense of the grand vizier, "the Sublime Port." He made extensive use of the secret police and imposed censorship on the Turkish press, as inept as it was severe, barring words like "fatherland" for fear it might stir nationalist opposition to the dynasty and opposition to the Islamic religion. "Liberty, explosion, bomb, regicide, murder, plot," and similar words were also proscribed. Abd al-Hamid undertook a number of building projects, especially railways, the most famous of which was the Hijaz Railway to Medina, completed in 1908 and destroyed by Lawrence of Arabia a few years later. Europeans branded Abd al-Hamid as the "Red Sultan" after his suppression of revolts in Macedonia, Crete, and in Armenian regions of Turkey. The atrocities began before his time but lasted through and after it. Although Abd al-Hamid may not have been directly implicated in the violence, he did little to prevent it. See "'Abd al-Hamîd II," in *EI*, 1: 63.

104. For praise of the sultan, see *MWVI*, May 1895: 2; June 1895: 3; December 1895: 1, 4; February 1896: 1. The Armenian question did appear in the *Moslem World* (see "A Tribute to Islam," *MW*, November 1893: 7) but was conspicuous throughout the *Moslem World and Voice of Islam*. See *MWVI*, February 1895: 3; March 1895: 2; April 1895: 1; December 1895: 2; and January 1896: 1.

105. "Special Notice," *MWVI*, October 1895: 2. See December 1895: 2.

106. "Special Notice," *MWVI*, November 1895: 2.

107. Ibid., January 1896: 3.

108. Khan, "Mohammed Alexander Russell Webb," 10.

109. Melton, "Webb, Muhammad Alexander Russel," 304.

110. *MW*, October 1893: 17.

111. See Khan, "Mohammed Alexander Russell Webb," 10.

112. Ibid.

113. Webb, *Islam in America*, 7.

114. Ibid., 10.

115. Ibid., 33.

116. See ibid., 43-45.

117. Ibid., 51-55.

118. Ibid., 43.

119. Ibid., 45.

120. Ibid., 26-27, and "Not a Personal God," *MWVI*, June 1895: 4. For al-Ghazali (d. 1111), one of the greatest scholars and religious reformers in Islamic history, see "Al-Ghazâlî, Abû Hâmid Muhammad b. Muhammad al-Tûsî," in *EI*, 2: 1038.

121. See Webb, *A Guide to Namaz*, 14.

122. Ibid., 7.

123. See Dannin, *Black Pilgrimage*, 43-44.

124. Webb, *A Guide to Namaz*, 3, 6.

125. Ibid., 5.

126. See *MWVI*, January 1895: 1. Webb stated: "The word Mussulman or Moslem is applied to one whose religion is Islam, *i.e.*, submission and obedience to one God, the creator of all things."

127. Webb, *A Guide to Namaz*, 5.

128. *A Few Facts* is sixty-seven pages in length, making it comparable in size to *Islam in America*. *The Armenian Troubles* is thirty-five pages long. *A Few Facts* was ascribed to an "American Observer," and *The Armenian Troubles* was attributed to a "Correspondent."

129. *MWVI*, May 1895: 2.

130. See "Armîniya" in *EI*, 1: 634.

131. "In Defence of the Right," *MWVI*, December 1895: 1 and 4; and "To His Imperial Majesty, Sultan Abdul Hamid II," *MWVI*, February 1896: 1. Webb cited lengthy pro-Ottoman statements on the Armenian issue from the pope and the Armenian patriarch and advertised another pro-Turkish pamphlet on the question by a "Señor S. Ximenez," described as a Spanish traveler and fellow of the Geographical Society of England. Webb also reprinted Ximenez's pamphlet in the main body of *The Armenian Troubles*. See *MWVI*, January 1895: 3; August 1895: 1; and Khan, "Mohammed Alexander Russell Webb," 28-29.

132. *MWVI*, May 1895: 3.

133. Ibid., 3-4.

134. An American Observer [Webb], *A Few Facts*, 7.

135. Ibid., 23, 30.

136. Ibid., 11.

137. Ibid., 37.

138. Ibid., 40.

139. Ibid., 52-56

140. Ibid., 56, 62-63, 65.

141. *MWVI*, January 1896: 1.

142. A Correspondent [Webb], *The Armenian Troubles*, 8.

143. Ibid., 8.

144. Christian Armenians constituted one of the oldest and most important Christian minorities of the Ottoman empire. Until 1828, the Ottomans controlled all Armenian regions in Anatolia, the Caucasus, and Central Asia, but ceded large parts of Eastern Armenia to the Russian empire that year, which made the Armenians a point of political contention in Russian and Western bids for greater influence in Ottoman realms under the auspices of defending Armenian interests. The Armenian issue became an international issue from the closing decades of the nineteenth century through World War I, and its magnitude at the time was not unlike the Arab-Israeli crisis today. It remains hotly contested between Turks and Armenians, and relevant sections of the Ottoman Archives have yet to be opened to the public. The crisis passed through different levels of intensity, reaching its peak during World War I with the alleged "Armenian massacres" of 1915. See "Armîniya" in *EI*, 1: 634.

145. A Correspondent [Webb], *The Armenian Troubles*, 9 and 18.

146. Ibid., 9. Sassoun (Sasun) is in the Kurdish region of Turkey's Eastern Taurus Mountains not far from Lake Van. It had a large Armenian population and was at the center of the ethnic troubles of 1895–1896.

147. An American Observer [Webb], *A Few Facts*, 57.

148. A Correspondent [Webb], *The Armenian Troubles*, 10.

149. Ibid., 9.

150. Ibid., 14.

151. An American Observer [Webb], *A Few Facts*, 66–67.

CHAPTER 9

1. See Chappell, *Expomuseum*, "History," "1851–1878" and "1884–1900"; Zwick, *World's Fairs*, "Homepage" and "Centennial Exposition."

2. See Schlereth, *Victorian America*, 174; Chappell, *Expomuseum*, "History," "1851–1878," and "1884–1900"; Zwick, *World's Fairs*, "Homepage" and "Centennial Exposition."

3. See Schlereth, *Victorian America*, 174; Chappell, *Expomuseum*, "History," "1851–1878," and "1884–1900"; Zwick, *World's Fairs*, "Homepage" and "Centennial Exposition."

4. See Marlowe, "Zalabia and the First Ice-Cream Cone," 2–5, and Younis, "The First Muslims," 21. As Marlowe points out, there are other claimants, although all versions "involve the same setting, characters, and plot: an Exposition ice-cream vendor who runs out of cups and a Syrian vendor (or Turkish—the terms were roughly interchangeable at the time) who saves the day with a combination of *zalabia* and ambition." Hamawi's story is based on a letter he wrote to the *Ice Cream Trade Journal* in 1924, and the International Association of Ice Cream Manufacturers has generally recognized its validity. Hamawi was a Syrian Muslim from Damascus. On a sweltering July day at the fair, an American ice cream concessionaire next to Hamawi was selling ice cream in bowls, as was the custom, but the muggy heat made the ice cream melt almost instantaneously. Hamawi's stand was selling sugared doughnuts (*zalābiyya*) and thin pancakes (*qaṭā'if*; colloquial: *'aṭā'if*), generally eaten with confectionary. Hamawi demonstrated to the unhappy ice cream vendor that he could solve his problem

by rolling Hamawi's wafer-thin Syrian pancakes into cones and putting the ice cream inside. The ice cream would melt more slowly, and the cone would be even more delicious when it melted. Marlowe's account, the standard American version of the story, is that the vendor ran out of cups. This early Muslim-American cooperation gave birth to the all-American ice cream cone. Hamawi's pancake ice cream cones were so popular that he had to hire a host of Arab-American immigrants to grill more pancakes.

5. See Younis, "The First Muslims," 21.

6. Ibid., 19. Younis contends that Amir 'Abd al-Qadir, the Algerian resistance leader against French colonial occupation, was an official guest of honor and that President James Buchanan presented him with a fine pair of gold-plated pistols and that fountains were built in 'Abd al-Qadir's honor. Younis's documentation is obscure, and there is obviously some confusion. Ulysses S. Grant was president during the 1876 Exposition; Buchanan had died eight years before. There is no evidence that 'Abd al-Qadir came to the United States or attended the Centennial. Both Britain and the United States sent "a brace of pistols inlaid with gold" to 'Abd al-Qadir out of appreciation for his intervention to save Christian lives in the Damascus riots of the 1860s. See Blunt, *Desert Hawk*; Boutaleb, *L'émir Abd el-Kader*; Churchill, *The Life of Abdel Kader*; Clayton, *The Phantom Caravan*; Danziger, *Abd al-Qadir and the Algerian*; Klein, *President James Buchanan*; and Elbert Smith, *The Presidency of James Buchanan*.

7. Seager, *The World's Parliament of Religions*, 72.

8. Younis, "The First Muslims in America," 21.

9. Ziolkowski, "The First World's Parliament of Religions," 3.

10. Ibid.

11. Abu-Lughod, *New York, Chicago, Los Angeles*, 109.

12. Menand, *The Metaphysical Club*, 292; and Turner, *Islam in the African-American Experience*, 62. Menand puts the fair's attendance around twenty-seven thousand.

13. Ziolkowski, "The First World's Parliament of Religions," 8.

14. Abu-Lughod, *New York, Chicago, Los Angeles*, 100.

15. See Seager, *The World's Parliament of Religions*, 23; and Abu-Lughod, *New York, Chicago, Los Angeles*, 53, 100.

16. Abu-Lughod, *New York, Chicago, Los Angeles*, 100, 109.

17. Seager, *The World's Parliament of Religions*, 44.

18. Houghton, *Neely's History*, 22. Webb was impressed by Rev. Alfred Momerie's attitude toward Islam at the Congress of Liberal Religion in Chicago in 1895, and described him as speaking "most reverently and respectfully of our Prophet." See *MWVI*, August 1895: 3.

19. Ziolkowski, "The First World's Parliament of Religions," 8.

20. Ibid.

21. See *Weather People and History*, "The Windy City." The nickname probably antedates the fair but became popularized as a consequence of the manner in which Chicago bid for it.

22. Abu-Lughod, *New York, Chicago, Los Angeles*, 100.

23. Ziolkowki, "The First World's Parliament of Religions," 3; Jack, "The World's Parliament of Religions," 1.

24. Jack, "The World's Parliament of Religions," 1.

25. Ziolkowski, "The First World's Parliament of Religions," 3.

26. Jack, "The World's Parliament of Religions," 2.

27. Menand, *The Metaphysical Club*, 292; and Schelereth, *Victorian America*, 175.

28. Jack, "The World's Parliament of Religions," 2–3; Abu-Lughod, *New York, Chicago, Los Angeles*, 109.

29. Seager, *The World's Parliament of Religions*, 194; and Ziolkowski, "The First World's Parliament of Religions," 3.

30. Houghton, *Neely's History*, 19–20; and Jack, "The World's Parliament of Religions," 2–3.

31. Ziolkowski, "The First World's Parliament of Religions," 2–4.

32. Seager, *The World's Parliament of Religions*, 193.

33. Ibid., 23.

34. Ibid., 24; and Ziolkowski, "The First World's Parliament of Religions," 2–4.

35. Seager, *The World's Parliament of Religions*, 52–54.

36. Ibid., 16, 47.

37. Ibid., 47, 52–53.

38. See Campbell, *Campbell's Illustrated History*, 2: 416; Younis, "The First Muslims," 19–20.

39. See Seager, *The World's Parliament of Religions*, 56–57; Campbell, *Campbell's Illustrated History*, 2: 416–417; Younis, "The First Muslims," 19–20.

40. See the *New York Times*, 14 July 1894: 9; Seager, *The World's Parliament of Religions*, 193; Menand, *The Metaphysical Club*, 292.

41. Schlereth, *Victorian America*, 175; Seager, *The World's Parliament of Religions*, 193.

42. Seager, *The World's Parliament of Religions*, 193–194.

43. Ibid., 206.

44. Menand, *The Metaphysical Club*, 292; Schelereth, *Victorian America*, 175.

45. Ibid.; Seager, *The World's Parliament of Religions*, 194.

46. Seager, *The World's Parliament of Religions*, 193; Menand, *The Metaphysical Club*, 292.

47. Seager, *The World's Parliament of Religions*, 194.

48. Houghton, *Neely's History*, 19–20; Jack, "The World's Parliament of Religions," 1–3; Abu-Lughod, *New York, Chicago, Los Angeles*, 105.

49. Bonet-Maury, *Le congrès des religions*, 15.

50. See Seager, "The World's Parliament of Religions," abstract; and Houghton, *Neely's History*, 20–21.

51. See Bonney, "The Genesis of the World's Religious Congresses," 74–78.

52. Seager, *The World's Parliament of Religions*, 93–94.

53. Ibid., 234–235.

54. Bonet-Maury, *Le congrès des religions*, 13–14.

55. *MWVI*, March 1895: 2. Webb commended Jones's journal, *Unity*, highly: "We advise our Oriental brothers to read *Unity*; it will do them good." He commended Jones for a sermon he gave in Chicago on the Islamic "Pilgrimage," in which he "spoke most kindly and fraternally of this Islamic pillar of practice." Webb asserted that Jones was a witness for Muslims that "at least one Church-Christian minister in

America [was] not afraid to speak kindly of Islam from his pulpit." See *MWVI*, November 1895: 3.

56. Seager, *The World's Parliament of Religions*, 95–96.

57. Jones, *A Chorus of Faith*, inset.

58. Seager, *The World's Parliament of Religions*, 93.

59. See Bonney, "The Genesis," 89; and Barrows, *The World's Parliament of Religions*, 1: 18.

60. See Houghton, *Neely's History*, 19; Jack, "The World's Parliament of Religions," 3.

61. Seager, *The World's Parliament of Religions*, 203.

62. Ziolkowski, "The First World's Parliament of Religions," 4.

63. *Inter Ocean*, 28 September 1893.

64. Druyvesteyn, "The World's Parliament of Religions," 142.

65. See Jack, "The 1893 World's Parliament of Religions," 9.

66. Barrows, *The World's Parliament of Religions*, 1: 20.

67. Sayyed Ameer Ali—also referred to in this text as Ameer Ali and Justice Ameer Ali—was known for his modernist interpretations of Islam, which were generally well received in the West, where his writing generally created a favorable impression of Islam. *The Spirit of Islam* first appeared in 1891 and had a profound effect on Webb. See "Amir 'Ali, Sayyid," in *EI*, 1: 443. Seager, *The Dawn of Religious Pluralism*, 247; Jack, "The World's Parliament of Religions," 3; Jack, "The 1893 World's Parliament of Religions," 9.

68. *Inter Ocean*, 21 September 1893; Houghton, *Neely's History*, 498.

69. Barrows, *The World's Parliament of Religions*, 1: 18.

70. Bonet-Maury, *Le congrès des religions*, 321.

71. Barrows, *The World's Parliament of Religions*, 1: x; see Kidd, "Anecdotes," 14.

72. Fannie Barrier Williams was part of the African Methodist Episcopal delegation and protested "against the attempt of white Christians to establish the mean sentiment of caste in religion and degrade [blacks] to a footstool position at the shrine of Christian worship," noting how Christianity, "like every other force in America," had been essentially "an instrument and servant of slavery." She elaborated on how slavery had destroyed the black family, denouncing the "demoralizing gospel preached to the American slave for two hundred years" and speaking of how "mothers saw their babes sold by Christians on the auction block in order to raise money to send missionaries to foreign lands." Barrows deleted most of Williams's criticisms, leaving little indication of the original substance. See Williams, "What Can Religion Further Do to Advance the Condition of the American Negro?" in Barrows, "What Can Religion Do to Advance the Condition of the American Negro?" 2: 1114–1115 (her photograph appears on page 2: 1146); compare *Inter Ocean*, 24 September 1893.

73. Druyvesteyn, "The World's Parliament of Religions," 65; Kidd, "Anecdotes," 14.

74. See Barrows, *The World's Parliament of Religions*, 2: 1590.

75. Seager, *The World's Parliament of Religions*, 96.

76. Jones, *A Chorus of Faith*, 176.

77. Houghton, *Neely's History*, frontispiece.

78. *MWVI*, July 1895: 2.

79. Seager, *The World's Parliament of Religions*, 89.

80. See Bonet-Maury, *Le congrès des religions*, 320. The Pentecost is an ancient Christian feast based on the New Testament with earlier Jewish parallels. It is held on the seventh Sunday after Easter and commemorates the descent of the Holy Spirit upon the apostles in preparation for carrying the message of Christ to the nations. In reference to the World's Parliament of Religions, the Pentecost metaphor reflected millennial expectations that the event would prove a universal spiritual revival, culminating in a conversion of non-Christian peoples and faiths to Christianity.

81. Seager, "The World's Parliament of Religions," abstract.

82. Houghton, *Neely's History*, 20–21.

83. Carus, *The Dawn*, 18–19.

84. Ziolkowski, "The First World's Parliament of Religions," 4.

85. Houghton, *Neely's History*, 57–58, 772.

86. Ibid., 28.

87. Ibid., 22–23.

88. Seager, *The World's Parliament of Religions*, iii.

89. Barrows, *The World's Parliament of Religions*, 2: 1182.

90. Ibid., 1: 20–22; Jack, "The World's Parliament of Religions," 3, 9.

91. Druyvesteyn, "The World's Parliament of Religions," 164–165.

92. Ibid.

93. Cook's two presentations were titled "The Worth of the Bible, or Columnar Truths in Scripture" and "Certainties in Religion." See Barrows, *The World's Parliament of Religions*, 2: 1072–1075; *Inter Ocean*, 15 and 21 September 1893; Marty, *Pilgrims*, 329; Kidd, "Anecdotes," 3.

94. *Inter Ocean*, 21 September 1893; Marty, *Pilgrims*, 329; Kidd, "Anecdotes," 3.

95. *MW*, October 1893: 8.

96. Kidd, "Anecdotes," 3.

97. Houghton, *Neely's History*, 19–20; Jack, "The World's Parliament of Religions," 7; Bonet-Maury, *Le congrés des religions*, 16.

98. Bonet-Maury, *Le congrés des religions*, 16; Houghton, *Neely's History*, 28; Lawrence, "A History of the 1893 Parliament," 1; Ziolkowski, "The First World's Parliament of Religions," 4; Seager, *Parliament of The World's Religions*, iii.

99. Bonet-Maury, *Le congrès des religions*, 28.

100. Ibid.

101. See Kidd, "Anecdotes," 13.

102. *Inter Ocean*, 21 September 1893.

103. Seager, *The World's Parliament of Religions*, 174, 262; Houghton, *Neely's History*, 64; Jackson, *Vedanta for the West*, 26–27.

104. Seager, *The World's Parliament of Religions*, iii, 9.

105. Houghton, *Neely's History*, 22–23.

106. See Seager, *The World's Parliament of Religions*, 96.

107. Ibid., 206.

108. Ibid., 11–12.

109. Catholics and Jews filled the slums of America's big cities during the last half of the nineteenth century. Initially unwelcome, they remained largely social outsiders. The parliament helped them find psychological space and avenues of "respectability" beyond the tenements into the American mainstream. By the end

of World War II, more than half a century later, Jews and Catholics had been incorporated into the matrix of American religious culture and began to enjoy a social legitimacy comparable to that of Protestants. See ibid., iii, 11–12.

110. See ibid., 247; Bonet-Maury, *Le congrès des religions*, 119–121; and Jack, "The World's Parliament of Religions," 3, 9. Jack mistakenly observes: "Two [Muslims] came from India, but the Muslim who spoke was a convert from America. The two Indians were Jinda Ram and Siddhu Ram. Both were on the platform at the opening ceremonies, but neither gave addresses." The Rams, as their names indicate, were Hindus and not Muslims. At the time, it was customary for Hindus to wear turbans, as did Swami Vivekananda. Perhaps their dress convinced Jack that they were Muslims.

111. Sayyed Ali Belghrami graduated from Patna College in Sanskrit in 1874 and continued studies primarily in science at the University of London. He mastered a number of ancient and modern Indian tongues in addition to English, French, German, Arabic, Persian, and Latin. The Indian government gave him the honorific title of *Shams al-'Ulamā'* (the sun of the scholars). His fame rested chiefly on his language skills as a translator from French and English into Urdu. See "Bilgrami," in *EI*, 1: 1219.

112. Seager, *The Dawn of Religious Pluralism*, 247.

113. Ziriklî, *Al-A'lâm*, 8: 198; Kahhâla, *Mu'jam al-Mu'allifîn*, 13: 248. Webb probably established contact with Abou Naddara. He made reference to the latter's newspaper, *Le journal d'Abou Naddara*, and cited an account there of "a young French Orientalist, who made it his mission to investigate the true doctrine of Islam" and embraced the faith. See *MW*, November 1893: 9.

114. See Abou Naddara, "The Koran and Other Scriptures: Letter to the Parliament from J. Sanua Abou Naddara, Paris," in Barrows, *The World's Parliament of Religions*, 2: 1146–1148; Houghton, *Neely's History*, 653–654; *Inter Ocean*, 24 September 1893. Both Houghton and the *Inter Ocean* mistakenly render his name as "Sanna."

115. See Abou Naddara, "The Koran and Other Scriptures," in Barrows, *The World's Parliament of Religions*, 2: 1146–1148; Houghton, *Neely's History*, 653–654.

116. Compare Abou Naddara, "The Koran and Other Scriptures," in Barrows, *The World's Parliament of Religions*, 2: 1146–1148, with Houghton's, *Neely's History*, 653–654; *Inter Ocean*, 24 September 1893.

117. Bonet-Maury, *Le congrès des religions*, 17, 119, 190.

118. Druyvesteyn, "The World's Parliament of Religions," 223; see also Barrows, *The World's Parliament of Religions*, 2: 1590; Bonney, "The Genesis of the World's Religious Congress," 85.

119. See *Inter Ocean*, 16 September 1893.

120. See Druyvesteyn, "The World's Parliament of Religions," 223; Seager, *The World's Parliament of Religions*, 157.

121. Barrows, *The World's Parliament of Religions*, 1: 565; Houghton, *Neely's History*, 235.

122. Barrows, *The World's Parliament of Religions*, 1: 572; Houghton, *Neely's History*, 239–240.

123. Barrows, *The World's Parliament of Religions*, 1: 578; Houghton, *Neely's History*, 243–244.

124. See "Al-Nasafî," in *EI*, 7: 969; Barrows, *The World's Parliament of Religions*, 1: 569; Houghton, *Neely's History*, 237.

125. Barrows, *The World's Parliament of Religions*, 1: 570–571; Houghton, *Neely's History*, 238–239.

126. Barrows, *The World's Parliament of Religions*, 1: 572; Houghton, *Neely's History*, 240.

127. Barrows, *The World's Parliament of Religions*, 1: 574; Houghton, *Neely's History*, 240.

128. Barrows, *The World's Parliament of Religions*, 1: 577; Houghton, *Neely's History*, 242.

129. Barrows, *The World's Parliament of Religions*, 1: 575–576; Houghton, *Neely's History*, 241–242.

130. Barrows, *The World's Parliament of Religions*, 1: 579–580; Houghton, *Neely's History*, 244–245.

131. Barrows, *The World's Parliament of Religions*, 1: 579–580; Houghton, *Neely's History*, 244–245. Compare Seager, *The World's Parliament of Religions*, 157–158.

132. Barrows, *The World's Parliament of Religions*, 1: 579–580; Houghton, *Neely's History*, 244–245. Compare Seager, *The World's Parliament of Religions*, 157–158.

133. Carus, *The Dawn of a New Religious Era*, 14–15.

134. See Macfie, *Orientalism*, 1–8; Kurzman, *Modernist Islam*, 3–27, 277–303.

135. See Barrows, *The World's Parliament*, 2: 1587.

136. Post, "The Ethics of Islâm," in Barrows, *The World's Parliament of Religions*, 2: 1096–1098; Houghton, *Neely's History*, 613–115; *Inter Ocean*, 23 September 1893.

137. *MW*, October 1893: 8.

138. Houghton, *Neely's History*, 613–615; Barrows, *The World's Parliament of Religions*, 2: 1096–1098; *Inter Ocean*, 23 September 1893.

139. See Druyvesteyn, "The World's Parliament of Religions," 224. Compare Post, "The Ethics of Islâm" (Barrows), 2: 1096–1098; (Houghton), 613–615; *Inter Ocean*, 23 September 1893.

140. Houghton, *Neely's History*, 613; *Inter Ocean*, 23 September 1893 (personal translation).

141. *MW*, October 1893: 8.

142. See Seager, *The World's Parliament of Religions*, 96.

143. "The Women of Turkey," *MW*, October 1893: 5.

144. Ibid.; and *MW VI*, January 1895: 4.

145. Barrows, *The World's Parliament of Religions*, 2: 1587. His photograph appears on page 2: 1245.

146. See *Inter Ocean*, 21 September 1893; Herant Kiretchjian, "A Voice from the Young Men of the Orient," in Barrows, *The World's Parliament of Religions*, 2: 1276–1279; Houghton, *Neely's History*, 498, 806–810.

147. *Inter Ocean*, 26 September 1893.

148. Houghton, *Neely's History*, 654; *Inter Ocean*, 24 September 1893.

149. "The Death of the Prophet," *MW*, November 1893: 4.

150. Houghton, *Neely's History*, 699.

151. Ibid., 700; and *MW*, October 1893, insert page. Webb spells Jibara's name with a "G," Gibara, and renders the book's title as *Unity in Faiths and Harmony in Religions*.

152. Houghton, *Neely's History*, 699–700.

153. Ibid., 700.

154. Barrows, *The World's Parliament of Religions*, 1: 196, 202. Carpenter's citation was a marred rendition of the Qur'anic verse: "To each there is a particular orientation to which he shall turn. So strive with each other in doing [various types of] good deeds. Wherever you may be, God will ultimately bring you back together: In truth, God has power over all things" (Qur'an 2: 148).

155. Barrows, *The World's Parliament of Religions*, 1: 210.

156. Houghton, *Neely's History*, 275.

157. See Bonet-Maury, *Le congrès des religions*, 148–149.

158. *Inter Ocean*, 16 September 1893.

159. Barrows, *The World's Parliament of Religions*, 1: 196, 202; Webb, "The Spirit of Islam" (Barrows), 2: 989–996; (Houghton), 459–464.

160. *Inter Ocean*, 21 September 1893.

161. Ibid., 22 September 1893.

162. See *Inter Ocean*, 21 and 22 September 1893; Kidd, "Anecdotes," 13.

163. *Inter Ocean*, 22 September 1893; Webb, "The Influence of Social Condition" (Houghton); Webb, "The Influence of Islam on Social Conditions" (Barrows), 2: 1046–1052; Seager, *The World's Parliament of Religions*, 46.

164. Bonet-Maury, *Le congrès des religions*, 15.

165. Webb, "The Spirit of Islam" (Barrows), 2: 989; (Houghton), *Neely's History*, 459.

166. Shalton, "Mohammed Alexander Russell Webb," 12.

167. *Inter Ocean*, 21 September 1893; Webb, "The Spirit of Islam" (Barrows), 2: 989; (Houghton), 460.

168. Webb, "The Influence of Social Condition" (Houghton), 544.

169. Webb, "The Spirit of Islam" (Barrows), 2: 989; (Houghton), 460.

170. See *Inter Ocean*, 21 September 1893; Kidd, "Anecdotes," 13.

171. Webb, "The Spirit of Islam" (Barrows), 2: 990; (Houghton), 460.

172. Compare Webb, "The Spirit of Islam" (Houghton), 459–464, and in (Barrows), 2: 989–996.

173. *Inter Ocean*, 22 September 1893; Webb, "The Influence of Social Condition" (Houghton), 544–550; Webb, "The Influence of Islam on Social Conditions" (Barrows), 2: 1046–1052.

174. Compare Webb, "The Influence of Social Condition" (Houghton), 544–550, with Webb, "The Influence of Islam on Social Conditions" (Barrows), 2: 1046.

175. Barrows, *The World's Parliament of Religions*, 1: 221. Barrows did not delete Webb's entire reference to medieval Islamic civilization, only the following words about Spain: "Her fertile provinces, rendered doubly prolific by the industry and engineering skill of her conquerors, bore fruit in a hundred-fold. Cities innumerable sprang up in the rich valleys of the Guadalquiver and Gaudiana, whose names, and names only, still commemorate the vanished glories of their past." He deletes Webb's reference to Muslim "ship-building" and his remarks: "Whatsoever makes a kingdom great and prosperous, whatsoever tends to refinement and civilization was found in Moslem Spain." See Houghton, *Neely's History*, 549–550.

176. See Jones, *A Chorus of Faith*, 176; Webb, "The Influence of Social Condition," (Houghton), 544–545; Webb, "The Influence of Islam on Social Conditions" (Barrows), 2: 1046; *Inter Ocean*, 22 September 1893.

177. Bonet-Maury, *Le congrès des religions*, 190, 201–202.

178. Carus, *The Dawn of a New Religious Era*, 16.

179. Ibid., 7. As for Carus's participation, see Druyvesteyn, "The World's Parliament of Religions," 171.

180. Seager, *The Dawn of Religious Pluralism*, 247–248.

181. *Inter Ocean*, 21 September 1893; Webb, "The Spirit of Islam" (Houghton), 459–460; (Barrows), 2: 989. Most of the detail is deleted from Barrows's account.

182. See "Interview of a Correspondent," in Webb, *Lectures on Islam*, 31.

183. Seager, *The Dawn of Religious Pluralism*, unnumbered inserts between 270 and 271.

184. OA, document C.

185. Shalton, "Mohammed Alexander Russell Webb," 12; Jack, "The 1893 World's Parliament of Religions," 10.

186. Ron Kidd, "Anecdotes and Descriptions," 14, quoting from *Inter Ocean*, September 22, 1893: 6.

187. Kidd, "Anecdotes," 14.

188. *Inter Ocean*, 21 and 22 September 1893.

189. Ibid., 21 September 1893; Webb, "The Spirit of Islam" (Barrows), 2: 989; (Houghton), 460.

190. See Druyvesteyn, "The World's Parliament of Religions," 65; and Jack, "The 1893 World's Parliament of Religions," 10.

191. Bonet-Maury, *Le congrès des religions*, 148.

192. *MW*, March 1895: 3.

193. Lancaster, *The Incredible World's Parliament of Religions*, 16.

194. "A California Editor," *MW* October 1893: 7.

195. Ibid.

196. *MWVI*, April 1895: 3.

197. *MW*, October 1893: 8.

198. *MWVI*, October 1895: 2.

199. Ibid., July 1895: 2.

200. *MW*, October 1893: 9.

201. Ibid., 8–9.

202. *MW*, October 1893: 8.

203. *MWVI*, March 1895: 3.

204. "*Republic* Reviews Alex Webb's Life."

205. Webb's mission was not launched at the parliament, of course, but preceded it by several months. Unlike Buddhism, Hinduism, and Islam, Baha'ism had no official presence at the parliament. Much later, during World War II, Baha'i officials declared the Christian missionary Rev. Henry Jessup's favorable mention at the parliament of their faith and the "Christ-like" teachings of Baha'-Allah as their formal debut in the United States. See Seager, *The World's Parliament of Religions*, v, 13; Perry, "The Chicago Baha'i Community," 9–10; Druyvesteyn, "The World's Parliament of Religions," 74–75.

206. "The Parliament of Religions," in *MW*, October 1893: 9.
207. Ibid.
208. Ibid., November 1893: 8.
209. Ibid., October 1893: 9.
210. Ibid., 8.
211. Ibid.
212. Ibid., 8–9.
213. Ibid.
214. Ibid.
215. Ibid., 8.
216. Ibid., 9.
217. Ibid., 8–9.
218. Ibid.

CHAPTER 10

1. See "To My Oriental Brothers," *MWVI*, January 1895: 3. Webb wrote the statement in his defense to explain why the *Moslem World* had been discontinued.
2. Ibid.
3. Eraslan, "Muhammed A. R. Webb'in," 89.
4. Based on a personal communication from Dr. Sevket Pamuk, professor of Economics at the Atatürk Institute of Modern Turkish History at Boğaziçi University, Istanbul. During the period from 1844 till World War I, one hundred Ottoman *kuruş*, a silver coinage, equaled one gold Ottoman lira. During the same period, one Ottoman lira was equivalent to £0.9 or $4.4.
5. Eraslan, "Muhammed A. R. Webb'in," 87.
6. Ibid., 89. Muhammad states that "when financial support from India became irregular, an association with the Ottoman Sultan Abdul Hamid II gained for Webb . . . an alternative source of aid," but I have not come across explicit proof of such assistance other than what has just been mentioned. See Muhammad, "Muslims," 199.
7. Eraslan, "Muhammed A. R. Webb'in," 87–88.
8. Within six months, Webb wrote in a vein recalling his earlier optimism: "There is abundant evidence that Islam, the true faith, is soon to become the universal religion." See "The True Faith," *MWVI*, January 1895: 1.
9. Eraslan, "Muhammed A. R. Webb'in," 87–89.
10. "Mohammed Webb Locked Out," *New York Times*, 14 July 1894: 5.
11. "Nafeesa Keep Breakfasts."
12. Eraslan, "Muhammed A. R. Webb'in," 89–91.
13. "Nafeesa Keep Breakfasts."
14. "Mohammed Webb Locked Out," *New York Times*, 14 July 1894: 5. See also Ferris, "Immigrant Muslim Communities," 210. Ferris writes: "Dissension within the organization ultimately undermined Webb's efforts. On July 12, 1894, Nefeesa Keep locked herself in the *Moslem World*'s editorial offices and accused Webb of financial chicanery. Keep alleged that Webb failed to pay her and other staff members, that he used misleading tactics when soliciting funds from abroad, and that he bought a

lavish farm and land in upstate Ulster County with money earmarked for spreading Islam throughout the country."

15. "Nafeesa Keep Breakfasts."

16. "Mohammed Webb Locked Out," *New York Times*, 14 July 1894: 5.

17. "Nafeesa Keep Breakfasts."

18. Ibid.

19. "Mohammed Webb Locked Out," *New York Times*, 14 July 1894: 5.

20. Eraslan, "Muhammed A. R. Webb'in," 89–91.

21. "Nafeesa Keep Breakfasts."

22. "Mrs. Keep Visits the Consul."

23. "*Republic* Reviews Alex Webb's Life."

24. Baroda and Basoda are both Indian cities, the former larger and more famous than the latter. The Urdu inscription on the nawab's photograph reproduced in the *New York Times* described him, however, as "the *ra'īs* of Basoda." *Ra'īs* was a Mughal title similar to "nawab" that was used in British India for traditional landholders. The *ra'īs* class tended to be patrons of Mughal culture, and Sayyid Ahmad Khan's reform efforts were focused on their class. See "Fall of Islam"; Ferris, "Immigrant Muslim Communities," 210–211; Case, "The Aligarh Era," 21.

25. "Fall of Islam"; Ferris, "Immigrant Muslim Communities," 210–211.

26. For exchange rates see Economic History Services, *What Was the Exchange Rate Then?* In 1895, the exchange rate for £1 was $5, inversely $1 was valued at £.2; the rates in 1893 and 1894 varied only slightly: $1 was worth £.21. I have taken the 1895 rate, since the article was written that year.

27. "Fall of Islam"; Ferris, "Immigrant Muslim Communities," 210–211.

28. Ibid.

29. Ibid.

30. See also Ferris, "Immigrant Muslim Communities," 211; Turner, *Islam*, 255 n. 39.

31. Based on a visit to Ulster Park in June 2002. It is to the north of New Paltz and about five miles south of Kingston.

32. All citations that follow are taken from "Fall of Islam."

33. Irish servants were common in the last quarter of the nineteenth century. The Irish "Bridget" or "Biddy" was the ethnic stereotype of the American domestic servant. Having servants was the necessary mark of middle-class affluence, and even those who were not well-to-do had the requisite "live-in maid," who received her pay in room and board and minimal wages. Such servants often resided in "sparsely furnished areas of the house generally above or beside the kitchen or in the attic." See Schlereth, *Victorian America*, 71–73; and Fishburn, *The Fatherhood of God*, 11–12.

34. Webb, "Philosophic Islam," 51.

35. The Ulster Park station manager indicated to the *New York Times* reporter that Webb bought his property in Ulster Park in 1893. Keep referred to Webb's move to Ulster Park during the July 1894 scandal, indicating that his move there had taken place sometime earlier.

36. Tunison, "Mohammed Alexander Russell Webb," 18.

37. Ferris, "Immigrant Muslim Communities," 211.

38. Shalton, "Mohammed Alexander Russell Webb," 2–3.

39. Ibid., 83–84.

40. "To My Oriental Brothers," *MWVI*, January 1895: 3–4.

41. Ibid.

42. Ibid., February 1895: 3–4.

43. Ahmad, *Mujaddid-e Azam*, 160–161; Osman, "The Story" (1995), 17.

44. Ahmad, *Mujaddid-e Azam*, 159.

45. OA, Document B.

46. The property records of Ulster Park need to be studied. According to Mary Howell, Columbia County historian, land records for Ulster Park during the 1890s are kept in Kingston, New York, near the Old Church.

47. Tunison, "Mohammed Alexander Russell Webb," 18.

48. See Menand, *The Metaphysical Club*, 291; McDannell, *The Christian Home*, 9; Schlereth, *Victorian America*, xiv; Seager, *The World's Parliament of Religions*, 17.

49. See Roy, *The Economic History of India*, 63, 161; Rothermund, "Problems of India's Arrested Economic Growth," 5; and Dutt, *The Economic History of India*, 453–454.

50. See Ahmad, *Mujaddid-e Azam*, 160.

51. Haberly, *Newspapers*, 11; Bird, "The Press of Bergen County," 203.

52. *MWVI*, April 1895: 3.

53. Webb, "Philosophic Islam," 51.

54. Webb, *Islam in America*, 9.

55. Ibid., 10.

56. Schlereth, *Victorian America*, 22.

57. Ibid., 25; Fishburn, *The Fatherhood of God*, 97.

58. See *St. Louis Post-Dispatch*, 1 October 1916.

59. Fishburn, *The Fatherhood of God*, 97.

60. Schlereth, *Victorian America*, 174; Fishburn, *The Fatherhood of God*, 97; *History of Columbia County*, 170. Telephones were introduced in the late 1870s. By the 1880s, they had become an important part of American life. They had reached rural America by 1900. Phone books began to appear at that time.

61. Schlereth, *Victorian America*, xii–xiii, 84, 188–189, 191–193, 198–202.

62. Fishburn, *The Fatherhood of God*, 97.

63. Menand, *The Metaphysical Club*, 374.

64. Welter, "A Century of Protestant Anti-Catholicism," 43.

65. See Menand, *The Metaphysical Club*, 381–382, 387; Balkin, "History Lesson," 45–46; Gunn, *New World Metaphysics*, 223.

66. Frazier, "The New Poetry," *New Yorker*, 22 July 2002: 34.

67. See "Obituary: Alexander R. Webb." Directory records for Rutherford are very scant, in part because Rutherford was generally listed as part of the Passaic, New Jersey, directory but was included some years and excluded others. Webb appears in *Haring's Passaic Directory* in 1904, and his Rutherford residence is given as 149 Chestnut (294). There was a 1911 directory exclusively for Rutherford and vicinity, but I found only a microfilm of its title page without contents: Richmond, *1911–1912 Directory of Rutherford*. There is no mention of Webb in the following directories. Morris, *Directory of Passaic, N. J.* (1895–1896; I could find no directory for 1896); *Directory of*

Passaic, N. J. (1897–1898); *Directory of Passaic, N. J.* (1899); *Griffith's Passaic Directory* (1900), (1901), (1902), (1903); *Passaic Directory* (1906); Richmond, *Richmond's Directory of Passaic* (1907), (1908), (1909); *Richmond's Fourth Annual Directory of Passaic* (1910); Richmond, *1911 Volume 5 Directory of Passaic*; Richmond, *Richmond's Annual Directory of Passaic* (1912), (1913), (1914), (1915), (1916); Richmond, *Richmond's Eleventh Annual Directory of Passaic* (1917).

68. Abu-Lughod, *New York, Chicago, Los Angeles*, 76.

69. *Twelfth* [U.S.] *Census of Population 1900: New Jersey, Bergen County, Rutherford Burrough, Vol. 5.*

70. *Thirteenth* [U.S.] *Census of Population 1910: New Jersey, Bergen County, Rutherford Burrough, Vol. 5.*

71. "Obituary: Alexander R. Webb"; Haberly, *Newspapers*, 10–11; and Osman, "The Story" (1944), 7.

72. Ibid.

73. Haberly, *Newspapers*, 11; and Bird, "The Press of Bergen County," 203.

74. "Obituary: Alexander R. Webb"; Osman, "The Story" (1944), 7.

75. See ibid.; Tunison, "Mohammed Alexander Russell Webb," 18; Muhammad, "Muslims," 199; Bektashi, "Mohammed Alexander Russell Webb," unnumbered; Melton, *Religious Leaders*, 595.

76. Tunison, "Mohammed Alexander Russell Webb," 18.

77. "Sultan Honors an American."

78. See "Obituary: Alexander R. Webb."

79. Osman, "The Story" (1944), 7.

80. Tunison, "Mohammed Alexander Russell Webb," 13.

81. "Mr. Webb on Turkish Life"; Haberly, *Newspapers*, 11. Webb's lecture was described as pleasing from beginning to end. He presented his audience with several "stereopticon pictures" of Turkey: "[Webb] described humorously the famous dogs of Constantinople, told how they give a fire-alarm in the city and how the firemen turn out; pictured the Turkish horse car, and told of some of the famous sites of interest with which Constantinople abounds. Altogether, the lecture, by a man in thorough sympathy with his subject, was interesting and of educational value."

82. Ferris, "Immigrant Muslim Communities," 211.

83. "Obituary: Alexander R. Webb"; "A. H. Webb, Former St. Louisan Dies."

84. Osman, "The Story" (1944), 7.

85. "Obituary: Alexander R. Webb"; Bunker, *Bits and Pieces*, 282; Osman, "The Story" (1944), 7.

86. Osman, "The Story" (1944), 7.

87. "Obituary: Alexander R. Webb"; Tunison, "Mohammed Alexander Russell Webb," 18; Osman, "The Story" (1944), 7.

88. "Obituary: Alexander R. Webb"; Osman, "The Story" (1944), 7.

89. Tunison, "Mohammed Alexander Russell Webb," 18; "Obituary: Alexander R. Webb."

90. Based on a visit to the site in January 2001; "Obituary: Alexander R. Webb"; Tunison, "Mohammed Alexander Russell Webb," 18.

91. "Obituary: Alexander R. Webb"; Osman, "The Story" (1944), 7.

92. Tunison, "Mohammed Alexander Russell Webb," 18. Similarly, Melton concurs that "Webb continued to advocate Islam until the end of his life" (*Religious Leaders*, 595.)

93. Bird, "The Press of Bergen County," 203. Bird confused Islam and Hinduism. He stated, among other things, that "on one occasion Mr. Webb, attired in the garb of his rank, assisted at a Mohammedan service held by a delegation of Hindus in Washington."

94. Osman, "The Story" (1944), 8. According to Osman, Ella "did not continue to share her husband's interest in Islam in her later years." Osman makes no mention of Webb's children, but there is no indication that any of them continued to adhere to their father's religion.

95. Literally: "The exception has no ruling." The expression originally refers to logical and legal matters that constituted "exceptions to the rule," but is used metaphorically for exceptional people.

CONCLUSION

1. Osman, "The Story" (1944), 8.
2. Ali, "Preface," 5.
3. Nyang, *Islam*, 41, 70, 73.
4. Bousquet, "Moslem Religious Influences," 44.
5. Muhammad, "Muslims," 199.
6. Muhammad, "Muslims," 199; Nyang, *Islam*, 64, 104.
7. Nyang, *Islam*, 64, 104.
8. *MWVI*, March 1895: 3.
9. Webb, "The Spirit of Islam" (Barrows), 2: 989; (Houghton), 460.
10. Ibid.
11. Webb, *Islam in America*, 11.
12. Kurzman, *Modernist Islam*, 4.
13. Ibid., 277–290, 316–324. For Webb's acknowledgment of his indebtedness to Syed Ahmad Khan, see Webb, "Sectarian Exclusiveness," *Allahabad Review*, December 1891: 177.
14. Ibid., 5, 19.
15. Jackson, *Vendanta for the West*, 48–49.
16. See Haddad and Lummis, *Islamic Values*, 12.
17. See Smith, *The Babi and Baha'i Religions*, 101, 105; Perry, "The Chicago Baha'i Community," 348.
18. See Dannin, *Black Pilgrimage*, 36–37; Clegg, *An Original Man*, 19.
19. Quilliam, "Letter to the Editor," *Allahabad Review*, February 1892: 17. Quilliam did not base his opinion on a contemporary notion of agency, but on the prejudice of the English-speaking peoples of the West, especially Britain, against foreigners. He suggested a course of action that was essentially what he and Webb followed: "The proper course to adopt is to establish in England a Moslem Publication Society to issue works on Mohammadanism and if possible a weekly or monthly journal. This is one way to reach the masses. In a few years by sowing the seed in this manner you will have opened the door for preaching efforts."

20. Poston, *Islamic Da'wah*, 40.

21. Webb, "Philosophic Islam," 51; *MWVI*, April 1895: 3.

22. Khan, "Mohammed Alexander Russell Webb," 57.

23. *MWVI*, February 1896: 2.

24. Webb, "To the Editor," *Allahabad Review*, July 1891: 110; Webb, "Progressive Mohammedanism"; Webb, "Sectarian Exclusiveness."

25. Osman, "The Story" (1944), 8.

26. Shalton, "Mohammed Alexander Russell Webb," 8, 34–35, 90.

27. Ibid., 90–91.

28. "Always Truthful," *MW*, October 1893: 12.

29. Ibid., 8; see Webb, *The Three Lectures*, 34; OA, Document B.

30. Khan, "Mohammed Alexander Russell Webb," 17, 56.

31. *Inter Ocean*, 21 September 1893; and Webb, "The Spirit of Islam" (Barrows), 2: 992; (Houghton), 462.

32. Seager, *The World's Parliament of Religions*, 5–7.

33. Ibid.

34. Ali, "Preface," 5.

35. Webb, "Philosophic Islam," 52.

Bibliography

"A. H. [*sic*] Webb, Former St. Louisan Dies." *St. Louis Republic*, 3 October 1916: 8.

Abu-Lughod, Janet [Lippman]. *New York, Chicago, Los Angeles: America's Global Cities*. Minneapolis: University of Minnesota Press, 1999.

Ahmad, Basharat. *Mujaddid-e Azam*. N.p.: n.p., n.d.

Ahmad, Mirza Ghulam. "Letter to Alex. R. Webb, 4 April 1887." In Mirz Ghulam Ahmad, *Shahna-e Haqq*. N.p.: n.p., n.d.: 443–444.

———. *Shahna-e Haqq*. N.p.: n.p., n.d.

Ahmadiyya Anjuman Insha'at Islam Lahore. *Alexander Russell Webb*. Available at http://www.ahmadiyya.org/islam/webb1.htm. Accessed February 2003.

Aijian, M. M. "The Mohammedans in the United States." *Moslem World* 10 (1920): 30–35.

"Alexander H. [*sic*] Webb." *New York Times*, 3 October 1916: 11.

"Alexander R. Webb Dies: Former U.S. Consul Was Newspaper Man." *St. Louis Post-Dispatch*. 3 October 1916: 7.

Ali, Hassan, "Preface." In Mohammed Alexander Russell Webb, *The Three Lectures of Mohammed Alexander Russell Webb, Esq. Delivered at Madras, Hyderabad (Deccan) and Bombay, with a Brief Sketch of His Life Published by Moulvi Hassan Ali (Mohammedan Missionary)*. Madras: Lawrence Asylum Press, 1892, 3–5.

Allievi, Stefano. *I nuovi musulmani: I convertiti all'islam*. Rome: Edizioni Lavoro, 1999.

Allison, Robert J. *The Crescent Obscured: The United States and the Muslim World 1776–1815*. Chicago: University of Chicago Press, 1995.

An American Observer [Mohammed Alexander Russell Webb]. *A Few Facts about Turkey under the Sultan Abdul Hamid II*. New York: J. J. Little, 1895.

"Annie Besant on Islam." *Islamic Review and Muslim India.* October 1915: 504–510.

America's Obituaries and Death Notices. NewsBank Incorporated. Available at http://
www.newsbank.com/public/obit.html. Accessed January 2005.

Armstrong, Karen. *Islam: A Short History.* New York: Modern Library, 2000.

Armstrong, Orland Kay. "Beginnings of the Modern Newspaper: A Comparative Study
of St. Louis Dailies from 1875 to 1925." In *Deskbook of the School of Journalism,*
revised by Robert S. Mann, 1–39. Columbia, Missouri: n. p., 1924.

Arnold, T[homas] W[alker]. *The Preaching of Islam: A History of the Propagation of the
Muslim Faith.* Westminster, England: Archibald Constable, 1896.

———. *The Preaching of Islam: A History of the Propagation of the Muslim Faith.*
London: Constable, 1913.

Asani, Ali S. "Studying Islam in America: A Report." *Journal of Muslim Minority
Affairs* 13, 1 (1992): 278–280.

"Asked to Turn Moslems: Mohammed Webb, in a Dress Suit, Tells of the Beauties
of the Mohammedan Religion." *New York Herald,* 28 February 1893: 7.

Austin, Allen D. *African Muslims in Antebellum America: Transatlantic Stories and
Spiritual Struggles.* New York: Routledge, 1997.

"Awakening of Moslems in America." *The Moslem Sunrise,* July 1935: 18.

Balkin, Jack M. "History Lesson: Five Supreme Court Justices Think Congress Doesn't
Have the Power to Pass New Laws Against Discrimination. They're Forgetting
about the Civil Rights Movements of the Nineteenth and Twentieth Centuries."
Legal Affairs (July–August 2002): 44–49.

*Ballenger and Hoyes First Annual City Directory of the Inhabitants, Manufacturing
Establishments, Business Firms Etc. in the City of St. Joseph 1876.* Leavenworth, Kan.:
J. H. Ketcheson, n.d.

———. *Second Annual City Directory of the Inhabitants, Manufacturing Establishments,
Business Firms Etc. in the City of St. Joseph 1877.* Leavenworth, Kan.: J. H.
Ketcheson, n.d..

———. *Third Annual City Directory of the Inhabitants, Manufacturing Establishments,
Business Firms Etc. in the City of St. Joseph 1878.* Leavenworth, Kan.: J. H.
Ketcheson, n.d..

Barclay, Harold. "The Muslim Experience in Canada." In *Religion and Ethnicity,* ed.
Harold Coward and Leslie Kawamura, 101–114. Waterloo, Ontario: Wilfrid Laurier
University Press, 1977.

Barrows, John Henry, ed. *The World's Parliament of Religions: An Illustrated and Popular
Story of the World's First Parliament of Religions, Held in Chicago in Connection with
the Columbian Exposition of 1893.* 2 vols. Chicago: Parliament Publishing Co., 1893.

Bektashi, Muhammed A. Al-Akhari. "Mohammed Alexander Russell Webb, Islam in
America, and the American Islamic Propagation Movement." In the DePaul
University Library Archives on the World Parliament of Religions, Box 21 A.
CPWR Administration: Research Committee, 1993, pages unnumbered.

Bellah, Robert. "The Protestant Structure of American Culture: Multiculture or
Monoculture?" *Hedgehog Review: Critical Reflections on Contemporary Culture* 4,
1: 7–28.

Bellah, Robert and Frederick E. Greenspahn, eds. *Uncivil Religion: Interreligious
Hostility in America.* New York: Crossroad, 1987.

Bird, Eugene K. "The Press of Bergen County." In *The History of Bergen County, New Jersey, 1630–1923*, ed. Frances A. Westervelt, 203. New York: Lewis Historical Publishing, 1923.

Braden, Charles. "Islam in America." In *The International Review of Missions* 48, 191 (1959): 309–317.

Blavatsky, H[elena]. P. *Isis Unveiled: A Master-Key to the Mysteries of Ancient and Modern Science and Theology*. 2 vols. 1877. Reprint, Pasadena, Calif.: Theosophical University Press, 1998.

Blunt, Wilfrid. *Desert Hawk: Abd el Kader and the French Conquest of Algeria with 16 Gravure Plates and a Map*. London: Methuen, 1947.

Bonet-Maury, Gaston. *Le congrès des religions à Chicago en 1893*. Paris: Librairie Hachette, 1895.

Bonney, Charles Carroll. "The Genesis of the World's Religious Congress of 1893." In the DePaul University Library Archives on the World Parliament of Religions, Box 21 A. CPWR Administration: Research Committee: Essay Charles Carroll Bonney, 1993. Photocopied from the *New-Church Review*, January 1894: 73–100.

Bousquet, G. H. "Moslem Religious Influences in the United States." In *Moslem World* 25 (January 1935): 40–44.

Boutaleb, Abdelkader. *L'émir Abd el-Kader de la Nation Algérienne*. Algeria: Éditions Dahlab, 1950.

Bulwer-Lytton, Lord Edward. *Zanoni*. New York: Harper & Brothers, 1842.

Bunker, Frederick C. "Profile of Alexander R. Webb." In *Bits and Pieces of the History of Rutherford, New Jersey*, 282. Unpublished book.

Campbell, J. B. *Campbell's Illustrated History of the World's Columbian Exposition: Compiled as the Exposition Progressed from the Official Reports, and Most Profusely Illustrated with Copperplate Engravings*. 2 vols. Chicago: J. B. Campbell, 1894.

Carus, Paul. *The Dawn of a New Religious Era and Other Essays*. Chicago: Open Court, 1916.

Case, Margaret H. "The Aligarh Era: Muslim Politics in North India, 1860–1910." Ph.D. diss., University of Chicago, 1970.

Century Club of American Newspapers. St. Louis: St. Louis Republic & George Knapp, 1909.

Chappell, Urso S. A. *World's Fair History, Architecture, and Memorabilia*. Available at http://www.expomuseum.com/. Accessed February 2003.

Chicago Tribune Historical Archives. NewsBank Inc. Available at http://www.newsbank.com/. Accessed January 2005.

Churchill, Henry Charles. *The Life of Abdel Kader*. London: Chapman & Hall, 1867.

Clark, Peter. *Marmaduke Pickthall: British Muslim*. London: Quartet Books, 1986.

Claverack Academy and Hudson River Institute Register 1855–1865. Manuscript in the Claverack Free Library and Reading Room, Claverack, N.Y.

[Claverack Academy and Hudson River Institute] Record 1857–1871. Manuscript in the Claverack Free Library and Reading Room, Claverack, N.Y.

Clayton, Vista. *The Phantom Caravan*. New York: Exposition Press, 1975.

Clegg, Andrew Claude III. *An Original Man: The Life and Times of Elijah Muhammad*. New York: St. Martin Griffin, 1997.

Cole, Juan R. I. *Modernity and the Millennium: The Genesis of the Baha'i Faith in the Nineteenth-Century Middle East*. New York: Columbia University Press, 1998.

A Correspondent [Mohammed Alexander Russell Webb]. *The Armenian Troubles and Where the Responsibility Lies.* New York: J. J. Little, n.d.

Cranston, Sylvia. *HPB: The Extraordinary Life and Influence of Helena Blavatsky, Founder of the Modern Theosophical Movement.* New York: G. P. Putnam's Sons, 1993.

Dannin, Robert. *Black Pilgrimage to Islam.* Oxford: Oxford University Press, 2002.

Danziger, Raphael. *Abd al-Qadir and the Algerians: Resistance to the French and Internal Consolidation.* New York: Holmes & Meier, 1977.

DeCaro, Louis A. *On the Side of My People: A Religious Life of Malcolm X.* New York: New York University Press, 1996.

Dewey, Clive, ed. *Arrested Development in India: The Historical Dimension.* New Delhi: Manohar, 1988.

Diouf, Sylviane A. *Servants of Allah: African Muslims Enslaved in the Americas.* New York: New York University Press, 1998.

Directory of Passaic, N.J., Together with Garfield, Clifton, Carlstadt, Wallington, Lodi, Rutherford, East Rutherford, Woodridge, Hasbrouck Heights, Lyndhurst, Kingsland 1897–1898. Passaic, N.J.: Passaic Daily News, n.d.

Directory of Passaic, N.J., Together with Garfield, Clifton, Carlstadt, Wallington, Lodi, Rutherford, East Rutherford, Woodridge, Hasbrouck Heights, Lyndhurst, Kingsland 1899. Passaic, N.J.: Passaic Daily News, n.d.

"Dispatches from United States Consuls in Manila, Philippine Islands 1817–1899." Rolls 4–5: 4 October 1887 to 19 December 1893. National Archives Microfilm Publications, Microcopy No. 455. Washington, D.C.: National Archives and Records Services General Services Administration, 1969.

Downey, Dennis B. *A Season of Renewal: The Columbian Exposition and Victorian America.* Westport, Conn.: Praeger, 2002.

Druyvesteyn, Kenten. "The World's Parliament of Religions." Ph.D. diss., University of Chicago, 1976.

Dry, Camille N. *Pictorial St. Louis: The Great Metropolis of the Mississippi Valley: A Topographical Survey Drawn in Perpective, A.D. 1875.* Designed and edited by Richard J. Compton. Reprint, n.p.: McGraw-Young, 1997.

Dutt, Romesh. *The Economic History of India in the Victorian Age: From the Accession of Queen Victoria in 1837 to the Commencement of the Twentieth Century.* London: Routledge & Kegan Paul, 1956.

Economic History Services. *What Was the Exchange Rate Then?* Available at http://eh.net/hmit/exchangerates. Accessed March 2006.

Edwards, Doug, Matthew Whitecar, and Shannon Harrison. *The DMS Stephen Crane Page.* Available at http://www3.uakron.edu/english/richards/edwards/crane.htm. Accessed 2002.

Edwards, Richard, ed. *Edward's Annual Director to the Inhabitants, Institutions, Incorporated Companies, Manufacturing Establishments, Business, Business Firms, etc., etc., in the City of Chicago, for 1869–1870.* St. Louis: Richard Edwards, n.d.

———. *Edward's Annual Director to the Inhabitants, Institutions, Incorporated Companies, Manufacturing Establishments, Business, Business Firms, etc., etc., in the City of Chicago, for 1870–1871.* St. Louis: Richard Edwards, 1870.

————. *The Fire Edition: Edward's Chicago Directory, Containing the Names of All Persons in Business in the City Whose Location Could Be Ascertained to December 12, 1871 Also, a Business Directory Embracing a Classified List of Trades, Professions and Pursuits* . . . Chicago: Richard Edwards, n.d.

————. *Edward's New Chicago Directory, City and County Record* . . . *for 1872*. Chicago: Richard Edwards, 1872.

————. *Edward's New Chicago Directory, 1873*. Chicago: Richard Edwards, 1873.

Elazar, Daniel J. "The American Cultural Matrix." In *The Ecology of American Cultures,* ed. Daniel J. Elazar and Joseph Zikmund II, 13–42. New York: Thomas Y. Crowell, 1975.

The Encyclopedia of Islam. WebCD ed. Leiden: Brill Academic Publishers, 2003.

Eraslan, Cezmi. "Muhammed A. R. Webb'in Amerika'da İslâm Propagandasıve Osmanlı Devleti'yle İlişkileri (1893–1896)." *Ilmi arastirmalar* 2 (1996): 79–94.

Elazar, Daniel J. "The American Cultural Matrix." In *The Ecology of American Cultures,* ed. Daniel J. Elazar and Joseph Zikmund II, 13–42. New York: Thomas Y. Crowell, 1975.

Eliot, T. S. *The Complete Poems and Plays 1909–1950.* New York: Harcourt & Brace, 1962.

Etzioni, Amitai. "Individualism—within History." *Hedgehog Review: Critical Reflections on Contemporary Culture* 4, 1 (spring 2002): 49–56.

"Fall of Islam in America: Story of a Mussulman Propaganda That Came to Grief: Moslems Fail to Agree: The Nawab of Basoda Says Between £40,000 and £50,000 Was Sent Here to Convert the United States: Webb Says Less than £2000 Were Sent: The Ex-United States Consul at Manila, Who Was to Establish Mohammedanism in This Country Living in Poverty." *New York Times,* 1 December 1895: 21.

Family Search Database. Available at http://www.familysearch.org/. Accessed January 2005.

Ferris, Marc. "To 'Achieve the Pleasure of Allah': Immigrant Muslim Communities in New York City 1893–1991." In *Muslim Communities in North America,* ed. Yvonne Yazbeck Haddad and Jane Idleman Smith, 209–230. New York: State University of New York Press, 1994.

Fink, Sam. *Index of Chicago Marriages.* Available at http://www.sos.state.il.us/GenealogyMWeb/MarriageSearchServlet. Accessed January 2005.

Fishburn, Janet Forsythe. *The Fatherhood of God and the Victorian Family.* Philadelphia: Fortress, 1981.

"For the Faith of Islam. Mr. Webb Opens His Moslem Temple—To Have a School of Morality." *New York Times,* 8 October 1893: 21.

Fortune City: 1895 Stephen Crane's The Red Badge of Courage. Available at http://www.fortunecity.com/tinpan/quickstep/1103/book57.htm

Foster, Lawrence. "Cults in Conflict: New Religious Movements and the Mainstream Religious Tradition in America." In *Uncivil Religion: Interreligious Hostility in America,* ed. Robert N. Bellah and Frederick E. Greenspahn, 185–204. New York: Crossroad, 1987.

Frazier, Ian. "The New Poetry." *New Yorker,* 22 July 2002: 34.

Friedmann, Yohanan. *Prophecy Continuous: Aspects of Ahmadi Religious Thought and Its Medieval Background*. Berkeley: University of California Press, 1989.

Garcin de Tassy [Joseph-Heliodore-Sagesse-Vertu]. *La langue et la littérature hindoustanies en 1875: Revue annnuelle*. Paris: Librairie Orientnale de Maisonnneuve, 1876.

Gaylord and R. H. McDonald Maps. Available at www.press.uchicago.edu/books/grossman/images/C2-C3_fireprogress.pdf. Accessed January 2005.

"Got a Consulship: Mr. Alex R. Webb of St. Louis Appointed to Represent this Country at Manila, in the Philippine Islands." *Missouri Republican*, 30 September 1887: 8.

Gould's St. Louis Directory for 1877. St. Louis: David B. Gould, n.d.

Gould's St. Louis Directory for 1878. St. Louis: David B. Gould, n.d.

Gould's St. Louis Directory for 1879. St. Louis: David B. Gould, n.d.

Gould's St. Louis Directory for 1880. St. Louis: David B. Gould, n.d.

Gould's St. Louis Directory for 1881. St. Louis: David B. Gould, n.d.

Gould's St. Louis Directory for 1882. St. Louis: David B. Gould, n.d.

Gould's St. Louis Directory for 1883 (for the year ending April 1st, 1884). St. Louis: David B. Gould, n.d.

Gould's St. Louis Directory for 1884 (for the year ending April 1st, 1885). St. Louis: Gould Directory Co., n.d.

Gould's St. Louis Directory for 1885 (for the year ending April 1st, 1886). St. Louis: Gould Directory Co., n.d.

Gould's St. Louis Directory for 1886 (for the year ending April 1st, 1887). St. Louis: Gould Directory Co., n.d.

Gould's St. Louis Directory for 1887 (for the year ending April 1st, 1888). St. Louis: Gould Directory Co., n.d.

Grebsonal, L. "The Mohammedan Propagandist." *Frank Leslie's Illustrated Week*, 30 March 1893: 204–205.

Griffith's Passaic Directory Including Clifton, Lake View, Garfield, Lodi, Wallington 1900. Passaic, N.J.: Passaic Daily News, n.d.

Griffith's Passaic Directory Containing Clifton, Lake View, Garfield, Wallington, 1902. N.p.: n.p., n.d.

Griffith's Passaic Directory Contiaing Clifton, Lake View, Garfield, Wallington, 1903. N.p.: n.p., n.d.

Griffith, Joshua. *Griffith's Passaic Directory Containing Clifton, Lake View, Garfield, Wallington 1901*. Paterson, N.J.: Joshua Griffith, n.d.

Gunn, Giles, ed. *New World Metaphysics: Readings on the Religious Meaning of the America Experience*. Oxford: Oxford University Press, 1981.

Haberly, Lord. *Newspapers and Newspaper Men of Rutherford*. N.p.: Rutherford Committee of the New Jersey Tercentenary & Fairleigh Dickinson University, n.d.

Haddad, Yvonne Yazbeck. "Make Room for the Muslims." In *Religious Diversity and American Religious History: Studies in Traditions and Cultures*, ed. Walter H. Conser Jr. and Sumner B. Twiss. Athens: University of Georgia Press, n.d.

———. "Muslims in Canada: A Preliminary Study." In *Religion and Ethnicity*, by Harold Coward and Leslie Kawamura, 71–100. Waterloo, Ontario: Wilfrid Laurier University Press, 1977.

Haddad, Yvonne Yazbeck, ed. *The Muslims of America*. Oxford: Oxford University Press, 1991.

Haddad, Yvonne Yazbeck, and John L. Esposito, eds. *Muslims on the Americanization Path?* New York: Oxford University Press, 2000.

Haddad, Yvonne Yazbeck, and Adair T. Lummis. *Islamic Values in the United States: A Comparative Study.* New York: Oxford University Press, 1987.

Haddad, Yvonne Yazbeck, and Jane Idleman Smith, eds. *Muslim Communities in North America.* New York: State University of New York Press, 1994.

Hamdani, Daood Hassan. "Canada's Muslims: An Unnoticed Part of Our History." *Hamdard Islamicus* 20, 3 (1997): 97–100.

———. "Muslims and Christian Life in Canada." In *Islam in North America,* ed. Michael Köszegi and J. Gordon Melton, 253–263. New York: Garland, 1992.

Hanson, J. W., ed. *The World's Congress of Religions.* Chicago: Monarch Book Co., 1894.

Haring, Frank. *Haring's Passaic Directory Containing Clifton, Lake View, Garfield, Wallington, Rutherford, East Rutherford, and Carlton Hill 1904, revised 1904–1905.* Paterson, N.J.: Frank Haring, n.d.

Hart, Jim Allee. *A History of the St. Louis Globe-Democrat.* Columbia: University of Missouri Press, 1961.

Headley, Al-Hajj. "Is Our House in Order?" *Islamic Review,* September 1928: 322–333.

Heritage Quest. ProQuest Co. Available at http://www.heritagequestonline.com/. Accessed at January 2005.

Historical New York Times. ProQuest Co. Available at http://www.proquestcompany.com/. Accessed at January 2005.

History of Berkshire County, Massachusetts, with Biographical Sketches of its Prominent Men. New York: J. B. Beers, 1885.

History of Columbia County, New York: Illustrious and Biographical Sketches of Some of Its Prominent Men and Pioneers. Philadelphia: Everts & Ensign, 1878.

Hermansen, Marcia. "Conversion." In *Encyclopedia of Women and World Religion,* ed. Serenity Young, 1:204–207. New York: Macmillan, 1999.

———. "Roads to Mecca: Conversion Narratives of European and Euro-American Muslims." *Muslim World* 89, 1 (January 1999): 56–89.

History of Adair, Sullivan, Putnam and Schuyler Counties, Missouri originally printed 1888, the Goodspeed Publishing Company. Astoria, Ill.: Stevens Publishing, 1972.

History of Buchanan County, Missouri, Containing a History of the County, Its Cities, Towns, Etc., Illustrated, indexed Edition. St. Joseph: St. Joseph Steam Printing Co., 1881.

Holmes, Mary Caroline. "Islam in America." *Moslem World,* July 1926: 262–266.

Houghton, Walter Raleigh, ed., *Neely's History of the Parliament of Religions and Religious Congresses at the World's Columbian Exposition: Compiled from Original Manuscripts and Stenographic Reports,* 2 vols. in one. Chicago: Frank Tennyson Neely, 1893.

Hyde, William and Conard, Howard L., eds. *Encyclopedia of the History of St. Louis: A Compendium of History and Biography for Ready Reference.* 4 vols. New York: Southern History Co., 1899.

Hudson River Institute, Claverack, Columbia County, New York, September 11, 1865–1885. Manuscript in the Claverack Free Library and Reading Room, Claverack, N.Y.

Illinois Census 1860. Available at http://persi.heritagequestionline.com/hqoweb/library/do/census/results/image/print?urn=urn. Accessed January 2005.

Inter Ocean. Clippings of the World's Parliament of Religions. University of Chicago, Regenstein Library.

Index of Male Marriage Records 1871–1881. Archives Department, St. Louis Assessor's Office, St. Louis, Missouri.

Islam—Our Choice: Impressions of Eminent Converts to Islam. Abridged ed. Edited by Ebrahim Ahmed Bawany. Karachi: Begum Aisha Bawany Wakf, 1961.

Islam—Our Choice: Impressions of Eminent Converts to Islam. Abridged ed. Edited by Ebrahim Ahmed Bawany. Karachi: Begum Aisha Bawany Wakf, 1970.

"Islam in England." *Moslem World*, June 1914: 310.

"Islam in Liverpool." *Moslem World*, July 1911: 345–346.

"The Islamic Propaganda." *New York Times*, May 28, 1893: 4.

Islamic Review and Muslim India: Religion, Ethics, Politics, Literature, Art, Commerce: A Monthly Journal devoted to the Interests of the Muslims. Edited by Khwaja Kamal-ud-Din. London: Woking Mosque, J. S. Philips, 1913.

Islamic Review and Muslim India: Religion, Ethics, Politics, Literature, Art, Commerce: A Monthly Journal devoted to the Interests of the Muslims. Edited by Khwaja Kamal-ud-Din. London: Woking Mosque, J. S. Philips, 1914–1920.

Islamic Review. Edited by Khwaja Kamal-ud-Din. London: Woking Mosque, 1913–1963.

Iyilik, Betul. *The Unveiling of an Historic Mosque*. Available at http://www.muslimnews .co.uk/hmosque102.html. Accessed on October 31, 1997.

Jack, Homer A. "The World's Parliament of Religions." DePaul University Library Archives on the World Parliament of Religions, Box 21 A. CPWR Administration, Research Committee, December 1988.

———. "The 1893 World's Parliament of Religions: How Some Religions Participated: II: The Eastern Religions." DePaul University Library Archives on the World Parliament of Religions, Box 21 A. CPWR Administration, Research Committee, Sept. 11, 1991.

Jackson, Carl T. *Vedanta for the West: The Ramakrishna Movement in the United States*. Bloomington: Indiana University Press, 1994.

Jackson, Kenneth T., ed. *The Encyclopedia of New York*. New Haven, Conn.: Yale University Press, 1995.

Jackson, Ronald Vern, et al., eds. *Missouri—North—1870 Federal Census Index*. Salt Lake City: Accelerated Indexing Systems International, 1989.

Jessup, Henry H. "The Religious Mission of the English Speaking Nations." In *The World's Parliament of Religions*, ed. John Henry Barrows, 2:1125–1126. Chicago: Parliament Publishing Co., 1893.

Johnson, K. Paul. *Initiates of Theosophical Masters*. Albany: State University of New York Press, 1995.

Jones, Jenkin Lloyd. *A Chorus of Faith as Heard in the Parliament of Religions Held in Chicago, Sept. 10–27, 1893*. Chicago: Unity Publishing Co., 1893.

Kahhāla, 'Umar Riḍā. *Mu'jam al-Mu'allifīn: Tarājim Muṣannifī al-Kutub al-'Arabiyya*. 15 vols. Beirut, Lebanon: Dār Ihyā' al-Turāth al-'Arabī, n.d.

Kaushal, G. *Economic History of India: 1757–1966*. New Delhi: Kalyani, 1979.

Kidd, Ron. "Anecdotes and Descriptions." DePaul University Library Archives on the World Parliament of Religions, Box 21 B, CPWR Administration, Research Committee, 1991.

Khan, Fareeha. "Mohammed Alexander Russell Webb: A Nineteenth Century American's Impressions of the Religion of Islam." Master's thesis, University of Chicago, 2002.

Klein, Philip. *President James Buchanan*. University Park: Pennsylvania State University Press, 1962.

Klos, Stan. "Frank Hatton." In *Virtual American Biographies*. Available at http://64.233.167.104/search?q=cache:88GWenvJmpQJ:www.famousamericans.net/fr. Accessed February 2005.

———. "John Russell Young." In *Virtual American Biographies*. Available at http://www.famousamericans.net/johnrussellyoung/. Accessed February 2005.

Khulusi, S.A., ed. *Islam Our Choice*. 1st unabridged ed. Woking, England: Woking Muslim Mission & Literary Trust, 1961.

Köszegi, Michael A., and J. Gordon Melton, eds. *Islam in North America: A Sourcebook*. New York: Garland, 1992.

Kurzman, Charles, ed. *Modernist Islam 1840–1940: A Sourcebook*. Oxford: Oxford University Press, 2002.

Kur, Abdulla Budruddin. "Mohammadan Propaganda in America: To the Editor of the 'Bombay Gazette.'" 12 September 1892. In Mohammad Alexander Russell Webb, *Lectures on Islam: Delivered at Different Places in India*, 15–16. Lahore: Mohammadan Tract and Book Depot, 1893.

———. "Mohammadan Propaganda in America: To the Editor of the 'Bombay Gazette.'" In Mohammed Alexander Russell Webb, *Islam: A Lecture on Islam Delivered at the Framji Cowasji Institute, Bombay, India, Thursday Evening 10th November 1892*, 7. Bombay: Bombay Gazette Steam Printing Works, 1892.

———. "To the Editor of the Times of India." 16 November 1892. In Mohammad Alexander Russell Webb, *Lectures on Islam: Delivered at Different Places in India*, 18. Lahore: Mohammadan Tract and Book Depot, 1893.

———. "To the Editor of the Times of India." 16 November 1892. In Mohammed Alexander Russell Webb, *Islam: A Lecture on Islam Delivered at the Framji Cowasji Institute, Bombay, India, Thursday Evening 10th November 1892*, 8. Bombay: Bombay Gazette Steam Printing Works, 1892.

1874–1875, The Lakeside Annual Directory of the City of Chicago Embracing a Complete General and Business Directory. 2 vols. Chicago: Williams, Donnelly, 1874–1875.

1875–1876, The Lakeside Annual Directory of the City of Chicago Embracing a Complete General and Business Directory. Chicago: Williams, Donnelly, 1875–1876.

Lancaster, Clay. *The Incredible World's Parliament of Religions at the Chicago Columbian Exposition of 1893: A Comparative and Critical Study*. Fontwell, Sussex: Centaur, 1987.

Lant, John A. "A Message to the Faithful All Over the World." *Allahabad Review*, January 1894: 12–14.

Lant, J. H. *The Hudson Directory, for 1870, Containing the Names of the Inhabitants*. Hudson, N.Y.: Bryan & Webb, 1870.

Lavan, Spencer. *The Ahmadiyah Movement: A History and Perspective*. Delhi: Manohar Book Service, 1974.

Lawrence, Judith. "A History of the 1893 Parliament." DePaul University Library Archives on the World Parliament of Religions, Box 21 B. CPWR Administration, Research Committee, December 1988.

LeBeau, Bryan. *Religion in America to 1865*. New York: New York University Press, 2000.

Littell, Franklin Hamlin. *From State Church to Pluralism: A Protestant Interpretation of Religion in American History*. New York: Macmillan, 1971.

Logan, Sheridan A. *Old Saint Jo: Gateway to the West, 1799–1932*. N.p.: Stinehour, 1979.

"Lotos Leaves." In *Online Eximious Books and Autographs*. Available at http://64.233.167.104/search?q=cache:TxDK1ask7yMJ:www.eximiousbooks.com/cgi-. Accessed February 2005.

Macfie, Alexander Lyon, ed. *Orientalism: A Reader*. New York: New York University Press, 2000.

McCloud, Aminah Beverly. *African American Islam*. New York: Routledge, 1995.

McDannell, Colleen. *The Christian Home in Victorian America, 1840–1900*. Bloomington: Indiana University Press, 1986.

McMullin, Jean Brice. *Hudson Revisited*. N.p.: n.p., 1985.

Maass, John. *The Gingerbread Age: A View of Victorian America*. New York: Bramhall House, 1957.

Magnan, William B. *Streets of St. Louis*. Groton, Conn.: Right Press, 1994.

Magnan, William B., and Marcella C. Magnan. *The Streets of St. Louis: A History of St. Louis Street Names*. 2nd ed. N.p.: Virginia Publishing, 1994/1996.

Mann, Robert S., ed. *Deskbook of the School of Journalism*. 8th ed. Columbia, Missouri: N.p., 1924.

Marlowe, Jack. "Zalabia and the First Ice-Cream Cone." *Saudi Aramco World*, July–August 2003: 2–5.

"Married." *Chicago Tribune*, 6 May 1870.

Marty, Martin E. *The Infidel: Freethought and American Religion*. Cleveland: Meridian, 1961.

———. *Pilgrims in Their Own Land: Five Hundred Years of Religion in America*. New York: Penguin, 1984.

———. *Religion and Republic: The American Circumstance*. Boston: Beacon, 1987.

Marty, Martin E., and Micah Marty. *When True Simplicity Is Gained; Finding Spiritual Clarity in a Complex World*. Cambridge, England: William B. Eerdmans, 1998.

Matar, Nabil. *Islam in Britain 1558–1685*. Cambridge: Cambridge University Press, 1998/1999.

———. *Turks, Moors, and Englishmen in the Age of Discovery*. New York: Columbia University Press, 1999.

May, Elaine Tyler. *Great Expectations: Marriage and Divorce in Post-Victorian America*, Chicago: University of Chicago Press, 1980.

Mead, Sidney E. *The Nation with the Soul of a Church*. New York: Harper & Row, 1975.

Melton, J. Gordon, ed. *Encyclopedia of American Religions*. Detroit: Gale, 1996.

———. *Religious Leaders of America*. 2nd ed. Detroit: Gale, 1999.

———. "Webb, Muhammad Alexander Russel [sic] (November 18, 1846, Hudson, New York—October 1, 1916, Rutherford, New Jersey)." *Biographical Dictionary of American Cult and Sect Leaders*, 303–304. New York: Gale, 1986.

Menand, Louis. *The Metaphysical Club: A Story of Ideas in America*. New York: Ferrar, Straus, & Giroux, 2001.

*Merchant's Chicago Census Report, Embracing a Complete Directory of the City,
    Showing Number of Persons in Each Family, Male and Female—Birth Place and
    Ward Now Residing In.* [Chicago]: n.p., 1871.

Mills, Joy. *One Hundred Years of Theosophy: A History of the Theosophical Society in
    America.* Wheaton, Ill.: Theosophical Publishing House, 1987.

*1880 Missouri Census of the City of St. Louis (Second Enumeration), Wards 6–9:
    Inhabitants in the City of St. Louis in the County of St. Louis, State of Missouri,
    enumerated by me on the 11th Day of November 1880, Conrad Blumengard.*
    Missouri Historical Society, Columbia, Missouri, role 729, house # 1218.

Missouri Census 1880. Available at http://persi.heritagequestionline.com/hqoweb/
    library/do/census/results/image/print?urn=urn. Accessed January 2005.

Missouri River Heritage Association. *The Heritage of Buchanan County, Missouri.*
    Dallas, Texas: Missouri River Heritage Association, 1886.

Morgan, H. Wayne. *Victorian Culture in America 1865–1914.* Itasca, Ill.: F. E. Pea-
    cock, 1973.

Morris, J. F. *Directory of Passaic, N.J. Together with Rutherford, Garfield, Clifton,
    Wallington, East Rutherford and Carlstadt 1895–1896.* Passaic, N.J.: News Pub-
    lishing Co., n.d.

Moslem Sunrise. July 1921–October 1922. Highland Park, Mich.: Karoub House, 1921.

Moslem World. Edited by Rev. S. M. Zwemer. 1911–1952.

Moslem World to Spread the Light of Islam in America. Edited by Mohammed Alexan-
    der Russell Webb. October and November 1893.

"The Mosque at Woking England." *Moslem World,* January 1914: 91–92.

Muhammad, Akbar. "Muslims in the United States: An Overview of Organizations,
    Doctrines, and Problems." In *The Islamic Impact,* ed. Yvonne Yazbeck Haddad,
    Byron Haines, and Ellison Findly, 195–217. Syracuse, N.Y.: Syracuse University
    Press, 1984.

———. "Some Factors Which Promote and Restrict Islamization in America."
    American Journal of Islamic Studies 1, 2 (August 1984): 41–50.

Missouri Census 1880. Available at http://persi.heritagequestionline.com/hqoweb/
    library/do/census/results/image/print?urn=urn. Accessed in January 2005.

"Mrs. Keep Visits the Consul: Delighted to Hear the Sultan Has Nothing to Do
    with Webb's Crusade." *New York Times,* 17 July 1894: 1.

"Muhammed [sic] Webb Locked Out: Nefeesa Keep Will Not Admit Him to the
    Moslem Brotherhood's Offices." *New York Times,* 14 July 1894: 5.

"Muhammad Webb's Mission to Establish the Faith of Islam Here." *New York
    Times,* 25 February 1893: 1.

Murad, Abdal Hakim. "The Great Dive: The Unusual Life of William Williamson."
    Seasons: Semiannual Journal of Zaytuna Institute (autumn–winter 2003–2004):
    23–31.

———. "Marmaduke Pickthall: A Brief Biography." *Seasons: Semiannual Journal of
    Zaytuna Institute* (spring–summer 2004): 23–39.

"Nafeesa Keep Breakfasts: 'Something Told' Her She Was to Have Roast Chicken."
    New York Times, 16 July 1894: 1.

Naipaul, V. S. *Among the Believers: An Islamic Journey.* New York: Random House,
    1982.

National Archives. Available at http://monitor.nara.gov/cgi-bin/starfinder/13875/ micfilm.txt. Accessed February 2005.

New York 1840 Sixth Census, Fulton County: Schedule of the Whole Number of Persons within the Division Allotted to Michael Thompson by the Marshall of the Northern District of New York. Missouri Historical Society, Columbia, Missouri, role 284.

New York 1850 Census Index, Columbia County: Schedule I: Free Inhabitants in the 2nd Ward City, Hudson in the County of Columbia, State of New York enumerated by me on the 5th day of August, 1850, Ass't Marshall. Missouri Historical Society, Columbia, Missouri, role 491.

New York 1860 Census Index, Columbia County: Free Inhabitants in the 1st Ward City of Hudson in the County of Columbia, State of New York enumerated by me on the 14th day of June, 1860, John Reynolds, Ass't Marshall. Missouri Historical Society, Columbia, Missouri, role 738.

New York Civil War Records (1861–65). Available at http://search.ancestry.com/cgi-bin/ sse.dll?gsfn=alexander&gsln=webb&gskw=&rank=1&d. Accessed February 2005.

New York Public Library—Ask Librarians Online. Available at http://www.questionpoint .org/crs/servlet/org.oclc.ask.AskPatronQuestion. Accessed at February 2005.

Newspapers in Missouri: A Union List 1994—Staff of Missouri Newspaper Project 1988– 1994, A Component of the United States Program. 2 vols. Kansas City: University of Missouri, Kansas City, 1994.

Noll, Mark A. *The Old Religion in a New World: The History of North American Christianity.* Grand Rapids, Mich.: William Eerdmans, 2002.

Nyang, Sulayman S. *Islam in the United States of America.* Chicago: Kazi, 1999.

NYS Civil War Soldier Database. Available at http://iarchives.nysed.gov/CivilWarWeb/ soldierServlet. Accessed February 2005.

Obeidat, Marwan M. "Washington Irving and Muslim Spain." *International Journal of Islamic and Arabic Studies* 1 (1987): 27–44.

"Obituary: Alexander R. Webb." *Rutherford Republican and Rutherford American,* 7 October 1916: 1.

Obituary Collection. Ancestry.com. Available at http://www.ancestry.com/search/obit/. Accessed January 2005.

"Obituary: Margaret Sanger Is Dead at 86; Led Campaign for Birth Control." *New York Times on the Web Learning Network: On This Day, September 7, 1966.* Available at http://www.nytimes.com/learning/general/onthisday/bday/0914.html. Accessed January 2005.

"Obituary Notes." *Editor and Publisher* 49, 17 (October 7, 1916): 34.

Olmstead, Clifton E. *History of Religion in the United States.* Englewood Cliffs, N.J.: Prentice-Hall, 1960.

Osman, Nadirah Florence Ives. "The Story of the First American Convert to Islam: Muhammad Alexander Russell Webb—A Scholar of Fame—Social Worker— Leading Journalist—Editor of Many Papers—Consul General for U.S.A.— Founder of First Islamic Mission and Islamic Periodical in America." *The Light,* 8 April 1944: 6–7, and 16 April 1944: 5–8.

———. "The Story of the First American Convert to Islam: Muhammad Alexander Russell Webb, Editor and Owner of Newspapers, Scholar, Consul-General of U.S.A." *The Light,* March–April 1995: 14–18, and May–June: 6–10.

Ottoman Archives. Yıldız Arşivi Sadâret Hususî Mârûzâtı (Y.A.HUS): 2/8/1314: "Amerika'da Islam dinine geçmiş Aleksandr Russel Webb Efendi'nin Müslümanlığa dair ve Daily Express Gazetesi'nde münteşir musâhabesi hakkinda." Document A.

———.Yıldız Arşivi Sadâret Hususî Mârûzâtı (Y.A.HUS): 15/4/131: "Amerikalı mühtedî Muhammad Webb Efendi'nin, Islâmiyeti müdafaa yolundaki beyânât ve teşebbüsâtının menfaat temîni maksadına mebnî olmadığı." Document B.

Parkinson, John Yehya-en-Nasr. "The Liverpool Muslim Movement." *Islamic Review and Muslim India* (May 1914): 166–168.

Passaic Directory Containing Clifton, Lake View, Garfield and Wallington, 1906. Passaic, N.J.: A. L. Freeman, n.d.

"Paul Belloni Du Chaillu." In *Columbia Encyclopedia,* 6th ed. Available at http://64.233.167.104/search?q=cache:gosYPım8IjYJ:www.bartleby.com/65/du/DuC. Accessed February 2005.

Perry, Mark. "The Chicago Baha'i Community, 1921–1939." Ph.D. diss., University of Chicago, 1986.

Phillips, Sarah Lemen. *Putnam County, Missouri Cemeteries: Information Obtained by Stone Readings and Additional Data from Unionville Republican: Readings to 1980 Inclusive.* Kirksville, Mo.: Simpson, 1990.

———. *Putnam County, Missouri Estate Records: Estate Records for Putnam County, Missouri 1845–1909.* Kirksville, Mo.: Simpson, 1989.

Pickthall, Marmaduke. "The Prophet's Gratitude." *Islamic Review and Muslim India* (January 1917): 35–39.

Pool, John J. *Studies in Mohammedanism: Historical and Doctrinal with a Chapter on Islam in England.* Westminster, England: Archibald Constable, 1892.

"Poor Mustapha Arjawalli: Once a Man of Some Consequence, He Is Now Standard in This City." *New York Times,* 22 July 1894: 21.

Portrait and Biographical Record of Buchanan and Clinton Counties Missouri Containing Sketches of Prominent and Representative Citizens Together with Biographies and Portraits of All the Presidents of the United States. Chicago: Chapman Brothers, 1893.

Post, George. "The Ethics of Isâm." In *The World's Parliament of Religions: An Illustrated and Popular Story of the World's First Parliament of Religions, Held in Chicago in Connection with the Columbian Exposition of 1893,* ed. John Henry Barrows, 2:1096–1098. Chicago: Parliament Publishing Co., 1893.

———. "The Ethics of Islam." In *Neely's History of the Parliament of Religions and Religious Congresses at the World's Columbian Exposition: Compiled from Original Manuscripts and Stenographic Reports,* ed. Walther Raleigh Houghton, 613–615. Chicago: Frank Tennyson Neely, 1893.

Poston, Larry. *Islamic Da'wah in the West: Muslim Missionary Activity and the Dynamics of Conversion to Islam.* New York: Oxford University Press, 1992.

Price, Kenneth M., and Susan Belasco Smith, eds. *Periodical Literature in Nineteenth-Century America.* Charlottesville: University Press of Virginia, 1995.

"The Progress of Islam." *Allahabad Review,* July 1893: 1.

Queen, Edward L. II, Stephen R. Prothero, and Gardiner H. Shattuck Jr., eds. *Encyclopedia of American Religious History.* 2 vols. New York: Facts on File, 2001.

Quilliam, W[illiam] H[enry]. "Letter to the Editor," *Allahabad Review* (February 1892): 17–18.

Rambo, Lewis R. "Theories of Conversion: Understanding and Interpreting Religious Change." *Social Compass* 46 (September 1999): 259–271.

Rammelkamp, Julian S. *Pulitzer's Post-Dispatch 1878–1883.* Princeton: Princeton University Press, 1967.

Rancés diccionario ilustrado de la lengua española. Barcelona: Editorial Ramón Sopena, 1983.

"*Republic* Reviews Alex Webb's Life: Former Editor of *Unionville Republican*," *Unionville Republican*, 31 January 1917: 12.

Richmond, W. L. *1911–1912 Directory of Rutherford Including East Rutherford, Carlstadt, Lyndhurst, Kingsland, Wood Ridge Issued June 1st 1911.* Passaic, N.J.: W. L. Richmond, 1911.

———. *Richmond's Annual Directory of Passaic, Garfield, Clifton, Wallington, Athenia, Allwood, Delawana (New Jersey) 1912.* Passaic, N.J.: W. L. Richmond, 1912.

———. *Richmond's Annual Directory of Passaic, Garfield, Clifton, Wallington, Athenia, Allwood, Delawana (New Jersey) 1913.* Passaic, N.J.: W. L. Richmond, 1913.

———. *Richmond's Directory of Passaic, Garfield, Clifton, and Wallington (New Jersey) 1907.* Yonkers, N.Y.: W. L. Richmond, n.d.

———. *Richmond's Annual Directory of Passaic, Garfield, Lodi, Clifton, Wallington, Athenia, Allwood, Delawana (New Jersey) 1914.* Passaic, N.J.: W. L. Richmond, 1914.

———. *Richmond's Annual Directory of Passaic, Clifton, Garfield, Lodi, Wallington, Athenia, Allwood, Delawana (New Jersey) 1915.* Passaic, N.J.: W. L. Richmond, 1915.

———. *Richmond's Annual Directory of Passaic, Clifton, Garfield, Lodi, Wallington, Athenia, Allwood, Delawana (New Jersey) 1916.* Passaic, N.J.: W. L. Richmond, 1916.

———. *Richmond's Directory of Passaic, Garfield, Clifton, Wallington and Delawana (New Jersey) 1908.* Passaic, N.J.: W. L. Richmond, n. d.

———. *Richmond's Directory of Passaic, Garfield, Clifton, Wallington, Athenia, Allwood, and Delawana (New Jersey) 1909.* Passaic, N.J.: W. L. Richmond, n.d.

———. *Richmond's Fourth Annual Directory of Passaic, Garfield, Clifton, Wallington, Athenia, Allwood and Delawana (New Jersey) 1910.* Passaic, N.J.: W. L. Richmond, n.d.

———. *Richmond's Eleventh Annual Directory of Passaic, Clifton, Garfield, Lodi, Wallington, Athenia, Allwood, Delawana (New Jersey) 1917.* Passaic, N.J.: W. L. Richmond, 1917.

———. *1911 Volume 5 Directory of Passaic, Garfield, Clifton, Lake View, Wallington, Athenia, Allwood, and Delawana (New Jersey).* Passaic, N.J.: W. L. Richmond, 1911.

Rippin, Andrew. *Muslims: Their Religious Beliefs and Practices.* London: Routledge, 2001.

Roberts, Frank A. *Autograph Book 1861.* Manuscript in Claverack Academy records at the Claverack Free Library and Reading Room, Claverack, N.Y.

Rocher, Lisbeth, and Fatima Cherquaoui. *D'une foi, l'autre: Les conversions à l'islam en Occident.* Paris: Éditions du Seuil, 1986.

Rose, Anne C. *Victorian America and the Civil War*. Cambridge: Cambridge University Press, 1992.

Rosenau, Pauline Marie. *Post-Modernism and the Social Sciences: Insights, Inroads, and Intrusions*. Princeton, N.J.: Princeton University Press, 1992.

Rothermund, Dietmar. "Problems of India's Arrested Economic Growth under British Rule." *Arrested Development in India: The Historical Dimension*, ed. Clive Dewey. New Delhi: Manohar, 1988.

Roy, Tirthankar. *The Economic History of India 1857–1947*. New Delhi: Oxford University Press, 2000.

The Rural Repository: A Semi-Monthly Journal Embellished with Engravings. Hudson, N.Y.: n.p., 1824–1851.

"Mr. Webb on Turkish Life: His Interesting Talk at the Church of Our Father on Monday Night." *Rutherford America* (27 February 1902): 1.

Rutt, Chris L. *History of Buchanan County and the City of St. Joseph and Representative Citizens: 1826–1904*. Chicago: Biographical Publishing Co., 1904.

Ryan, Charles J. *H. P. Blavatsky and the Theosophical Movement*. Available at http://www.theosociety.org/pasadena/hpb-tm/hpbtm-18.htm. Accessed February 2005.

Sadiq, Mufti Muhammad. "No Polygamy." *Moslem Sunrise* (July 1921): 9–10.

Samson, Jim, ed. *The Late Romantic Era: From the Mid-Nineteenth Century to World War I*. Englewood Cliffs, N.J.: Prentice-Hall, 1991.

Sarna, Jonathan D. "Jewish-Christian Hostility in the United States: Perceptions from a Jewish Point of View." In *Uncivil Religion: Interreligious Hostility in America*, ed. Robert N. Bellah and Frederick E. Greenspahn, 5–22. New York: Crossroad, 1987.

Saunders, Randall Neefus. "Remembering Claverack College." In *Index of Various Papers and Materials Collected by the Historical Committee of the Claverack Woman's Club*, 59–74. Claverack Free Library and Reading Room, Claverack, N.Y.

———. *Remembering Claverack College*. Hudson, N.Y.: Hudson Evening Register, 1944.

Schlereth, Thomas. *Victorian America: Transformations in Everyday Life, 1876–1915*. New York: Harper Collins, 1991.

Schild, James J. *Houses of God: The Historic Churches and Places of Worship of the St. Louis Area*. Florissant, Mo.: Auto Review, 1995.

Seager, Richard Hughes, ed. *The Dawn of Religious Pluralism: Voices from the World's Parliament of Religions, 1893*. La Salle, Ill.: Open Court, 1993.

———. "The World's Parliament of Religions, Chicago, Illinois, 1893: America's Religious Coming of Age." Ph.D. diss., Harvard University, 1987.

Shalton, Seira B. "Mohammed Alexander Russell Webb and Islam in Nineteenth-Century America." Master's thesis, Arizona State University, May 1999.

Shoemaker, Floyd C., ed. *The Missouri Historical Review*. Vol. 11, October 1916–July 1917. Columbia, Missouri: State Historical Society of Missouri, 1917.

Smith, Elbert B. *The Presidency of James Buchanan*. Lawrence: University of Kansas Press, 1975.

Smith, Jane I. *Islam in America*. New York: Columbia University Press, 1999.

Smith, Peter. *The Babi and Baha'i Religions from Messianic Shi'ism to a World Religion*. Cambridge: Cambridge University Press, 1987.

Stanton-Hope, W. E. *Arabian Adventurer: The Story of Haji Williamson.* London: Robert Hale Limited, 1951.

1880 Census of City of St. Joseph, Buchanan County, Missouri, excluding Washington Township: Population Schedule of the Tenth Census of the United States 1880—City of St. Joseph Buchanan County. 2 vols. in 1. Edited by Dixie Painter. Washington, D.C.: National Archives and Record Service, 1978–1979.

St. Joseph Gazette, 6 January 1877; 24 June 1877.

St. Louis Republican, 26 September 1887; 30 September 1887.

Steven, Walter B. *One Hundred Years of the St. Louis Republic.* St. Louis, Mo.: St. Louis Republic, 1908.

Stiletto. "Face Studies: Alexander Russell Webb." *Frank Leslie's Illustrated Weekly,* 30 March 1893: 204.

Sullivan, James. "Paul Dana." In *The History of New York State.* Available at http://64.233.167.104/search?q=cache:eJcbK4wtaCwJ:www.usgennet.org/usa/ny/st. Accessed February 2005.

"Sultan Honors an American: Appoints A. R. Webb, the Mohammedan Missionary, Honorary Consul General Here." *New York Times,* 1 October 1901: 9.

Taft, William H. *Missouri Newspapers.* Columbia: University of Missouri Press, 1964.

Tocqueville, Alexis de. *Democracy in America.* Translated by Harvey C. Mansfield and Delba Winthrop. 2 vols. in 1. Chicago: University of Chicago Press, 2000.

"To Preach Moslemism. Ex-Consul Webb, Backed by Mohammedan Cash, Returns to America to Teach the Koran." *New York Herald,* 26 February 1893: 21.

Truesdell, Paul E. Jr. *Descendants and Ancestors of Samuel Truesdell of Newton, MA.* Available at http://petjr.crosswinds.net/GENE/pafg01.htm. Accessed October 2004.

Tunison, Emory H. "Mohammed Alexander Russell Webb First American Muslim." *Arab World* 3 (1945): 13–18.

Turner, Richard Brent. *Islam in the African-American Experience.* Indianapolis: Indiana University Press, 1997.

Turmel, Joseph. "Immaculate Conception." In *The Encyclopedia of Religion and Ethics,* ed. James Hastings. 12 vols., 7:165–167. Edinburgh: Clark, 1913.

Twain, Mark. *Tom Sawyer Abroad; Tom Sawyer, Detective.* Edited by John C. Gerber and Terry Firkins. Berkeley: University of California Press, 1982.

Tweed, Thomas A. *The American Encounter with Buddhism 1844–1912: Victorian Culture and the Limits of Dissent.* Bloomington: Indiana University Press, 1992.

Unionville Republican, 18 December 1873; 25 December 1873; 8 January 1874; 9 March 1876; 16 March 1876; 23 March 1876; 20 July 1876; 27 July 1876; 3 May 1877.

United States City Directories, 1861–1881, St. Louis, Missouri, 1876: Directories of the Principal Cities in the United States on File at Gould's Directory Office, reel 9.

United States City Directories, 1861–1881, St. Louis, Missouri, 1877: Directories of the Principal Cities in the United States on File at Gould's Directory office, reel 10.

United States Code: Congressional and Administrative News, 89th Congress, First Session. St. Paul, Minn.: West Publishing Co., 1965.

U. S. *National Archives and Records Administration.* Available at http://www.archives.gov/publications/genealogy_free_content.html. Accessed February 2005.

Washington, Peter. *Madame Blavatsky's Baboon: A History of the Mystics, Mediums, and Misfits Who Brought Spiritualism to America*. New York: Schocken, 1995.

Weather People and History: Naming the Windy City. Available at http://www.islandnet .com/~see/weather/history/chicago-nickname.htm. Accessed February 2005.

Webb, F. H. *Claverack: Clover-Reach*. Claverack, N.Y.: F. H. Webb, 1892.

Webb, Alexander Russell. "Harmony." *Allahabad Review*, February 1892: 13–15.

———. "A Letter." *Allahabad Review*, July 1892: 77–78.

———. "Letter to Mirza Ghulam Ahmad," 24 February 1887. In Mirza Ghulam Ahmad, *Shahna-e Haqq*. N.p.: n.p., n.d.: 439–443.

———. "Progressive Mohammedanism." *Allahabad Review*, November 1891: 156–158.

———. "Salutatory." *Unionville Republican*, 8 January 1874: 2.

———. "Sectarian Exclusiveness." *Allahabad Review*, December 1891: 174–177.

———. "To the Editor." *Allahabad Review*. August 1891: 109–111.

———. "To the Editor." *Allahabad Review*. May 1892: 60–61.

———. "Two Remarkable Phenomena." In *The New Californian*, January 19, 1892: 248–251. Los Angeles: New Californian Publishing Society, 1891.

Webb, Mohammed Alexander Russell. Diary. 29 August 1892 to 15 December 1892. Duke University Library, Special Collections, Durham, N.C.

———. *A Guide to Namaz: A Detailed Exposition of the Moslem Order of Ablutions and Prayers with a Review of the Five Pillars of Practice*. New York: Moslem World Publishing Co., 1893.

———. *Islam: A Lecture Delivered at the Framji Cowasji Institute, Bombay, India, Thursday Evening 10th November 1892, by Muhammad Alexander Russell Webb, Esq., Late of the American Consular Service*. Bombay: Bombay Gazette Steam Printing Works, 1892.

———. *Islam in America: A Brief Statement of Mohammedanism and an Outline of the American Islamic Propaganda*. New York: Oriental Publishing Co. & Acton Press, 1893.

———. *Lectures on Islam: Delivered at Different Places in India*. Lahore: Islamia Press, 1893.

———. Letter to Budrudin [sic] Abdulla Kur, Esq., Bombay, 4 July 1892. In Alexander Russell Webb, *Lectures on Islam: Delivered at Different Places in India*, 16–18. Lahore: Mohammadan [sic] Tract and Book Depot, 1893.

———. Letter to Budrudin [sic] Abdulla Kur, Esq., Bombay, 4 July 1892. In Mohammed Alexander Russell Webb, *Islam: A Lecture IslamDelivered at the Framji Cowasji Institute, Bombay, India, Thursday Evening 10th November 1892*, 7–8. Bombay: Bombay Gazette Steam Printing Works, 1892.

———. "Influence of Islâm on Social Conditions." In *The World's Parliament of Religions: An Illustrated and Popular Story of the World's First Parliament of Religions, Held in Chicago in Connection with the Columbian Exposition of 1893*, ed. John Henry Barrows, 2 vols., 2:1046–1052. Chicago: Parliament Publishing Co., 1893.

———. "The Influence of Social Condition." In *Neely's History of the Parliament of Religions and Religious Congresses at the World's Columbian Exposition: Compiled from Original Manuscripts and Stenographic Reports*, ed. Walter Raleigh Houghton, 544–550. Chicago: Frank Tennyson Neely, 1893.

———. "The Spirit of Islam." In *The World's Parliament of Religions: An Illustrated and Popular Story of the World's First Parliament of Religions, Held in Chicago in*

Connection with the Columbian Exposition of 1893, ed. John Henry Barrows, 2:
989–996. Chicago: Parliament Publishing Co., 1893.

———. "The Spirit of Islam." In *Neely's History of the Parliament of Religions and
Religious Congresses at the World's Columbian Exposition: Compiled from Original
Manuscripts and Stenographic Reports*, ed. Walter Raleigh Houghton, 459–464.
Chicago: Frank Tennyson Neely, 1893.

———. "The Three Lectures of Mohammed Alexander Russell Webb, Esq. Delivered at
Madras, Hyderabad (Deccan) and Bombay, with a Brief Sketch of His Life Published
by Moulvi Hassan Ali (Mohammedan Missionary)*. Madras: Lawrence Asylum
Press, 1892.

Weitbrecht, H. U. "A Moslem Mission to England." *Moslem World*, April 1914:
195–202.

Weller, Charles Frederick. "The Contribution of the Ahmadiyya Movement to the
World Fellowship of Faiths—A Second Parliament of Religions." *Moslem Sunrise*,
April–July 1933: 43–44.

Welter, Barbara. "From Maria Monk to Paul Blanshard: A Century of Protestant
Anti-Catholicism." In *Uncivil Religion: Interreligious Hostility in America*, ed.
Robert N. Bellah and Frederick E. Greenspahn: 43–71. New York: Crossroad, 1987.

"William Henry Quilliam/Sheikh Abdullah Quilliam." Available at http://www.pcweb
.liv.ac.uk/guild/islamic/history.htm. Accessed February 2004.

Williams, Fannie Barrier. "What Can Religion Do to Advance the Condition of the
American Negro?" In John Henry Barrows, ed., *The World's Parliament of
Religions: An Illustrated and Popular Story of the World's First Parliament of Religions,
Held in Chicago in Connection with the Columbian Exposition of 1893*, 2:1114–1115.
Chicago: Parliament Publishing Co., 1893.

White, L. Mitchell. "The Press." In *Missouri: Its Resources, People, and Institutions*,
ed. Noel P. Gist, 369–376. Columbia: Curators of University of Missouri, 1950.

Whitman, Walt. *Leaves of Grass: The First Edition 1855*, ed. Malcolm Cowley. New
York: Barnes & Noble, 1997.

Winter, Timothy. "Conversion as Nostalgia: Some Experiences of Islam." In
Previous Convictions: Conversion in the Real World, ed. Martyn Percy, 93–111.
London: Society for Promoting Christian Knowledge, 2000.

Winther, Oscar Osburn. *A Classified Bibliography of the Periodical Literature of the
Trans-Mississippi West, 1811–1957*. Bloomington: University of Indiana Press,
1961.

Wohlrab-Sahr, Monika. *Konversion zum Islam in Deutschland und den USA*. Frankfurt,
Germany: Campus Verlag, 1999.

Wolfe, Michael, ed. *One Thousand Roads to Mecca: Ten Centuries of Travelers Writing
about the Muslim Pilgrimage*. New York: Grove, 1997.

*World Christian Encyclopedia: A Comparative Survey of Churches and Religions in the
Modern World*. 2 vols. Edited by David B. Barnett, George T. Kurian, and Todd M.
Johnson. Oxford: Oxford University Press, 2001.

Yearbook of American and Canadian Churches 2001. Edited by Eileen W. Lindner.
Nashville, Tenn.: Abingdon, 2001.

Younis, Adele L. "The First Muslims in America: Impressions and Reminiscences."
Journal of the Institute of Muslim Minority Affairs 5 (1984): 17–28.

Zelinsky, Wilbur. *The Cultural Geography of the United States.* Englewood Cliffs, N.J.: Prentice-Hall, 1992.

Ziolkowski, Eric J. "The First World's Parliament of Religions and the Columbian Exposition (Chicago, 1893): Twin Legacies in American Literature and Religious Sensibility." DePaul University Library Archives on the World Parliament of Religions, Box 21 B. CPWR Administration, Research Committee, 1987.

Zirikli, Khayr al-Dīn al-. *Al-A'lām: Qāmūs Tarājim li-Ashhar al-Rijāl wa al-Nisā' min al-'Arab wa al-Musta'ribīn wa al-Mustashriqīn.* 8 vols. Beirut, Lebanon: Dār al-'Ilm li-al-Malāyīn, 1992.

Z[wemer], S[amuel] M. "The Birth of Mormonism." *Moslem World,* January 1918: 95.

———. "Mormonism." *Moslem World,* October 1918: 436.

Zwick, Jim, ed. *World's Fairs and Expositions Defining America and the World, 1876–1916.* Available at http://www.boondocksnet.com/expos. Accessed February 2004.

Index

[American]), 36. Work cited: *Uncle Tom's Cabin*

Streator, Ill., 323n

Strong, Josiah, 263. Work cited: *Our Country* suicide, 251, 308n

Sultan Abdul Hamid II. *See* Abdul Hamid, II (sultan of the Ottoman Empire)

Sunderland, Elizabeth (*see also* Parliament of Religions, First World's): 235. Work cited: "Lessons from the Study of Comparative Religion"

Sunderland, Reverend J. T., 197

Supreme Court (U.S.), 31, 36, 86, 92, 263, 304n

Surrey (England), 74

Sweden, 178

Swedenborg, Emanuel, 219

Swedish, 34

Swami Vivekananda. *See* Vivekanda, Swami

synagogue (*see also* Hudson, N.Y.: religious and quasi-religious societies), 27

Syrian Protestant College of Beirut (now American University of Beirut), 232

Taghkanic, N.Y. (*see also* Columbia County), 35

Tangier (Morocco), 105

Tarboro, N.C., 323n

Tarrytown-on-the-Hudson, N.Y., 250

Tchéraz, Mina, 238

Teachings of Islam (Ghulam Ahmad) (*see also* Ahmadiyya; Ahmad, Mirza Ghulam Ahmad), 19

Temple, Moorish Science: Islamic publications of, 183

Tennyson, Sir Alfred Lord, 220

Terry, M. S. (*see also* Parliament of Religions, First World's), 235

Texas, 22, 35, 37, 323n

Thaumatopolis (city of wonders and miracles) (*see also* Exposition, Fourth Columbian Centennial: White City, the), 213

theology, Swedenborgian, 219

Theosophical Society, the, 5, 56–58, 60, 65, 70–71, 93, 119, 131, 157, 170, 176, 178, 189, 294n

Theosophy, 5, 48, 53–60, 65, 70, 93, 101, 116, 119, 136, 170, 181, 268, 274, 277, 278, 293n, 298n

Third Order of Mejidi (one of Webb's Turkish medals of honor), 266

Thoreau, Henry David, 14, 56. Work cited: *Walden*

Three Lectures (Webb) (*see also* Propaganda, American Islamic; Webb, Alexander Russell): 182, 184–190; contents of, 186–90; editions of, 186; as incomplete record of Indian lectures, 184

Tiffany, House of (New York) (*see also* Webb, Alexander Russell: jewelry career of), 83

Tilden, Governor Samuel J. (*see also* Webb, Alexander Russell: "in the middle of it all"), 88

Times-Journal. See St. Louis Times-Journal

Titanic (steam ship), 264

"To His Imperial Majesty, Sultan Abdul Hamid II" (Wilburn), 205

Tocqueville, Alexis de, 12, 27, 33, 36–37, 41, 43, 190

Tom Sawyer, 12, 49, 174, 291n

Tom Sawyer Abroad (Twain), 12, 174

Transcendentalism, 70

Transcendentalists, 14, 57, 69

Trinity (doctrine of), 48, 51, 185, 230, 278

Tripoli (North African regency of), 14

Tunison, Emory H., 9, 15, 19, 52, 66, 87

turbans (*see also* Webb, Alexander Russell: dress), 8–9, 129, 142, 226, 239, 282, 334n

Turner, Richard Brent, 9, 178, 283n

Twain, Mark (pseud. Clemens, Samuel Longhorn). *See* Clemens, Samuel Longhorn

Tyler, Joseph C., 108

Ulster Park, N.Y., 6, 163, 166, 248, 251–57, 259–60, 264, 339nn, 340n

"Uncle Sam" (*see also* Wilson, Samuel Wilson; Webb, Alexander Russell: "in the middle of it all"), 11, 282n

Uncle Sam Bridge, 282n

Uncle Tom's Cabin (Stowe), 36

Union, the (*see also* Civil War, the), 22, 37–38, 84–86, 90, 288n

Union Pacific Railroad, 208

Unionville, Mo., 12, 14, 83–84, 86–89, 91, 299n, 300n, 301n, 302n

Unionville Republican, 84, 87–88, 96, 98, 289n, 300n

Unionville Weekly Argus, the, 84

Unitarians, the, 12, 14, 57, 68, 176, 197, 261, 267–68, 276, 277, 286n, 288n

"Unity of Faith and Harmony of Religions" (*also Unity of Faiths and Harmony of Religions*) (Jibara), 234

Universalists, the, 52, 64, 261

University of Chicago, 17, 213

Urban, Eusebio. *See* Judge, William Quan

Urdu language (*see also* Webb, Alexander Russell: language knowledge of), 61–63, 125, 128, 150, 153, 168, 317n, 334n, 339n

Utah, 31

Utah War, the (Mormon War, the) (*see also* Latter-Day Saints, Church of), 31

Valley, Hudson River. *See* Hudson River Valley